Middle East Studies
History, Politics, and Law

Edited by
Shahrough Akhavi
University of South Carolina

A Routledge Series

Middle East Studies: History, Politics, and Law

Shahrough Akhavi, *General Editor*

New Pythian Voices
Women Building Political Capital in NGOs in the Middle East
Cathryn S. Magno

Turkey in Germany
The Transnational Sphere of Deutschkei
Betigül Ercan Argun

Islamic Law, Epistemology and Modernity
Legal Philosophy in Contemporary Iran
Ashk P. Dahlén

Gender, Literacy, and Empowerment in Morocco
Fatima Agnaou

Trapped Between the Map and Reality
Geography and Perceptions of Kurdistan
Maria T. O'Shea

Kurdish Nationalism and Political Islam in Turkey
Kemalist Identity in Transition
Omer Taspinar

Organizations, Gender, and the Culture of Palestinian Activism in Haifa, Israel
Elizabeth Faier

Palestinian Identity in Jordan and Israel
The Necessary 'Other' in the Making of a Nation
Riad M. Nasser

Strategies of Resistance in the Dramatic Texts of North African Women
A Body of Words
Laura Chakravarty Box

Islam, Democracy, and the Status of Women
The Case of Kuwait
Helen Mary Rizzo

Legislating Authority
Sin and Crime in the Ottoman Empire and Turkey
Ruth A. Miller

War and Migration
Social Networks and Economic Strategies of the Hazaras of Afghanistan
Alessandro Monsutti

WAR AND MIGRATION

Social Networks and Economic Strategies of the Hazaras of Afghanistan

Alessandro Monsutti

Translated by
Patrick Camiller

Routledge
Taylor & Francis Group
NEW YORK AND LONDON

Originally published as *Guerres et Migrations: Réseaux Sociaux et Stratégies Économiques des Hazaras d'Afghanistan* (2004). This English translation is being published with kind permission of the Editors: Editions de l'Institut d'ethnologie, Neuchâtel, Switzerland & Editions de la Maison des Sciences de l'Homme, Paris, France.

Published in 2005 by
Routledge
Taylor & Francis Group
711 Third Avenue
New York, NY 10017

Published in Great Britain by
Routledge
Taylor & Francis Group
2 Park Square
Milton Park, Abingdon
Oxon OX14 4RN

Routledge is an imprint of the Taylor & Francis Group, an informa business

First issued in paperback 2012

International Standard Book Number-13: 978-0-415-97508-7 (Hardcover)
International Standard Book Number-13: 978-0-415-65478-4 (Paperback)
Library of Congress Card Number 2005001551

Library of Congress Cataloging-In-Publication Data

Monsutti, Alessandro.
[Guerres et migrations. English.]
War and migration : social networks and economic strategies of the Hazaras of Afghanistan / Alessandro Monsutti ; with a foreword by Dale F. Eickelman; translated by Patrick Camiller.-- 1st ed.
p. cm. -- (Middle East studies: history, politics, and law)
Includes bibliographical references.and index.
ISBN 0-415-97508-5 (alk. paper)
1. Hazåaras. I. Title. II. Series: Middle East studies (Routledge (Firm))
DS354.6.H3M6613 2005
305 89'42--dc22 2005001551

T&F informa
Taylor & Francis Group
is the Academic Division of T&F Informa plc.

Visit the Taylor & Francis Web site at
http://www.taylorandfrancis.com

and the Routledge Web site at
http://www.routledge-ny.com

Contents

To my mother,
To my father,
who have never left me

Be in the world below as a stranger, or a passer-by

Hadith

After a few steps the dervish stopped and said: "Travel the World!"
He squatted beside the steam and plunged his hand in the water.
"When water stagnates it become unhealthy. It turns earth into mud.
Be as the water that slips through your hand!"

Atiq Rahimi

Foreword

War and Migration breaks with established ethnographic conventions. Until recently, ethnographers focused on a single village or region and then traced the complex social ties with the rest of the world. Alessandro Monsutti is distinguished from most of his predecessors. He forms part of a new generation of ethnographers that no longer considers a specific geographic place as the focus of study, but instead the extended and reliable networks of trust and mutual obligation. This book offers a solid multi-sited ethnography that takes the study of networks as its central theme instead of a single place. The networks of solidarity in question are those developed by the Hazaras—and by neighboring groups—for mutual support and communication. The regional wars and internal struggles that Afghanistan has sustained over the course of the past thirty years have been especially destructive, but they are not unprecedented. Monsutti describes a "network society" that existed long before Manuel Castells in the early 1990s made the term a sociological standard.

War and Migration depicts Hazara economic and social ties as total social facts in Marcel Mauss's sense of the term. Monsutti explains the extent to which social and economic ties overlap and how their imbrication allows individuals to anticipate the actions of others. This mutual anticipation is essential for a society for which migration is neither temporary nor permanent and which neighbors perceive the Hazaras as politically marginal and religiously heterodox. In such circumstances, the economic worth accorded to goods and money is highly relative. It is challenging to place a reliable exchange value on the banknotes of Iran, Afghanistan, Pakistan, and other countries. Equally daunting is the challenge of reliably sending goods, funds, and messages over long distances, especially when they are subject to long delays and political insecurity. Nonetheless, the concurrent and overlapping use of letters of credit, secret codes, telephone calls, and messages passed along a chain of intermediaries facilitates economic exchange and sustains ties of family and community. Monsutti convincingly shows that these overlapping ties cannot be depicted as a series of concentric circles that spread out from family and household to encompass progressively kin, village or community, and ethnic or religious group. These various forms of identity overlap and imply one another. They form the background understandings that allow the Hazaras to adapt to changing social, political, and economic circumstances. As the author emphasizes, the trust and reliability placed on social ties flows from the density of ties maintained with particular persons or groups rather than from kinship or tribal identity alone.

This study is based on the ties of belonging and trust that the Hazaras have elaborated in spite of their geographical dispersion and not on any single point of common origin or locale. The study of Hazara networks entails three basic questions: How do Hazara migrants cross state frontiers, often in the absence of formal documents or permits? How do emigrants send funds to their family or households in the absence of reliable banking or state institutions? Finally, how do the Hazaras send reliable messages through multiple intermediaries, and often not in written form? Of course, prior knowledge of the character of close relatives and neighbors allows the Hazaras to anticipate their future reactions. Yet Hazaras cannot often rely on close relatives alone or on members of their community of origin. Their dispersion constrains them to take risks and to rely on others to obtain visas and cross borders.

This book offers ethnographic insight into how the Hazaras assess and overcome these risks, although not always successfully. Their strategies for migration form an integral part of their social life. It would be inappropriate for them to be seen as traumatized by migration, contrary to common conventional ethnographic understandings. Monsutti makes use of quantitative data whenever it is available, but the main strength of this book is in tracing in compelling detail the migratory itineraries and choices of a dozen Hazaras who chose to emigrate at different periods in their lives from Afghanistan to Iran or Pakistan.

The network society created by these migrant workers and merchants has been stretched to the limit by Afghanistan's tumultuous recent history. Yet the intertwined and durable ties of this network society, formed by reciprocal economic and social obligations, show a strong capacity to endure and adapt. Multilateral Hazara networks encompass Afghanistan, Pakistan, and Iran and in recent years have extended to the Arabian Peninsula, Europe, Southeast Asia, and North America, creating channels for moving goods, people, and information more reliable than those provided by state authorities or formal banking channels.

The author's description of the *hawâla* system for the transfer of funds is especially incisive. Few readers will henceforth consider *hawâla* networks an anachronism, nor consider them merely as a means to transfer funds illegally to sustain rogue states or criminal and terrorist groups. Just as is the case with modern banking, the *hawâla* system can be abused. Nonetheless, in regions where banks are absent, inefficient, or insecure, *hawâla* offers an excellent means to overcome the obstacles of geographical distance and insecurity. Finally, the ease with which *hawâla* traders adapt to modern forms of communications and banking technologies—using them whenever they are more efficacious than conventional means—provides a rich exemplar for those interested in facilitating economic and social development.

War and Migration has a clarity that evokes the classic work of Henri Pirenne on the movement of goods and commerce in the insecure context of medieval Europe. It describes in convincing detail the workings of informal institutions—including that of the *hawâla*—that are often unknown or viewed with suspicion by administrators, politicians, and officials in international humanitarian and relief organizations. Knowledge of how such "informal" institutions work can make a significant contribution to building a better future for Afghanistan. This book will suggest to readers ways of encouraging sustainable economic and social development in Afghanistan's more remote regions. *War and Migration* is essential reading for scholars, officials, and all those interested in Afghanistan and neighboring countries.

Dale F. Eickelman,
Ralph and Richard Lazarus
Professor of Anthropology and
Human Relations, Dartmouth College (USA)

Introduction

In its scale and duration, the conflict that has been tearing Afghanistan apart is one of the gravest humanitarian disasters of the second half of the twentieth century. Between the Communist coup of 1978 and the Soviet withdrawal of 1989, a third of the population fled abroad, eleven percent became refugees inside the country, and nine percent were killed (Sliwinski 1989: 51–52). At the beginning of the 1990s Afghans formed the largest group of displaced persons on earth, accounting for nearly half the total under the responsibility of the United Nations High Commissioner for Refugees (UNHCR) (Colville 1998: 6). In 1990 there were 6.22 million Afghan refugees in the world (HCR 1997). Large numbers returned after the Soviet withdrawal (1989) and the capture of Kabul by resistance forces (1992), but over the following years this trend was reversed as more outward flows accompanied the new outbreaks of fighting, especially in the Mazar-e Sharif and Kabul regions. The fall of the Taliban regime, the establishment of a government in Kabul backed by the international community between autumn 2001 and summer 2002 and the prospect of a restoration of normality have caused an unprecedented wave of returns. In the summer of 2002 the UNHCR estimated that more than a million and a half refugees had made their way back to the country, and that 230,000 internally displaced persons had regained their villages in the space of a few months.[1] Nevertheless, the number of Afghans living abroad is still considerable.

Afghanistan and Afghans have experienced some curious changes of fortune in the West. Whereas, in the 1980s, the media praised the heroism of a people resisting Soviet occupation at the highest possible cost to themselves, the image gradually worsened in the 1990s as the talk turned to a revival of tribalism, smuggling and drug-trafficking, or "Kalashnikov culture" and international terrorism. Yet neither of these opposing views can possibly do justice to the complexity of the Afghan situation.

In my own first encounters with Afghans, I was struck by how frequently they made two statements: *mosâfer astim* and *e'tebâr nist. Mosâfer astim:* "we are travellers," in the sense of "we are only travellers" or "we are not at home," but also and perhaps especially "we are only passing through this world." *E'tebâr nist:* "there is no trust" or "who can be trusted?" *Amnyat nist:* "there is no security." These expressions are mainly intended in a general or existential sense, as we can see from the fact that they were in use before the Communist coup of 1978. They tersely remind us of two major phenomena that have constrained the lives of Afghans throughout their troubled history: war and migration.

Nevertheless, Afghans are not passive victims of a fate totally external to them. Faced with endemic insecurity, scattered among a large number of countries, they have developed social and economic strategies based upon spatial mobility and group solidarity. Life has gone on in spite of the fighting, the bombing and the massacres; people and goods cross the fighting zones, as Afghans have grown used to the difficulties of the situation. In this context, I soon realized the centrality of trust in Afghan society. The cleavages and conflicts do not exclude close social ties, as I saw for myself while talking, living and travelling with Afghans, taking risks alongside them and developing over time a number of strong personal relations.

Two of my principal conclusions are that migration is a way of life rather than merely an external constraint, and that, although war and exile certainly bring great insecurity, they do not prevent the reproduction of relations of solidarity and trust. The idea of the voyage, so dear to my Afghan friends, has a spatial but also a metaphysical and moral dimension, for it expresses the uncertainty dominating our lives. We are all travellers and are united by this common fate.

My first real contact with Afghans goes back to 1993, when I and a group of students from the Institute of Ethnology of the University of Neuchâtel spent the months from July to October in Quetta, the capital of Pakistani Baluchistan, working under the guidance of Pierre Centlivres and Micheline Centlivres-Demont. The object of our research was the migration and integration of Afghans who had left the refugee camps to settle in an urban environment. Our preparation for the trip began in 1991, with the learning of Dari (the form of Persian spoken in Afghanistan) and the study of such issues as relations between refugees and host countries, new occupational and civil identities, the position of women and educational problems.

Contacts made during this first trip led me to take up the study of the Hazaras, an oppressed minority originating in the center of Afghanistan. During subsequent stays in 1995–96 and, more briefly, in 1998 and 2001, I extended my investigations to Afghanistan and Iran. Most of my field research took place in the period between two landmarks in recent Afghan history: the defeat of the Hazara forces of Hezb-e wahdat, in Kabul in March 1995, when they were caught in a pincers between the troops of Massoud/Sayyaf and the Taliban, suffered heavy losses (including that of their leader, Abdul Ali Mazari) and had to withdraw to the Hazarajat; and the Taliban capture of the capital in September 1996. But the work and its conclusions cover a longer time span.

Despite these events, in 1995 and 1996 the Hazaras were still able to cross fairly easily the Pashtun Belt in the south and east of the country, where the Taliban movement (which first appeared in late 1994) had won some popularity by ending the terrible anarchy due to merciless Pashtun commanders and the systematic racketeering in migrants and refugees. Subsequently, however, the situation became much worse. In May 1997 the Taliban briefly occupied the town of Mazar-e Sharif, but in the ensuing rout two thousand of their fighters were summarily executed and the remainder driven out. In the summer, the Taliban imposed a blockade of Hazarajat to undermine the military positions of the Wahdat. But it was only in the months after August 8, 1998, when they captured Mazar and reportedly massacred 2,000 people (although the figure was probably as high as 3–6,000, most of them Hazara), that the Taliban extended their control, however imperfectly, over the region.[2]

In this escalation of the conflict, the Hazaras were the main target of the Taliban on account of their Shiite beliefs and their stubborn resistance; the mistrust and fear reported by my informants thus proved largely justified. Yet the truly Hobbesian situation of latent warfare, together with the general lack of trust, did not prevent the establishment of huge networks specializing in migration and trade.

The American intervention following the attacks of September 11, 2001 in New York and Washington led to the victory of forces opposed to the Taliban. The future of Afghanistan is still uncertain. Migratory flows from Hazarajat, one of the country's poorest regions, began long before the war and have become a cultural model largely independent of external circumstances. It is unlikely that they will come to an end, even in the most optimistic scenario of a return to normality.

The study of Hazara migratory strategies has several dimensions: it forms part of the theoretical debate on migration and transnationalism, and addresses the methodological doubts that have been shaking the world of anthropology since the mid-1980s; it calls into question the cut-and-dried distinction between economic migrants and refugees; it reveals the effectiveness of money-transfer networks and their role in the reproduction of social relations; and it helps to correct the relative lack of attention to the Hazaras in Western ethnography.

The work consists of two sets of three chapters presenting field material, framed by a number of theoretical considerations. Chapter 1 assesses the contribution of the literature on migration and transnationalism to debates in anthropology, and identifies aspects that may be useful for an understanding of the Afghan case. Chapter 2 considers a number of works that have a bearing on Afghan refugees, the methods used in the present research and the population that forms its object. A number of individuals are introduced here who will reappear from time to time later in the text. In the ethnographic section, chapters 3, 4 and 5 look at the main foci of the Hazara migration: that is, Hazarajat (Afghanistan), Quetta (Pakistan) and a number of urban centers in Iran. My intention here is not to offer a detailed monograph on each locality, but to highlight the social organization and modes of cooperation specific to the different contexts. Chapters 6, 7 and 8 explore the flows linking Afghanistan, Pakistan and Iran, in particular the ways in which people move among the three countries, the transfers of money and goods, and the modes of communication within the transnational community under investigation. For the sake of clarity, the presentation will look first at the various localities and then at the migration flows, but this is not meant to imply any logical precedence or to reflect the actual chronology of the fieldwork. Chapter 9 discusses the notion of trust and the forms of cooperation specific to the insecure migratory situation of the Hazaras, and presents some ideas on the importance and limits of kinship ties. In the light of the social-economic and political strategies developed by the Hazaras, the conclusion and epilogue consider possible solutions to the Afghan conflict and the future reconstruction of the country, and outline what has become of my principal interlocutors.

It is customary to acknowledge one's intellectual debts in a preface, and this is a custom with which I am happy to comply. Pierre Centlivres accompanied me in my discovery of Afghanistan. He played an important role in my intellectual formation, and in the development of a conceptual and methodological framework for my research. Richard Tapper made me feel welcome during my research stay at SOAS in 1999–2000 and kindly shared with me various insights. Christian Ghasarian was always unstinting in his encouragement. Micheline Centlivres-Demont guided my first steps in Persian. Gilbert Rist attentively read a first draft of the text, and his rigour greatly helped to improve it.

My work would have been impossible without the friendship of Haji Barkat Ali, Ghulam Sakhi Khatibi and Chaman Ali, as well as of their families. I am also grateful to a large number of people who gave me assistance and advice at various stages: Abdul Karim Abawi, Maaike and Shahin Ashkan, Abdul Wahhab Bahoner, Fabrice Boulé, Jérôme Brandt, Yvan Droz, Raphy Favre, Catherine Fragnière-Haro, Sylvia and Fabrice Gaussen, Tina Gehrig, Roman Gehring and his family, Marie-Christine Hauser, Taiba Krähenbühl, Ishaq Ali Mohammadi, Sayyed Askar Mousavi, Haji Mohammad Quli Mukhi, Obaid A. Nejati, Major Niaz Ali, Sima Samar, Michel Schnarenberger, Soleiman Seraj, Shah Wali Shafayee, Mohammad Akbar Shahristani, Timur Shah, Paul Titus, Elsa Truze, Philippe Truze, Claude Voillat, Abdul Ghafur Wahdat, Raymonde Wicky, Ehsan Zahine and Shahir Zahine.

Several institutions gave invaluable financial assistance for my research. My first study trip to Pakistan was organized and partly funded by the Institute of Ethnology in Neuchâtel, and later stays in Afghanistan, Pakistan and Iran were made possible by grants from the Human Rights and Humanitarian Division and the Swiss Agency for Development and Cooperation of the Ministry of Foreign Affairs of Switzerland. A brief trip to Iran in 1998 was supported by the Association suisse des amis de l'Afghanistan, and a stay in Pakistan in 2001 was made possible by a grant from the Graduate Institute of Development Studies in Geneva. I spent the 1999–2000 academic year at the Department of Anthropology and Sociology of the School of Oriental and African Studies in London, thanks to a grant from the Swiss National Science Foundation. I also had the benefit of a small grant from Crédit Suisse.

During my periods in the field, several international agencies and non-governmental organizations gave logistical support that helped to improve my working conditions: the UNHCR, the ICRC, the Shuhada Organization, AVICEN, DHSA and Global Partners. I had access to a number of libraries: most especially, the library of the Institute of Ethnology in Neuchâtel, the personal collection of Pierre and Micheline Centlivres, the Bibliotheca Afghanica in Liestal (recently moved to Bubendorf) under the direction of Paul Bucherer-Dietschi, the SOAS library, the British Library (particularly the documents of the British India Office) and the Public Record Office in London, as well as the library of the University of Baluchistan in Quetta and the documentation center of the ARIC (ACBAR Resource and Information Centre) in Peshawar.

I wish to particularly thank to Patrick Camiller, who has excellently translated the text from French. This English version would not have been possible without the financial support of the Swiss Agency for Development and Cooperation, the Graduate Institute of Development Studies in Geneva, the Academic Society of Neuchâtel, Christian Nef, the Department of Arts and Human Sciences of the University of Neuchâtel, and the Association suisse des amis de l'Afghanistan.

My gratitude goes out to all who welcomed me and were kind enough to answer my questions in the field; they enabled me to understand much that went beyond the framework of academic research. Faced with the most trying conditions of life, the people of Afghanistan have shown an exemplary dignity and dynamism. Let my work be homage to their courage. Last but not least, this work would never have seen the light of day without Alice's support. In agreeing to let me leave so often, sometimes without receiving news from me for months on end, she gave proof of a truly Afghan patience.

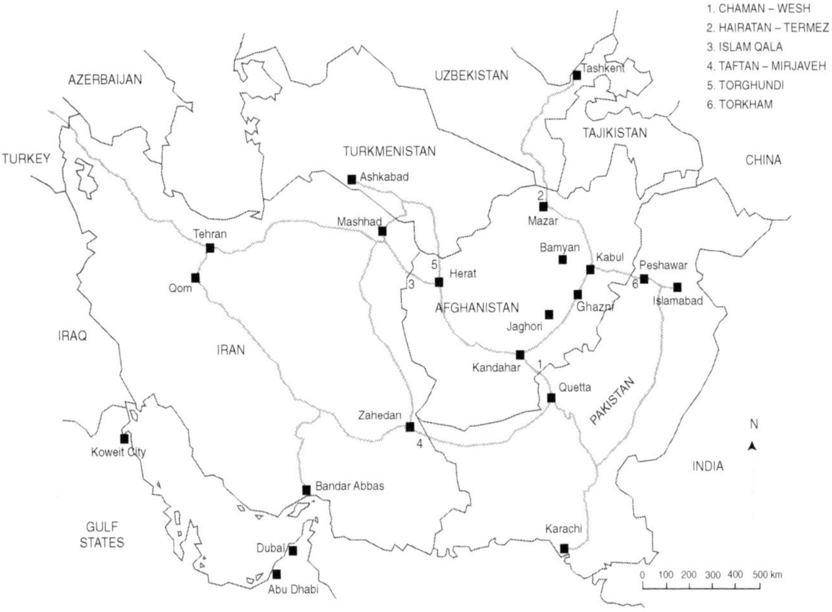

Figure 1. Afghanistan, Pakistan, and Iran

PART ONE

ISSUES AND METHOD

Chapter One

Migration and Transnationalism in the Anthropological Debate

TOWARDS A NEW PARADIGM IN ANTHROPOLOGY

At the junction between two millennia, many anthropologists feel deeply uneasy about the object and method of their discipline. Although there are scarcely any more grand systems of explanation, the theoretical debate remains intense and many authors are hoping that a new paradigm will take shape. In this rich if disorganized intellectual climate, there have been important advances in the study of migration and refugee flows, in connection with the theme of transnationalism and globalization, and this has had a wider impact on anthropology and the human and social sciences in general.

A lot of research remains caught up in a conceptual framework that may appear out of date. Since the 1980s, however, a new epistemological thinking (originating mostly among North American authors who adopt the perspective of postmodern anthropology) has broken with the previously dominant model that conceived of communities as discrete units, each woven together and rooted in a particular territory. Although numerous voices have been raised against the excesses of this new current, and against its oversimplification of the history of the discipline, it is no longer possible to keep doing anthropology as it was done in the 1950s, 1960s or even 1970s. The study of migration has played a major role in this turn (Kearney 1986: 332).[1]

Migration is often explained in terms of violent conflicts or the attraction of labor markets in rich countries or urban centers. Although other factors may be in play, such as natural disasters (earthquakes, floods, prolonged drought, etc.) or certain kinds of development project (dam construction, landholding reforms, programs to settle nomadic populations, etc.), it is political or economic causes which are ordinarily used to distinguish between involuntary or forced migration and voluntary migration; the media and public opinion in the West echo this by readily contrasting political refugees with economic migrants, seeing the latter as bogus refugees who use asylum procedures to come and work in Western Europe or North America.

It is becoming increasingly clear that this mainly causal framework cannot do justice to the complexity of today's global migration flows. We have to go beyond anthropological conceptions in which cultures and communities appear as spatially located phenomena; we should no longer think of migration as movement from one place to another, but rather as:

> multidirectional (sometimes circular) relocation which changes place of residence but not always the places where time is actually spent, the intensity of social relations but not systematically their structure. It is therefore a complex social phenomenon involving much more than flight or attraction towards prosperous lands. The conception of a definitive resettlement or irreversible move does not take account of the social reality, for the migratory phenomena observable today are mostly bidirectional or circular (Droz and Sottas 1997: 70).

In many cases, spatial dispersion is a survival strategy that makes it possible to use a variety of ecological and socio-economic niches. Migration flows, then, should no longer be seen in terms of "flight by individuals in search of a better life"; for, although migrants do leave, "at the same time—through family circulation strategies—they remain at home" (Dros & Sottas 1997: 86).

Group mobility by no means signals a recent change from a world of homogeneous and mutually separated social-cultural entities. From the very beginnings, migration has been a major constituent of human history. In the eighteenth century, for example, Iran experienced huge and compulsory resettlement, which lastingly altered the geographical distribution of its population (Perry 1975), and in the following century Afghanistan was the scene of intermingling whose effects are still visible today (Centlivres and Centlivres-Demont 1983, 1988a; Mousavi 1998). The Middle East and Central Asia have always had large nomadic populations, with migration not limited simply to seasonal relocation by shepherds. To be sure, population movements have been particularly intense in the last part of the twentieth century, but this is not enough to explain the current theoretical infatuation with the problems of migration and refugees. We need also to bear in mind other factors, such as the rise of postmodern theories in philosophy and social science, the accompanying crisis of grand systems of explanation in anthropology, and the gradual institutionalization of development aid and humanitarian action in two distinct stages (after the Second World War and then after the end of the Cold War).

The aim of this introductory chapter will be to assess the scope and limits of the existing literature on migration. Thought needs to be given to an open conception of the relationship between social-cultural groups and territories, in a way that goes beyond the assumption of sedentariness and the opposition between voluntary economic migrants and involuntary political refugees. Finally, we must take a critical look at the idea that migration shatters social ties and inevitably induces psychological traumas.

THE FIGURE OF THE REFUGEE IN OFFICIAL INTERNATIONAL TEXTS

The office of the United Nations High Commissioner for Refugees was created in the years following the Second World War. The international definition of a refugee may be found in the first article of the 1951 Convention Relating to the Status of Refugees, which was adopted on July 28, 1951 and came into force on April 22, 1954, but with application only to events in Europe prior to January 1, 1951. In 1967 a Protocol extended both the time frame and the geographical field of validity:

> The term 'refugee' shall apply to any person who, owing to a well founded fear of being persecuted for reasons of race, religion, nationality, membership of a particular social group or political opinion, is outside the country of his nationality and is unable or, owing to such fear, is unwilling to avail himself of the protection of that country; or who, not having a nationality and being outside his country of former habitual residence as a result of such events, is unable or, owing to such fear, is unwilling to return to it (HCR 1996a).

At the time of writing, 133 countries have ratified this Protocol.[2] The purpose of the two documents is to protect fundamental rights (first of all, the right to life and physical safety) of people who are forced to flee their homes. When individuals are no longer protected by their own government, it falls to the international community (in the shape of the signatories) to intervene on their behalf. The UNHCR is supposed to complement governments by encouraging the signature of international conventions, by ensuring that refugees are treated accordingly and not forced to return to the country from which they have fled, and by seeking permanent solutions to refugee problems (HCR 1996a, 1996b).

This definition calls for a few remarks. First, international legal usage does not accord refugee status to "internally displaced persons" (IDPs), that is to persons who have not left the national territory in question (Hein 1993: 44; Marx 1990: 190; Zetter 1991: 40). Second, a person who, in the country of asylum, continues military activities against his or her country of origin is not considered a refugee.[3] And, lastly, these texts imply a distinction between refugees and economic migrants: whereas the former are persecuted, or fear persecution, and have no other choice than to flee, the latter continue to enjoy the protection of their government and are supposed to have left their country voluntarily in search of a better life.

International organizations concerned with refugee aid allow for three long-term solutions: repatriation to the country of origin, integration into the first country to provide asylum, and resettlement in a third country (Hein 1993: 48; Malkki 1995a: 505; Stein 1986: 265, 268).

The last scenario remains a rarity, for Third World countries are both originators and hosts of the great majority of refugees (Stein 1986: 265). On January 1, 2001, nearly 22 million persons came under the mandate of the UNHCR. (This figure included 3,580,400 Afghans—before, that is, the return of several hundreds of thousands in the months following the overthrown of the Taliban regime in autumn 2001.) On the same date, a total of 6,694,800 refugees were distributed among Europe, North America and Australasia.[4] Thus, while the issue of asylum-seekers and refugees fills the headlines in the West, the reality is that nearly 70 percent of the world's refugees are living in Third World countries. This is not least of the paradoxes of globalization: the industrial countries, whose immigration policy is shaped by the dichotomy between political refugees and economic migrants, have accompanied their advocacy of the free circulation of capital with a complex legal and police apparatus to control immigration from the poorest regions of the world. This situation often forces would-be immigrants to apply for political asylum, which they have little chance of obtaining.

Repatriation to the country of origin, which is considered the optimum solution, is a rather infrequent occurrence (Zetter 1988b: 101; Stein 1986: 269, 272). In Europe, after the huge movement of population resulting from the Second World War, most later refugees (between the 1950s and 1970s) came from countries fighting a colonial regime; the eventual success of this struggle and the achievement of independence then made it possible for them to return. Since the mid-seventies, however, most of the world's refugees have come from independent countries—from Afghanistan, of course, but also from various other countries in Asia and Africa, where a long-drawn-out conflict makes repatriation more and more of a hypothetical solution (Stein 1986: 265–66).

Thus Western barriers to immigration, combined with the political difficulties of repatriation to the country of origin, mean that humanitarian agencies consider integration in the first country of asylum to be the most feasible, if not the best, solution. In this optic, although the paid activity of migrants is usually in the informal sector and not in the official labor market (Kearney 1986: 349), integration is the only real solution in the long term (Stein 1986: 277).

The definition of a refugee in the international texts is supposed to be binding on states that have signed up to them, and therefore to provide millions of people with a legal status that protects them from arbitrary treatment. Yet, as Richmond stresses (1988: 23), it is not a fruitful analytic or descriptive starting-point for researchers in the social sciences. The Hazaras, for instance, are constantly on the move among Afghanistan, Pakistan, Iran and the countries of the Arabian Peninsula. War and poverty have compelled them to leave their native regions, but they have developed (with scarcely any international aid) a number of social-economic strategies based on high levels of circulation. Whereas the international texts, with their stress on the legal and normative dimension, conceive of the refugee as a resourceless individual removed from any cultural context, social relationships remain very strong among Afghans.

The wish has often been expressed that academic research and refugee aid should be closer to each other. In an attempt to enrich the definition in the international texts Harrell-Bond and Vourtira, for example, write that:

> anthropologically, refugees are people who have undergone a violent 'rite' of separation and, unless or until they are incorporated as citizens into their host state (or returned to their state of origin), find themselves in transition, in a state of liminality. This betwixt-and-between status may contain social and economic dimensions as well as legal and psychological ones. Moreover, encoded in the refugee label are images of dependency, helplessness, and misery (Harrell-Bond & Vourtira 1996: 1077).

Beyond the vocabulary of anthropology, however, we find in this definition all the elements of a refugee as conceived in international law: separation followed by assimilation or return; violence, dependence, and so on. Although the authors in question seek to distance themselves from this overly juridical definition, they do not manage to shake off the all too common metaphor of rootlessness, nor to abandon a highly sombre vision of the refugee experience. It is true, of course, that refugees face a dramatic situation, yet they have resources which they know how to mobilize effectively.

Thus, although we can be happy at the rise of an applied anthropology that has much to contribute to humanitarian and development aid, and although it is desirable that anthropologists should serve as intermediaries between humanitarian agencies and local communities (Howell 1982), it is regrettable that most of the relevant texts abandon any critical perspective. The closing of the gap between reflection and action most often seems to concern only particular assignments for which anthropologists adopt the vocabulary of international documents. Sometimes, it is even hard to distinguish academic research from the humanitarian reports whose terminology has invaded the whole field of refugee studies.

Malkki (1995a) has shown that refugee studies took shape, first, in relation to displaced persons in Europe after the Second World War, and then through a whole series of discursive and institutional developments in international law, development studies, refugee studies, UN activity, the work of special refugee agencies, and so on. The figure of the refugee thus made its cognitive and legal appearance in a period marked by the creation of special camps and the spatial concentration of refugees under initially military administration (Malkki 1995a: 498). After the 1951 Convention and the 1967 Protocol, the international institutions began to relate to the question of refugees—not, however, as a political problem requiring a political solution, but as a matter of directing charity towards people who were seen as the mere victims of events outside their control. The two main characteristics of the resulting "international refugee system" (Malkki 1995a: 504) were therefore depoliticization and bureaucratization, and it is from this system that academic research has uncritically imported most of its ideas. The term "refugee" is here not so much an analytic category enabling us to identify a certain kind of person or situation, but rather a legal category that allows very different cases to be grouped within one or other element of a debatable dichotomy: either as economic migrants or as refugees. As Malkki puts it:

> The 'international refugee regime' [. . .] has been instrumental in the recent emergence of 'refugee studies' as an academic or 'applied academic' specialization. Much social scientific research—whether resulting in policy recommendations, development reports, or academic articles—has been conducted in more or less formal connection with (and often funded by) these international organizations. It can hardly be surprising that these institutional, organizational settings have had subtle (and sometimes not-so-subtle) effects in shaping the questions that scholars have formulated about displacement and refugee settlement (1995a: 506).

To avoid this pitfall, it has become urgently necessary for new research to focus on the international system, UN agencies and non-governmental organizations. The opposition between political refugee and economic migrant, already implicit in the 1951 Convention and the 1967 Protocol, has scarcely any descriptive or analytic relevance, even though it remains part of national immigration policies. Any anthropological approach to migratory phenomena must move beyond this conception, and bring it under appropriate scrutiny.

TYPOLOGIES AS A GENERAL THEORY OF MIGRATION

Many authors consider that a general theory of migration should take the form of a typology, centring mainly upon the rational choice of the people involved. Their approaches, which claim to have predictive power, set out a bipolar opposition between societies that send and receive migrants, and distinguish between "push factors" impelling departure and "pull factors" attracting migration.

Ravenstein (1885 & 1889) and Fairchild (1925) were among the first to present a general theory of migration, the latter's four categories of invasion, conquest, colonization and immigration remaining influential until after the Second World War (Connor 1987b: 153–154). One of the most elaborate typologies has been that of Petersen (1958), who also had the great merit of weakening the opposition between push and pull factors. In his view, the supposedly universal tendency to a settled existence that is implicit in that opposition has no historical or psychological foundation.

Petersen starts from a general distinction between "conservative" and "innovating" migration: people migrate, in the former case, to preserve their living conditions, and in the latter case to improve them. He further subdivides migration into five classes: primitive, forced, impelled, free and mass (1958: 258–259).

Primitive migration is the result of ecological pressure. Its conservative form Petersen describes as either "wandering" (when there is no clear destination) or "ranging" (when it involves hunter-gatherers or nomadic shepherds). Its innovating form he calls "flight from the land," since it is usually a question of people leaving the countryside for the town.

Where political factors are determinant, Petersen distinguishes between "forced" migration (under compulsion from a state or an institution within society) and "impelled" migration (if people have some power over their decision to leave); the two conservative forms of these he calls respectively "displacement" and "flight," and the two innovating forms "slave trade" and "coolie trade."

Free migration corresponds to the wish of the migrants themselves. The difference between pioneering and group movement consists in the mode of departure (individual or communal) and the number of persons involved.

Free migration often paves the way for mass migration—for instance, the settling of peasants from Europe in North America, or the urbanization of a rural population across or within an international frontier.

More recently, Kunz (1973, 1981) and du Toit (1990) have also argued that a typology is integral to any general theory of migration. Kunz starts with the following definition: "With a different past and with motivations at variance with those affecting voluntary migrants, the refugee moves from his homeland to the country of his settlement against his will. He is a distinct social type" (Kunz 1973: 130), whose aim is one day to rediscover community ties by returning to his homeland. Although Kunz's central distinction is between voluntary and involuntary migration (characterized by push and pull factors respectively), he further uses a classical model to identify the diverse combinations of motives and external circumstances that enter into the latter. Thus, he speaks of "anticipatory refugee movement," where refugees move to the host country in anticipation of a worsening situation at home, and "acute refugee movement," where they flee, often in difficult conditions, a context of violence and insecurity (1973: 131). In both cases, it is true, "push factors" are the decisive ones, but the urgency gives them much greater prominence in "acute movement." Pull factors may then often play a role in the choice of an (at least temporary) host country.

Kunz (1973) offers a first set of distinctions regarding the forms of exile and arrival in the initial host country. He uses the term "push-permit" to characterize anticipatory movements; the refugee, faced with impending calamities, tries to leave his homeland and to find official residence elsewhere. If the situation has already become dramatically urgent, however, Kunz speaks of "push-pressure"; the refugee then has neither the time nor the means to consider pull factors, and heads for the first available place of refuge. Further distinctions are possible with regard to the refugee's insertion into the host country: "push-pressure-plunge" when the situation in the first host country forces him to move on to another; "push-pressure-stay" when he receives permission to settle in the country of refuge; and "push-pressure-return" when he is induced to return to his country of origin.

A second typology is based on a distinction between waves of refugees, since the members of a society react differently to the same events and will not all leave at the same moment or for the same reasons. Kunz here uses the term "vintages" to refer to groups who left at the same time, had similar experiences and often share the same ideas.

A third distinction relates to the forms of departure. Among the urgent forms, Kunz lists flight, forced population transfer and relocation through absence (that is, people who leave their country in normal circumstances and refuse to return because of subsequent events).

Like many others, du Toit counterpoises voluntary and forced migration. He distinguishes among seasonal migrants, refugees, planned relocation and voluntary migration (1990: 305–306) and attempts to draw up a model embracing various aspects of migration: spatial flows, push and pull factors, physical movement, the taking of decisions. While advocating measures to prevent flight from the countryside and to promote more harmonious development, he calls for special attention to be paid to migration routes and the multiplicity of factors involved in migration. He recognizes that migration is not an act but a process, yet his definition of it remains rather limited:

> Migration is a relatively permanent moving away of a collectivity, called migrants, from one geographical location to another, preceded by decision making on the part of the migrants on the basis of a hierarchically ordered set of values or valued ends and resulting in changes in the interactional system of the migrants (du Toit 1990: 308).

A number of different stages are often identified in the experience of refugees: perception of a threat; the decision to flee; the period of extreme danger and flight; the arrival in safer areas; life in the camps; repatriation, settlement in the first host country or departure for another country; the various phases of creating a new home; adaptation and acculturation; changes in behaviour as a result of these experiences (Stein 1981: 321).

The wish to develop a general theory of refugee movement beyond particular cases, and to achieve greater conceptual clarity and terminological precision, is certainly praiseworthy in itself. But it is regrettable that the suggested definitions are little more than labels, providing rigid frameworks that do not allow the complexity of situations in the real world to be expressed. Thus, the distinction between "push" and "pull" factors is not unimportant, but we may doubt the relevance of the options that are considered to be open to refugees: departure for a third country, return to their country of origin or settlement in the first host country. The framework here remains the nation-state, and fails to do justice to the rich, polysemous experience of refugees and migrants. Its reductionism rules out any open and multiple view of space, as well as the existence of back-and-forth movements and transnational links.

These approaches emphasize the dramatic side of forced migration, with its profoundly traumatic effects. Many authors speak of populations being completely "uprooted" (e.g. Zetter 1988a: 1) or cast into "limbo" (Stein 1986: 264). But this is to overlook the strategies that refugees develop, as well as their social-cultural resources, with the result that the frequently multidirectional and recurrent character of migratory movements becomes blurred in a generally linear vision.

THEORIES OF MODERNIZATION AND DEPENDENCE

Approaches to the phenomenon of migration are often divided into microtheories and macrotheories. Microtheories focus on individual rational choice in a world where chances are not evenly distributed, so that migration is seen as a population movement from regions poor in capital but rich in labor to economically prosperous regions that need a large workforce. Most of the contributions reviewed in the previous section may be grouped under this category. Macrotheories adopt explanations with a more global reach, laying stress on demographic and economic structures in the context of a capitalism organized on a world scale (Richmond 1988; Zolberg 1981).

This distinction ties up with the two theoretical approaches to North-South relations: modernization theory and the theory of dependency and world systems. Bocco has this to say about the former:

> The modernization theorists of the 1950s and 1960s thought of national and international migration as a necessary, sometimes even an inevitable, phenomenon—or anyway as a stage in the process of human evolution. Considered as veritable catalysts of social change, migratory flows were supposed to have given traditional societies access to modernity. Within this framework, the large refugee flows from the South triggered by the creation of new postcolonial states were seen as a transitional phenomenon, destined to die out with the emergence and consolidation of a modern 'national' spirit (Bocco 1994: 15–16).

Modernization theory dominated debate until the mid-1960s. Descended from an ancient Western philosophical tradition, it based itself upon the belief in progress and explained the decisions of individuals to migrate in terms of how they assessed the information at their disposal. It was easy for critics to point out that in many cases the effects of urbanization were rather more pernicious than the economic development predicted by modernization theory (e.g. Kearney 1986: 334), and that the whole process had to be seen in the light of the worldwide expansion of capitalism and the accompanying rise of nationalist discourses and practices limiting the mobility of labor (Bocco 1994: 16). Dependency theory thus emerged on the basis of a Marxist critique of modernization theory, its aim being to study the "development of underdevelopment" (Kearney 1986: 338). The industrial countries and the Third World, like urban and rural areas, did not have separate economies but were linked together in relations of dependence that served the needs of the core at the expense of the periphery. Far from being an instrument of modernization, migration and development were exploitative mechanisms within what Wallerstein (1974, 1980, 1989) called the capitalist "world-system."

Kearney (1986) emphasized some of the limitations of dependency theory: it was too general to provide good directions for research in specific fields; it neglected cultural factors and laid too much stress on economic as opposed to political questions; it did not take into account strategies of resistance and reappropriation in the periphery; and it thought of the world as having a single rather than several centers.

Accepting that the great migratory flows could not be isolated from economic disparities in the contemporary world, Kearney argued that they had to be studied in conjunction with issues of development and underdevelopment. His proposed third way, which he called articulation theory, was meant to look into social practices and their cultural dimension, while still remaining attentive to local initiatives and relations of domination. Kearney was interested more in systems of production and reproduction than in the sphere of circulation; he did not retain the idea of a world-system unified by the capitalist economy, because he thought that the periphery had a dynamism of its own and perhaps also modes of production distinct from those of the core. The domestic unit thus remained the pertinent analytic level for empirical research. At the same time, the "articulatory migrant network" offered a fertile interpretive key enabling us to represent the movement of persons, goods, services and information as a huge vascular system (1986: 353).

In a full review of the social and economic literature on migration, Massey and his colleagues have widened the discussion by identifying four distinct currents:

1) *Studies inspired by neoclassical economics (both macro and micro)* highlight income and employment differences, explaining migratory flows by geographical variations in supply and demand; there is movement of workers "from labour-abundant to labour-scarce countries," with migration the outcome of a wage-gap between countries (Massey et al. 1993: 433f.). Microeconomically, this means that individuals rationally choose to migrate after making a cost-benefit calculation and seeking to maximize their interests.
2) *The new economics of migration* does not consider only the labor market but extends the decision-making process to the whole of

the domestic group. Households seek not only to maximize their interests but also to minimize risks by diversifying their economic resources (Massey et al. 1993: 436). In this view, then, migration is to developing countries what social security is to developed countries.

3) *The dual labor-market theory* does not rest upon an individual or family model of rational choice but explains migration by the permanent need for labor in modern industrial societies—by demand factors rather than by supply. Migrants meet the requirements of employers, since they regard the low-paid work on offer to them as a mere source of income, not as a means of social advancement (Massey et al. 1993: 440–442).

4) In *world-systems theory,* international migration results not only from the organization of production and labor in the industrial countries, but more generally from the structures of the world market. Migratory flows are thus brought about by economic globalization—that is, not by wage and employment differences, but by the penetration of the capitalist market into developing countries and the resulting social, cultural and economic upheavals. Persons move in the opposite direction from commodities and capital (Massey et al. 1993: 447–448).

Massey and his colleagues stress that the factors which induce migration are not necessarily the same as those which perpetuate it. They accordingly speak of "cumulative causation" (Massey et al. 1993: 448): migrants weave networks of contacts that make it ever easier to move between different countries. Furthermore, the gap between demand (the number of people wishing to enter an economically developed country) and supply (the number of visas available) creates a lucrative niche. A whole black market of forgers and people-smugglers comes into being to get round controls in the destination country, while NGOs justify their own existence by defending migrants and refugees from state repression and providing them with legal forms of assistance (Massey et al. 1993: 450–451).

In short, the factors triggering and sustaining migratory flows come to form more or less stable systems (Massey et al. 1993: 462). Given the multiplicity of causes—political, economic, social, cultural and psychological—it is hard to imagine a theory that could integrate them all into a coherent whole.

NEW APPROACHES OF MIGRATION

In their critical reflection on the object and methods of anthropology, numerous (mainly North American) authors inspired by *Writing Culture* (Clifford and Marcus eds 1986) consider the links among social-cultural groups, territorial areas and the phenomenon of migration. For a long time, anthropologists saw their object of investigation as consisting of culturally and linguistically homogeneous territorial groups—until migrants came along to shake that perception. Then it was thought that migrants simply moved from one place or culture to another, in a one-way process that ended with varying degrees of successful integration.

Beginning in the 1980s, an anthropological current sought to shift the focus from clearly defined territorial groups to the trajectories of migrants crossing political and cultural boundaries. There was growing interest in cultural hybridity, creolization, public culture or global economics, in transnationalism and diaspora existence, as aspects of a world undergoing massive change in which the metaphor of rootedness no longer seemed to apply. The success of the term "diaspora"—which reached its peak in 1991 with the founding of an eponymous journal—testifies to the rise of migration studies. It derives from a Greek word meaning "dispersion" and has been used historically to refer to the Jews within the Roman Empire (Tölölyan 1996: 10). In a programmatic text that appeared in the first issue of the journal, Safran defined its referent as follows:

> expatriate communities whose members share several of the following characteristics: 1) they, or their ancestors, have been dispersed from a specific original 'centre' to two or more 'peripheral,' or foreign, regions; 2) they retain a collective memory, vision, or myth about their original homeland—its physical location, history, and achievements; 3) they believe that they are not—and perhaps cannot be—fully accepted by their host society and therefore feel partly alienated and insulated from it; 4) they regard their ancestral homeland as their true, ideal home and as the place to which they or their descendants would (or should) eventually return—when conditions are appropriate; 5) they believe that they should, collectively, be committed to the maintenance or restoration of their original homeland and to its safety and prosperity; and 6) they continue to relate, personally or vicariously, to that homeland in one way or another, and their ethnocommunal consciousness and solidarity are importantly defined by the existence of such relationship (Safran 1991: 83–84).

Although this definition still reflects the Jewish origin of the concept and its extension to certain other communities (Armenians and Greeks), the term has been used to denote a large number of dispersed peoples—from the Turks of Germany to the Asians of Britain and the Chinese of South-East Asia, or even the Palestinians (Bruneau 1994; Tedlock 1996; Tölölyan 1996; Schnapper 2001). Nevertheless, it remains too formal and restrictive to provide the basis for a general theory of migration. Clifford, in a critique of Safran's text (1994), suggested that the concept should be widened as part of an anthropology of travel in the changing global conditions of our time. In his view, it was not useful to define a term such as "disapora" by reference to an "ideal type," so that various groups then became more or less "disaporic" by virtue of various qualities they did or did not have. Instead, he argued for an anthropology that could offer an open, non-normative account of decolonization, migration, global communication, transport, and any other phenomenon linked to multilocality and mobility. In the rapidly changing world of the late twentieth century, social links were becoming diffuse and transnational relations more widespread. Diaspora discourses therefore reflected a general tendency of belonging to transnational networks that included a person's place of origin as one "mooring" among others.

Although diasporas are often brought about by political and economic inequality, Clifford stressed the capacity for resistance of displaced peoples. Diaspora communities such as the Jews contradict the idea of self-sufficient cultures turned in on themselves and tied to a single place. They cannot be reduced to an epiphenomenon of the nation-state or global capitalism, for they have become a constituent feature of the contemporary world. This should impel us to define a new set of conceptual tools.

Clifford's points concerning diasporas are part of his wider attempt to redefine the method of anthropology (1986, 1988, 1992, 1997). He is aware that there have always been dissident tendencies, but he reflects the legacy of Malinowski in stressing that the field was conceived in terms of joint residence rather than a trip or visit. In other words, the dominant concept of the field implied a stay in a given place. This method had its source in a conception of culture as an integrated, homogeneous entity within a clearly defined space. Clifford, by contrast, saw culture in terms of travelling—not only in the literal sense, but as a whole series of more or less allegorical or imaginary relocations. He also thought that anthropology should draw its inspiration from certain techniques in travel writing, to allow greater room for the author's emotions. Fieldwork was therefore no longer the study of distant peoples, of an essentialist Other, but involved a (not only spatial) experience of decentring.

In a text originally published in 1990, Appadurai (1999) also asked how anthropology could apprehend the contemporary world, and attempted to go beyond such dichotomies as global/local or North/South. He proposed five conceptual categories as a way of organizing the anthropology of global culture and economy: *ethnoscapes*, produced by the movement of persons (refugees and migrants, of course, but also seasonal workers and tourists); *technoscapes*, constituted through the circulation of technologies;

finanscapes, that is capital flows and stock exchanges; *mediascapes,* consisting of information and images produced by radio, television, newspapers, cinema and other media; and *ideoscapes,* deriving from state or non-state political ideologies (freedom, public good, rights, sovereignty, etc.). Far from culturally homogenizing the world, these five types of flow produce new differences and resurgent identities. Appadurai made further use of these distinctions in another text that appeared shortly afterwards (1991):

> As groups migrate, regroup in new locations, reconstruct their histories, and reconfigure their ethnic 'project,' the ethno in ethnography takes on a slippery, nonlocalized quality [. . .] groups are no longer tightly territorialized, spatially bounded, historically unselfconscious, or culturally homogenous (Appadurai 1991: 191).

In Appadurai's view, the movement of persons is an essential characteristic of the contemporary world. He argues for a "cosmopolitan ethnology" based upon new research strategies that enable us to understand the deterritorialized world in which we live (1991: 196); it should not only study actual movement but also focus on the imagination and its various representations. Gupta and Ferguson (1992, 1997) have further elaborated this theoretical effort, in reflections on field practice and its links with a localized conception of culture. The fact that societies, cultures and nations appear to be distinct from one another derives from a particular conception of space, whereas migrants and refugees call into question the conjunction of culture and territory.

In some respects, theories of transnationalism extend these general theoretical efforts into the field of migration studies, since their promoters no longer consider their object of study to be closed units or localized communities. Glick Schiller, Basch and Szanton Blanc have specialized in the theory of transnationalism, defining it as a social process whereby migrants establish relations across geographical, political and cultural boundaries and link together their country of origin with their country of resettlement. They call "transmigrants" those individuals who develop and maintain multiple relations—familial, economic, social, religious or political—across political, cultural and geographical frontiers, and whose identity is therefore linked to networks stretching across several nation-states (Glick Schiller et al. 1992: ix, 1; cf. Glick Schiller et al. 1995: 48, 54, and Basch et al. 1994: 7).

According to these authors, globalization is characterized by the intensification of relations among distant places, so that a local situation is influenced by events taking place far away. Anthropologists cannot take cultures in isolation, but must study the flows of persons, objects, capital, images and information. The perfect example of a transnational phenomenon is therefore a migratory process affecting several countries, but globalization has a more abstract dimension less directly linked to particular countries (Kearney 1995: 548 referring to Glick Schiller et al. 1992). Both concepts, however, point beyond a world divided between a core and a periphery; both involve a more complex view in which different social-cultural spheres interpenetrate. The research object for anthropology thus shifts from territorial (or supposedly territorial) communities within a nation-state towards discontinuous spaces whose nations are only one component and not the overarching frame of reference. This raises a number of theoretical and methodological issues (Kearney 1995: 548–549).

Globalization may be seen as an increase in the number of links and flows across state frontiers. It brings new types of movement of goods and information, as well as new feelings of belonging. Nation-states lose some of their decision-making power in relation to economic phenomena (the globalization of capital seems more critical here than the globalization and acceleration of trade flows), but this tendency—as many researchers have pointed out—goes together with the rise of ethnicist political discourses and "essentialist nationalism" (Glick Schiller et al. 1995: 52; cf. Appadurai 1999). Benedict Anderson, for his part, speaks of "long-distance nationalism" (1992: 12). There are two very different evaluations of this process. Some authors consider that the homogenizing force of Western social-economic imperialism threatens the cultural diversity of the world, while others stress that transnational flows are locally reinterpreted or that, as Marcus points out (1992: 313), the homogenization process encounters resistance and goes together with the creation of new differences. For Anderson (1992) this bodes nothing but ill, whereas for Appadurai (1995) it marks a new opening out (Centlivres 2000: 11–12).

The work of Malkki, already mentioned above (1992, 1995a, 1995b, 1997), is mainly concerned with refugees but expresses the same drive to rethink the whole problematic of migration. She attacks the metaphor of rootedness, which has metaphysical implications in so far as it naturalizes the ties between people and territories; the concept of a place of origin is indeed becoming hard to use, since more and more people identify with deterritorialized categories. The study of people on the move points to a new theoretical sensitivity, whose main interest is in frontiers and border-crossing. This paradigm shift allows us to cast a critical eye on the effects that a national frame of reference may have on research relating to refugees and other displaced persons.

Migration appears as an anomaly to social scientists for whom societies and cultures are rooted in a land, with the result that many academic studies adopt a quasi-medical or psychologistic perspective. But it is also anomalous in relation to the political organization of the world, divided as it is into a multiplicity of nation-states (Zolberg 1981: 6). The usual conceptions of culture tend "toward rooting rather than travel," writes Malkki (1992: 33) with reference to Clifford. Like Glick Schiller et al. (1995) and many others,[5] she lays bare the sedentarist presuppositions in xenophobic anti-immigrant discourse. The "order of things" of which she speaks is that of the natural division of the world into a number of sovereign states.

Malkki sums up her argument in four points: 1) The world of nations tends to be seen as a compartmentalized space of disjointed territories. 2) The relationship of local populations with space tends to be naturalized through botanical metaphors. 3) The concept of culture has many points in common with the concept of nation, since both imply rooting in particular places; this reveals a "metaphysical sedentarism" or a "metaphysic of sedentariness." 4) Naturalization of the links between populations and spaces implies that relocation is an anomaly—an idea expressed in the metaphor of "uprootedness."

This overview has brought out at least three features of transnational studies: the phenomena in question cross the frontiers of autonomous political entities; the links are established over a long distance; and a diversity of meanings and cultural forms is implied. Hannerz has proposed the term "global ecumene" (1992a: 37) to take us beyond a mosaic world-view consisting of disjointed social-cultural units, and to emphasize that social relations are more decisive than places.[6] While he criticizes what he calls, after Janet Abu-Lughod, "the rhetoric of globalbabble" (1992a: 34), Hannerz stresses the contribution of anthropology to the study of transnational processes in many research fields: "translocalities," "border studies," "migration," "diasporas," "transnational corporations and occupations," "tourism," "cyberspace," "media" and "commodities" (1998: 237).[7]

MIGRATION, TRANSNATIONALISM AND GLOBALIZATION

How should we assess the contributions of the old typologies and the new approaches? This question goes beyond the debate on migration and refugees; it concerns the significance of the epistemological turn in post-structuralist anthropology. What has to be considered is whether the post-modern perspective corresponds to a passing disorder or to a genuine theoretical regeneration.

The typologies go no further than a causal approach based upon people's motives for migration. The distinction between voluntary and forced migration does not, however, stand up to the reality of migratory strategies and possible changes over time. The view that migrants cross cultural frontiers simply by moving from one point in space to another, that migration is a linear phenomenon and the world a mosaic of nation-states, leaves us unable to see that population movement is most often circular and recurrent and that spatially distant places may together form a single system.

Transnational studies appear to be a more fruitful approach, because it takes account of the rich diversity of migrant situations beyond the narrow framework of nation-states. It takes on board the fact that migrants retain links with their country of origin; it concerns itself not only with adaptation processes and the forging of new identities but also, and above all, with the social relations that migrants develop. This goes beyond the idea that migration is a single event involving relocation from A to B, a one-way and irreversible occurrence. Contrary to what push-pull theory implies, the migrant is not simply an agent executing rational choices to maximize his or her interests. Without going to the opposite extreme (the idea that migrants are submerged by social forces on which they have no purchase), it is necessary to consider the social field and political context in which the lives of migrants and refugees unfold. In other words, we must avoid two pitfalls: "an undersocialized view of migration in which all action reflect(s) individual wishes and preferences," and "an oversocialized view in which people (are) passive agents in the migratory process" (Boyd 1989: 641). This also takes us beyond dependency and world-systems theory, which rests upon an overly schematic opposition between core and periphery.

More generally, the current that takes a special interest in globalization and transnationalism raises questions about the object and methods of anthropology. Many are those who claim that the impossibility of demarcating and territorializing social groups should make us abandon the concept of culture. But it is not always clear whether this is bound up with empirical considerations—that is, with the changing features of migration since the 1960s—or whether it is a theoretical statement. Does the altered perspective correspond to an objective evolution of the contemporary world, or does it stem from a new awareness of the limitations of the old anthropological and social-scientific paradigms? Are we speaking of a response to external changes or a conceptual adjustment? It is essential to distinguish these two levels, which the critical movement in North American anthropology often tends to confuse. In fact, we may reproach it with two interrelated defects: a misguided view of the social and economic history of the world, and a simplistic conception of the history of anthropology. Let us consider these in turn.

Authors who specialize in transnationalism and globalization usually argue that the flows of persons, capital, commodities and information acquired an unprecedented scale in the second half of the twentieth century. Glick Schiller and her colleagues clearly opt for the view that this was a novel phenomenon and seek to outline a corresponding field for research (Glick Schiller et al. 1992: x, 1).[8]

Theories of transnationalism and globalization would therefore seem to originate in a view of the faster cross-border circulation of persons, goods and money, as well as of information and ideas. But is this really so new? Many authors remain sceptical (e.g. Shami 1996: 4) and criticize the performative dimension of the statements in question, the quest for special effects, and the use of various stylistic figures. It is perfectly legitimate to take an interest in human groups on the move. But Mintz, for example (1998), wonders whether the term "transnational" introduces anything new. He does not deny that separate places may be linked through the continual movement of individuals, money, goods and information. Basing himself on the experience of the Caribbean, however, he shows that globalization has been characterized by periodicity. In the nineteenth century several hundred million people migrated; roughly half of these were Europeans who left to become citizens of the United States, Canada, Argentina, Uruguay, South Africa, New Zealand or Australia; but the other half—Africans, Chinese or Indians—migrated as a labor force from colonized countries to other colonized countries. This vast movement therefore expressed a certain relationship of forces and division of labor at international level. It is true that migration took new forms in the twentieth century, as many Africans, Chinese or Indians settled in the West, but that was only one stage in a larger process that had begun several centuries earlier. Only a profound shortsightedness makes the bards of transnationalism overlook this fact. Mintz concludes in polemical but convincing fashion:

> The massive movement of people globally is centuries old. The identification of persons with more than one community is similarly ancient. [. . .] The new theories of transnationalism and globalization are not respectful enough of history, especially of the history of exploration, conquest and the global division of labour (1998: 131).

Gupta (2000), who bases himself on the spread of agricultural products and new food habits, also situates globalization in a broader historical and geographical perspective. From the Middle Ages on, the tastes of Westerners were influenced, or even fundamentally altered, by food supplied from China, India or Africa, while in a symmetrical process many of the ingredients in Indian cooking originated in the New World. Northern Europe played a minor role until the Industrial Revolution, although dense trade flows linked Southern Europe, North Africa, the Middle East, the Indian subcontinent and the Far East. What mainly characterizes the contemporary period, therefore, is not globalization but a crisis of sovereignty affecting the nation-states that developed in the West after the Treaty of Westphalia (1648). Discourses centered upon globalization mostly emanate from Western academics immersed in a specific political model. They are not really aware that, in many other parts of the world, the nation-state remained a fiction while social, cultural and commercial relations maintained a stable existence. As a lot of research has shown,[9] migration and trade are age-old phenomena that acquired particular intensity in the last few centuries and in regions outside Europe.[10] The acceleration of recent times is largely a question of degree.

Another frequent element in definitions of globalization is the emergence of deterritorialized identity-referents. The dispersion of certain peoples combined with a persistent sense of unity is certainly not a new phenomenon, it was long masked by the nation-state model yet is an integral part of human history. Without denying that the circulation of capital and information is nowadays unprecedented in both speed and scale, we need to keep in mind that the rise, triumph and relative weakening of nation-states in the nineteenth and twentieth centuries took place at a particular historical moment. After a long period in which it was held back, the expression of transnational relations and loyalties has gained new visibility in the contemporary world (Schnapper 2001). Nevertheless, far from being specific to postmodernity or globalization, this "polycentric" mode of "discontinuous and reticulate" organization is older than the nation-state, with its characteristic "homogeneity and centralization" (Bruneau 1994: 13). This is especially true of the Islamic world, which throughout history has formed a "trans-state" and "trans-societal" space of people, goods and ideas (Shami 1996: 17).

It is a particular historical angle of vision that makes us think of transnationalism as a recent phenomenon, whereas in reality (as Gellner (1983), Anderson (1983) and Hobsbawm (1990) have shown) the nation-state is a novelty linked to the development of capitalism and industrialization, which resulted in a new system of representing space and community ties. Today people travel and communicate faster than in the past, but it is the scale rather than the nature of the phenomenon which has changed

(Gupta and Ferguson 1997: 40). Perhaps what best defines the present day is the fact that a division of space into sovereign nation-states is superimposed onto multiple movement across state frontiers linked to the spread of postindustrial capitalism. In sum, we should neither overestimate nor underestimate the changes that have come with the emergence of a global society.

How do the main North American researchers working on the conditions of production of anthropological knowledge see the history of their own discipline? They argue in favor of opening up or disembedding the field, so that the links between culture and territory are weakened and the whole approach becomes more pluralist and less totalizing (e.g. Marcus 1989: 8). Their criticisms cannot be lightly dismissed; indeed, they are a key aid in helping us to understand migratory phenomena and the contemporary world. Unfortunately, however, they are in danger of rapidly becoming new academic clichés, which are not always built around in-depth ethnography.

In order to present their own discourse as innovative, such authors as Glick Schiller, Basch and Blanc-Szanton claim that classical anthropology conceived of each society as a "discrete and bounded entity," with its own distinctive economy, culture and historical trajectory, and that it was tied to a "bounded view of society and culture," "static models" (Glick Schiller et al. 1992: 6) or "bounded social science concepts" (Basch et al. 1994: 22). But these pictures of the history of the discipline are too crude and schematic. Nor can one refrain from criticizing the search for stylistic effect when they speak of the "discovery" of transnationalism (Basch et al. 1994: 4–7).

At the same time, however, it is necessary to look critically at the tradition defined by Malinowski and then taken up by the whole of the discipline; to rethink the anthropology of refugees and migration through a critique of the idea of the rootedness and territoriality of human groups. The more or less functionalist conceptions implicit in the work of many anthropologists have led them to see relocation as an anomaly that requires psychological services to provide a new framework for those who have been subjected to the trauma. Regrettably, Glick Schiller, Basch and Blanc-Szanton confuse the part with the whole; what they denounce is in fact the result of Malinowski's reaction to diffusionism. As Gupta and Ferguson point out (1997: 19–21), the diffusionist current represented by Rivers, for example, laid great stress on contact between cultures; Boas also took an interest in the history of migration and seriously doubted whether there were primitive societies that had never had any contact with the outside. Rather than simply emphasizing the undeniable changes in the contemporary world, it is therefore crucially important to reflect on the history of anthropology and on its way of constructing its object of study.

In one polemical text, whose starting point is not migration but the concept of culture, Brightman (1995) makes an incisive critique of the new thinking among American anthropologists. Questioning the significance of the postmodern "epistemological turn," he argues that their contributions often aim to do no more than express old problems in a new vocabulary, with a superficial reading, or even ignorance, of the classical texts. This is what he calls "relexification." Malkki, for instance, invoking Clifford, writes that for classical anthropology "the idea of culture carries with it an expectation of roots, of a stable, territorialized existence" (1992: 29), whereas Brightman attacks this prejudice through a detailed reading of certain texts. The same charge may be made against Appadurai (also quoted by Malkki (1992: 29)), when he claims that "natives are not only persons who are from certain places, and belong to those places, but they are also those who are somehow *incarcerated*, or confined, in those places" (Appadurai 1988: 38).

Brightman argues that such critiques involve a "construction of defective culture" (1995: 526), in the sense that they deny the diversity of previous definitions. In reality, the object of study in classical anthropology was much more fluid, and its use of the term "culture" indicated a shared terminology but by no means substantive conceptual agreement. Many of the criticisms of the concept of culture actually represent rhetorical strategies in which the wealth of usage is selectively narrowed down. For all the talk of post-Foucault discursive practices and post-Bourdieu theories of practice or habitus, there is often no more than a new nomenclature without any real conceptual innovation. Brightman does not deny the interest of contemporary debates, nor that many questions need to be posed differently in the changed intellectual context, but he does reproach many authors for their performative utterances and appeal for greater attention to the classical legacy:

> And to be sure, certain of the recent criticisms of culture gamble rather poignantly for their topicality on an increasingly pervasive disciplinary amnesia, a lack of familiarity with what has gone before. [. . .] Neither in earlier disciplinary history nor as deployed in recent anthropological writing does the culture concept consistently exhibit the attributes of ahistoricism, totalization, holism, legalism, and coherence with which its critics selectively reconstitute it. These are invented images of culture, both arbitrary and partial with respect to a much more diverse and versatile field of definition and use. Such images, nonetheless, are rapidly acquiring more authoritative perlocutionary effects (1995: 540–541).

We should not be duped, then, by the relexification manoeuvres of those authors who blithely attribute to their predecessors what they themselves intend to oppose with their "rhetoric of discontinuity" (Darnell 1995). In Darnell's eyes, the claim to theoretical novelty by the authors of *Writing Culture* (Clifford and Marcus 1986), a veritable manifesto of postmodern anthropology, largely rests upon a camouflaging of the work of their predecessors. Mintz also expresses surprise that the promoters of transnationalism appear so ignorant both of world history and of the history of anthropology (1998: 120, 131). In the same vein, Sahlins (1999) denounces the hegemonic tendencies of what he calls "afterology" (postmodernism, poststructuralism, postcolonialism, etc.), and defends Firth, Boas, Kroeber, Herskovits, Linton or Radin against the charge that they regarded cultures as self-sufficient entities closed in on themselves (Sahlins 1999: 411).

Thus, the abandonment of the term "culture" advocated by American authors such as Lila Abu-Lughod (1991) cannot in itself constitute a solution, based as it is upon a very partial (in both senses of the word) reading of the history of anthropology. As to the proposed alternatives, we may doubt whether Abu-Lughod's "ethnography of the particular," for example, is likely to prove a fertile project, or whether she is right to claim that "'culture' operates in anthropological discourse to enforce separations that inevitably carry a sense of hierarchy" (1991: 137–138). Analytic thought itself is called into question by the attachment of such value to particularity.[11] In assailing the generalizations of previous authors, Abu-Lughod herself engages in improper generalization and simplification; her stereotyped presentation of functionalist-inspired monographs leaves whole swathes of the discipline out of the picture.

Amselle, in his most recent work (2000), regrets the use that has been made of notions of mixing or creolization, which he himself helped to popularize.

> Starting from the postulate of discrete cultural entities called 'cultures,' one ends up with a hybrid conception of a postcolonial or post-Cold War world. [. . .] If, as postmodern anthropologists assert, our epoch is radically different from all previous ones, in the sense that it brings all cultures on earth into a relation of total interdependence, there must have been a time in human history when certain societies were closed in on themselves. [. . .] Contrary to the implicit postulate of the supporters of globalization, which allows them to reproduce the distinction between primitive and modern societies at the core of the definition of anthropology, we would like to show here that closed societies have never in fact existed (2000: 209–210, 213–213).

For Amselle, then, we are not witnessing the disappearance of a primitive world of isolated and homogenous societies, because no such world has ever existed. Basing himself on knowledge of West Africa, he forcefully asserts the flexible and historical character of extra-European societies. What distinguishes the contemporary epoch is not contact between cultures or large-scale international migration, nor even the pace of such movement, but rather particular identity reflexes and a redefinition of the role of nation-states (Schnapper 2001).

Friedman (1994, 2000), an author much interested in relations between the global and the local, also criticizes the new tendency in North American anthropology both for its schematic picture of the theories and methods of classical anthropology and for its inaccurate view of world history. The fact that contacts have always existed does not, he stresses, mean that the idea of place loses all meaning. Global contacts must be placed in a wider historical perspective, so that the world is understood as a system in which cultural frontiers undergo cycles of shrinkage and expansion. Unlike the theorists of transnationalism, Friedman tries to draw out the historical, political and social forces that impel people to build exclusive identities. Not content with the moral point of view for which hybridity is a solution to the major problem of essentialism, he does not mince his words about the new "transnational vulgate" (2000: 193). He follows Brightman and Sahlins in lambasting the view that authors such as Appadurai or Malkki have of the history of anthropology: they may think they are reforming the discipline through the deconstruction of old categories, but for the most part they just "add the prefix 'trans' to the words that used to connote that which was closed" (Friedman 2000: 194). Some argue that Western colonial expansion imposed uniformity and that the true hybridity of the world is once again manifesting itself in the postcolonial age, whereas a larger group of authors insist that globalization is blurring what was originally a mosaic of distinct cultural identities. In either case, however, globalization is seen as having profoundly changed the world.

The point here is not to deny the existence of global flows, but to think of them as the product of specific historical conditions that did not eliminate all local causality. The temptation of seeing societies as isolated entities must be resisted, and ways found to study closure mechanisms and essentialism as social phenomena rather than moral or political transgressions. The construction of local identities should be understood in connection with the encompassing regional systems that have existed since time immemorial. Friedman points out that a new period of "economic *deglobalization*" began after 1920 and was reversed only in the 1950s—which implies that globalization is not without precedent but has appeared cyclically in close connection with the dynamics of the world capitalist system (2000: 203). What we are witnessing is not the emergence of a new world, but a complex historical and economic process made up of periods of expansion and retreat.[12]

Now, it is certainly true that we must find the means to understand transnational (or simply multilocal) phenomena and go beyond a limited territorial view of culture and society; mainstream anthropology did for a long time treat populations as metaphysically tied to a particular land and perfectly adapted to their ecosystem. It is also true that refugees represent an anomaly with regard to this conception. But we must beware of stylistic effects. The invention of a new vocabulary does not always regenerate ethnographic practices and very often overlooks the complexity of the history of the discipline.

It is not my intention to downplay the significance of transnational studies, which are undoubtedly one of the most interesting attempts to tackle the doubts besetting anthropology since the exhaustion of functionalism and structuralism. The real task is to disentangle what amounts to an intellectual flirtation from a genuine theoretical enrichment capable of leading to a new ethnographic practice.

The movement of individuals to seek work, to escape drought or to flee war is a common experience in Afghanistan. It is an exaggeration to attribute a "sedentary metaphysic" (Malkki 1992: 31) to the whole of Middle Eastern or Western scholarly literature on the area. Although refugee studies and the practice of humanitarian organizations do tend to regard movement as pathological, or at least anomalous, it is hard to think what might correspond to the "nomadology" that Malkki (1992: 31) invokes by quoting the French philosophers Deleuze and Guattari.

Large-scale migratory and economic circuits spanning state frontiers are not a new development, and they do not dissolve either places or belonging to social groups. Migratory trajectories may insert themselves into a local framework of self-representation and representation of the life-cycle. The circuits studied in the present work have been apprehended through a mixture of ultimately very classical methods with a perceptual effort or intellectual sensitivity that owes much to the postmodern current.

Summary: Broadly speaking, he argues that caution should be used of these claims made by transnational studies. Not that they aren't valid in some ways, but don't over estimate it. Be sure to recognize that so much of this migration has been going on long time & it does not deterritorialize or de-social group their people and their identities.

Chapter Two

From Theory to Field: Research in a Context of Conflict and Migration

ORIGIN AND THEME OF THE RESEARCH

In the previous chapter, we saw that neither the figure of the refugee defined in international documents nor the various typologies of migration offer a satisfactory theoretical framework to explain and understand mass population movements. The new approaches to the phenomenon, whatever criticisms may be levelled against them, open up more interesting perspectives.

The aim was not to discover the motives impelling Afghans to migrate, but to throw light on the social-cultural resources that they mobilized in response to the dislocating effects of war and exile. The research centered on the Hazaras from Ghazni province, especially the district of Jaghori, but not on any particular village community, as my intention, in following the strategies and networks of relations that an initially small number of interlocutors established over time, was to develop a clear and vivid picture of the ties of solidarity among groups dispersed in Afghanistan, Pakistan and Iran. How do people move around? What are the main stages in the process of migration? Where do they stay for the night? To whom do they turn to obtain employment, a residence permit, a visa or even an identity card or passport? How do they send money or goods from one country to another? How do they keep in touch, when the technical means at their disposal are very limited? What kinds of solidarity can they rely upon? My knowledge developed through personal involvement, and the necessary intellectual detachment did not eliminate all affective closeness.

The above questions were meant to guide my study of the forms and structures of the Hazara transnational community, with a special role for documents and the presentation of ethnographic data. Two dimensions may be distinguished: (i) a state of affairs—that is, the dispersion of families (and, more generally, groups of solidarity) as a result of war; and (ii) a strategy involving huge migratory and economic networks to revive or maintain contact across geographical distance. It is to this dual aspect that I refer when I speak of "multilocation" (Centlivres 1995a; Centlivres-Demont 1998). Family strategies for multilocation among Afghanistan, Pakistan and Iran were studied through detailed examination of individual movement, ways of transferring money and goods, and the circulation of information. By focusing more on what social players said and did than on the characteristics and external causes of migration, I was able to see that Afghans have continued to make constant journeys back and forth (*raft o âmad*). Very few never travelled outside their country after 1978, and very few refugees did not return to it at least once. Contrary to a widespread idea, migration is a dynamic process that leads to complex adjustments; it is a veritable cultural model, not a simple act of going somewhere followed by integration or assimilation in the host country or return to the country of origin.

The definition of refugee in the official international texts is therefore seriously out of tune with the life of Afghans in exile. The massive population transfers, together with the dramatic situation in Afghanistan, should not lead us to see refugees as passive victims, outside any historical, political or social-cultural context. Migration is not necessarily experienced as a trauma or even an exceptional event. Indeed, despite harsh living conditions, many Afghans derive a certain benefit from dispersion by diversifying their social-economic activity (Titus 1999: 3), with the result that they do not actually return to their country of origin. Afghans have responded with courage to their changed circumstances, and not been dependent solely on international aid.[1] Besides, the Hazaras have made little use of the refugee camps in Pakistan and the humanitarian infrastructure. They are a particularly striking illustration of the strengthening of relations based upon spatial fragmentation and constant movement within huge migratory networks, but the situation has scarcely been different for Pashtuns, Tajiks and Uzbeks.

War and exile have also been the setting for major political changes, especially the emergence of new forms of power and a profound recomposition of identity marked by narrower solidarity support groups and the rise of ethnicist demands. The central issue in Afghan society seems to be the quest for trust. In the absence of a true rule of law, the success of any transaction depends on the degree of trust binding together those involved in it.

Since the various players clearly prefer to interact with people close to themselves socially, war and exile have tended to deepen an already pronounced social fragmentation. Yet, despite the ethnicization accompanying the war, the migratory networks have mainly been organized at a sub-ethnic level, parallel but distinct in the case of solidarity groups with roots in areas quite distant from each other. The many international networks are all strongly marked by geographical origin or tribal affiliation, whereas mistrust still dominates local relations between communities.

The sense of space among Afghans is not divided between a place of origin and a place of exile; their movements are complex and never-ending. More than the cause of massive but reversible exile, war has been the framework in which group identities have been profoundly redefined in terms of mutual support across a diversity of complementary economic and geographical situations. The method of investigation in the present work mirrors that diversity.

AFGHAN REFUGEES: CAMPS, TOWNS AND THE WEST

The literature on Afghan refugees consists of a small number of books, together with various articles in academic journals[2] and reports commissioned by humanitarian organization.[3] Because of the constant overlap between the academic and the humanitarian, it often raises "the prevention of new migration," "the voluntary return of refugees" or "integration in the host country" as problems to be addressed (Centlivres and Centlivres-Dumont 1992: 1), all within the official definitions of these terms. (See, for example, the collective work edited by Anderson and Hatch Dupree, 1990[4]).

Most of the academic works relate to the camps in Pakistan, where Pashtuns are clearly in the majority, and for this reason they offer only a partial view of the migrant experience (Centlivres 1993). The number of studies concerning Iran is accordingly very low, and only a few authors have tried to judge in a more detached light the role of humanitarian aid in Afghanistan.[5] On the other hand, a number of researchers have put themselves forward as cultural translators between Afghan refugees and the aid agencies, bringing a better understanding of the social structure, political organization, position of women, tribal code and religious values of the refugees (Ahmed 1986; Christensen 1983, 1984; Christensen and Scott 1988). Some writers have taken a particular interest in the cultural context of the Pashtuns, who form the majority group in Pakistan as well as the largest single population in the North-West Frontier Province (NWFP) and northern Baluchistan where many Afghan refugees are concentrated.

Whereas the Pakistani anthropologist Akbar Ahmed emphasizes the identity breakdown and social-cultural decomposition among Afghan refugees in Pakistan, Centlivres and Centlivres-Demont (1988d) explore the strategies for recomposition and restructuring in exile and demonstrate how the various humanitarian discourses are out of tune with the shifting social relations in the Afghan Refugee Villages (ARVs). Although the prestige of the old tribal leaders and mullahs has not disappeared, a new category of influential persons has emerged alongside them, distinguished by their adaptability to the new context and their capacity to establish and exploit the new networks.

All the values associated with the definition of refugees in the international texts conflict with one of the most important values of Afghan society: namely, the quest for autonomy. When Afghans went to Pakistan, a whole series of agencies took responsibility for them and defined them in a novel manner; acceptance of aid placed them in a subaltern position, so that the imposed image of the refugee became more destructuring than the exile itself. Nevertheless, they proved capable of mobilizing cultural resources to reorganize their social existence and relations. In Pakistan they could appeal to three figures of the refugee (Centlivres 1988a).[6] The first of these, conveyed by the international organizations and NGOs, drew its inspiration from the 1951 Convention and the 1967 Protocol, where the refugee is defined in terms of individuals rather than groups, of victims in need of help who must be taken into care. Second, the *paštunwali,* the tribal code of the Pashtuns, emphasizes the temporary asylum that armed and organized groups can find among their peers. The third semantic field refers to the religious dimension: "the term *mohâjer* (plur. *mohâjerin*), an Arab word used in all Islamic countries, (may be) translated by 'refugee'" (Centlivres 1988a: 137); and Afghans who left their infidel-ruled country justified their decision by reference to the life of Mohammed, using the term *ansar* (originally one of the inhabitants of Medina who welcomed the Prophet and his companions) to denote the Pakistanis. In turn, both these terms also referred to the image of the *mujâhed* or fighter, who wages the *jihâd.*

The situation was different in three respects, however, for those Hazaras who went to Pakistan: they mostly avoided the UNHCR-backed refugee villages and settled in Quetta, capital of Baluchistan province; they could not appeal to *paštunwali* values to gain acceptance of their presence from the local Pakistani population; and their Shia affiliation, which set them apart from other Afghans and Pakistanis, meant that religious solidarity operated only in limited ways.[7]

Few writers have turned their attention to the many Afghans who, like the Hazaras, settled outside the camps within the urban centers of Pakistan.

One exception is the work of Connor (1987a, 1987b, 1989) on "self-settled refugees" in Peshawar, which starts from the assumption that choice of residence is influenced by the refugee's past history and cultural framework, including geographical and ethnic origin, social position (educational level, occupational experience) and political involvement (membership of a resistance movement), time of departure from Afghanistan, and reasons for the decision (1989: 908).

Connor seeks to close the gap between studies of voluntary migrants and refugees, and to move beyond the idea that the route taken by the latter is always "forced, chaotic, generally terror-stricken" (1987b: 152). Following Kunz (1973), she argues that a general theory of refugees must formulate causal typologies and include the notion that different "vintages" of refugees share a number of distinct characteristics (Connor 1987b: 155). Connor admits that she pays greater attention to what Afghans say than to what they do. After analysing the responses of 771 heads of families, she identifies ten reasons for the decision to leave Afghanistan: fear for life (14.53%) or livelihood (9.86%) in the wake of bombing and military hostilities; avoidance of conscription (23.48%); anti-Communism (12.06%); recent imprisonment (8.82%) or fear of arrest (6.74%); suspect family member (3.76%); harassment due to membership of a pro-Communist organization (2.98%); being in Pakistan at the time of the 1978 coup (0.91%); other reasons (1.82%).

Connor spends little time on the religious dimension of a protest exodus against the Communist government. Her conclusion, in which it is certainly possible to follow her, is that Afghans left their country after events related in some way to their own particular sociology; they did not flee en masse (1987b: 183). Her mapping of Afghan refugees in Peshawar is most interesting, but the significance of her information on the reasons for departure from Afghanistan is open to some doubt. In fact, the results are rather disappointing. It comes as no surprise that the bombing and fighting, together with general pressure from the Soviet army and the Communist government, were the main reasons driving Afghans into exile (rural populations were more like to suffer bombing and massacre, whereas city dwellers had more to fear from wrongful arrest (Connor 1987b: 184).[8] The percentages given by Connor do not take account of the inevitable overlap in motives. Moreover, her chronological section focuses particularly on the moment of departure; she says nothing about back and forth movements, and takes no interest in refugee movements within a diachronic perspective. She gives the impression that Afghans left at a precise moment and for precise reasons, which might certainly have varied from person to person or group to group but were unambiguous in each particular case, whereas in reality the taking of decisions was an uninterrupted process. Categorization by "date of departure" does not allow us to draw out medium to long-term strategies. It was one thing to leave Afghanistan, and another to choose not to return. In seeking to group refugees by "vintage" and by social-cultural, status and ethnic factors (1989: 927–929), Connor neglects the planned "multilocation" of families and kinship groups, as well as the complementarity of places of residence and occupations. Driven by poverty as much as by war, Afghans have been constantly on the move. They have woven an intricate web of transnational relations, and it would pointless to try to specify the moment at which the decision to leave Afghanistan was taken.

Gradually a number of researchers have come to take an interest in Afghans who settled abroad after 1978, either in Europe or in North America.[9] For the most part, they were city dwellers from the middle and upper classes, and large Pakistani cities such as Karachi, Islamabad and Peshawar were often the stopover points in their exodus (Centlivres and Centlivres-Demont 2000: 153). The forms and networks of the migration from Jaghori district were different (Gehrig and Monsutti 2003), and yet the Hazaras, like their fellow-countrymen who emigrated to the West, put in place a number of transterritorial and transnational networks. For them too, "the networks replaced a homogeneous collective organized in a given territory" (Centlivres and Centlivres-Demont 2000: 153).

The literature on Afghan refugees has only marginally and belatedly taken account of the fact that geographical dispersion is a lasting phenomenon which results from explicit individual and collective strategies. My interest in individual trajectories and cross-border networks led me to go beyond the idea that refugees are resourceless victims. Once we focus more on the strategies and cycles of migration, rather than the words and motives of migrants, mobility no longer appears as an anomaly or trauma. The Hazara migration cannot be one-sidedly defined as something forced. For young men, in particular, it is a means of realizing a certain idea of personal autonomy and plays an important role in the construction of masculinity; they often marry only after they have spent a number of years in Iran. Migration is an economic diversification strategy, and therefore a survival strategy, but also a kind of rite of passage to adulthood. We should not think of it in terms of a break, since it enters into the picture that people have of a human life span.

FROM NETWORKS TO A MULTILOCATIONAL ETHNOGRAPHY

In presenting the voluminous literature on migration, globalization and transnationalism, we have seen how essential it is to move beyond the image of societies as discrete territorial entities, and of refugees as pure victims torn from their habitual setting. New approaches partly rehabilitate, both as observational perspective and as object of study, a methodological tool that seemed to have become obsolete: namely, the network.[10]

Network analysis already made some headway in the 1950s, but it was mainly in the next two decades that it flourished, before exhausting itself in the 1980s. The eventual discredit into which it fell may be put down to its undifferentiated conception of social relations (an interest in the structure of social relations and the frequency of interactions rather than the content of individual exchanges and relations), together with excessive formalism, problems in gathering empirical data to fit the theory, and a concentration on relatively marginal themes. Nevertheless, networks remained a methodological tool with which to understand the characteristic mobility situations of contemporary societies. In one old but still famous study of a Norwegian parish, Barnes gave a definition of network that remains useful by its very simplicity:

> The image I have is of a set of points some of which are joined by lines. The points of the image are people, or sometimes groups, and the lines indicate which people interact with each other. We can of course think of the whole of social life as generating a network of this kind (Barnes 1954: 43).

In other words, this approach takes a person or group of persons as its starting point for the reconstruction of social relations. Society is no longer seen in functionalist terms as a series of distinct integrated communities, but rather as interpenetrating sets of social relations that branch out from each individual, not tied to a particular territory and without precise spatial or social boundaries. Links between two distant persons may be intense, while certain relations with close neighbors may be slack. Networks may be thought of as a criss-crossing of the social relations actually or potentially mobilized in particular situations.

If it is used with care, and cleansed of the formalist and individualist excesses of sixties or seventies "network analysis," the concept of social networks may still provide invaluable service. The works of Hannerz (1967, 1986, 1992a, 1992b, 1996) are representative of this trend, and the more recent among them reduce the weight of individuals and attach considerably greater scope to the strategies of groups such as households, lineages, neighborhood circles, or even tribal segments. The flexibility of the network tool makes it possible to study the cultural complexity of the present-day world (which may be seen as a "network of networks"), to explain how the local level connects with the global system, and to put in perspective the links among dispersed members of solidarity groups.

In this connection, the concept of "multilocality" first introduced by Rodman (1992)[11] and adapted by Centlivres (1995a) proves rich and open:

> Migration [. . .] also means porous frontiers, a 'culture' of survival and a need for anthropologists to change from a paradigm of rootedness in a given environment to a paradigm of multilocation. Tens of millions of people find in mobility a resource, not only a constraint. Except in the case of traditional nomadism, the significance of mobility, multilayered lives and archipelagos of family, tribal or ethnic groups has until now been too little appreciated. The identity spaces relevant for so many families or kinship groups are no longer fixed locations but transnational networks; and the new mobility is not, or is no longer, linked only to crises but has become integral to the existence of individuals and communities. This growing trend implies that an initially imposed dispersion is turned to advantage, with the result that the concept of original group or kinship group loses its territorial basis, just as the concept of productive activity loses its roots in a particular area. Finally, it implies the constant transfer or exchange of persons, messages and goods (Centlivres 1995a: 38).[12]

In his studies of Mexican migrants in the United States, Rouse (1991, 1992) fleshes out what a new ethnography of migration and multilocal populations might look like. His starting point is that we live in a situation of "transnational capitalism" that is blurring the image of a world divided into nation-states and cohesive communities, as well as the division between core and periphery. The view of migratory phenomena as movement from one social environment to another, involving a process of gradual, more or less profound adaptation to a new way of life, remains dependent upon a bipolar model in which migrants eventually lose contact with their place of origin. It does not enable us to understand how migrants can keep up an active involvement in several places. By contrast, Rouse lays great stress on the coexistence of different sets of values among migrants and the widening of their cultural repertoire; migration thus appears as a more complex process in which individuals may become fully-fledged social players in a number of different places. This leads to what he calls "cultural bifocality" (Rouse 1992: 41): that is, a capacity to see the world in alternating and non-exclusive ways, through different lenses. The Mexicans with whom Rouse worked migrate to California but do not usually settle there on a permanent basis; their plans remain geared to their place of origin, and they regularly send back the money they manage to save. They therefore evolve in a transnational space, whose different locations are connected through constant movement:

> Indeed, through the continuous circulation of people, money, goods, and information, the various settlements have become so closely woven together that, in an important sense, they have come to constitute a single community spread across a variety of sites, something I refer to as a 'transnational migrant circuit' [. . .] Today, it is the circuit as a whole rather than any one locale that constitutes the principal setting in relation to which Aguilillans orchestrate their lives (1991: 14).

These transnational migrant circuits correspond to the new forms of capitalism beyond national frontiers. But, as Rouse remarks, the fact that migrants develop within different social environments does not lead to cultural homogenization, since each site in the circuit is characterized by a different way of life. Faced with this multidirectional migration, cultural juxtaposition and fragmentation of reference spaces, in the conditions of "postmodern hyperspace" (Rouse 1991: 18), it becomes difficult to demarcate communities and social spaces from one another.

These methodological considerations have implications beyond the study of migration, as the work of Marcus testifies. Like Molière's Monsieur Jourdain, who spoke in prose without realizing it, I have unwittingly practised the "multi-sited ethnography" that Marcus (1995) advocated in a text that was published when I was working in the field.[13] His various "tracking" strategies to implement his program (Marcus 1995: 105–110) are termed "follow the people," "follow the thing," "follow the metaphor" (especially in the media), "follow the plot, story or allegory" (as in Lévi-Strauss's structural analysis of myths), and "follow the life or biography." I myself have followed the people and reconstituted the circulation of goods and the life trajectories of my informants. The point was not to conduct an intensive ethnographic investigation in one locality, but to consider how the research object fits into a world system and to study the circulation of persons, objects and goods, as well as symbols. This relocation of ethnographic analysis is not an academic trick but corresponds to the everyday living conditions of a growing number of people. In contrast to classical fieldwork, with its long periods in a small-sized community, the contrast between local and global becomes less sharp as the focus shifts to the links between different sites.

Nevertheless, the wish to rethink the object and method of anthropology does not render obsolete the classical ethnographic approach. It does not abandon the idea of decentring in relation to the evidence, which is implicit in the field. And it retains a place for participant observation, without fetishizing it or regarding it as the only possible technique of investigation. Thus I travelled from Pakistan to Afghanistan and Iran, but I also met Hazaras in Switzerland, France, England, the United States and even Turkey.[14] In a sense the field caught up with me, as may be seen from my correspondence by letter and e-mail with Afghans in Pakistan and elsewhere.

By working in several different places, one risks dispersal of effort and a certain loss of ethnographic depth. Yet the population or phenomenon under research can still be small in scale; the point is to gain an overview by carrying out research in a number of key locations in the relevant flows. Rather than limit myself to one place, I therefore reconstituted the links that a migrant population forged between different places of settlement which, despite the spatial dispersion, formed a coherent social field. The field research was multilocal not only in the sense that the localities were diverse, but above all by virtue of a wish to understand the structural links between them. In focusing especially on the two-way flows, I accumulated material on families and family strategies (alternating migration among brothers, decision-making processes, etc.), and I attempted to understand how people travelled, communicated and transferred funds.

The limits to the group I studied were not fixed in advance by the researcher or his informants. It was in the course of the investigation that I tried gradually to reconstitute the actual social ties among a certain number of people—"strong ties" (within the kin and the circle of close friends) and "weak ties" (with acquaintances) (Granovetter 1973a and 1973b). Both of these must be studied if one is to understand migratory phenomena. As Emmanuel Marx stresses (1990: 195), the researcher should not concentrate only on permanent institutionalized relations, as passing ties also hold essential information about social practices. In the present case, this meant going beyond the apparent weight of official kinship relations and ancestral, tribal or ethnic affiliation, in order to bring out the actual relations of my informants throughout the course of their migration.[15]

The concept of network, or of trajectory or multilocality, offers a means of linking the actual choices of people with the organization of society. Afghans, for example, are both relatively autonomous agents carrying out rational choices and, at the same time, members of collectives within which relations of trust and cooperation are woven. The study of family networks involves taking an interest in individual trajectories, but without neglecting the social dimension of migration that results from strategies charted at the level of the domestic unit, or even of larger groups. For the Hazaras, to migrate is not simply a response to war and violence; it is a planned strategy at the level of the family, which makes it possible to generate income through money-transfers, but also at the level of the solidarity group, which provides an information and support network making migration easier to accomplish.

Edwards (1994) expressed the disarray of an anthropologist interested in Afghanistan who had to abandon his original plan of working in a clearly defined community, whether a mountain village or a nomadic tribal group. Circumstances forced him to conduct his fieldwork in a variety of places—in Peshawar and the NWFP refugee camps, on a trip inside Afghanistan, in work among Afghans in Washington, and in research about internet users. In this way, Edwards worked out a new way of performing field study that was both multilocal (from Peshawar to Washington) and non-local (internet). My own experience was comparable, although the bulk of my work was conducted in Afghanistan (especially Hazarajat, but also the great commercial and migratory crossroads of Kandahar, Ghazni, Kabul and Mazar-e Sharif), Pakistan (mainly Quetta and the nearby coal mines) and Iran (the urban centers of Tehran and Qom, as well as Zahedan, Shiraz and Mashad). The multilocality of the research corresponded to the multilocality of the population group.

PROFILES AND ITINERARIES OF THE PRINCIPAL INFORMANTS

For reasons that are hard to evaluate, the Hazara people originating in the center of Afghanistan occupy only a minimal place in the historical and anthropological literature.[16] They are a large group (estimates range from 10% to 25% of the Afghan population) but a marginal one, an ethnic and religious minority (Shia, unlike the Sunni majority) who interact little with their neighbors. The Hazara networks are therefore distinct and easily identifiable.

Long-range "multi-site" research on the Hazaras can enrich the ethnography of Afghanistan. In following certain kinship groups from one country to another, I was able to develop a less abstract conception of multilocality and of the factors impelling Afghans to move around as much as they do. The population group in question came essentially from the southern fringes of Hazarajat, and above all from the district of Jaghori in the east of Ghazni province. Personal contacts I had made in 1993 led me to concentrate on the Dahmarda valley, in the extreme south of Jaghori. There I mostly interacted with members of the Dawran lineage, as my intensive research related to a group of cousins belonging to the Awlad-e Atay sublineage (see chapter 3). In following the networks from one end to the other, I was able to form a precise idea of living and working conditions in the various places where members of an enlarged kinship group settled. In Tehran I encountered many people I had known in Dahmarda, or come across in Quetta. The following were my chief informants:[17]

- Mardan Ali. Born between 1952 and 1954, he never attended school and left Dahmarda at the age of seventeen following a quarrel. He joined the Pakistani army in 1971, at the time of the war with India. Four years later, he left to marry the sister of a Hazara, also originally from Jaghori, whom he had got to know in the army. He then performed two more years of military service in Afghanistan, and was stationed in Kandahar barracks at the moment of the Communist coup in April 1978. He deserted a few months later, and then spent the years of Soviet occupation (1979–1989) either in Quetta (where he worked in the coal mines during the winter months) or as a Hezb-e islami fighter in the summer. His family remained in Dahmarda throughout those years. He gave up combat after the Soviet withdrawal, gradually lengthening his stays in Quetta (where he continued to work in the mines and was given some responsibilities) and spacing out his trips back to Hazarajat. In the winter of 1995–96, after fighting divided the population of his home village, he brought his family to Pakistan and built a house there. He has two sons and four daughters (the eldest having been born in 1978–79).
- Mohammad Ali. He is the brother of Mardan Ali, born in or around 1966. He attended some classes with a mullah. He left Dahmarda for the first time in 1981, and since then has spent most of his life as a migrant alternating between work as a miner, a mason and a quarryman. He spent four periods in Iran (1985–86, 1987–88, 1990–93, 1994–97) and two in Quetta (1981, 1983–85), returning four times on a visit to Dahmarda (1982, 1986, 1988–90, 1993–94). He married a woman from the line on his mother's side (originally from Dawud, a village close to Dahmarda) and had two sons and a daughter at quite an early age.[18]
- Aziz Azizi. He is the third brother, born in 1968 or 1969. The most educated of the three, he attended a religious school in Quetta between 1984 and 1985 and again in 1989. In 1989–90 he worked in Iran as a guard for a construction company. After returning to Dahmarda, he opened a shop in the bazaar. He is married to a close relative of Mohammad Ali's wife, and has three daughters.

- Mohammad Hasan. He is the patrilateral cousin (FBS) of Mardan Ali and his brothers, born in 1969 or 1970. In the second half of the 1980s he worked in the Quetta coal mines (1987–88) and fought intermittently in the ranks of the Nasr in Afghanistan.[19] He spent a year and a half in Tehran, between 1992 and 1993, then married a woman from his mother's kin (to whom he had been engaged since 1990). He has a young son. In Dahmarda he works alongside his father on the family land.

- Mohammad Husayn. Born in 1976 and not yet married, he is the brother of Mohammad Hasan, with whom he worked in Tehran in 1992–93. He returned in 1994 and worked as a mason with his cousin Mohammad Ali. He had a serious work accident early in 1996.
- Mohammad Yusuf. He is the patrilateral cousin (FBS) of the latter two, born in or around 1962. He took up arms in 1979, but soon left for Quetta and Iran (where he spent the three years from 1980 to 1982); he spent further periods in Quetta (1984–86) and Tehran (1991–92), during which he worked as an ordinary laborer. Although he had no education, he went into business in 1993 with a small sum he had managed to save. He married a woman from his lineage in 1984 and had two sons and a daughter by her. In 1992 he married the widow of his elder brother Ramazan Ali, who had been killed in combat, and had a daughter by her (in addition to his brother's five children).
- Husayn Bakhsh. Born in or around 1959, he is the cousin (FZS) of Hasan and Husayn as well as their brother-in-law (ZH). He has no children. In 1980 he joined his sister in Quetta (their father having died when they were children). Since then he has spent several periods in Iran (1981–83, 1987–90, 1992), but has only twice returned briefly to Dahmarda (1993, 1996). He attended several courses with a mullah and played an important role as a link man between Iran and Hazarajat. He earns his living as a construction worker.

Other individuals related to the foregoing were also important for my research:

- Mohammad Jawad. Born in 1971, he is a more distant member of the Dawran lineage and the brother-in-law (WB) of Mohammad

Yusuf. He has spent three periods in Iran (1989–92, 1993–95, and since 1996), interspersed with brief trips back to Dahmarda (which he used to become engaged in 1993 and married in autumn 1995[20]). He works as a laborer, but is the financial partner of Mohammad Yusuf; they pooled their savings and jointly own a shop in Dahmarda that remains shut when they are both away.

- Hazrat Ali. Originally from Rash, a village close to Dahmarda where he was born in the late forties, he is the brother-in-law (ZH) of Hasan and Husayn. He has been only once to Iran, in 1981–82. A poor peasant, he has worked every winter since 1983 in the Quetta coal mines (he took advantage of his first trip there in 1977 to obtain a Pakistani identity card). He has five daughters and three sons.

- Mohammad Reza. He is the half-brother of Mardan Ali's wife and is married to a sister of Hasan and Husayn. Born in 1945 in Patu, a village close to Dahmarda. His father had one wife in Hazarajat (his mother) and another in Quetta (the mother of Mardan Ali's wife), and regularly travelled between the two places. Reza spent a year in Qom (Iran) around 1976 as a laborer, then another year in Tehran in 1992. Each winter since 1980 he has gone to work in the Quetta coal mines. He received no schooling. He has six sons and six daughters. The eldest, Alidad, married young and went to work in the mines for the first time in winter 1995–96.

- Mohammad Hanif. Born around 1964, he is a member of the Dawlatjam lineage. Talks are under way with a view to marriage between his younger sister and Abdul Karim, the eldest son of Mardan Ali. He comes from a fairly well-off family and he and his two elder brothers are in business together, with activities stretching from Mazar-e Sharif and Herat to Quetta and Iran. Having long been in charge of the shop in Dahmarda, he began to travel on family business in 1994 and makes at least one trip a year to Quetta and Iran. He is married with two sons and a daughter.

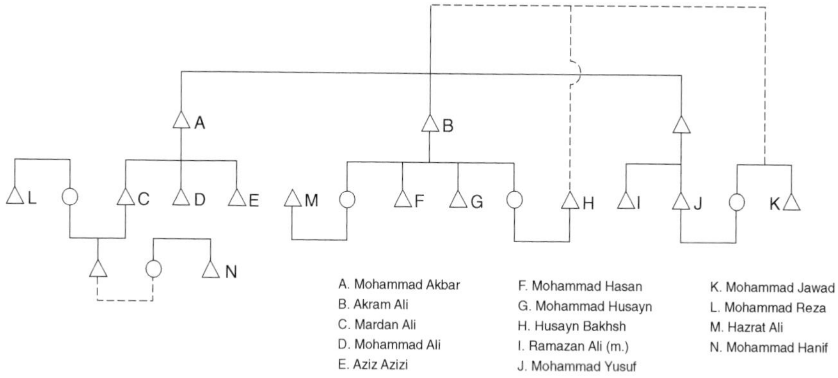

Figure 2. Simplified kinship relations of principal informants

To give some chronological depth, we should also mention:

- Mohammad Akbar. He is the father of Mardan Ali, Mohammad Ali and Aziz Azizi, born in or around 1935. In addition to a few short periods in Quetta, he has twice been to work in Iran, once in the early seventies and once around 1986.
- Akram Ali. He is the half-brother of the foregoing and father of Mohammad Hasan and Mohammad Husayn. Born around 1930, he went to Quetta as a child to work as an ordinary pedlar, and again in the 1970s. He also spent some time in Iran shortly before the Communist coup in 1978.

These few brief biographies suffice to illustrate the complex migratory paths of the Hazaras, as well as the different strategies on offer to them. The Communist coup and the ensuing war meant that people from Jaghori moved around much more, but many men had already been going to work in Iran or Quetta (at quite a young average age in the case of my informants).

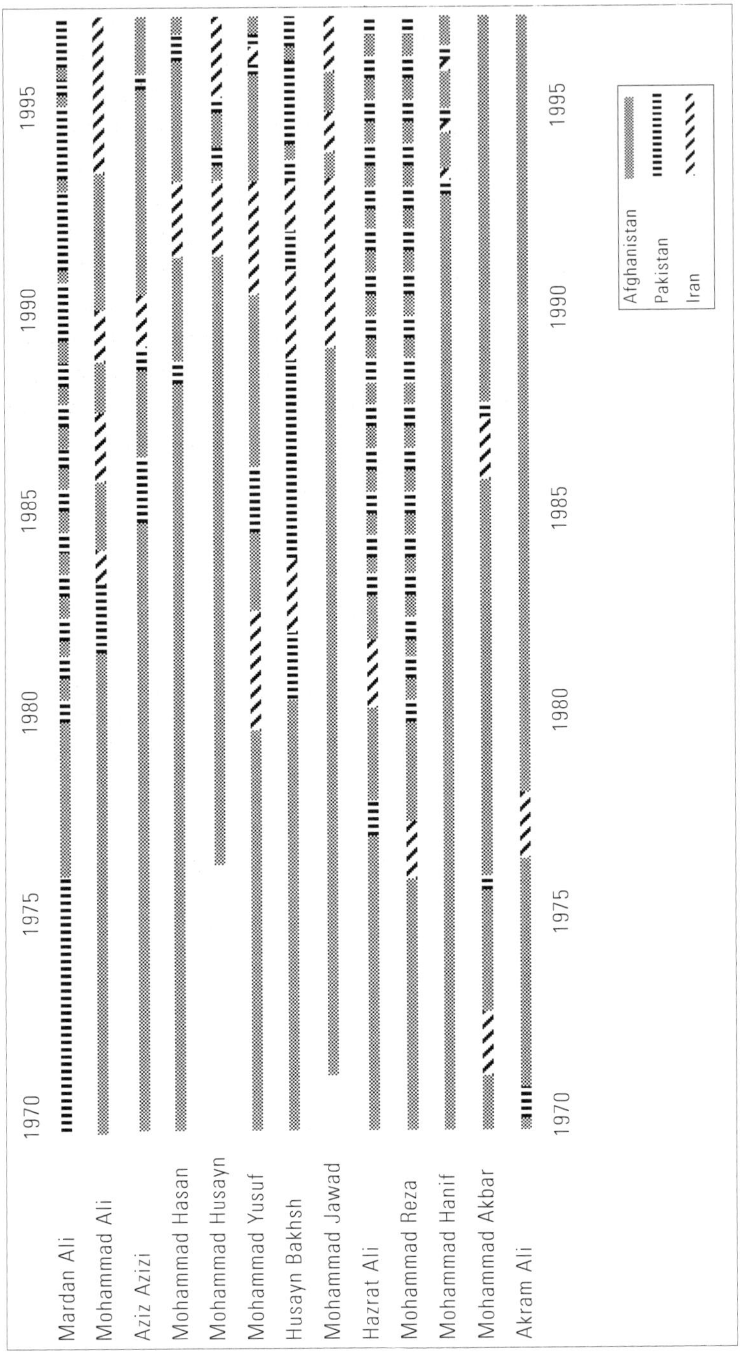

Figure 3. Itineraries of principal informants

Four models of migration emerge from the sample: (i) permanent settlement in Quetta (the case of Husayn Bakhsh); (ii) quite long periods in Iran, often involving young men saving up to marry or to start up a business; (iii) annual migratory movement between Afghanistan and Pakistan, involving peasants or fighters who go to work in the Quetta mines during the winter (the case of Mardan Ali, but also of Hazrat Ali and Mohammad Reza, who prefer not to leave their families for too long); (iv) quite short but recurrent trips between Hazarajat, Quetta and Iran for business purposes (the model recently adopted by Mohammad Yusuf and Mohammad Hanif). The same individual may, of course, switch from one model to another during a lifetime. None of my informants left Afghanistan without ever returning; all travelled backwards and forwards between their native village in Hazarajat, Pakistan and Iran, in accordance with their strategic choices, skills and preferences. (Mardan Ali is the only one never to have gone to work in Iran.)

RESEARCH TECHNIQUES

Writing is one of the main activities of the ethnologist. In the field he takes notes and keeps a journal, and back home he produces a text that respects a number of academic norms. As Gupta and Ferguson point out:

> The distinction between 'the field' and 'home' rests on their spatial separation. (A contrast) differentiates the site where data are collected from the place where analysis is conducted and the ethnography is 'written up.' To do ethnographic work is thus to do two distinct types of writing. One kind is done 'in the field.' These 'fieldnotes' are close to experience, textually fragmentary, consisting of detailed 'raw' documentation of interviews and observations as well as subjective reactions [. . .] The other sort, done 'at home,' is reflective, polished, theoretical, intertextual, a textual whole—this is the writing of ethnographic papers and monographs (1997: 12).

The anthropological current represented by such authors as Clifford or Marcus (Clifford 1988; Clifford and Marcus eds. 1986; Marcus and Cushman 1982; Marcus and Fischer 1986) has taken a keen interest in the production of ethnographic texts and in the relationship between researcher and informants. Nowadays it is scarcely an option to use the scientific, disembodied present of the classical monographs. As Marcus notes, this creates "new opportunities for innovations in ethnographic writing to break out of old narrative constraints by constituting a much more complex object for ethnographic study and representation" (1989: 8). Unfortunately, attempts at dialogic or reflexive writing in which the informants are given a voice mask the fact that the author remains the ethnographer. The multiplication of perspectives and juxtaposed styles, in the name of an intellectual and moral alliance between observer and observed (Marcus 1989, 1992), certainly faces up to the limits inherent in any vantage point, but it runs the risk of blurring the relations of power that exist within any society and between different parts of the world.

In the course of their training, ethnographers learn to ask questions and to interpret the answers they are given. But an important part of their work consists in answering questions that their informants ask in return; this is an essential aspect of the exchange that fieldwork can promote. I was often asked about European customs (marriage and the family, work, religious practices, etc.), but also about the political actions of Switzerland, Europe or the United States in favor of the Hazaras: "What can you do for the Hazara nation? What can you contribute? Why hasn't Europe helped us?" Well-intentioned people regularly tried to convert me to Islam. A foreigner is the object of great curiosity which, though usually benevolent, sometimes causes safety problems by drawing attention to a potentially tense and envy-arousing presence.

Afghan society has long been familiar with writing and has a rich scholarly tradition. Yet only a small proportion of Afghans are literate. Educated men are surrounded with respect, but the rural population looks with suspicion upon city intellectuals, who are thought to have rejected the values of Islam. The researcher does not escape this kind of ambivalence. Moreover, as a foreigner with bizarre ways, he attracts not only playful curiosity but also mistrust and even, more rarely, open hostility. The discovery is therefore mutual, and it is necessary to participate with good grace in such exchanges.

My research took place mainly in Dari (the Persian of Afghanistan), a language that is understood and spoken by the great majority of Afghans.[21] It was essential to cross-reference questions and answers and to tackle the same themes with different individuals. Except for ad hoc tasks such as the reading or translation of letters or printed material, I never had recourse to a guide or interpreter. Working mainly among country people with no formal education, I decided to conduct interviews directly in their language rather than allow any screen to interfere with the establishment of interpersonal relations. To improve my overview or to clarify certain points, I supplemented my information with long conversations in English, or sometimes French, with a few individuals who had received a higher education.

I practised the classical techniques of ethnographic investigation, such as participant observation and free or semi-structured interviews. I questioned individuals about their personal histories and the activity of other family members. Whenever possible—and this presupposed a strong bond with my informants—I collected written documents such as letters to family or close friends, letters of credit or account books. I also took a large number of photographs, although it was not always possible to use my camera. Afghans have two extreme attitudes in this respect: some, especially children, clamor to be photographed, while others refuse to appear in a picture, for a mixture of religious and superstitious reasons. With a few exceptions (above all, a long account of his travels by a Hazara I had known for a long time), I did not tape-record these conversations, both to avoid eliciting overly formal statements and because I felt that the laborious work of transcription did not really make it worthwhile.

Apart from the crossing of the Pakistan-Iran frontier and a few flights on the ICRC aeroplane inside Afghanistan, I travelled like most Afghans by bus or lorry, on mule or on foot, following my main informants on their peregrinations from Hazarajat to Quetta and on to Iran. I spent the longest in Quetta (Pakistan), a city that had the twin advantage of being relatively safe and occupying a strategic place on the Hazara migration route to Iran.

I endeavoured to stop over along the way, either with private individuals or in the offices of Afghan NGOs. In Afghanistan itself I was usually in the company of Hazara informants on their way back home, but unforeseen complications sometimes meant that I had to continue the journey alone. I always made every effort not to stand out, for the sake of my own safety. I wore local clothing suited to the lifestyle and climate—the wide trousers and long shirt, at once comfortable and discrete, the little skullcap and the beard (the last two elements being the Afghan passport, as Afghans often jokingly say)—but I never tried to pass myself off as an Afghan or a Muslim. My difference was highly visible in the evening, when I washed my face or brushed my teeth, and during the prayer stops that punctuate any journey in the region.

Accommodation was a delicate issue, as a place had to be found that was both neutral and embedded in the society. In Quetta I stayed in the Hazara neighborhood, either in the garage annexes of a Pakistani Hazara who ran some coal mines, or in a room sub-let from a friend. In Hazarajat I usually put up with private individuals, and more rarely in the offices of an NGO or a simple roadside inn. In Iran I mostly lived with my informants on the construction sites where they worked.

Like Afghans themselves, I several times altered my itinerary inside Afghanistan to bypass the combat zones. The fascination of danger and a thirst for adventure can have their effect on the research worker in the field, but I tried to resist this by keeping in mind Claude Lévi-Strauss's opening remarks in *Tristes tropiques:*

> I hate travelling and explorers. [. . .] Adventure has no place in the anthropologist's profession; it is merely one of those unavoidable drawbacks, which detract from his effective work through the incidental loss of weeks or months; there are hours of inaction when the informant is not available; periods of hunger, exhaustion, sickness perhaps; and always the thousand and one dreary tasks which eat away the day to no purpose and reduce dangerous living in the heart of the virgin forest to an imitation of military service. [. . .] The fact that so much effort and expenditure has to be wasted on reaching the object of our studies bestows no value on that aspect of our profession, and should be seen rather as its negative side. The truths which we seek so far afield only become valid when they have been separated from this dross (Lévi-Strauss 1976: 15).

These points are certainly well taken. But we may fail to share the positivist spirit informing his remarks, so different from recent emphasis on the subjectivity of the players and of the ethnographer himself. In fact, one of the riches of the ethnological approach is the reliability of the human relations that are established with the people; emotion operates as a methodological tool, a procedure of discovery whereby little facts picked up almost by chance are rendered significant. By a series of impressionistic touches, an ethnologist can make visible, audible and palpable a moving little world whose tragic fate profoundly disturbs us. He evokes places and people, sketches an atmosphere, without overlooking his own personal and scientific misgivings. In this sense, my adventure was above all a human adventure, and the most intractable difficulties were those related not to war and insecurity but to the management of human relations and the opaqueness of the events unfolding before my eyes.

The relationship between the ethnologist and his informant is ambiguous. The former is paid to make the first contact; he comes from afar, gathers his information and leaves. For him a personal investment in the relationship is the only means of collecting reliable data. It is through other people's stories and confidences that he deepens his knowledge and conducts his investigation. One of the difficulties, however, is that there is a fine line between legitimate and improper use of his contacts.

Yet the satisfactions and the emotions are there aplenty. One of my most regular informants, Mahmad Nur (see chapter 7), said in the course of one conversation that he loved talking with me. When I thanked him for the time and expressed all the respect I had for people like him who work hard to keep their family, he replied that it was he who owed me a debt of thanks: "This is the first time a stranger has stopped and asked me questions about my life and work, when intellectuals from my own country take no interest in illiterate people like me." And he added: "The Hazara are a forgotten people; you will be our ambassador." His words deeply affected me. It is through this kind of experience that the ethnographic approach gains its full meaning. What Mahmad Nur said to me made up for all the little intrigues to which I may have been subjected.

Many indications soon convinced me that the money-transfer networks were a very important phenomenon. I thought it advisable to go more deeply into a small number of cases that seemed exemplary in relation to two categories: (i) all kinds of persons involved in financial transfers, the transport of goods and cross-frontier movements; and (ii) a cross-section of the main ethnic groups, each offering distinctive features related to place of origin, ties with the host society, strategies for social-economic advancement (attitude to education or trade, for example), and so on. The idea, then, was to collect the life paths of my informants (professional and political development, chronology of relocations, etc.) while at the same time putting together particular genealogies. I compiled a list of kinship terms from the spoken language in Jaghori and carefully noted their social usage. This is an especially useful way of seeing how solidarity groups form on the basis of kinship yet go beyond it. This is a lengthy procedure that presupposes relations of trust, but it allowed me to trace the active partners within the kinship group (those with whom my informant was associated in his economic activity) and thus to uncover the structure and functioning of the multilocal family networks.

My approach therefore had a clearly qualitative orientation. But certain quantitative information (economic data, types of occupation, number of repatriations, etc.), which I found in reports commissioned by international organizations such as the UNHCR or various NGOs, formed an indispensable complement to my work. These sources enabled me to see my own results in a different light, and to verify the relevance and recurrent character of the phenomena under investigation. I also tried to make a list of the inns used by Hazaras along their migratory route, so as to assess indirectly the amount of movement and the scale of the money-transfers.

To supplement what I gathered from observation and numerous informal discussions, I devised a double-entry interview grid, where the columns contained questions (place of residence, change of residence, type of activity, location and function of any partners, location and occupational activity of any kin, etc.) and the rows represented the years starting from the present.[22] I completed the data by taking supplementary notes, drawing up brief genealogies and asking my interlocutors about the ties of kinship and friendship that they called upon in the context of migration. In a perspective that was both diachronic and synchronic, this research technique made it possible to visualize the migratory paths and the solidarity networks.

For the sake of comparison, I tried to gather data on various occupational activities and the major ethnic groups, while continuing to focus mainly on Hazaras from Jaghori district. Despite a number of drawbacks (my informants were generally happy to answer my questions, but this type of interview was too much like a "survey" by a humanitarian organization and threatened to heighten the ambivalence of my position), this proved an invaluable methodological tool in addition to less directed interviews. Out of a total of 89 completed interview grids, 65 (or 73.0%) related to Hazaras and another four (4.5%) to Shiite Sayyeds living in a Hazara milieu (giving a total of 77.5%). Among the Hazaras, 38 were from Jaghori (21 from the Dahmarda valley alone) and a further 27 from other areas. In gathering data on all the ethnic and social groups, with a progressive emphasis on the Hazaras, the Jaghori district, the Dahmarda valley and, finally, members of the Dawran lineage and the Awlâd-e Atay sub-lineage (around Mardan Ali, Mohammad Ali, Aziz Azizi, Mohammad Hasan, Mohammad Husayn and Mohammad Yusuf), I conducted intensive research on a precisely defined population group while still adopting a comparative approach.

It should be noted that ethnic affiliations are not always as clear as one might think; they are often negotiated in accordance with the context. For example, one of my informants was the son of a Tajik civil servant who had settled down in Hazarajat, having converted to Shiism and married a Hazara; another had a Qizilbash[23] mother and a father who, though of Pashtun origin, was from a "Hazarified" family. Depending on circumstances, these individuals knew how to play on this diversity and to vary the register of their ethnic affiliation. Besides, how should we place the Sayyeds, those self-styled descendants of the Prophet Mohammed? They are conscious of their distinctive identity, as embodied in clearly endogamous practices, but they can be found among all the main ethnic groups: Persian-speaking Shiites in Hazarajat, Persian-speaking Sunnis among the Tajiks, Pashtu-speaking Sunnis among the

Pashtuns, and so on. I chose to group them together here by religion rather than language, in order to keep a separate place for "Hazara Sayyeds."

The range of occupations in my sample was not very large. The two largest groups were those of trader (a term covering quite different activities, not always easily distinguishable within a single individual's multiple practice as money-transfer specialist, wholesale merchant, shopkeeper, etc.) and money-changer, with 22 instances (24.8%). The number of miners and workers was as high as 20 (22.5%). The liberal professions, managers, teachers and employees of humanitarian organizations were also well represented (with a total of 24 persons, or 26.9%). The greatest part of my research concerned individuals who in one way or another were involved in financial networks, as well as ordinary workers who used them to send money to their family back in Afghanistan. The different categories are not pure: I decided to place each person under the activity that seemed to occupy most of his time; but there is a lot of overlapping, especially in the case of students and jobless persons, who nearly always engaged in a little activity on the side. Only one of my informants described himself as a peasant at the time of the interview. But it should be made clear that most of the miners and workers had some land in Afghanistan, so that the category in which I placed them had to do with the fact that I met them in a migratory context. Finally, only one woman features in the investigation. I very soon realized that my questionnaire would be geared chiefly to male informants, but that was mainly due to the characteristics of Afghan society, with its pronounced seclusion of women.

The legitimacy of the investigative techniques and the representativeness of the examples are guaranteed by the depth of the data: the collection of eventful life-stories uncovered a host of links among a large number of individuals, and the matching up of individual trajectories yielded a representative and lifelike portrait of the conditions in which Afghans live.

DIFFICULTIES IN THE FIELD

Working in a difficult context, I encountered several kinds of problems in the field: insecurity and war; the irregular legal situation of many informants; police controls; distrust towards me; the issue of prestige that I presented for Afghans; lack of understanding with regard to my work; confusion between research and humanitarian aid; expectations of material advantage; lack of privacy . . .

One of the most serious limitations, however, was the impossibility of conversing with women. I met very few in the course of my various periods in the field, and those I did manage to interview freely were nearly all educated city women. Although the tactless mistakes of the ethnologist are usually excused and can be full of lessons, it is a delicate matter to ask Afghan men about women. Most of my informants did not hesitate to tell me, sometimes even with a hint of amusement, the sum they had paid to obtain favors from a particular civil servant. But it was unthinkable to ask them the name of their mother or wife, so that when I tried to reconstitute family relationships I used the circuitous route of asking about brothers-in-law (ZH: *dâmâd,* WB: *xosur-bura*) rather than sisters or a wife. As to perceptions of war and migration, I was able to obtain little information about how women saw them. It is true that men were the mobile element in family groups, but this itself meant that women played an essential role that was actually strengthened in the course of the war, since they took on more and more central tasks of the domestic unit in the village of origin. Involving themselves more than men cared to admit in family choices and strategies, they played a role in decision-making whose complex rules were hard to understand for a male anthropologist overexposed to stereotypical conceptions of the gender division of labor.[24]

Afghanistan was a country at war, where security conditions were seriously compromised. Even outside the main combat zones and frontlines, small-scale hostilities were a frequent and unpredictable occurrence, acts of banditry were always to be feared, and tensions ran high within local communities. On several occasions I found myself caught up in an exchange of gunfire or an armed robbery.

Since danger could suddenly appear in peaceful-looking spots, it was often hard to keep a level head. In fact, it was a trivial incident that gave me the greatest fright. One night in 1996, when I was sleeping in a school in Jaghatu district (Ghazni province), I was awakened by an armed man who slammed the door as he entered my room, his face menacingly illuminated by a petrol lamp. Fighting between two Shiite factions was taking place nearby, and it was said that several involved commanders had kidnapped foreigners in the past. As the man leaned over the sleeping bodies and seemed to looked for one in particular, I made myself as small as possible beneath the blanket and barely suppressed a nervous tremor—until it finally dawned on me that he was the guard looking for a colleague to relieve him.

In Iran it was the police controls that caused me problems. You cannot simply walk in the street and strike up a chance conversation in the hope of meeting someone from Afghanistan, for Afghans in Iran are fearful and suspicious and do not let anyone stop them without reason or a prior introduction. This means that it impossible to conduct research without exact and reliable addresses. I was afraid of endangering my Afghan friends, most of whom did not have the necessary papers, and I constantly wondered whether I was being followed by the police. I always took great precautions when I went to visit one of my interlocutors, walking around for a long time in a bazaar before suddenly jumping into a taxi. By comparison, Pakistan offered the best conditions for research: Afghans could move around freely there, and in Quetta I was able to walk in the streets picking up more and more information from countless little conversations.

The fact that my research sometimes touched on illegal activities, such as the crossing of frontiers, caused me some problems but scarcely bothered my Afghan informants. They described such practices in an uninhibited way as if they were a matter of course, often feeling buoyed up my interest and soon passing from mistrust to boastfulness. Only large-scale smugglers and businessmen were reticent when answering my questions.

The greatest difficulty of all, however, was the management of human relations in a society marked by intense competition, violence and constant mistrust. The little problems of everyday life can prove more daunting than the most spectacular dangers;[25] people constantly change their plans and require you to adjust accordingly; you never know what is going to happen, when you are going to leave or return. It is hard to know where you are going to sleep that night, and you always have to bring along your toothbrush as well as such tools of the trade as notebooks, pens or a camera.

Lack of privacy is a great source of tension that eventually takes a heavy toll on your morale. In the case of private individuals, propriety dictates that a guest should never be left alone, and so there is virtually no time when you can cut yourself off for a few moments, even to satisfy a call of nature. When I used to write up my journal in the evening, children devoured by curiosity would attach themselves to me and observe my least action or gesture. My left-handedness and my general way of writing amazed them to such an extent that they frequently asked whether it was a cultural phenomenon due to the direction in which Latin characters are written.

The art of speech occupies a central position in Afghan culture. Afghans appreciate oratorical jousting, joke a lot and are often in a cheerful mood; they find any occasion right to strike up a conversation. In a society with an egalitarian ideal, where competition and a sense of honor are keenly felt, hospitality is an extremely important value. A foreigner is thus both a focus of competition and a confidant.[26] Travellers provide an opportunity for distraction and the exchange of information, but the solicitude of which are the object can become invasive. Sometimes I was forced to make a detour to avoid having to make a stop for tea in one shop or another. The touching hospitality of Afghans can have pernicious effects, for it becomes a fetter on movement. As Dorronsoro writes, "the rules of politeness are designed to limit the potentially disturbing action of the traveller. Welcomed in a special room for guests, he has no contact with the women of the house and is rarely able to move around on his own" (2000: 8).

Despite the hospitality, one sometimes has the sense of being in the way.[27] Fieldwork involves a subtle mix of necessary (or anyway inevitable) indiscretion and respect for the privacy and work of others. My presence occasionally drew suspicion, and I was several times accused of being a spy. To overcome this, it is sometimes necessary to be introduced by someone who has the trust of the informant, to adopt a frank attitude, to give repeated explanations of one's work, and to avoid at all costs any ill-considered promises. Things cannot be done in a hurry. The ice is often broken when one shows proof of detailed geographical knowledge, such as the story of a trip or a listing of the villages through which one has passed. Reassured, the informant will say: "Ah, he was really there! And he came back!"

In crisis situations, the presence of aid workers weighs heavily upon the relations that the ethnographer is able to build. Whereas humanitarian agencies are geared to action and ask questions for specific purposes, the anthropologist must chiefly try to understand which are the right questions to ask of others and himself without imposing his own way of thinking. This difference constitutes one of the most difficult methodological and ethical problems in the field. It is essential to clear up any confusion. Through his presence, the researcher arouses hopes that he is unable to satisfy; people in distress approach him to intercede on their behalf and to help resolve all manner of administrative problems. Thus, I found myself having to answer endless questions about how to go the West, whether I could procure a visa, whether I could help in finding a job in an aid agency, and so on. My informants often oscillated between feelings of prestige at the interest I showed in them and a certain unease and misunderstanding in relation to my work. It was therefore crucially important to keep explaining that my reason for being there was not to help refugees directly but to write a book on the Hazara migrants and, in this way, to make Western public opinion a little more aware of the situation in Afghanistan.

My difficulties were especially acute during my stay in Dahmarda in autumn 1995, when everyone I met insisted on showing me their irrigation channels (*kârez*). At the time the valley was experiencing grave tensions between two rival factions (see chapter 3), and Mardan Ali, in order to make things easier and to make himself appear important, had spread it around without telling me that I worked for an NGO active in agriculture. The false hopes he thereby raised among the farmers caused me huge methodological problems. Many people asked me to come and see that their *kârez* had run dry and then appealed for me to help them. When I asked them anything in connection with my research, they inevitably brought the conversation round to the issue of irrigation: "Come and see my *kârez;* it's blocked up with stones. There are lots of stones here and not much water! Put my name down!" I tried to get out of it by saying that, as long as the Dahmarda population was divided, it could not make any demands for outside aid. I even had to make a speech in Persian before an assembly of local notables.

Afghanistan is a highly fragmented country. It was certainly against my better judgement that I allowed myself to become caught up in these matters, especially as Mardan Ali had not explained in advance the situation in his village. I agreed to speak to representatives of the different factions, never promising anything and always making it clear that my work was different from that of an NGO employee. But, although I resisted any temptation to play the demiurge, a series of minor events gradually entangled me in the local factional strife. In that winter of 1995–96, tensions linked to the general political and military situation in Afghanistan led to the killing of a dozen people, and it came to my ears that plans were afoot to kidnap me. I found it hard to judge the truth of these rumors, as it was possible that people were trying to make me take sides in some way. But earlier kidnappings of foreigners made me decide not to go to the area again during my second trip to Afghanistan in 1996, even though my research partly concentrated on the people of the Dahmarda valley.

An ethnologist must avoid the humanitarian label, but that does not mean he can ever insert himself into the same relational schema as an Afghan. For an Afghan, friendship is defined not only emotionally but also by clear and precise criteria: the amount of time spent together, the favors done, etc. One of my informants said that in his view there were four stages in a friendship: a period of observing the other, trying to understand his character and deciding whether it is worth investing in the relationship; next, a period of mutual favors that also serve as tests of sincerity, emotional honesty and strength of commitment; then the real friendship, when greater freedom is possible and each knows that he can ask the other for favors; and a final stage when each feels entitled not only to ask the other for favors but to demand them. It is a symmetrical relationship characterized by empathy and mutual giving.

Although the ethnologist cannot fully enter into this schema, and although his chief reason for being in the area is professional, he is able to develop quality relationships. Of course, he remains an outsider and cannot escape the complicated power play, rivalry and jealousy of which he is the object. But the very fact that he will return from whence he came means that some people can confide in him in a way that they would not with even a close Afghan friend. Here we see all the ambiguity of the ethnographic approach.

PART TWO

THE LOCATIONS

Chapter Three

Hazarajat: Kinship and Neighborhood in the Village

MEMORY OF MIGRATION IN EARLIER TIMES AND THE MULTIPLE REGISTERS OF SOLIDARITY

In this chapter, we shall first look at the types of organization in Hazara society and then turn to changes that have taken place in the recent period. As we have seen, my main work was with people from the Dahmarda[1] valley (or, more precisely, Dahmarda-ye Gulzar), in the extreme south (*uluswâli*) of the district of Jaghori. This choice, resulting first of all from chance encounters, was justified by the intensity of migratory movement among the local population.

The boundaries of Hazarajat are imprecise. In 1999 the United Nations estimated its population at between 1.6 million and 2.5 million (Johnson 2000: 46).[2] It is a mountainous region, which reaches a maximum height of more than 5,000 meters. The climate is harsh: winter snowfall can cut villages off for weeks at a time, and the summers are mild but short. It is densely populated in relation to the climatic conditions, altitude and soil. Hazaras to the south of the Koh-e Baba chain (Day Zangi, Day Kundi, Behsud, Ghazni) are sedentary farmers, whereas those immediately to the north (between Yakawlang and Bamyan) make a subsistence living in which animal farming plays a greater role (Schurmann 1962: 112). Unlike on the southern fringes of Hazarajat, a distinction is made between a high-altitude settlement (*aylâq*) and a permanent village (*qišlâq*) (Huwyler and Meyer 1979: 25–26, 45). Use is made of each plot suitable for cultivation. Wheat, barley, maize, potatoes, broad beans, onions, carrots, turnips, clover and alfalfa are grown on the irrigated lands. Dry farming is also practised on the mountain slopes, and a number of orchards (mulberry, apple, apricot, walnut, almond, etc.) dot the landscape. Poplars provide wood for the construction industry.

Apart from some intellectuals and political leaders who claimed in support of their demands that the Hazaras are the real native people of Afghanistan, most of my interlocutors traced their ancestry back to population movements and intermingling. Memory of ancient migration, often linked to the idea that they are descended from Genghis Khan's soldiers, is compounded by the often painful experience of recent migration. Thus, many Hazaras were displaced in the late-nineteenth century, when their original homeland was subjugated by the emir of Kabul and they found refuge in neighboring countries, especially in Iranian Khorasan and in Quetta (British-ruled Baluchistan, today in Pakistan). A smaller group left to settle in Central Asia.[3] The food shortage that hit Afghanistan in the early 1970s, then the war that tore the country apart in the 1980s and 1990s, again drove many Hazaras abroad, although those affected think of this trauma not as a unique or irreversible experience but as a repetition of past events. Already in the nineteenth century, many Hazaras were driven by poverty in the winter to seek work as porters in the lowland towns (Burnes 1986: 175; Maitland 1891: 370). Before the Communist coup of 1978, seasonal migration might involve as much as thirty to fifty percent of males in the poorest villages. Temporary migration led many inhabitants of the central provinces of Afghanistan to the big cities and the main agricultural regions, and several authors mention the large community from Jaghori who settled in Quetta (Etienne 1972: 211; Canfield 1976: 116; Huwyler and Meyer 1979: 22–23). At the end of the twentieth century, with the infrastructure of Afghanistan devastated by more than two decades of fighting, migration was evidently a way of escaping the violence and insecurity, but also a social and economic strategy. The war profoundly altered social relations in Hazarajat, making the region ever more dependent on outside funding and leading to the emergence of a new political class.

In Jaghori, as elsewhere in Hazarajat and Afghanistan, there are several different sources of solidarity and cooperation: kinship is certainly one of these, but other factors such as neighborly relations also play a role. This does not mean that we are dealing with concentric circles. Rather, there is a more subtle overlapping of identity registers that only partly cover one another.

THEORIES ABOUT THE ORIGINS OF THE HAZARAS

The historical origins of the Hazaras are a matter of dispute, as are the conditions under which they converted to Shiism (Bacon 1951a, 1951b, 1963;

Ferdinand 1959; Schurmann 1962; Poladi 1989; Mousavi 1998). Even the etymology of the word is in doubt. As *hazâr* means "thousand" in Persian, most authors consider that it goes back to the Mongol word *minggan*, which has the same meaning. In the age of Genghis Khan (early-thirteenth century), it served to denote the basic thousand-man unit of the Mongol armies, and by extension it could also have the sense of "tribe." Thus, it is argued that the word *hazâra* replaced *minggan* in the area of present-day Afghanistan, where it eventually came to designate a specific group. This evolution may also be found elsewhere. Troops organized in units of a thousand are said to have gone to India with the armies of Tamerlane (who died in 1405), and the district of Hazara, to the north of Islamabad (in present-day Pakistan), supposedly derives its name from regiments based there at the time.

The term *hazâra* appears in the early-sixteenth-century memoirs of Babur, founder of the Mongol dynasty in India, who used it several times to denote various partly Mongol-speaking peoples living in geographically disconnected areas, such as the Rûstâ-hazâra of Badakhshan or the inhabitants of mountainous regions west of Kabul up to the historical province of Ghor and Ghazni (1987: 196, 200, 207, 214,218, 221).[4] Babur also speaks of the Turkmân Hazâra, an unsubdued mountain tribe against which he fought in 1506 (1987: 251–253). If the term *hazâra* has several referents, it already serves to denote a population with strong Mongol elements that was present in the center of present-day Afghanistan.

Bacon (1951b) considers that the Hazaras are directly descended from the Jaghatai Mongols of Central Asia, whereas Schurmann (1962) thinks they are for the most part Nikudari Mongols from the eastern fringes of Iran who mixed with local Iranian-speaking peoples. Kakar (1973), reconciling these two views, holds that the Hazaras arrived in what is now Afghanistan between 1229 and 1447; a first wave consisted of Jaghatai from Central Asia and was followed by Ilkhans expelled from Iran, Turks, Turco-Mongols, Timurids and others, so that by the sixteenth century the Hazaras formed a distinct group already living in their present region. Under the influence of the Safavids of Iran, they then converted to Shiism between the late-sixteenth and early-seventeenth centuries (Mousavi 1998). Owtadolajam (1976), a sociologist who carried out research in Quetta in the early 1970s, came out firmly in support of a Mongol ancestry. Following Kakar, however, he identifies two distinct origins:

- peoples driven out by the advance of Genghis Khan (most notably, Uighurs): region of Ghazni, Jaghori and its surroundings (lack of Day prefix in name of tribes);

- Genghis Khan Mongols properly so called, who may be subdivided into two groups: Ilkhans, that is Mongols from Iran who took refuge in central Afghanistan (Day Chopan, Day Khitai); and Jaghatais, that is Turkized Mongols expelled from Transoxania through the emergence of new powers (Day Kundi, Behsud, Day Mirdad, Polada, Sheikh Ali).

Without taking sides in the dispute between Bacon (1951b, 1963) and Schurmann (1962),[5] we may consider it historically likely that Turkic and Mongol groups gradually driven into the Hindu Kush between the thirteenth and fifteenth centuries (from Central Asia and Iran) mixed with the local Iranian peoples and adopted their language. Nevertheless, such theories rest upon a too rigid and substantive definition of ethnicity. Barth, in a celebrated text outlining his radically different theory (1981a: 198–227), argued that ethnic identity involves not a set of objective traits (origin, language, territory, etc.) but a construct ceaselessly renegotiated within the framework of social interactions. The Middle East has long been familiar with the constitution, in marginal areas, of heterogeneous groups resulting from a continual process of inclusion and exclusion, distinction and resistance to the central power. The history of the region displays numerous examples of heterodox religious groups that have settled in remote areas to escape persecution, strengthening their social-cultural identity (Canfield 1973a: 10–12 and 1973b: 1511–13; Planhol 1993).

In other words, a shared identity does not necessarily imply a common historical origin. In the case that concerns us here, the Hazara sense of belonging rests not upon a Mongol ancestry but on a process of marginalization that must have begun at quite an early date. Since its first appearance in the sixteenth century, the term *hazâra* has served to denote a number of different populations, and today it is used for certain heterogeneous Sunni groups in the districts of Rustaq (province of Takhar) and Nahrin (province of Baghlan) who have virtually nothing in common with the Hazaras proper other than their marginal geographical and political situation (Centlivres and Centlivres-Demont 1988a: 42, 50–51, 62). This indicates that the term refers more to a social position than to a single historical origin. Similarly, rather than being due to direct action on the part of the Safavids, the conversion of the Hazaras to Shiism might be the result of a process of detachment from neighboring peoples.

THE HAZARA TRIBAL SYSTEM: A HISTORICAL PERSPECTIVE

Between the sixteenth and nineteenth centuries, Hazarajat mainly escaped the control of the great regional empires. Only with the second reign of Emir Dost Mohammad (1842–1863) did the central power in Kabul extend its control over Bamyan and impose tribute on certain peripheral areas in the region (Noelle 1997). It was the war of conquest under Abdur Rahman (1891–1893), accompanied with profound ethnic-religious polarization and a whole series of massacres and atrocities (Kakar 1973 and 1979; Poladi 1989; Mousavi 1998), which finally put an end to the independence of Hazarajat. The conflict led to a number of population transfers: whole swathes of Hazarajat (especially in what is now Uruzgan province) were emptied of their population and occupied by Pashtuns. The former inhabitants went abroad (to Iran, present-day Pakistan and even Central Asia) or to the north of the country, especially the region of Mazar-e Sharif (Sholgara, Char Kent, Dara-ye Suf). Other Hazaras sought refuge in neighboring areas: for example, some inhabitants of Day Chopan (in Zabul province) migrated to the contiguous district of Jaghori; over the last twenty years their descendents, economically vulnerable landless peasants, have left in droves to chance their luck in Pakistan and Iran. The painful memory of these events is very present and shows through in the revolutionary songs of the 1980s (Bindemann 1988).

The Hazara tribal system was partly dislocated by the bloody war of 1891–1893 and the gradual penetration of the state administrative apparatus down to local level (Canfield 1971). We have little information about the preceding period, when society was dominated by powerful tribal chieftains or *mirs* (Roy 1985: 194; Mousavi 1998: 47, 91–92) whose sphere of influence might extend over several valleys. Constantly divided by conflicts (Elphinstone 1992 II: 211), the *mirs* owned land and controlled the principal means of production. In general, their functions were handed down from father to son. Social-political entities and tribal affiliations mainly consisted of clientelist networks, which were symbolically invested with a genealogical ideology according to which each tribal segment had a common male ancestor. Social relations thus appear to have been strongly hierarchical.

Apart from the works of Elphinstone (1992 (1815)), by British travellers and scholars such as Burnes (1992 (1834)), Moorcroft and Trebeck (1979 (1841)) and Masson (1997 (1842)), one of the best sources of information on the nineteenth-century Hazaras are the reports of the Afghan Boundary Commission, especially those of Maitland, who headed a mission to Afghanistan between 1884 and 1886, shortly before the wars of Abdul Rahman. According to one local tradition reported by Maitland, the Hazara were originally divided into eight tribes (1891: 284):[6] Dai Zangi; Dai Kundi; Dai Chopán; Dai Kalán (the modern Shekh Ali); Besud; Faolád; Khatai; Dáhlá. All of Maitland's sources mention the first five, whereas one of the last three is sometimes replaced with Dai Mirdád. He provides a list of the main territorial and tribal divisions of the Hazara at the time of his journey (1891: 286):[7]

Table 1: The main Hazara tribal sections, as listed by Maitland (1891)

Tribes	Places	Number of families
1. Besud	District of Besud, north of Náwar, north-eastern Hazarajat	15,000
2. Dai Zangi	Dai Zangi land, northern and north-western Hazarajat, with Yák Walang	13,000
3. Dai Kundi	Dai Kundi land, western Hazarajat	11,000
4. Independent Hazaras (several tribes)	Yaghistán, south-eastern and southern Hazarajat (today's Uruzgan)	44,500
5. Ghazni Hazaras	Hazara-populated areas closest to Ghazni	22,000
6. Shekh Ali Hazaras	The valleys of Shekh Ali, Turkoman, Pársá; Jalmish and Surkháb; Doshi, Khinján, Ghori, Andaráb, etc.	13,000
7. Bámián Hazaras, etc. (portions of Hazára, Tátár and Habash tribes)	Bámián, Doáb and Rui	5,500
8. Hazaras from district of Balkh-áb, Dara Yúsúf and elsewhere in Afghan Turkistan (fragments of tribes)	Dispersed, but nearly all in the region between Yák Walang and Mazár-i-Sharif	8,000
Total		132,000

Maitland concludes that the Hazaras were a population numbering roughly half a million. Among the "independent Hazara," he lists the following tribes (1891: 347): Jirghai Usi Muhammad, Dáyah, Faoládi, Zaoli, Sultán Ahmad, Urusgán, Kalandar, Kolián, Dai Chopán (or Khatai, or Bábali), Dai Zangi Pitai (or Southern Dai Zangi). The author points out that a large proportion of the Shekh Ali was Sunni by religion, especially in the lower Shekh Ali valley (Parwan province), and that in his view they had converted recently under pressure from Pashtun neighbors. As to the Turkmen valley, he thought its inhabitants to be of Turkmen origin but to have been integrated with the Hazaras at least since the early sixteenth century. He also mentions

Table 2. The main Hazara tribes in the Ghazni region, as listed by Maitland (1891)

Tribes	Places	Number of families
1. Jaghatu	West of Ghazni, up to Náwar	8,470
2. Muhammad Khwája	In Náwar, up to Karábágh in the south	3,330
3. Chahár Dasta	Karábágh	1,850
4. Jághuri	Upper Arghanbáb valley, west of Karábágh, south-west of Náwar	6,290
5. Faoládi of Málistán	In Málistán, north-west of Jághuri	2,040
Total		21,980

the presence of Ismailis in the Surkhab and Andarab valleys and the fact that they mixed there with Tajiks, a group more and more dominant upstream (1891: 389, 392) and also present around Bághak (between Jalmesh and Doab-e Mikhzarin) (1891: 386). Maitland's Shekh Ali appear to have been a heterogeneous group. In this region, the division among Sunnis, Shiites and Ismailis is more important than tribal affiliations (Canfield 1973a and 1973b). In Maitland's account, there were Tatars living in the lower and middle Kahmard valley, and Habashs in the Roy-e Doab region (Sunnis, who were not thought of as Hazara). Tajiks were present in the Bamyan region proper, but apparently Hazaras still represented 80% of the population there (Maitland 1891: 395): Khatai, Faoládi, Ditto and Dai Zangi, divided into numerous branches (1891: 398).

As to the Ghazni region, Maitland (1891: 377) presents a table of Hazara tribal affiliations that still seems largely applicable today (see table 3). Among the Jaghatu, Maitland recorded the following sections (1891: 361): Aludáni, Islám, Kataghán, Shákhá, Kimlut, Iliás, Biát, Khwája Míri, Kari Suf, Aishghi, Farash, Lághri, Kargháni and Ahmada, the most numerous being the Aludáni (2,500 families), the Biát (1,300) et the Kataghán (1,000). Jaghatu is a geographically based grouping, which scarcely corresponds to the way in which the people in question designate themselves. Some sections identified by Maitland did not really think of themselves as Hazara, especially the Bayats (part of the Qizilbash federation that is said to have come from Iran in the eighteenth century, in the age of Nader Shah Afshar) and the Qataghan (self-styled Turks originally from northern Afghanistan). As to the Alawdini from Nawur, some of whom claim to be descended from Ala-ud-Din, the Ghurid ruler who sacked Ghazni in the middle of the twelfth century. The Foladi were one of the original divisions of the Hazara, but were then scattered through various regions: Bámián (Dara Faoládi), Dara Yúsúf, Málistán and the Ujaristan valley (Ajrestan, province of Uruzgan), which had the largest group (5,000 families).

Maitland (1891: 369–375) also lists the tribal branches in the comparatively more homogeneous population of Jaghori. Without counting the *mir* and his branch, the territory was divided into seven *dastas* or "sub-districts"[8], each with three to seven sections governed by a *mehtar*[9] that were usually known by the name of the principal branch.

Table 3: The main tribal sections in Jaghori, as listed by Maitland (1891)

Dastas or sub-districts	Sections	Places	Number of families
I. Ezdari (total 700 families)	1. Khwája Ali	Aludán and Kharbed	400
	2. Bághochari	Kamrak and Surkhjui	300
II. Hájíbíní (total 750 families)	1. Hájíbíní	Lomán	300
	2. Beg	Bárik	100
	3. Busaid	Lomán and Shahar-i Zaida	200
	4. Shoghla	Shoghla	150
III. Geri (total 900 families)	1. Geri	Tezao and Nairun	400
	2. Angúrí	Angúrí	300
	3. Haidar	Saosang and Kadi	200
IV. Maska (total 1,420 families)	1. Maska	Gazak and Tanachob	100
	2. Átá	Maska and Sang-i Sulákh	300
	3. Oki	Udkol (Aokol?)	600
	4. Dámardah	Gulzár	100
	5. Khosha	Chalmadak	100
	6. Pátú	Pátú	120
	7. Bábá	Bábá	100
V. Kalandar (total 1,000 families)	Unknown	Kalandar	1,000
VI. Sherdágh (total 500 families)	Unknown	Sherdágh	500
VII. Pashé (total 800 families)	Unknown	Pashé	800
VIII. The branch of the Mír (total 220 families)	Álam Beg	Sang-i Másha	100
	Zardak	Zardak	120

It was impossible for me to check the accuracy of this list. Local people concurred with Hazara researcher Mohammad Isa Gharjestani (1989) in distinguishing four main branches and sub-branches:

1) The Baighani or Âta, divided into Oqi (including the lineage of the *mir*), Maska, Bâbâ, Dahmarda,[10] Yâr Mohammad and Khosha.
2) The Yazdari or Ezdari: Sa'id Ahmad, Allâhudâl, Khwâja Ali, Mirdâd.
3) The Bâghocari: Busayd, Khodâdâd, Bâya, Lomo (or Lumân).
4) The Gari: Dolsha, Dâwud, Zerak, Haydar.

Other groups present in the region were not directly affiliated to the Jaghori tribal group and were thought to have different origins:

5) The Qalandar[11] (late-nineteenth-century refugees from Day Chopan and Arjestan).
6) The Pashi (present in Jaghori and Malistan districts and thought by many to be directly descended from Genghis Khan's troops).

Throughout Jaghori one also finds groups who, though supposedly descended from the Pashtun tribe of the Shamulzay and have merged with the Hazara population.

It is difficult to collect tables that converge with one another. The affiliations are changing and follow the vicissitudes of history, reflecting the political conditions of the time as well as migratory patterns and the absorption of one group by another. Thus, several informants placed the Busayd and Lumân among the Gari, which was sometimes also said to include such groups as the Anguri or the Dawlatshâh. Another branch, the Hecha, was often included among the Âta. It is therefore impossible to draw up a complete and univocal typology for the population of Jaghori in which all the levels and affiliations systematically interlock. Information given by different individuals rarely coincides, and the imposition of an arbitrary "order" or "meaning" would not do justice to the complexity of the social relations (Tapper R. 1988, 1989).

The subjugation of Hazarajat by Abdur Rahman not only disorganized the Hazara tribal system but also opened up the region to Pashtun nomads, who secured the best pastures for their herds.[12] Relations between the two communities have always been difficult, with the religious divided compounded by divergent economic interests. The Pashtun nomads are not only herdsmen but also traders: money-lending and trade in manufactures give them ascendancy over the Hazara farmers, who are sometimes forced to sell their possessions to repay creditors and become tenant farmers on their own land (Ferdinand 1962).

In the twentieth century, then, the Hazaras experienced a long period of marginalization. At the social, political and economic levels Hazarajat lagged considerably behind the rest of the country (Etienne 1972: 209–214), and many poor peasants were forced to look for work as laborers in towns such as Ghazni, Mazar-e Sharif and Kabul. Hazarajat was shaken by a number of revolts, most notably the one in the second half of the forties led by Ibrahim Khan, *bace gawsawâr* ("son of the cow-rider"), who fought against a tax in clarified butter that the Hazaras had to pay on every animal in their possession, even on non-milked horses and donkeys.[13] Popular tales recount the exploits of honorable bandits (*yâghi*) such as Yusuf Beg, who fought against arbitrary rule and reputedly eluded the authorities for nineteen years in Shahristan before he was finally captured and executed (Edwards 1986a: 208–211; Poladi 1989: 384–385, 396–397; Mousavi 1998: 163). Fayz Mohammad Kateb (Abdur Rahman's secretary, who left an account of the bloody conquest of Hazarajat[14]), Abdul Khaleq (the young man who assassinated King Nader Shah in 1933), Sayyed Ismael Balkhi (an important Hazara religious leader who was imprisoned between 1949 and 1964) are all celebrated as heroic fighters against an oppressive government. Indeed, Hazara identity has been built around the evocation of past injustices and protests against exploitation.

Central government control considerably weakened the power of the *mir*, who remained large landowners but became little more than intermediaries between the population and (mostly Pashtun) civil servants. The word *mir* itself gradually fell into disuse, so that today people use the term *xân* to denote someone whose influence is based upon personal wealth, kinship or other social relations.

After the Communist coup and the ensuing war, Hazarajat regained its old autonomy. The region was relatively spared by the Soviet occupying forces and hardly witnessed any major military operations. Dahmarda, for instance, suffered only three incursions by tanks, plus a few bombing raids that left some spectacular but inconsequential craters in the fields. On the other hand, factional struggles often took a deadly turn, and wrenching internal tensions led to major changes in the social-political structure (Roy 1983, 1983–1984, 1985: 194–205; Bindemann 1987; Grevemeyer 1988; Akram 1996; Harpviken 1996). In a first phase young clerics trained in Iran, often of humble origins, supplanted the old tribal and religious elites. Then a process of unification took place around the ethnic discourse of the Hezb-e wahdat, a political movement that came into being in the late 1980s

(Harpviken 1996). The war saw the emergence of a new elite and a new political consciousness that spurned any return to the status quo ante. Previously excluded from power and treated as second-class citizens, the Hazaras desperately sought national recognition and international attention (Monsutti 1996b, 1996c, 1997b), and their hopes were enormously raised in the post-9/11 climate that brought about American intervention and the fall of the Taliban. After the *loya jirga* and establishment in Kabul of a government backed by the international community, the Hazaras demanded a state in which their rights would finally be recognized.

DAHMARDA: TERRITORY, POPULATION AND ECONOMY

The district of Jaghori lies in the east of Ghazni province, on the southern fringes of Hazarajat. It occupies an area of 1,855 sq. kms. in the upper Arghandab valley, but despite the high altitude (between approximately 2,000 and 3,600 meters) the terrain is not particularly uneven. The low rainfall (approx. 300 millimeters a year (Geokart 1984)) makes agriculture difficult. According to an estimate produced by the Democratic Republic of Afghanistan, the total population in 1979 was 99,126 (AVICEN 1990: 20; UNIDATA 1992: 9); there were 15,477 households, with an average of 6.4 members (UNIDATA 1992: 9). A more recent estimate by humanitarian organizations present in the area put the population at more than 150,000 with an average of 6.7 persons per household (156,285 according to GRSP 1996: 5; 152,567 according to Johnson 2000: 46). The estimated density therefore ranges from 53 to 84 inhabitants per sq. km. It is difficult to be more precise in the present circumstances.

Dahmarda lies in a small valley on the left bank of the Arghandab which has its back turned to the rest of the district. Mountains tower over the valley, rising to 3,142 meters in the north and 3,038 meters in the south. Downstream (to the west) it is enclosed by gorges, while upstream it opens out to form quite a wide basin with a small altitude variation between 2,400 and 2,500 meters (*Gazeteer of Afghanistan* 1985, vol. 6, map VI-18-A at 1:300,000). Compared with the rest of Jaghori district, Dahmarda is poorly endowed with water and trees. The main road suitable for vehicles takes the Rasana pass, nearly 2,700 meters south-east of the bazaar, and then enters the district of Gelan (populated by Pashtuns, mostly from the Taraki tribe). From there, one can descend to the Tarnak valley and either join the Kabul-Kandahar road or go back up through Hutqol to the other part of Jaghori. Two other roads, both of them bad, lead into the Arghandab valley (province of Zabul): the first across the Qâro pass to the south, at a height of just over 2,500 meters; the second along the valley to the west.

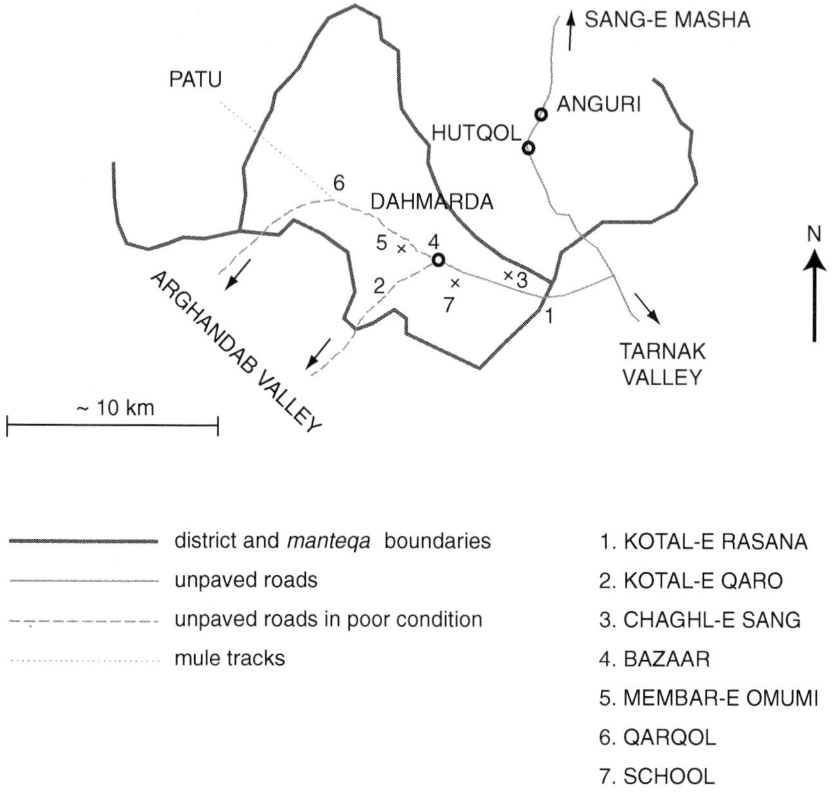

Figure 4. Map of Dahmarda

I recorded my arrival in Dahmarda in my diary of October 11, 1995:

> *After the Rasana pass, at the foot of which stretched the almost treeless Dahmarda basin, it was not long before we reached Mardan Ali's house, one of the first on the road. A few women were in the vicinity: they went up to Mardan Ali, and the usual polite formulas were exchanged. The younger ones quickly kissed Mardan Ali's right hand, while he affectionately passed his other hand over their heads. When the woman was older, it was he who bowed with respect.*
>
> *We went into the* awli *(house with a yard): high walls, an irregular wooden gate, a small inner courtyard, enclosures for goats, sheep and cows (the troughs built directly into the walls), and upstairs the living quarters. These were divided into two: on the left Mardan Ali's family; on the right the families of Aziz Azizi and Mohammad Ali (who is currently in Iran). All told, some twenty people live in these premises.*

We go into the main room of Mardan Ali's quarters. It is slightly raised and connects with the kitchen through a low door: from time to time I see an arm or, a head bent surreptitiously in my direction. The layout is simple but functional: some gelim *(woven carpets) on the floor,* tošak *(thin quilted mattresses) on the sides, two or three tinplate chests in an alcove in the pisé wall, a few photographs on the walls (I am told they are of Mardan Ali's two brothers, Mohammad Ali and Aziz Azizi, and of Ramazan Ali, their* bace kâkâ *(FBS), who was killed in combat four years earlier.*

I am surprised to see several women there: they lean against one another on the other side of the room and timidly peer at me while exchanging greetings with Mardan Ali. He briefly presents them to me without mentioning their names (using kinship terms such as "the wife of my kâkâ*" or "my brother's wife"); his sister is also present, completely shrouded in a flowery white veil, and so is his mother. I feel myself being scrutinized, but the women's faces remain covered, except for that of Mardan Ali's mother, who seems bolder and more communicative: she talks to me directly with bursts of half-embarrassed, half-excited laughter. When I look at her as I reply, she modestly puts her hand in front of the lower part of her face. Mardan Ali hands out money lavishly to the children and women: 1,000 afghanis (roughly 0.25 dollars) to the former, and as much as 4,000 afghanis (roughly one dollar) to the latter. A neighbor suddenly arrives and the women disappear like a puff of air.*

Later in the evening I get to meet the men. Abdul Karim, the bright teenage son of Mardan Ali, Aziz Azizi, his brother, Mohammad Akbar, his father, and Akram Ali, the kâkâ *(both are quite tall and thin, unlike Mardan Ali and his son, who are rather squat), as well as Mohammad Hasan, the* bace kâkâ, *who squints horribly but proves to be jovial enough. When Mardan Ali greets an elder, they embrace and Mardan Ali puts his forehead on the other's shoulder. The couples hold each other closely and kiss effusively on the cheeks. As for me, some warmly shake me by the hand, while others openly hug me and almost lift me off the ground.*

The population consists of 450 to 500 households (*xâna*), or 3,000 to 3,500 inhabitants, who live in some forty loosely clustered hamlets (*qaria* or *âghel*). More than two hundred families in Dahmarda have resettled in Quetta, and there are more than 350 unmarried workers and twenty families (roughly 500 persons in all) in Iran. It is a highly mobile population, but although individuals move around very often the total number must be fairly stable. Altogether, then, the *qawm* of Dahmarda consists of between 4,700 and 5,500 persons, roughly 64 percent in Jaghori, 26 percent in Quetta and 10 percent in Iran.

The economy basically depends on irrigation agriculture and money-transfers from men working in the coal mines near Quetta or as laborers in Iran (see chapters 6 and 7). The housing is quite scattered.[15] Downstream, where the valley has steep sides, the houses rarely have surrounding walls, but further up the landscape opens out and people live in larger homes with high mud walls (*qala*). It is here that the main community buildings are to be found: the mosque and a school recently converted by a local NGO. There is also a bazaar consisting of seventy shops,[16] but it is not very active and rarely has more than a dozen shops open at the same time; there are only a few craftsmen, a couple of blacksmiths, a joiner and two or three millers.

Each family has a small number of sheep and goats, and in some cases one or two cows. In summer a shepherd takes the flocks into the nearby mountains. Unlike in the high plateaux of northern Hazarajat, the families do not live for long periods in high-altitude hamlets.

The staple food is bread, which is usually baked on a thin metal plate or, less often, in a buried clay oven. People dip it in a thin soup prepared with dried mutton. Dried or fresh fruit, beans and dairy produce provide extra nutrition that is highly appreciated.

The lands are classified according to their use:

- *zamin-e âbi:* "irrigated land," arranged in horizontal terraces separated by little embankments;
- *zamin-e lalmi* or *dayma:* "non-irrigated land" allocated to pluvial agriculture, which has a lower yield but whose products—especially wheat—are considered superior in quality;
- *carâgâh* ("pasture") or more rarely *zamin-e alafcar* (from *alaf,* "forage"), reserved for an individual or more often a group such as the inhabitants of a hamlet or the members of a sub-lineage;
- *zamin-e omumi:* "common land"; everyone can use it, gather wild fruit there, pasture their flocks or take away forage and combustible brushwood. (Another fuel is cow dung, which is mixed with straw and dried in the form of flat cakes or *calma.*) In Dahmarda all the land has been distributed. Some stretches of mountain used for forage by the inhabitants of a particular hamlet may nevertheless be available for everyone to use as pasture.

Pluvial agriculture is quite uncommon in Dahmarda. Mardan Ali's famly, for instance, does not own any *lalmi.*[17] Irrigation is effected through underground channels or *kârez,* which capture ground water, and through open furrows (*juy*) which drain river water or continue a *kârez*. The valley contains tens of irrigation channels. When a *kârez* is constructed, the irrigated land is divided among those participating in the venture, as are the time-share water rights that are handed down from generation to generation. But these allocations are no simple matter: it is not enough to divide up the surface area and the hours of water use; it is also necessary to take into account the yield of each plot and the rate of flow of the various channels. The number of hours allocated to each right-holder is expressed in multiples of *roz* ("day") and *šab* ("night")—which in Jaghori correspond to twelve and twenty-four hours respectively. There is no local notable responsible for the distribution.

The lands are distributed in accordance with the origin of the property entitlement, which is part of the ancestral memory. (Many *kârez* are supposed to date from the founding of Dahmarda.) The relevant categories here are:

- *zamin-e ersi* (*ers:* "inheritance"): "inherited lands," in a paternal line from the ancestral founders who developed them for irrigation agriculture and built the adjoining *kârez;*
- *zamin-e ahiâi* (*ahiâ:* "rebirth, restoration, revival"): "lands brought into use" by one or more individuals, who thereby acquired ownership that was endorsed by the community;
- *zamin-e zarxarid* (or more rarely *zamin-e xaridâri*): "purchased lands" (from *zar,* "gold," and *xaridan,* "to buy"), so called even if the act of purchase goes back several generations.

The boundary markers are often simply stones taken from the ground that are in no way different from others in the area. In theory, the land purchase brings water rights with it. But, although private property is very important in this society of sedentary farmers, land is not regarded as a commodity: to sell a plot without first discussing it with paternal kin would be a serious transgression, and parents would have the right to pre-empt it. In any event, no one coming from outside would be able to purchase land.

Most of the properties are small. Agricultural holdings are customarily expressed not in area measurements but in the seed requirement or the labor time needed for ploughing or harvesting. My information concerning Jaghori tallies with Schurmann's concerning Yakawlang (1962: 153–154): an average family owns approximately six *jerib* of irrigated land (one *jerib* = 0.2 hectares).[18] In Dahmarda only a few rich families have more than twenty or thirty *jerib*.

4 hectares = 10 acres

.2
×20
4 hectar

In Jaghori, three kinds of agreement may exist between landowner and farmer:

- *gerawi:* "loan against security": the farmer pays the landowner a certain sum to use the land (or house); the landowner has to repay the loan to regain the use of his property;
- *ejâradâri:* "renting" (from *ejâra,* "lease" or "concession"): regardless of the amount produced from year to year, the farmer pays a contractually fixed rent (mostly in kind but sometimes also in money) and keeps the surplus;
- *dehqâni:* "sharecropping": the farmer (*dehqân*) has to deliver a certain proportion of his produce to the owner.

The northern Afghan principle (Centlivres 1970: 139) of dividing the harvest in accordance with five factors (land, irrigation water, seeds, draught animals, physical labor)—so that a peasant having nothing but his labor-power would receive only a fifth of the crop—appears to be unknown in Jaghori and elsewhere in Hazarajat. The world of Dahmarda is one of close mutual acquaintance: the farmer is often a relative or neighbor of the owner, and may help him out by looking after his land while he is away in Pakistan, Iran or elsewhere. The current practice is that the farmer keeps a quarter of the harvest and hands over three-quarters to the owner (who almost invariably supplies the irrigation water and seeds as well). This is the system that people usually invoke when they are away. They entrust their land to relatives or neighbors, so that both sides benefit and at the same time strengthen their links with each other. In fact, it is not uncommon for someone who is abroad with his family to ask nothing in return from the relatives who look after his land in his native village. The arrangement is very informal, as the mutual relations are part of a non-commodified cycle of gifts and services.

Work in the fields varies with the season. Spring sees the levelling and ploughing of irrigated plots, the pruning of trees, the clearing of channels and the sowing of potatoes, barley and maize. Summer is devoted to harvesting of the wheat sown the previous year, and of the potatoes and barley; farmers gather apricots and mulberries, and cut the alfalfa for the winter. Autumn brings the sowing of wheat for the following year, and the gathering of apples and almonds. Winter is used for work to maintain the *kârez* and the *juy.* People are then relatively free of agricultural labor, and it is the main season for temporary migration to Pakistan.[19]

Wheat, the main produce, exists in two varieties on the irrigated land: spring wheat (*gandom-e bahâri*) and autumn wheat (*gandom-e termâhi*).

The latter is the more common in Jaghori: to profit from melted snow water, the farmers sow it in October (after intensive irrigation lasting seven to ten days) and harvest it around August. Spring wheat is grown mainly in the high regions of central and western Hazarajat, where pluvial agriculture is also practised. The spring wheat and non-irrigated wheat are planted in April and harvested before the serious cold sets in. Output on irrigated areas may be as high as 1,500 kg of wheat per hectare when conditions are good, but often falls as low as 800 kg. The non-irrigated fields give a maximum of 600 to 700 kg per hectare.[20] According to my information, the yield is ten to twenty times the seed, depending upon the conditions and the type of agriculture (although in regions with the harshest climate it can be as low as two or three times the seed).

Less widely consumed produce may also be found. Barley (which is used mainly for fodder) is sown between April and May and harvested in August. Maize follows the same cycle, but it is very rare in Jaghori, as it requires a lot of water. Potatoes, which are also quite uncommon, are planted in spring and harvested at the end of August. Turnips are planted in August and harvested in October-November for the winter. Both onions and tomatoes are planted in spring and harvested in August. The small yellowish carrots are highly appreciated. Various kinds of beans are also grown.

Clover, an annual forage crop, is planted in late August and harvested after the winter, towards the end of March, so that it can be eaten fresh by livestock. Alfalfa, a perennial, is sown for a long period (between six and sixteen years, depending on conditions) and can be cut several times a year. Like two other forage plants, it is dried so that it can be fed to animals in the winter.

Special care is taken over the vineyards and orchards. Apricots are gathered in late August (just before the wheat), mulberries in July and apples in October; grapes are harvested in late September. Almonds are gathered from late September to early October, in time for migrants to the Quetta coal mines to pay for their journey by selling a few bags at the end. It is thus an important agricultural product, being easy to keep, transport and sell, and is also the only source of currency. Sometimes wheat or barley is sown among the various trees, which include poplars and willows. In comparison with the rest of Jaghori, however, Dahmarda does not have many trees.

Let us take the case of Mardan Ali. His father intended to marry him off against his will to his brother's daughter. But, with his characteristic independence and fighting spirit, Mardan Ali ran away from Dahmarda at the beginning of the 1970s, spent several years in Pakistan and even worked for a while in the plantations of Bangladesh, before joining first the Pakistani army and then the Afghan resistance forces. On returning to Dahmarda, he asked for and obtained his share of the legacy while his father was still alive.

By 1996 he had two sons and four daughters. Although he spent most of his time working in the Quetta mines, his family lived in the hamlet of Chaghl-e Sang,[21] where some two hundred people were spread around twenty-nine houses. Mardan Ali received a little more than two *jerib* of irrigated land from his father, plus four *jerib* of undeveloped land. He also had a few fruit-trees, especially almond trees. His water came from two *kârez:* Takht-e Sang-e Bâlâ or Nula (two *šab,* or 48 hours over an eight-day cycle) and Takht-e Sang-e Pâyn (two and a half *šab,* or sixty hours every twelve days). In 1996, as he was mostly in Quetta, he used the services of a *dehqân,* while his elder son, aged seventeen, ran a shop in the bazaar; the family owned eight sheep, which it left in the care of a shepherd. In 2001, however, the situation changed when Mardan Ali's family joined him in Quetta. He sold the shop and animals, and left his land in the care of his brother, Aziz Azizi, who kept all the produce from it.

Mardan Ali's father, Mohammad Akbar, has not yet divided the land between his two other sons (the daughters do not receive any real property). Together they hold a little more than four *jerib* and receive water from three *kârez,* including forty-eight hours every ten days from the *kârez* of Qockâr-e Pâyn, which is shared by sixteen families (roughly one hundred persons).

As to Akram Ali, the 65-year-old half-brother of Mohammad Akbar, he lives with his wife, his elder son Mohammad Hasan, the latter's wife and young son, and two unmarried daughters. His other son, Mohammad Husayn, works in Iran and sends his savings back home. They own five *jerib* of irrigated land (roughly one hectare) and have water rights over seven *kârez:* 6 hours (*nim-roz*) in an eight-day cycle at Qockâr-e Bâlâ; 6 hours every ten days at Qockâr-e Pâyn; 24 hours (*yak šab*) every ten days at Peshbughundi-ye Bâlâ; 24 hours in a ten-day cycle also at Peshbughundi-ye Pâyn; 12 hours (*yak roz*) every ten days at Lukh; 36 hours every ten days at Takht-e Sang-e Pâyn; and 24 hours every eight days at Takht-e Sang-e Bâlâ.[22] The land is divided among three purposes: (1) wheat; (2) fallow prepared for the next year's wheat; and (3) forage (especially alfalfa and barley). Rotation takes place every year.

In 1996, their almond crop rose to a little more than 2,000 kg. The elder son, Mohammad Hasan, would have to go to the Pakistani frontier (Wesh) to sell them, in the hope of making 8 million afghanis or approximately 2,000 dollars (see chapter 7); this would enable him to repay the loans he took on to build a new house. The other products are consumed by the family: a little more than 800 kg of wheat (they have to buy a similar amount at the bazaar, at a price of some 5,800 afghanis, or 1.45 dollars, per *ser* in 1995), some apricots (around 14kg), carrots and turnips, and some alfalfa and barley as forage. Their almonds (which can fetch 23,000 afghanis or $5.75 a *ser* at the Anguri bazaar) and dried apricots are the only produce to enter the commercial circuit.

The family owns fourteen sheep and three goats. In summer they slaughter around one sheep a month; they hang the semi-carcass up to dry and cook it as and when they need to. In winter they kill only two sheep and complete their diet with carrots and turnips. The cows and oxen remain close to the houses all year round, but in summer the sheep and goats—which give milk only in spring—are led each day to mountain pasture by a shepherd from Chaghl-e Sang. Every evening, the twenty-nine families living in the hamlet take it in turns to offer him a meal—one for each four animals that he looks after. Each also contributes a half-*ser*[23] of wheat (3.5 kg) per animal for the season.[24] In winter the sheep and goats remain in enclosures and are fed on forage plants.

Although the economy of Jaghori is mainly agricultural, the role of trade should not be neglected. Despite the isolation of Hazarajat from the main combat zones, or perhaps because of it, trade with Pakistan grew considerably through twenty years of war. Jaghori, in particular, protected by mountains though still close to the Kabul-Kandahar highway, became one of the main Hazarajat outlets to the south, as the great bazaars of Sang-e Masha and Anguri testify. The one at Dahmarda, which, though not very active, has a total of some seventy shops, seems disproportionate to the size of the population. One finds there manufactured goods (pots, fabrics, soap, etc.) and foodstuffs (rice, cooking oil, tea, sugar, etc.) from abroad—especially from Pakistan and Iran, but also from the former Soviet Union. Relatively open to the outside world—it has regular contacts with Quetta in Pakistan—the district of Jaghori plays a particularly important role in the vast transnational migratory and commercial circuits established by the Hazaras. It is more developed than the rest of Hazarajat, especially parts of the interior such as Shahristan or Lal-wa-Sarjangal, and there is a high level of movement into and out of the district, with active trade and a large number of (admittedly unasphalted) roads.

THE FAMILY AND MARRIAGE

Like other groups in the surrounding region, the Hazara are patrilinear (an individual belongs to his father's line of descent; members of a lineage are considered descendants of the same male ancestor) and patrilocal (after marriage the wife goes to live with her husband in his parents' home, and all the sons usually live under their father's roof). Marriage between cousins is very widespread, but there is no real preference for marriage between a man and his parallel patrilateral cousin. Parallel strategies for more diversified marriage do exist, however, among the *sayyed* (Kopecky 1982: 94–95) as in the rest of the population. Generally speaking, village and ethnic endogamy is very pronounced. The rare exceptions usually involve the union of a Hazara girl with a man from another ethnic group. As net donors of women, the Hazaras thus enter into an asymmetrical relationship that reveals their inferior position within the social hierarchy.

The domestic economy is based upon a strict division of labor. The men take charge of the heavy agricultural labor and relations with the outside world; it is they who go to the bazaar to buy the produce and other items that the household needs. The women do the cooking, gather the brushwood for fuel and look after the small livestock and farmyard animals. The degree of female seclusion depends on the context. The *parda* (literally "curtain") signifies first and foremost discretion and modesty. When Hazara women move around in the circle of village acquaintances, they wear a simple (often green) piece of cloth on their head and are usually content to turn their face away from a passing male while exchanging the customary greetings. On a journey or in a town, however, they wear the Iranian-inspired veil (*câdor*), which leaves the face partly exposed, or more rarely the *câdari*, a long piece of pleated fabric that covers the eyes with a kind of grid.[25] Given that many men go to fight or work abroad for long periods, women in rural areas take on a number of traditionally male agricultural tasks and have considerable weight within the domestic economy. They play an essential role in the migratory strategies of the Hazaras. Yet they are spatially less mobile than men and never leave their village unless accompanied by a male relative.

The influence of the Iranian revolution and its Islamist movements has discouraged ostentatious spending, so that the stages of the marriage ceremony have become simpler. In 1995 and 1996, for example, weddings in Dahmarda lasted only one day and no longer involved dancing or music—just a few bursts of gunfire to accompany the procession. As to the brideprice, it is usually set somewhere between the equivalent of 500 and 1,000 dollars.

Let us briefly review the marriages of the individuals introduced in chapter 2:

- Mohammad Akbar is a Dawran from Dahmarda. His wife is a Gari from Dawud, another region of Jaghori. This alliance outside the lineage would be repeated by his two sons, Mohammad Ali and Aziz Azizi.
- Akram Ali, Mohammad Akbar's half-brother, is married to a Wafa from Dahmarda. This alliance would be repeated by his elder son, Mohammad Hasan.
- Mardan Ali refused to marry his patrilateral parallel cousin (one of Akram Ali's daughters), as Mohammad Akbar and Akram Ali had agreed. He incurred the criticism of the family, and this was one reason why he left Dahmarda at the age of seventeen. He went so far as to burn his chest with a brazier, and this did eventually soften his father's position. In the end, he was able to marry a Hazara woman whose brother he had met in Quetta. Although she was born in Quetta, her family originated in Patu, a village near Dahmarda, with which other marital unions exist. Mardan Ali's father-in-law had two wives: one in Patu (Mohammad Reza's mother) and one in Quetta (the mother of Mardan Ali's wife). Akram Ali and Mohammad Akbar nearly fell out over the affair and have not spoken any more about marriage between their children.
- Mohammad Ali is the brother of Mardan Ali. His wife is a Gari from Dawud, from the same lineage as his mother.
- Aziz Azizi is Mardan Ali's youngest brother. His wife is also a Gari from Dawud, the first cousin of Mohammad Ali's wife.
- Mohammad Hasan married a girl from his mother's lineage—the Wafa.
- Mohammad Husayn is still unmarried.
- Husayn Bakhsh has been living for a long time in Quetta, but he is a Dawran from Dahmarda. He is married to a girl from his own lineage, the sister of Hasan and Husayn. She is also his matrilateral cross-cousin (MBD).
- Ramazan Ali is deceased. His widow married his younger brother, Mohammad Yusuf.
- Mohammad Yusuf is a Dawran from Dahmarda. He has two wives: the first is from his own lineage (Mohammad Jawad's sister); the second is the widow of his elder brother, an Omur like his father's second wife.

- Mohammad Jawad is a Dawran (on both his father's and mother's side) from Dahmarda. He married a girl from his own lineage while I happened to be there. She may be classified as a patrilateral parallel cousin, although the relationship is genealogically more distant.
- Mohammad Reza is from Patu, but his mother is a Wafa from Dahmarda. He is married to the youngest sister of Mohammad Hasan and Mohammad Husayn. Mardan Ali's wife is one of his two half-sisters. This is therefore a case of a repeated alliance.
- Hazrat Ali is a Baram from Rash, a hamlet of Dahmarda whose inhabitants are considered to have a different tribal origin. His wife is another sister of Hasan and Husayn, hence a Dawran from Dahmarda.
- Mohammad Hanif belongs to the Dawlatjam lineage from Dahmarda. He is married to a niece of his mother's. Both women are from the Omur line, to which Mohammad Hanif's family is linked by several other marriages.

This sample of fourteen persons evidently does not fully correspond to the wider picture, but it does express the different tendencies in Dahmarda, and more generally among Hazaras. The Hazaras draw a distinction between endogamous marriage (taking a wife "among our own people," *az xod*) and exogamous marriage (marrying an "outsider," *begâna*), the reference group here being patrilinear. Quite clearly we are not dealing with a single matrimonial model.[26] If we except Ramazan Ali and the case of levirate brought about by his death, we are left with thirteen conjugal unions. These were distributed as follows:

Table 4. Marital unions in Dahmarda

father's lineage (*az xod*)	mother's lineage (*az mâmâxel*)	other lineage (*begâna*)
3 (23.08 %)	6 (46.15 %)	4 (30.77 %)

own *manteqa*	other *manteqa*
8 (61.54 %)	5 (38.46 %)

Only three of my informants are married to women from their own lineage (women who may therefore be classified as patrilateral parallel cousins). That makes 23 percent of marriages—or, in other words, more than three-quarters of the marriages in questions were between persons who did not belong to the same lineage. Six men married women from their mother's lineage—equivalent to roughly 46 percent—although it is true that in two of these cases the women belonged to the same lineage as her husband and his mother.[27] The same number of marriages was contracted between persons from different *manteqa*, but then it was mostly a question of reactivating old alliances.

We can see that endogamy within the same lineage is not a dominant tendency. Marriage ties uniting two lineages tend to be perpetuated over generations, and it is current practice for a man to marry a woman from his mother's lineage (this scenario accounts for some of the unions contracted outside the *manteqa*). Although all the marriages considered here are between persons previously related to each other, lineage endogamy is involved in fewer than a quarter of marriages.

These figures seem to be confirmed by the interview grid material. Unfortunately, my data on this issue are complete for only thirty-seven (thirty-four of them married) out of the sixty-nine interviewees from Hazarajat. The breakdown is as follows:

Table 5: Marital unions in Hazarajat

	father's lineage (*az xod*)	mother's lineage (*az mâmâxel*)	other lineage (*begâna*)
Dahmarda	4 (26.67 %)	6 (40.00 %)	5 (33.33 %)
Jaghori	6 (26.09 %)	7 (30.43 %)	10 (43.48 %)
Hazarajat	10 (29.41 %)	8 (23.53 %)	16 (47.06 %)

	own *manteqa*	other *manteqa*
Dahmarda	10 (66.67 %)	5 (33.33 %)
Jaghori	16 (69.57 %)	7 (30.43 %)
Hazarajat	24 (70.59 %)	10 (29.41 %)

These figures call for some comments. Lineage endogamy is involved in twenty-five to thirty percent of marriages. The declining number of unions with a woman from ego's maternal line is linked to the fact that the genealogical information is more detailed for Dahmarda (to a lesser extent, this also accounts for the relative decline in marriages with women from other *manteqa*). It would not be improper to conclude, therefore, that the number of marriages with women from the *mâmâxel* is higher than with women from ego's lineage. In other words, men marry more often within their mother's lineage than within their father's. Marriage with the patrilinear parallel cousin is relatively infrequent.[28] On the other hand, village endogamy (within the *manteqa*) is high, accounting for roughly seventy percent of marriages. As to the rest, the overwhelming majority take place within the group defined both ethnically (Hazara) and religiously (Shiite). In Dahmarda, the only interethnic marriages (between Hazaras and Pashtuns) that my informants could recall were those contracted to end a cycle of vengeance.

Generally in Afghanistan marriage brings about a transfer of responsibility from the woman's father to her husband. What matters for a man is to marry a woman he knows who has a spotless reputation; it is not necessary that she should be from his own lineage (Tapper R. and Tapper N. 1992/1993). A father will try to introduce some diversity, however, by marrying one of his sons (often the eldest) within his own lineage, while marrying another to a girl from his wife's lineage. Women also play an important role in these matters. A mother is often happy to marry a son to one of her nieces or to a young cousin, thereby strengthening both her position within the host family and relations with her original family. But male discourse tends to mask these tendencies through a genealogical emphasis on patrilinear relations (Bourdieu 1972: 74–95, 137–140; Geertz 1979).

LINEAGE AND TYPES OF RESIDENCE IN DAHMARDA

In stressing the importance of tribal typologies and genealogies, Mousavi describes as follows the situation in Afghanistan:

> The Chinese Box of Afghanistan is made up of several smaller 'boxes' of different peoples and nations, all forming Afghanistan, such as: the Nuristanis, the Afghans, the Hazaras, the Tajiks, the Baluchis, etc.; with each in turn representing an independent Chinese Box (1998: 19).

This image expresses well a number of indigenous representations, but it does not allow for the fact that individual identity is multiple and ever open to negotiation. The identity affiliations and mutual support groups that each individual can activate change with the context. Hazara tribal genealogies, however pertinent historically, refer back to past migrations and to old splits and fusions. In this sense, they afford precious testimony that is very different from the efforts of certain leaders and intellectuals to construct an identity around autochthony and a common origin for the Hazaras.

Nowadays, as several authors have pointed out, the old tribal names of the Hazaras mainly refer to particular territories (Schurmann 1962: 121; Rosman and Rubel 1976: 559; Gawecki 1986: 16). This development is quite clear in the case of "Jaghori" and "Dahmarda," which used to designate a tribe and a section respectively, but which now refer to a district and part of a district. We know from Maitland (1891) that Dahmarda originally designated a branch of a tribe that had settled in Gulzar. Today, although everyone still knows it, the name Gulzar is tending to disappear from usage.

One multiform term, *qawm*, expresses well the complexity of Afghan social reality (Centlivres 1970: 158–159). Most often translated as "solidarity group" (Canfield 1973a: 34; Centlivres and Centlivres-Demont 1988a: 17–18, 36–37; Roy 1985: 23), it refers to the agnatic kin group but it may also denote wider relations, lineage, tribe or ethnic group, or even professional or religious group. The theory of a segmentary system and the accompanying concept of lineage were developed in anthropological research into exogamous groups in Africa (Barth 1953: 10). Lancaster, in his study of the Rwala Bedouin (1997: 30), gives up "lineage" and prefers to use the indigenous terms. Cohen (1965) speaks of "patronymic group," to underline the reference to a common ancestor as constitutive of group identity, although this does not exclude ongoing processes of recomposition. In a later text, he even goes so far as to use the expression "patronymic association" (Cohen H 1970). But this suggestion, which has been followed up by Eickelman (1998: 151–153), seems exaggerated as the idea of free and voluntary affiliation that it suggests is alien to indigenous representations. The opposite tendency, which seeks to uncover the true reference level of *qawm* beneath the diverse usages and interlocking levels (Orywal 1986, 1988), misrepresents the complexity of the practices and representations in question.

In this study, I shall stick with the term "lineage" to denote a set of individuals who present themselves as having a common ancestor from whom they derive their name, and who consider that this creates among them a number of mutual obligations. This being so, the lineage should in no event be thought of as a set of individuals with a common goal who function as a collective agent at the political or economic level. There is no planned migratory strategy at the level of the lineage, even if the presence of a relative in such or such a place may influence certain individual choices. In short, the lineage is only one of the possible sources of trust, mutual support and co-operation available to the social actors.

In Jaghori, when an individual is asked about his belonging to a *qawm,* he may reply by referring unambiguously to his lineage, his village or his home district, or by declaring himself to be a Hazara. This semantic richness does not correspond to any conceptual vagueness but expresses the suppleness of the notion itself: the pertinent identity register depends on the context and the knowledge that each supposes the other has. As we shall see, however, it is not altogether satisfactory to translate *qawm* by "solidarity group," as many sources of solidarity and cooperation among the Hazara escape the kinship model and cannot be subsumed under the concept of *qawm.*

In its spoken language and imagery, but also in its local practices, the district of Jaghori is divided into a little more than twenty zones or *manteqa* (literally "regions"), although these have never really been given administrative recognition.[29] Dahmarda is one of these divisions. Roussel and Caley (1994) argue that the *manteqa* should be considered the basic unit of the Afghan rural world, at a level between the village and the district. In their view, the village is a heterogeneous and imprecise notion, as may be seen from the fact that the various maps of Afghanistan never concur in the names they give to particular villages. The authors define *manteqa* as follows: "a geographical area grouping together a number of villages and identified by its own inhabitants, as well as the inhabitants of the surrounding area, by a single regional name" (1994: 5). During the war, the *manteqa* were the most significant referent of identity, the primary space of solidarity for the organization of resistance. Effective solidarity does not stem only from belonging to the same *qawm;* what really matters is a certain degree of closeness, which may be based on kinship but also on neighborly relations. Solidarity and cooperation develop only where there is a high probability of future encounters and interaction (see chapter 9).

In Jaghori, the number of *manteqa* does not seem to be definitive. Maps drawn up by such NGOs as AVICEN and the Shuhada Organization suggest the following list: Almetu, Anguri, Bâbâ, Busayd, Chilbâghtu-ye Oqi, Chilbâghtu-ye Pashi, Dahmarda, Dâwud, Haydar, Hecha, Hutqol, Kamrak, Lumân, Maska, Pâtu, Sang-e Mâsha, Sapâya or Khodaydâd, Sa'id Ahmad, Shashpar, Sherzayda, Shoghla, Siyâ Zamin or Posht-e Chob, Taberghân, Ulyatu, Zerak. That makes exactly twenty-five *manteqa* in Jaghori, but sometimes Shoghla and Taberghân are omitted, and sometimes Siyâ Zamin and Sang-e Mâsha are not distinguished from each other.

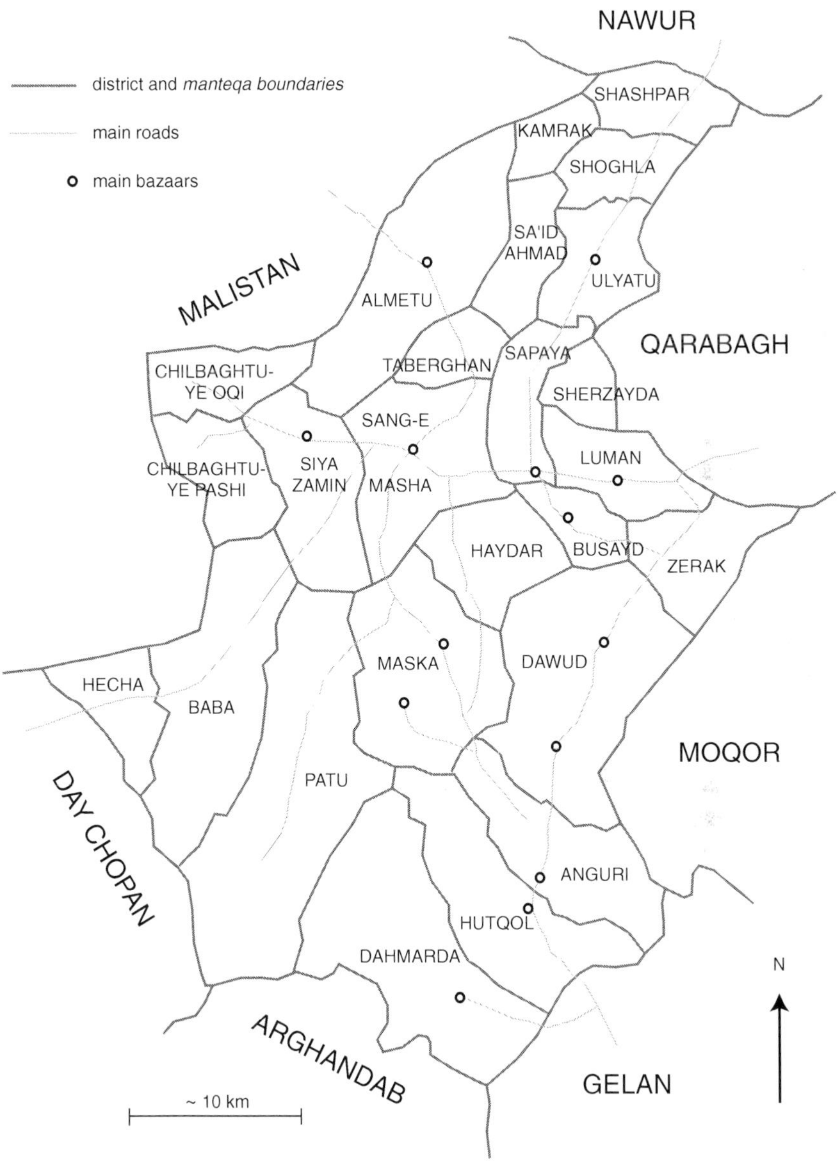

Figure 5. The district of Jaghori

Some of these *manteqa* (e.g. Dahmarda, Maska and Baba) bear the name of a tribal segment, while other names such as Sang-e Masha and Hutqol denote only the place. The relation between the *manteqa* names and tribal segments is far from clear-cut. Many groups are scattered—such as the Oqi, who may be found at both ends of the district, from Chilbaghtu-ye Oqi in the north to Hutqol in the south. There are many *manteqa* where the population has a mixed affiliation: such is the case of Sang-e Masha, to mention just one example, where Oqi, Maska and Dahmarda are quite numerous.

This is the settlement model in Dahmarda, most of whose inhabitants nevertheless think of themselves as belonging to the same tribal section. The locality owes its name to the ten original lineages (*dah,* "ten," *mard,* "man"), each of which derives its name from a supposed ancestor: Basmanay, Dali, Dawlatjam, Dawrân (or Dawro), Kharida (or Juma), Khoshdâd, Omur, Râzi, Tolgha, Wafâ. But some informants dispute this etymology and say that the name Dahmarda comes from Day Mirdâd, their supposed ancestral home in the region of Behsud. According to the most frequently mentioned version, the Gulzar valley was already inhabited by the ancestors of the Khoshdâd when migrants from Behsud settled there ten or a dozen generations ago (the nine other lines being descended from those ancestors). A eleventh lineage then came along at a later date: the Âhingar (or Ayngro in Hazaragi), that is, the "blacksmiths," who are presented as "Hazarized" Shamulzay Pashtuns converts to Shiism. The hamlet of Rash, usually included in the Dahmarda *manteqa* (in the northeast, on the road to Patu), is inhabited by the Bârâm, a group thought to come from different origins.

It is possible to reconstitute the meaning of the lineage names, which are mostly of Persian origin.[30] As we have just seen, *âhingar* (or *ayngro* in Hazaragi) is the Persian word for blacksmith. In Hazarajat the word *basmanay* denotes material assistance (sheep, money, etc.) for which a person in difficulties can ask from his kin. *Dali* is thought to be a word of Mongol origin meaning "like" or "similar." *Dawlat* means "government" but also "wealth," and *jam* "assembly." *Dawrân* (or *dawro* in Hazaragi) means "period." *Xarida* is the past participle of the verb *xaridan,* "to buy." *Juma* (from the same Arabic root as *jam*) denotes Friday; it is a common forename among the Hazara. *Xošdâd* means more or less "given with pleasure." *Omur* is the plural of *amr,* "order" or "command," but most often means "affairs." *Râzi* means "content" or "satisfied"; *tolga,* the top of the skull in Hazaragi; *wafâ,* "faith" or "fidelity."

In addition to these eleven lineages, one finds a few *sayyed* that account for little more than one per cent of the inhabitants of Dahmarda,[31]

Table 6: The lineages of Dahmarda

Omur:	115 houses	Khoshdâd:	20 houses
Dawrân:	90 houses	Basmanay:	15 houses
Wafâ:	70 houses	Âhingar:	15 houses
Dali:	40 houses	Qalandar:	5 houses
Tolgha:	30 houses	Sayyeds:	5 houses
Râzi:	25 houses	Kharida: (or Juma)	2 houses
Dawlatjam:	25 houses	Maska:	2 houses

The resulting total (459 houses) is only an approximation. But it can be seen that the two main lineages alone account for 45% of the total population.

although in some parts of Hazarajat, especially Yakawlang (Schurmann 1962: 112), *sayyed* villages can make up half the population. There are also some Maska, originally from Anguri, as well as Qalandar (known as *farâri,* "fugitives" or *hamsâya,* "neighbors" but also "clients, dependents") who came as refugees in the late nineteenth century from the Day Chopan region north of the present-day province of Zabul. As landless peasants, they were highly vulnerable socially and economically and in most cases went to try their luck in Quetta or Iran during the war. The largest lineages (especially the Omur and the Dawrân) are further divided into subgroups each with its own name, as a prelude to future segmentation. Within the Dawrân, for instance, there are the Ostâ (that is, Ostâd or "teacher") and the Atay or, to be more precise, Awlâd-e Atay ("father's children") to which Mardan Ali belongs.

In Dahmarda, no lineage is concentrated in a single place, and it is rare for a hamlet to be inhabited by a single lineage. Thus, each community of residents consists of several *qawm;* kinship ties and neighborhood ties are not the same. The lineage is not designated only by the term *qawm;* it is also possible to say *xân(a)wâr* ("family") ou *awlâd-e . . .* ("children of . . .") followed by the name of the eponymous ancestor. Locally, the term *xânawâda* ("family" or "dynasty") appears to have a narrower referent, while *xâna* ("house") is reserved for the people actually living under the same roof.

The vocabulary of kinship structures everyday relations and activities. Thus, an individual will call a male kinsman *kâkâ* (FB) if he is older than himself, or *bace kâkâ* (FBS) if he is of the same age. Similarly, the terms *mâmâ* (MB) et *bace mâmâ* (MBS) are used in dealing with members of the mother's lineage. The terminology is nevertheless fluctuating and strategic; its subtle use makes it possible to signal closeness and friendship, but also hostility and mistrust. More or less all social relations in Dahmarda are thought of in the mode of kinship. But, as Lancaster remarks about the Rwala Bedouin, although relations between groups are conceived in genealogical terms, the vocabulary of kinship is particularly fluid (1997: 154).

Hazaragi is richer in kinship terminology than Kabuli or Tehrani (Heslot 1984–85). Generally speaking, it is of the Sudanese type, but with traces of the Omaha terminology that is supposed to have been that of the ancient Turks and Mongols (Schurmann 1962: 140). In fact, some words are used to designate different generational levels: for instance, *xwar-zâda* and *jeya* (a word specific to the Shahristan region), which may designate men as well as women, has the primary meaning of ZS/ZD but also that of FZS/FZD, and by extension any person from a woman of ego's lineage, whatever the latter's relative age or gender.

The use of teknonyms is very extensive: the name of an elder relative or a woman is not spoken aloud, at least not in public. Thus, as we have seen, one of the branches of the Dawrân is called "the Awlâd-e Atay." And, since their eponymous ancestor is called *atay* ("father"), the members of the sub-lineage avoid using this term for personal address and reference and call their fathers *lâlây* ("elder brother").

As elsewhere in the Middle East, primogeniture is significant only for issues of precedence (see, for example, Barth 1953: 30; Bourdieu 1972: 126; Lancaster 1997: 153). Even if respect for elders is always affirmed, greater competence, resolution and enterprise often carry more weight than age in defining authority within the family circle.

Normally the inheritance is not divided before the father's death, but exceptions do exist (as we have seen in the case of Mardan Ali). Rather than seek an abstract rule, it is best to account for the possible configurations in terms of practical reason (Bourdieu 1972, 1980); brothers may separate before the father's death or remain together afterwards; apparently similar cases may stem from different or even opposite dynamics and choices. Kinship ties are not the only sources of solidarity and cooperation; the importance of neighborly ties, for example, may be seen in the way which an individual is placed by others. The same procedure is always used, which involves specifying his father's identity and his hamlet of origin, not the lineage.

Multiple differentiated obligations bind together the inhabitants of the valley. First of all, membership of a patrilinear group imposes various duties: vengeance, mutual financial support (for example, to collect the brideprice), joint participation in certain celebrations, etc.—in other words, diffuse solidarity and a sense of sharing a common destiny.

The other types of kinship relation (through the mother, sisters or female spouse) are often less constraining and may therefore leave greater scope for personal feelings. The term *mâmâxel* is used to designate the lineage of the maternal uncle (*mâmâ,* MB)—that is, the mother's lineage—*xeš* to designate the kinship by marriage, and *qawm o xeš* the whole of the kin.

A third type of relation is important: those who live in the same hamlet often own pasture in common, as well as several irrigation channels that they maintain and whose water they use in a fixed rota. If this can sometimes lead to conflict, it also imposes a need for concessions and a profound interdependence.

Finally, larger residence groups (usually covering several hamlets) play an important role by paying a *mullâ* to read from the Koran, to give young children a basic education, and to maintain a *membar* (derived from *minbar:* "pulpit"). In Hazarajat the term is used for places where people assemble during religious ceremonies, equivalent to what is called *hoseiniye* or *takya-xâna* in Iran. The Hazaras of Quetta speak of *imâmbârgâ* ("imam's court") or *imâmbâra,* a term in use among Shiites in the Indian subcontinent (see chapter 4). It consists of a set of rooms and yards that include the mosque.[32] The community gathers in the *membar* at the high points of social life (Edwards 1986a; Bindemann 1987: 43f.), and it is used particularly intensely during the *moharram* (first month of the Islamic lunar calendar) when Shiites commemorate the martyr Imam Husayn, grandson of the prophet Mohammed, who was killed in 680 AD in Kerbela (now in Iraq) at the instigation of the Omeyyad caliphate. It is a period of mourning and penance, with a large number of votive offerings (*nazr*) that often take the form of a meal for a departed relative or some other act of charity (*xayrât*). Other forms of redistribution are the *zakât* (legal alms for the needy) and the *xums* (a fifth of income collected and administered by the *sayyed,* in principle for actions to promote the public good (Kopecky 1982)).

In 1995 there were a dozen *membar* spread around the hamlets of Dahmarda; their role in the life of society was all the more important in that they were linked to neighborhood groups rather than particular lineages. Most often, they consisted simply of a large room that could be divided into two by a curtain (one part for men, the other for women). The *membar-e omumi,* which is a little below the bazaar and is shared by the whole valley, is used as a *madrasa* and serves as a meeting-place for the community; the large mosque is also situated there. The inhabitants of Dahmarda say that in principle everyone should gather there for prayers on Friday. But, since grave conflicts began to divide the population, this kind of meeting has no longer happened and the call to prayer has no longer been heard. Before the war the most important mullahs were *sayyed,* but this changed as many returned from Iran with a more or less sophisticated religious education.

LOCAL POWER

It is difficult to reconstitute the political structures of Hazarajat prior to Abdur Rahman's subjugation of the region. As we have seen, social relations appear to have been hierarchical, with powerful tribal chiefs or *mir* at the top; a large part of the population owned little or no land and made a living by working for a landowner. In the course of the twentieth century, the way in which Hazarajat was ruled underwent profound changes, most dramatically in the period after 1978.

In the 1880s Jaghori came under the control of Sardar Sher Ali Khan, a powerful *mir* from the tribal segment of the Oqi (Sang-e Masha) (Poladi 1989: 393), who was eventually executed on Abdur Rahman's orders in 1882 (Maitland 1891: 374). His descendants remained large landowners, and although their political power was gradually eroded they kept a strong influence over local society up to the Communist coup of 1978. As Olivier Roy noted (1985: 197), Hazara left-wing intellectuals, especially in Jaghori, are the sons of *mir* and property-owning families. The most notable examples were the brothers Sadeq and Akram Yari in the Maoist Shu'la-ye jawed movement, who disappeared in unclear circumstances during the time of Hafizullah Amin (1979). Others were killed during the twenty years of war by Islamist parties, and many sought refuge in Pakistan or the West. Sardar Yazdan Khan and his sons, General Musa Khan, Sardar Isa Khan and Sardar Isaq Khan, who long dominated political life among the Hazara of Quetta, also originated in that tribal section.

Whereas the power of the *mir* and later the *xân* has been based upon vast holdings of land and orchard, the *arbâb* or *malek* are the representatives of the population. Their appointment follows complex negotiations in which kinship groups, money and land carry a great deal of weight. There are no regular elections, and in principle the *arbâb* are chosen by the most affluent and influential heads of families. It is difficult to attain such a position without the approval of the *xân,* who are also called upon to settle certain disputes or administrative matters. Their role as intermediaries between local people and civil servants allows them to increase their power, but they also function as a protective screen in the face of outside intrusion (Centlivres and Centlivres-Demont 1981–82: 523–524). According to region, the *arbâb* may represent a village, a group of villages, a tribal segment, and so on.

In Dahmarda, for example, the whole of the *manteqa* had a leader, who used to be known by the name of *mehtar* and after the adoption of the 1964 Constitution was called *qariadâr.*[33] He was proposed by the heads of families throughout the valley and appointed by government representatives. Until the Communist coup of 1978, he usually came from the Omur or the Dawran, the two largest and most powerful lineages in the area, but, as we shall see, things have changed since then.

At a lower level, each lineage has its own *malek* or *arbâb* (the two terms are interchangeable). The representative of a hamlet, when there is one, is called *dârugha* All these notables are chosen by the relevant family heads after consultation with the *qariadâr;* they are usually designated more or less tacitly and remain in office as long as there is no major challenge. Sometimes, the position is handed down from father to son.

What is involved, then, is a layering of political functions whose reference groups are out of step. In fact, given the types of housing situation in Dahmarda, two individuals living in the same hamlet will recognize the same *dârugha* but not necessarily the same *malek,* while two members of the same lineage will recognize the same *malek* but not necessarily live in the same place.

There are numerous more or less formal occasions on which people meet: circumcisions, weddings, deaths, house-warming celebrations, religious festivities. Men sit for hours in the shade of a tree and exchange views about community affairs. The village elders, and any other males with some experience of life, are called *riš-safid,* "white beards," or *muy-safid,* "white hairs"; they are consulted whenever a decision has to be taken concerning the life of the community. When they have made a pilgrimage to the tomb of the Imam Husain in Kerbela (Iraq)—more common among Shiites than the journey to Mecca—they wear a blue turban and are respectfully called *karbalâ'i.*

Another category with influence among the Hazaras are religious figures, especially the *sayyed,* who are supposed to be descended from the Prophet Mohammed by his daughter Fatima. They form a kind of religious aristocracy, a wide network reaching beyond any particular tribe or region. They rarely give their daughters to non-*sayyed* (whom they call *'âm,* "common people"), but they marry Hazara women and constitute a social-cultural group inseparable from the rest of the population of Hazarajat. Many *sayyed* are ordinary farmers and have virtually the same lifestyle, but some become respected spiritual guides who, with their distinctive black turban and their position external to tribal genealogies, play a major role in public affairs and function as arbiters in disputes. Unlike the *mir,* they are influential because of their spiritual preeminence not because of any directly political or economic power (Kopecky 1982). Although they are few in number in Jaghori, and especially in Dahmarda, the *sayyed* have always had a distinguished place in village life. Individuals (often from humble families) who have been able to study in the great Shiite cultural centers of Iran or Iraq are given the name *šeyx, âxund* or *ruhâni.* The war meant that they came to play an ever larger role, at the expense of the old *mir, sayyed* and *arbâb* elites.

FACTIONS AND PARTIES

We can see that two systems of community organization overlap: the lineages, represented by *malek,* and the neighborhood groups, linked to one another by irrigation issues and a common *membar.* In Dahmarda, most of the lineages are geographically scattered, and as many as three different ones may coexist in a single hamlet. In general, religious structures seem to act as a counterweight to kinship groups and tribal links. Two mullahs are particularly respected in Dahmarda: one is a *sayyed,* the other a Maska from Anguri; in other words, neither of the two belongs to the *qawm* of Dahmarda. (This brings us close to the classical consideration in Middle Eastern anthropology that arbiters are external to the lineage segmentation: see, for example, Barth 1959.)

As we have seen, the authority of the *mir* or *xân* exists at district level, that of the *qariadâr* at *manteqa* level, that of the *malek* or *arbâb* at lineage level, and that of the *dârugha* at hamlet level. This said, however, the use of these terms varies and it would be misleading to view it as forming a strict system. As to the *sayyed,* their networks go beyond narrowly geographical boundaries.

Despite the many possible registers of solidarity, in the present day endemic insecurity and physical violence tend to overshadow social relations and everyday life. During the war, the clash of parties penetrated the local sphere. Jaghori (and especially Dahmarda) lies on the ethnic boundary between Hazaras and Pashtuns. In the early nineties, shortly after the Soviet withdrawal, there was heavy fighting between rival groups of *mujâhedin.* In 1995 and 1996, society seemed to be in a state of siege, yet incapable of overcoming its internal divisions. Road journeys were broken up by checkpoints in the hands of capricious young militiamen. Armed men patrolled the bazaars: Hezb-e wahdat at Sang-e Masha, Hezb-e islami at Hutqol . . . After a serious defeat at Kabul in March 1995, the Wahdat fell back on Hazarajat and tried to extend its control there at the expense of pro-government factions allied to Ahmad Shah Massoud; it scored a major success when it took Bamyan in October of the same year. During this period, the whole region was the scene of numerous unpredictable skirmishes. Early in 1996 pro-government forces were driven out of Jaghori and the fighting shifted towards Qarabagh. At the beginning of July, the Nawar region became the stage for fighting between Shiite factions—and then it was the turn of northern Hazarajat. Even after the Taliban captured Kabul in September, Hazara factions struggled to reach an agreement. Then the conflicts took a more dramatic turn at national level, until the Taliban laid siege to Mazar-e Sharif and Bamyan in 1998. Although their arrival in Jaghori in autumn 1998 took place without any major fighting, they never managed to crush certain pockets of resistance in other parts of Hazarajat, such as Yakawlang and Dara-ye Suf.

Dahmarda was relatively unscathed during the Soviet occupation: just a few bombs and two or three tank incursions. As elsewhere in Hazarajat, however, internal conflicts and social-political upheavals assumed proportions unknown in the code of tribal warfare; the settling of accounts could prove deadly (Centlivres 1997), especially as everyone had weapons (automatic rifles, even rocket-launchers or flame-throwers). The atmosphere was heavy: people mistrusted one another, the bazaar was usually deserted, and the *mullâ* had prohibited music and dancing, even at wedding celebrations. The first picture of Dahmarda, a peaceful valley living in splendid and harmonious isolation, gave way to one of deep divisions and economic dependence on migrant remittances. Local elections, self-defense militias, the prison, the irrigation committees, the well-stocked shops, the schools and dispensaries: these impressionistic elements of village autonomy broke up amid the violence within the local social life.

War overturned the delicate balances; new references and new sources of power, geared to regional or even international networks, made their appearance. The massive presence of weapons, together with the absence of the state, meant that it was possible to employ violent means. As leaders turned for support to the huge regional structures of political parties, local quarrels were fuelled by the clash of interests at regional and national level.

Although some dominant families managed to preserve their power, it became possible for a number of new men, often of humble origin, to thrust themselves forward through a mixture of personal ability and political skill. The actual relationship of forces was thus ratified by tacit acceptance. Resistance commanders (*qomândân*), for instance, ranging from intellectuals through clerics to simple illiterates, rose by virtue of their military and organizational talents and their connections with wider party networks. Apart from money, water, land and kinship, access to weapons via the resistance movements became more and more important as a source of power.

From the early eighties, two new political players began to play a major role: religious intellectuals and secular intellectuals. The latter, often from the wealthiest and most powerful lineages (even from the old *mir* layer), were proportionately more numerous in Jaghori than elsewhere in Hazarajat and tended to belong to Maoist-inspired parties. The early eighties saw them entering into a pitiless struggle with religious circles, and it was these who eventually carried the day (Roy 1985: 194–205; Harpviken 1996). Initially the leftist-nationalist Tanzim-e nasl-e naw-e Hazara-ye Moghol ("Party of the Mongol Hazara New Generation"),[34] founded in Quetta by Pakistani Hazaras, sank roots in the region by combining a discourse of ethnic emancipation with social reform projects. But it was soon ousted by the Shura-ye ettefaq-e islami ("Islamic Union Council"), a broadly based *sayyed*-controlled traditionalist movement.

Later, between 1982 and 1984, the pro-Iranian Sazman-e nasr ("Victory Organization") and Sepa-ye pasdaran ("Guards' Army") gained the upper hand, led by young clerics, often of humble origin, who had studied in Iran and were inspired by the Khomeini revolution. These two movements were distinct and often competed with each other, their division reflecting factional struggles inside Iran. The Nasr organization appeared to have connections with the people around Ayatollah Montazeri (close to Khomeini, but disowned by him shortly before the latter's death in 1989); the Sepa—which began to be talked about in summer 1982—was linked to the Iranian Pasdaran, the elite political-military formation. The tide of Islamist radicalism soon intensified the ideological nuances, with the former more attached to its independence and more alert to ethnic discrimination (Harpviken 1996: 88), the latter more intent on a Khomeini-style Islamist state.

In February 1989 the Red Army pulled out of Afghanistan. The Hazara leaders, fearing exclusion from the peace talks, realized that their salvation lay in unity—which, given the recent strife, could be built only on a new basis, that of Hazara identity. Spurred on by Iran, the main Shiite factions sought to bury their differences in a broad movement, the Hezb-e wahdat-e islami-ye Afghanistan ("Islamic Unity Party of Afghanistan"), which remained under clerical control but also incorporated many lay intellectuals, including former Marxists and Maoists (soldiers, engineers, doctors, teachers, etc.). These tried to make themselves indispensable by founding NGOs to take charge of health, education, road-building and so on. A more marginal current, consisting mainly of Sepa members, remained faithful to the Khomeini model and rejected the ethnicist turn. Nasr cadres thus formed the backbone of the Wahdat (people such as Abdul Ali Mazari and Mohammad Karim Khalili), while the historic leader of Sepa, Sheikh Akbari, threw in his lot with Massoud.[35]

In 1995 four main political groupings were present in Jaghori: Khalili's Hezb-e wahdat (mainly consisting of people from the Nasr), Akbari's Hezb-e wahdat (mainly consisting of people from the Sepa and the Nehzat),

Harakat-e islami and Hezb-e islami. The last of these, though mostly Pashtun, had solid roots in some parts of Jaghori: in particular, it controlled the Hutqol bazaar and therefore the main road into the district, although it was driven out at the end of the year by Wahdat forces loyal to Khalili. As to Harakat-e islami, it was not very strong at local level and lined up with the Akbari faction in the pro-government camp. Several commanders from this minority movement rallied to the Taliban after 1998.

The war meant that the power structures became extremely volatile, as the old *mir* were supplanted by the *šeyx* and the *sayyed* lost a lot of their prestige. Gradually, however, many Hazara leaders questioned the Iranian connection and Islamist ideology, in favor of ethnicist demands (Harpviken 1996). At regional level, clerics and lay intellectuals appear to have made common cause around a discourse of ethnic liberation. In Jaghori district, power was in the hands of the commanders.

Dahmarda underwent a similar evolution. At the beginning of the war, one of the first political parties active there was the Tanzim, and most influential local people (from the Omur and Dawran lineages) rallied to it out of sympathy with its national political demands. Young clerics returning from Iran, organized under the Sepa banner, rose up against the local notables and, with some regional support, managed to supplant the Tanzim in Dahmarda. Their local opponents then joined the ranks of the other Islamist party, the Nasr.[36]

After these events, three new functions took shape: the *ra'is*, a kind of mayor (a post held from 1984 to 1994 by a young pro-Iranian *šeyx* from the Dali lineage, not one of the two traditionally dominant), the *qomândân-e amnyat,* responsible for public order, who acted as a judge, and the *qomândân-e nezâmi,* the military leader responsible for defence. A village militia was formed to guard the bazaar and the main points of access (passes, roads, etc.). Ideally, these three figures were elected by family heads in the valley, but in reality they reflected the relationship of forces among the various factions in the area, each with its support at regional party level. In fact, there was only one proper election in the whole history of Dahmarda, in late November 1994, in an extremely tense atmosphere.

In Dahmarda, political issues came on top of the deep social divisions related to the scarcity of resources (agricultural land, water, etc.). In the first half of the 1980s, young clerics returning from Iran—most of them originally from humble backgrounds—used outside support to establish their dominance. But, ten years later, new elements appeared and the old notables counter-attacked.

Before the war, there was only the *madrasa* founded in the 1960s. From 1991, however, financial assistance from an Afghan NGO made it possible to introduce elementary education. The building of a school got under way in spring 1994, and its director was chosen from the powerful Omur lineage that alone accounts for nearly a quarter of the population of Dahmarda. He himself came from the Nasr majority that merged into the Wahdat (like many others in Dahmarda he had been a member of the Tanzim-e nasl-e Hazara-ye Moghol at the beginning of the war), whereas the *ra'is* was linked to the Sepa. The two men also differed in educational background (state schools for the former, religious studies in Iran for the latter), and it was not long before they fell out. Things took a dramatic turn during the elections of autumn 1994, when the Omur lineage, long divided politically, united behind the school director. The *qomândân-e amnyat* and the *qomândân-e nezâmi,* both kin of his, also lent their support and were confirmed in their posts; a new *ra'is* was elected. Fear that the Omur would become too powerful and start to run local life then prompted most members of the less well represented lineages to form an alternative coalition.

When two teachers were sacked after a quarrel with the director, and children from families sympathetic to the former *ra'is* stopped attending the school, violent clashes broke out and culminated in a series of thefts in the bazaar and the assassination of the former *ra'is* (December 1994). Tensions continued to run high and divided the village into two, and the recently elected *ra'is* soon gave up office. Supporters of the murdered *ra'is*—who was now presented as a *šahed* ("martyr")—undertook to build a new school, probably with financial support from the Rabbani government that was at war with the Hezb-e wahdat. Political labels circulated as so many insults: some spoke contemptuously of "the infidels" (*kâfer*), while others hit out at "Khomeini's mullahs."

In November 1995 the school director died in a landslide accident. But this did not calm people down—on the contrary, a new wave of violence culminated in the winter massacre of a dozen men linked to the Sepa, at the same time that the Wahdat was extending its grip almost everywhere in Hazarajat (Khalili's forces had taken Bamyan in October).

In Dahmarda, with the opposition crushed, the Nasr-Omur combination ruled almost untroubled down to the events of 1998, when the Taliban, after victories at Mazar-e Sharif and Bamyan, entered Jaghori in early October. During the intervening period, the Omur used the school to reassert their power, and in the end there was a repeat of the earlier division between pro-Iranians (party of the young *šeyk*) and anti-Iranians (party of the notables), despite the successive rallying of the latter to the Tanzim, Nasr and Khalili's Wahdat.

After the events of the winter of 1995–96 in Dahmarda, many individuals and some whole families left the region for Quetta. This was the case of Mardan Ali's family, which had remained in Dahmarda throughout the conflict with the Soviets and the ensuing civil war. It was only because of internecine strife that Mardan Ali decided to bring his family to Pakistan. His son, Abdul Karim, sold his shop for a mere 9,500 rupees, the whole of his stock (for 18 million afghanis) and his motorcycle (3.6 million afghanis)—the rough equivalent, all told, of 3,500 dollars. Mardan Ali bought some land in Quetta and built a house there costing 220,000 rupees (more than 6,000 dollars).

Many Afghan refugees gave up the idea of returning to their country of origin, because they could not expect to earn the same there as in Pakistan or Iran. Nevertheless, if the security conditions were favorable, men sent their wives and children to Afghanistan. This cut down on household expenses, as most families had a house and even some land there (whose produce could supply most of a family's diet); nor were there any bills to pay for gas, water or electricity. Movement in the opposite direction was always possible, as in the case of Dahmarda where local fighting led some families to resettle in Quetta.

Thus, a number of major issues and old resentments divided the inhabitants of the Dahmarda valley. It should be stressed that all the lineages were split between the two contending factions—all except for the Dali and the Âhingar, who lined up in their entirety behind the former *ra'is*. The Nasr comprised a majority of the Omur and a more or less sizeable minority of most of the other lineages, whereas the Sepa comprised a majority of members of the numerically secondary lineages, but also included a few Omur families. (After some hesitation, most of the members of the Dawran lineage—which had formerly shared power locally with the Omur—seems to have sided with the latter.) Most of the non-Omur were therefore supporters of the former *ra'is*, whereas the school director successfully lined up behind him the most influential members of his powerful lineage. There were also many waverers, and affiliations were not always clear-cut.

This political diversity within each lineage did not have only one explanation. Often the splits were tactical and strong ties of solidarity continued to provide a guarantee: if one faction was defeated, its supporters could always find protectors among the victorious. In some cases, however, such as a contested legacy, there were deep divisions within a lineage, as each side sought to assert its claim against those of its agnates. Thus, during the upsurge of violence in the winter of 1995–96, one Omur died after a beating from members of his own line who contested some land, while several influential members of the Sepa were left untroubled.

FORMS OF COOPERATION

The sources of solidarity and cooperation in Dahmarda are summarized in the following table:

Table 7: The main registers of solidarity in Dahmarda

Paternal kinship	Eleven dispersed lineages (*qawm, xânwâr*)
Maternal kinship and kinship through marriage	Mother's lineage (*mâmâxel*) and relatives by marriage (*xeš*); multiple links (between lineages and outside the *manteqa*)
Close neighborhood	Approximately forty hamlets (*qaria*); approximately one hundred irrigation channels (*kârez, juy*)
Wider neighborhood	A dozen places for prayer and meeting (*membar*)
Manteqa	*Membar-e omumi;* bazaar; school

Lineage and various neighborhood ties (from the hamlet to the *manteqa*) were the principal registers of solidarity. Paradoxically, they were also the framework for the principal rivalries, for the lineage was not a politically structured and unified group. Disputes at the wider level of the *manteqa* could sometimes be deadly, as a number of community structures situated at this level (the *membar-e omumi,* the bazaar, the school) were the sites of the most visible and acute tensions. The paternal cousin might be a rival. Kinship through the mother's line and through marriage was less well defined, and any issues that arose tended to be less problematic, so that this was an especially important source of cooperation in a migratory situation.

To grasp the multiplicity of social relations, it is not sufficient to attach a weaker meaning to the concept of lineage or to give it a different name—patronymic group or association, for instance, in the style of Cohen (1965, 1970). We must recognize that there are other positive sources of solidarity and mutual support, and that they do not come only in the form of kinship.

Apart from political leanings, there were also sociological foundations for the factional division in Hazarajat: on the one side were the old elites, the *xân* and the *sayyed,* as well as the lay intellectuals who often originated among them; on the other side were the new men, who generally claimed to adhere to Islamist ideology. Another key element was the generation gap between young intellectuals, whether secular or Islamist, and the older notables. According to region, party affiliations could follow a number of different lines. In Dahmarda, a young cleric from a relatively minor lineage challenged the pre-eminence of the Omur and the Dawran. After the troubles that lasted from late 1994 to early 1996 finally calmed down in Dahmarda, the two main lineages took things in hand in an effort to reassert their power.

Although Hazarajat was relatively spared during the Soviet occupation, it went through a veritable civil war. Hazara society may appear united in relation to the outside world, but numerous tensions arise as a result of demographic pressure, land scarcity and water shortage, as well as of competition for military and humanitarian aid. Simplistic explanations in terms of tribal or ethnic warfare fail to appreciate the constant intersection of subtle regroupment strategies. Not only does the play of alliances maintain a certain equilibrium among the various forces, preventing one faction or another from becoming too powerful; the fact that members of the same *qawm* may nearly always be found in opposing factions suggests a veritable strategy to diversify affiliations as a way of providing some assurance in the event of unfavorable political or military developments. Nevertheless, the most pitiless conflicts often take place within the same lineage. Paradoxical logics are therefore in play, and many actors change sides without prompting talk of treason. Tendencies develop at local level that recall the political evolution of Afghanistan as a whole.

At the same time, political-military developments at national level cannot be understood without reference to these local tendencies. The Taliban were able to advance mainly through the rallying of others to their side. Indeed, their declared hostility to Shiites did not prevent some Hazara leaders from joining forces with them. This was certainly the case in Jaghori, where several commanders from movements that had been marginalized by the unification within the main body of the Wahdat went over to the forces of Mullah Omar. Pakistani support is often blamed for the success of the Taliban, but that was not the only factor. For the Taliban knew how to exploit to the hilt the discontent among sections of the Afghan population, and to deepen the divisions among their enemies by supporting the pretensions of those who had earlier been defeated in internal strife.[37]

Chapter Four

Quetta (Pakistan): The Hazara Refuge

MIGRATORY CONTINUUM AND MUTUAL SUPPORT ASSOCIATIONS

The Hazara community is one of the largest in the urban area of Quetta, capital of Pakistani Baluchistan, successive waves having settled there since Abdur Rahman's conquest of Hazarajat in the late-nineteenth century. In fact, the migration has been virtually uninterrupted since that time. The terrible famine in large parts of Afghanistan in the early 1970s, followed by the Communist coup in 1978 and the Soviet intervention in 1979, greatly increased the number of departures and often gave them a more settled character. But, despite the vicissitudes of war, a seasonal migratory cycle has established itself over several decades, as many men from southern Hazarajat go to work each winter in the coal mines near Quetta and return in early spring to resume their farming activity. In other words, the flow is not one way. For all the variation in intensity, there is a migratory continuum between Hazarajat (especially the southern fringes in Ghazni province) and Quetta. Few Hazaras settled in the refugee camps in Pakistan; most preferred to try their luck in an urban environment and therefore benefited little from the UN (mainly UNHCR) or NGO refugee infrastructures.

City life imposed a series of new economic and social constraints, and in Quetta, even more than in Hazarajat, there were various sources of cooperation. As the Hazaras increased in number and spread through the urban fabric, they were less and less able to concentrate in groups according to their place of origin. They developed a complementary set of mutual support structures, especially *qawm* and neighborhood associations, but also committees of the numerous *imâmbâra* (the local equivalent of the Hazarajat *membar*).

In Quetta, unlike in Iran, the jobs market had little to offer (even if the day's wage of $2-$4 was roughly the same in the two countries), but those who had a little start-up capital could open a shop of their own. Although Quetta does not strike a European as calm and peaceful, it is certainly the place where Hazaras have found the safest refuge during the last few decades; they have not had to face either the insecurity endemic in Afghanistan or the police harassment that affects Afghans in Iran.

FROM THE BRITISH EMPIRE TO PAKISTAN

In the nineteenth century, the British opposed Russian penetration in Central Asia in what came to be known as the Great Game. In 1839, during the first Anglo-Afghan war, they temporarily occupied Quetta[1] because of its strategic importance. Then little more than a village, it was part of the sphere of influence of the Khan of Kalat,[2] whose power had grown in the eighteenth century and who recognized the suzerainty of the Emir of Afghanistan. After a serious setback, the British had to evacuate the region in 1842, but it was not long before they made their influence felt again. A treaty was signed in 1854 between the Khan of Kalat and the British Crown, then strengthened and extended in 1876 through the efforts of the indefatigable Robert Sandeman (Thornton 1979). In the following year, a British military contingent was established in Quetta. But it was only in 1887, after the second Anglo-Afghan war (1878–1880), that the whole of Baluchistan was declared a Crown territory. In 1879, evidently for strategic reasons, a start was made on the Bolan Pass railway linking the plains of Sind to the Quetta highlands and southern Afghanistan; in January 1880 it reached Sibi, and then, between 1887 and 1892, was extended through the Khojak pass to Chaman (Thornton 1979: 191, 207). Faced with the Afghan threat and the Russian advance in Central Asia, Quetta became the most important British garrison in the whole sub-continent. Afghanistan eventually had its existence recognized as a "buffer state" with fixed boundaries, but the Emir of Kabul did not really administer the territory of which he was nominal ruler. Abdur Rahman devoted his reign (1880–1901) to the assertion of control over all the areas allocated to him; the reduction of Hazarajat, between 1891 and 1893, was particularly difficult and bloody (Kakar 1973, 1979; Mousavi 1998; Poladi 1989).

In 1947, despite certain troubles, Quetta and Baluchistan joined the new state of Pakistan. The political situation remained unstable, with ever stronger rivalry between Baluch and Pashtuns and territorial disputes between Pakistan and Afghanistan (whose government questioned the legitimacy of the Durand Line traced by the British in 1893 which had served as an international frontier). The Soviets, for their part, based themselves on pro-independence currents among the Baluch population to extend their own sphere of influence. The massive inflow of Pashtuns into Quetta in 1978–1979 should be placed in this troubled local context. They became an important part of the city's population, forming a majority among Afghan refugees (Sliwinski 1989: 46)) and acquiring demographic weight at the expense of the Baluch.

Population movement is a longstanding feature of the region. Whether nomads or not, the inhabitants of Afghanistan have for a very long time been traveling to Iran or the Indian sub-continent to escape a war, to take part in rapine or to look for work. Many have kept a memory of past migration—like the refugees from Central Asia who fled the Russian advance and then Soviet forced collectivization (in the 1920s and 1930s), or the Hazaras who were robbed of their lands a hundred years ago and had to find refuge in the countries bordering Afghanistan. As to the Pashtuns, they have never experienced the frontier as a barrier and have even turned it to advantage by organizing profitable smuggling activities.

THE PHASES OF HAZARA MIGRATION TO QUETTA

The Hazaras have been present in Quetta since the end of the nineteenth century. Already they sought refuge in territory beyond the authority of the Emir of Kabul—either Qajar Persia or British India. The great drought of 1971, then the Communist coup of 1978, threw tens of thousands of Hazaras onto the roads, but migration between Hazarajat and Quetta had never completely dried up. Three historical periods may be distinguished.

From 1878 to 1891. Following the second Anglo-Afghan war, the first Hazaras went to Quetta to seek employment in British-run companies under the Raj and are thought to have worked on the building of roads and the Bolan Pass railway (Owtadolajam 1976; Poladi 1989: 261; Mousavi 1998: 142), as well as enlisting in the British Army of India. At that time there could have been no more than a few hundred in Baluchistan.

From 1891 to 1901. The subjugation of Hazarajat by Abdur Rahman, between 1891 and 1893, triggered a mass exodus of Hazaras to Turkestan, Khorasan and Baluchistan. In the following years there was terrible repression. Whole regions were forcibly emptied of their population and occupied by Pashtun settlers.

From 1901 to 1933. The situation in Afghanistan returned to normal under Habibullah (1901–1919), the son of Abdur Rahman. In an effort to calm tensions between the central government and the rebels, he offered an amnesty to the Hazaras and ensured that their lands were restored, but the exactions against them did not cease. The Hazaras felt unconcerned by the political troubles that shook the capital in 1929;[3] they no longer had confidence in the Afghan state, which they accused of promoting only Pashtun interests. In fact, in 1904 the British high command created a special regiment for those who left Afghanistan, the 106th Hazara Pioneers, which offered far greater career prospects, social recognition and economic success than they could have achieved in their country of origin (Bunbury 1949; Mousavi 1998: 142–144; Poladi 1989: 266–269). From that time on, refugees fleeing an oppressive regime have merged with migrants in search of work.

From 1933 to 1971. The regiment of Hazara Pioneers was disbanded in 1933. Deprived of this social and professional outlet, few Hazaras went to settle in Quetta between the 1930s and 1960s, although the migration never completely dried up. With the creation of Pakistan on 14 August 1947, the Hazaras were recognized as one of the "indigenous/local tribes"—a status confirmed on 15 June 1963 (Mousavi 1998: 145, 246; Owtadolajam 1976: 220).

From 1971 to 1978. The second large wave of migration dates from the early 1970s. In 1971 drought led to a terrible famine, whose full force hit the north-east and center of the country. Pressure on the land grew more intense and revived tensions between the Hazara farmers and Pashtun nomads; ever larger numbers of Hazaras then settled in Quetta or went to Iran in search of work. Between 1973 and 1978, tensions over the Pashtunistan issue between the Daud government and Pakistan were an additional factor in the Hazara migration, as the administration of Zulfikar Ali Bhutto—prime minister then president of Pakistan between 1971 and 1977—readily granted them Pakistani papers to offset Pashtun influence in the region. At the same time, the Afghan government made scarcely any effort to improve the social-economic situation of the Hazaras. In Quetta, Hazaras found not only a welcoming environment and various work opportunities (trade for some, coal mines for others), but above all a relatively peaceful atmosphere and great freedom of movement. Most of the families kept in touch with people in Afghanistan (a close relative, for example, who looked after the lands). People often spoke of plans to return, although these were rarely fulfilled.

After 1978. Following the Communist coup in April 1978 and the Soviet intervention in December 1979, the migratory movement assumed hitherto unprecedented dimensions. Hazarajat was one of the first regions to shake off the grip of the Communist regime. The Red Army barely took any interest in the area, but it was the scene of terrible factional strife and then became a target of the Taliban (see chapter 3). Migratory flows in several directions remained intense, but the really large-scale arrival of Hazara refugees in Quetta, as well as return flows, came in the wake of political and military events that shook Afghanistan (Soviet withdrawal in 1989; fall of the Najibullah government in 1992; fighting between resistance factions in Kabul between 1993 and 1995; the Taliban capture of the capital in 1996; the fall of Mazar-e Sharif and Hazarajat in 1998; American intervention and collapse of the Taliban regime in 2001).

Though numbering no more than a few tens of thousands, the refugees who fled Hazarajat for British India in the nineteenth century, as well as their descendants, achieved real political and economic success in their new host country. They maintained close relations with the British and, after the independence of Pakistan, occupied important positions in the army and state administration (Poladi 1989; Mousavi 1998). At the beginning of the 1970s, the capital of Baluchistan had fewer than 300,000 inhabitants; there were only 40,000 Hazaras in Quetta in 1971, but already 50–60,000 in 1975 (Owtadolajam 1976: 3). In the middle of the seventies the electoral rolls of Hazara-populated districts, which listed only men and women above twenty-one, contained fewer than five thousand names. By 1996 this figure had more than quintupled, to reach 26,200 names. This led a local NGO official to estimate that there were between 60,000 and 70,000 Hazaras of Pakistani nationality, out of a total population of approximately 120,000. At the end of the twentieth century, then, the Hazaras in Quetta were three times more numerous than at the beginning of the 1970s and formed the third-largest ethnic group in the urban area, after the Pashtuns and Baluch.

Back in the late-nineteenth century, a small group of Hazaras settled in Parachinar (North-West Frontier Province), in the territory of the Shiite Pashtun tribe of the Turi, with which intermarriage was not uncommon. Over the years, Hazaras also settled in less important centers of Baluchistan, such as Loralai, Pishin, Mach, Sanjawi, Harnai and Khuzdar; they often earned their living as sandal-makers. In the 1980s, some of the more affluent bought farmland in the Sind, north of Hyderabad in the districts of Nawabshah and Sanghar. Many families from Quetta also moved to Karachi.

The Hazaras of Pakistan mostly have their origins in southern Hazarajat (Jaghori, Qarabagh, Malistan, Ghazni, Nawur, Behsud and, to a lesser extent, Waras, Panjab and Shahristan). More than two hundred families have moved from Dahmarda to Quetta, whereas there are approximately four hundred and fifty in Dahmarda itself. As far as the Dawran lineage is concerned, ninety families live in Dahmarda, while almost eighty are in Quetta. So, nearly a third of the population of Dahmarda and almost a half of the Dawran lineage have resettled in Pakistan.

The population of Jaghori has looked towards Quetta for more than a century; the war only intensified the movement backwards and forwards. To expand their social and economic possibilities, many families have two houses: one in Quetta and another in Jaghori. This diversification calls to mind certain points that Salzman (1971) made about the nomads of Iranian Baluchistan, when he explained how regional economic systems are formed through differential use of ecological and social niches. He used the term "multi-resource economy" to refer to the resulting mix of goat, sheep and camel rearing; date-growing; caravan trade and pillage (replaced in the twentieth century with the migration of labor to the economic centers of Iran or the Arabian peninsula). Baluch nomads move around not only in relation to the pastoral cycle, but also to switch from one economic resource to another (for example, from zones of pasture to date-palm oases that may be several hundred kilometres away). Similarly, despite the different contexts, the Hazara migration to Quetta corresponds to a diversification strategy and is not just a response to violence. It did not commence with war (or recommence, if we bear in mind Abdur Rahman's earlier conquest of Hazarajat); there was a real continuity of migration between Hazarajat and Quetta throughout the twentieth century.

THE URBAN ENVIRONMENT

Quetta,[4] the capital of Pakistani Baluchistan, lies at an altitude of 1,680 metres, in a basin surrounded by mountains over 3,000 meters high. There is a (usually dry) river, the Lora Nadi, west of the urban area. The climate is dry: hot in summer (sometimes above 40°C) and cold in winter (with snow and a temperature often below zero). All year round, the average rainfall is as low as 300 millimeters.

Quetta is situated at the junction of the roads from Sind (across the Bolan Pass), Afghanistan (Khojak Pass and the town of Chaman) and Iran (through the high desert plateaux of Baluchistan). It already had a huge garrison in the days of the Raj,[5] and is still an important military area. The housing districts have grown up around the bazaars in the south of the city.

On 31 May 1935, the urban area of Quetta was virtually destroyed by an earthquake measuring 7.5 on the Richter scale, which left 20,000 to 30,000 victims. None of the old buildings has survived, and there are few new ones with more than one floor. This gives it the appearance of an enormous village. A university was founded there in 1970. There is little industry apart from a few brickyards, but handicraft activity is intense (carpet-making, embroidery, sandal-making, etc.). Numerous orchards are dotted around the region: grape, peach, plum, apricot, apple, cherry, almond and pomegranate are the main products.

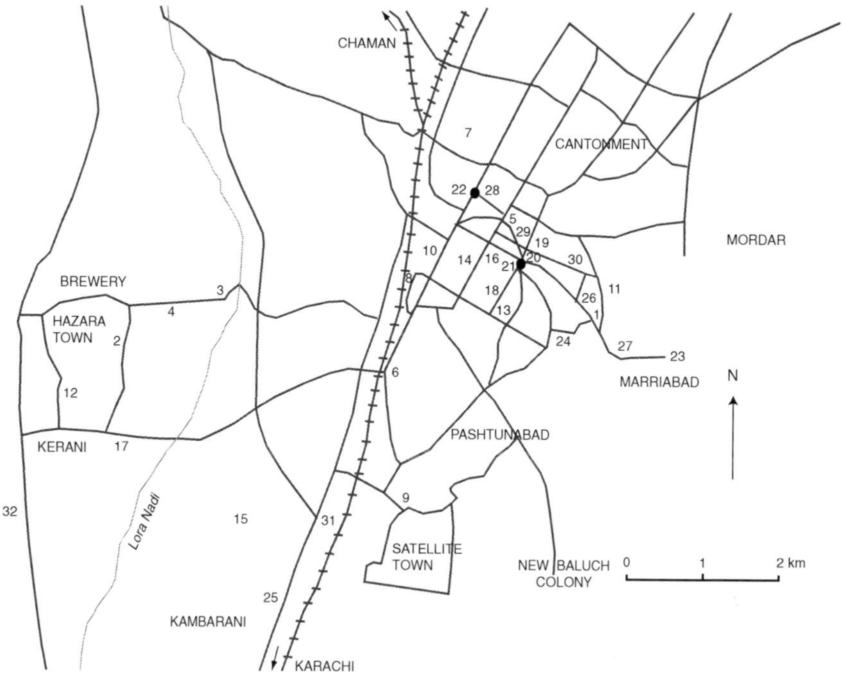

Key:

1. Alamdar Road
2. Aliabad
3. Bolan Medical Complex
4. Brewery Road
5. Circular Road (Old Ada)
6. Double Road
7. Fort
8. Railway station
9. Bus station (New Ada)
10. Governor's House, Civil Secretariat
11. Gulistan Town
12. Husaynabad
13. Main *imâmbârgâ* (Shiite)
14. Jinnah Road
15. Jungle Bagh
16. Kandahari Bazaar
17. Kerani Road
18. Liaqat Bazaar
19. Mission Road
20. Mizam Chowk
21. Main mosque (Sunni)
22. Provincial Assembly
23. Qabrestan (cemetery)
24. Qalandar Makran
25. Sariab Road
26. Saray-e Namak
27. Sar-e Maidani
28. Serena Hotel
29. Suraj Ganj Bazaar
30. Toghi Road
31. University of Baloutchistan
31. Western Bypass

Figure 6: The city of Quetta & Key to the map of Quetta

At the time of the 1981 census, the city had 285,000 inhabitants and the district 380,000.[6] According to official estimates (the only more recent source), the population of Quetta had risen by the mid-1990s to 800,000 or perhaps even one million. This impressive growth was due in part to the inflow of Afghan refugees, whose dynamism and willingness to make do with a low income enabled them to capture new sectors of the economy, sometimes at the price of conflicts with the local population. Moreover, their arrival upset the delicate political and demographic equilibrium of Baluchistan province, where Pashtuns today probably outnumber Baluch.

Quetta is on the edge of the areas of Pashtun and Baluch settlement, to the north and south respectively. Within the city itself, the different ethnic groups live in separate districts: the Pashtuns are a majority in Pashtunabad and Satellite Town (south); while the Hazara mostly live in the eastern districts of Alamdar Road, Toghi Road and Marriabad, and have recently moved into a large area in the west (Hazara Town, Brewery, Kerani Road . . .). Baluch and Brahwis are comparatively thin on the ground within the city, but they form the majority along the Sariab Road, in Kambarani and Kerani. The bazaar is a mixed area, but most of the traders are Pashtun.

The decline in Afghan refugee numbers since the Soviet withdrawal (1989) and the fall of Najibullah (1992)[7] is not attributable only to spontaneous or UNHCR-assisted repatriation. The Afghans immediately entered into daily contact with Pakistani society, being free to leave the official "Afghan Refugee Villages" and to become self-sufficient over time. Thus, many have chosen to settle in the urban centers of their host country and no longer show up as a special group in the statistics.

The law defines Pashtuns, Baluch, Brahwis and Hazaras as indigenous peoples. Theoretically reserved for Pakistani citizens, this status gives access to certain posts in the administration and has facilitated the integration of Afghan refugees from these ethnic groups. Communities originating in northern Afghanistan (Tajiks, Uzbeks, Turkmens, etc.) did not have the same opportunities and remained in a socially and economically precarious position, even if some were able to enrich themselves in the carpet trade. "Self-settled refugees" from northern Afghanistan are concentrated mainly in the south of the Quetta urban area, around Jungle Bagh, but also in Satellite Town, Pashtunabad and along the Sariab Road (see map). They live in makeshift accommodation on the waste ground between existing buildings. "Settlers"—a term used to describe Pakistani nationals from the Sind and Panjab, as well as refugees from India at the time of partition—complete the picture.

The history of migratory movements is clearly inscribed in the cityscape. Today scarcely a dozen families still live in the first Hazara areas near the large *imâmbârgâ* ("place of the imam") on McConaghey Road, a little south of the bazaar. Since the early-twentieth century, Hazaras have settled along the Alamdar Road, not far from the bazaar, to the east of Mizam Chowk, and it is there that most of their descendants still live. After the earthquake (1935) and the achievement of Pakistani independence (1947), the housing gradually extended as far as Sar-e Maidani (a previously uninhabited area), then climbed the slopes of Mordar. The influx of the 1970s soon saturated Marriabad, an area hemmed in by mountain (Mordar, to the east and south) and army ground (east of Toghi Road[8]). The topography put an end to the growth.

In the late-eighties, compelled to find new land to absorb their net influx and demographic growth, the Hazara turned to the other side of the city. Building rapidly spread south from Brewery to Hazara Town, Aliabad, Husainabad and Kerani Road, on former orchard land belonging to Baluch that the Hazaras bought up plot by plot. Although facilities remained rudimentary (most streets are bare earth, and not all homes are connected to the drains), these areas kept growing and growing—especially after the Taliban capture of Kabul in September 1996, the fighting with the Wahdat in summer 1997 and the fall of Bamyan in September 1998. Whereas the Kabuli Hazaras left to escape the repressive Taliban regime, those from Hazarajat were fleeing from drought and actual fighting.

The new Hazara districts in Quetta are not yet built-up. With roads that are dusty in summer and muddy in winter, with their straggling rows of shops and large open spaces between house walls that barely stand up, they look like a rather chaotic if booming frontier town. The constant influx and the population mix mean that acquaintance levels are not high in Brewery and Hazara Town. The streets often do not have properly fixed names, and so it is not always easy to find one's way around. Neighborhood or district solidarity is not yet solidly established.

Let us sum up. Hazara descendants of immigrants from the late-nineteenth and early-twentieth centuries live along the Alamdar Road and in adjacent areas. Families who arrived in the 1960s and 1970s occupy the hillier areas of Marriabad, which have running water, electricity, gas, schools, buses, and so on. The most recent immigrants, from the 1980s and 1990s, have filled up the few empty spaces in Marriabad, but mostly live in the new western parts of Quetta that are still in need of development. Today, the population level of the Brewery/Hazara Town area is tending towards parity with Marriabad and Alamdar Road.

The six-kilometer distance between the two Hazara areas is not without its problems. As it is expensive to travel by rickshaw, many Hazaras have bought Suzuki mini-vans and keep them constantly in use. But the transport industry is a highly sensitive issue in Baluchistan: it makes a lot of money and tends to crystallize ethnic tensions, since Baluch and Pashtuns both have monopoly control over certain areas (Titus 1996, 1997). Early in 2001, Baluch and Pashtun drivers protested against what they considered disloyal competition on the part of Hazara transport services between Alamdar Road and Hazara Town. Rioting broke out, and it took several days to reach an agreement permitting a few dozen Hazara drivers to operate.

The distance between the Hazara areas in Quetta does not by itself explain certain kinds of behavior; the social groups in question are also very different. Despite daily interaction, Pakistani and Afghan Hazaras rarely cross-marry and tend to have stereotypical images of one another. On several occasions I heard someone from a long-established Hazara group say to an excited child: *tu, az kujâ asti? bace Hazâra Tâwn asti?*, "Where are you from? Are you a Hazara Town kid?" These were scolding words for a kind of coarse behavior generally attributed to new arrivals from Hazarajat; whereas, on the other side, Pakistani Hazaras are often seen as arrogant and lazy. This discourse largely reproduces the urban-rural opposition inside Afghanistan.

Let us take two individual and family trajectories to illustrate the migratory continuum between Hazarajat and Quetta, as well as the paternalist relations between different strata of the Hazara population in Quetta.

Haji Sarwar lives in the Yazdan Khan Road area, not far from Saray-e Namak. His family is well known among the Hazaras of Quetta. His grandfather, Husayn Ali, left his family and Afghanistan (Nawur district, the *qawm* of the Alawdini) to go to British India at the end of the reign of Abdur Rahman. He passed through Parachinar on his way to Quetta, where he enlisted in the British army and went to fight in Iraq during the First World War. He then made his way back through Iran and married a woman from Shiraz. He formed a plan to return to Afghanistan, and it was on the journey there that his wife gave birth to a son. He then decided to settle for good in Quetta, where he started up a bakery. He died in 1936, shortly after being injured in the earthquake, and without ever hearing again from his first Afghan wife. His Iranian wife died in 1988. His son, Haji Karam, purchased a lorry and transported coal between the mines and the points of sale. Gradually he branched out, and today his offspring have good jobs and some real estate. Beginning in the mid-1980s, he purchased rights to work a number of coal mines.

Mardan Ali came to Quetta for the first time in the late 1960s. He spent the 1980s between Afghanistan and Pakistan, going to fight the Soviets in summer and travelling to Quetta in winter to work in the mines. In 1989, following the Soviet withdrawal, he laid down arms and returned to Afghanistan only to visit his family. He worked in Haji Sarwar's firm, starting as an ordinary worker and gradually moving up to become foreman. During all those years, his family remained in Jaghori: his wife, though born and bred in Quetta, preferred to live in Dahmarda as the mountain air was better for her tuberculosis. Only after the events that divided Dahmarda in the winter of 1995–1996 did Mardan Ali decide to bring his family to Pakistan.

NEIGHBORHOOD GROUPS AND ASSOCIATIONS OF PEOPLE FROM THE SAME PLACE OF ORIGIN

The insertion of Hazara into the social fabric of Quetta therefore varies with their date of arrival and the relative permanence of their settlement. Descendants of the first immigrants, who have long been Pakistani citizens, form quite a prosperous community, whereas more recent arrivals occupy a relatively subordinate position that is inscribed within the urban space, since they have to live in outlying hills or steppe and find it hard to break into many kinds of economic activity. A relationship of dependence, or even exploitation, exists between these two layers, the former often acting as protectors or employers of the latter. But tribal and ethnic affiliation is a backdrop that permits the establishment of stable relations and lasting reputations.

The power of the traditional leaders has been eroded with the change in social and political structures. In Hazarajat, the *mir* were politically and militarily supplanted by the *šeyk*, and the *sayyed* lost a lot of their prestige (Bindemann 1987; Harpviken 1996). Things happened differently in Quetta. The tribal chiefs did not always manage to maintain their distinction, since they lost the sources of their power (land, livestock, etc.) and had neither the social connections nor the necessary skills to make up for them. Others still show them formal respect, but do not ask them for advice when a problem has to be solved. The most influential persons are now those who can mediate with the Pakistani administration and know how it functions; their social position derives from their practical sense and their social connections.

In Quetta the types of residence, cooperation and mutual support are not the same as in Hazarajat. Hazaras are concentrated in certain parts of the urban area, but people from the same *qawm* do not group together. The nature of the property market is such that they live wherever they can find something to meet their needs. There is also a chronological factor, so that people from Dahmarda, for example, are distributed among Alamdar Road, Marriabad, Brewery and Hazara Town in accordance with their date of original settlement. Community life is organized around two parallel and complementary structures: neighborhood associations, and associations of people from the same place of origin.

Neighborhood associations consist of people living in one or two streets—a few dozen families. Family heads appoint one representative (sometimes called the *kalân-e mahalla; kalân* means "large") among the oldest inhabitants of the place, usually a Hazara of Pakistani nationality thought to know the ropes and to have important contacts. Each family pays ten to twenty rupees a month into a pool, which is used to help the poorest or recently bereaved families. Although members do not cooperate in agricultural labor, they have all kinds of other common interest (urban development issues, schools, clinics, and so on). By coming together, they are able to form a pressure group to influence the decisions of the competent authorities.

The other structure is the association of people from the same *qawm*, who, as we have seen, do not necessarily live in the same area. There are several dozen Hazara associations of this kind in Quetta. In reality, the membership criterion is not always the *qawm*. Depending on the size of the community, it may be the particular tribal segment or the precise geographical origin: one region (*manteqa*) or one or several districts (*uluswâli*).

People from Jaghori are particularly well represented in Quetta, but for that very reason they are split up according to tribal segment (Maska, Oqi, Dahmarda, etc.).[9] Family heads belonging to each association meet roughly once a month to discuss community affairs. They choose a head, or *kalân-e qawm*, by a complex process of selection: representatives of each lineage come together and weigh up various factors such as personal reputation, ties with Pakistan or previous responsibilities within the family. There is no formal election as such, and the *kalân-e qawm*, once chosen, keeps his position unless there is a major challenge. Usually he will be descended from one of the first immigrants, have held official responsibilities, and have many social connections outside the Hazara community. Known and recognized by others, he is expected to help new arrivals find a place in society and the Quetta labor market; to calm divisions within the community; and to represent the group in external dealings. He advises members of his *qawm* on various procedures or contentious issues (traffic accidents, trials, application for an identity card or a job, purchase of land, marital disputes, and so on). He must always try to fend off the Pakistani authorities and to provide a screen between them and the group. His function therefore resembles that of the *malek* or *arbâb* in Afghanistan (Centlivres and Centlivres-Demont 1981–1982; Dupree 1980: 249–150).

As in the case of neighborhood associations, the *kalân* collects and administers the monthly contributions, which may amount to several dozen rupees per family. Usually called the *canda* (from *cand*, "how much"[10]) or sometimes the *zaxira* ("reserve" or "treasury"), this fund is a kind of tontine: it can be sent to the place of origin in Afghanistan and spent there for the common good (schools, roads, *kârez*, etc.), but most often it is used in Quetta. In fact, the *kalân-e qawm* hands out assistance to those most in need, and to families faced with having to organize a funeral. He does not help with marriages, so as not to encourage lavish expenditure. The *qawm* associations only rarely take action to welcome migrants. In extreme emergencies, such as a sudden arrival en masse following some military event, the *kalân-e qawm* may collect food from regular contributors and distribute it to the new arrivals.

In the case of Dahmarda, divisions in the village of origin affected the situation in Quetta. Thus there were two *kalân-e qawm*, Haji Ejaz Ali (Dawran) and Abdullah Khan (Omur). The former, who played the more prominent role, arrived in Pakistan in the late sixties, where he soon acquired Pakistani papers and began to earn a living as an estate agent. He also held various public functions in Baluchistan. He collected thirty rupees a month from each family and, in the event of a death, he gave the surviving family a sum of between 5,000 and 10,000 rupees, according to their needs. As to the Maska, the main tribal segment from Jaghori living in Quetta, they are more numerous and have a more elaborate structure, with some 1,600 families divided among twenty lineages. The heads of these handle the monthly contribution, which varies from twenty to thirty rupees, and meet to elect a central president (*sadr*). The same person has held this office for more than a quarter of a century: he is a retired Pakistani army officer, who has also worked for the UNHCR.

In addition to the *qawm* and *mahalla* associations, the religious meeting-places form a third community structure. The Shiites of Quetta use the term *imâmbârgâ* ("court of the imam") or, more colloquially, *imâmbâra*, a local equivalent of the Iranian *takya-xâna* or the *membar* of Hazarajat. The term *masjid* ("mosque") is reserved for a part of these complexes set aside for prayers. The *imâmbâra* are generally *waqf* ("religious foundations"), whose revenue comes from donations and from their real estate. Their committees organize the meetings and processions that mark *moharram*, the first month of the Islamic lunar calendar, when Shiites commemorate the martyrdom of Imam Husayn.

The great *imâmbâra* of Quetta is at the corner of McConaghey Road and Khodadad Road, opposite a Sunni mosque. Some ten smaller *imâmbâra* are spread out along Alamdar Road, usually deriving their name from regional communities: the Panjâbi, the Qandahâri, the two Gilgiti, the Hazâra (very close to Saray-e Namak), the Baltistâni, and so on. But the actual attendance is based on local residence rather than place of origin. Many more are to found on Toghi Road, in Marriabad and in the new districts of Brewery, Hazara Town, Aliabad and Husaynabad. Behind their large gate topped with several flags, these places usually have a central courtyard with a room set aside for prayers and for meetings during *moharram*. Sometimes there is also a large-scale model of Imam Husayn's tomb in Kerbela.

Another religious meeting-place is the *idgâh*, which in the case of the Shiites is situated on Alamdar Road, approximately half way between Saray-e namak and Sar-e Maidani. It is a huge place where people gather for the two main Muslim festivals: the *id al-kebir* ("Great Feast") or *id-e qorbân* ("Feast of the Sacrifice"), commemorating Abraham's sacrifice, at the end of the annual period of pilgrimages to Mecca; and the *id al-fitr* ("Little Feast") or *id-e ramazân* ("Feast of Ramazan"), marking the end of *ramazân*, the ninth month of the Islamic lunar calendar, when people are supposed to fast from dawn to sunset.

A final important structure among the Hazara of Quetta is the Tanzim-e nasl-e naw-e Hazara-ye Moghol ("Party of the Mongol Hazara New Generation"), whose spacious center on Alamdar Road contains offices, classrooms and a concert hall. It is both a political and a cultural organization, founded in the early 1970s by a group of young Pakistani Hazaras. The party campaigns in support of Hazara emancipation, combining left-wing ideology with ethnicist demands. At the beginning of the war in Afghanistan, the Tanzim turned to activity inside the country with the support of the Pakistani secret services, but soon ran into the hostility of pro-Iranian movements and ceased operations in Hazarajat (see chapter 3). After the foundation of the Hezb-e wahdat in the wake of the Soviet withdrawal, tensions became less acute among the Hazaras, although there was still opposition between secular and religious forces.

Despite the differences, there are also parallels between the social organization of the Hazaras in Afghanistan and Pakistan. In Hazarajat (or anyway in Jaghori) the solidarity of neighborhood groups, on the basis of a *qaria* or around a *membar*, coexists with solidarity among the spatially dispersed members of lineages who have a common *arbâb*. In Quetta, each

Hazara also makes specific financial contributions to two structures: his *qawm* and his *mahalla*. Furthermore, in both Quetta and Jaghori, in both urban and rural areas, kinship groups and residence-based units do not coincide. Cooperation therefore develops within sociologically distinct groups for which the determining factor is proximity: territorial or residential in the case of the *mahalla*, lineage-based in that of the *qawm*. Within this framework, where people first meet and know they will continue to meet in the future, the penalty for lack of solidarity is a bad reputation (*badnâm*) and the unwillingness of others to take on commitments. A new kind of sociability, reducing the weight of kinship and neighborhood, comes to play a role which, though important, is not such a vital part of everyday life as community ties were in the village of origin. Here in the city, it is noticeable that individuals tend to develop within a broader circle, and that their social relations become more diverse.

Mutual support is a widespread phenomenon. Services are rendered without an expectation of immediate repayment; a return gift is made only in case of need. Reciprocity may be deferred and include persons other than the ones initially involved:

> T_1: A does B a service (gift).
>
> T_2 (for example, T_1 + 2 years): B does a service for C, the brother of A (return gift).

Such a system relates to what Sahlins calls "generalized reciprocity" (1965: 147). Goods and services circulate without the expectation of an equivalent in return (see chapter 9). This cycle of obligations creates ties and constitutes a community that cannot be reduced to the *qawm*. The fact of being in someone's debt ensures the continuity of the relationship with him, while also establishing a social hierarchy between donor and donee (Mauss 1985).

The life of Afghans is characterized by mobility and great insecurity. Neither states nor juridical bodies guarantee that contracts will be respected, and acts of violence are always a possibility. Individuals therefore have to fall back upon narrower forms of solidarity; cooperation and reciprocity can develop only if relations are lasting and recurrent. The existence of clearly defined Hazara areas in Quetta makes it easier to establish such ties. For, in the event of financial misconduct, the victim can strike back only if he has a minimum of information about the person responsible. (Usually it is enough to ruin the latter's reputation by spreading word about what he has done, but sometimes things can take a more violent turn.) According to Axelrod (1990), it can be more advantageous not to practice reciprocity towards individuals one will never meet again; the key element is social proximity, a common place of origin or a shared lineage. The density of relations and encounters (past, present and especially future) has greater weight than kinship as such, and so ties of neighborhood or friendship may prove more decisive. Nevertheless, the endogamous tendencies within Afghan society often cause these two levels to coincide (see chapter 9).

THE MALE WORLD OF THE COAL MINES

In a now quite old piece on the state of Middle Eastern anthropology, Antoun[11] wrote that "there are three types of urban population—long-term urbanites, fixed outsiders (who return from time to time to their place of origin), and a floating population (who come in crises such as drought and war and return when the crisis is over)" (1976: 178). As long as we do not make the compartments watertight, this categorization may be applied to the Hazaras of Quetta.

Thus, on the fringes of the established *qawm* and *mahalla* associations, there is a whole little world of essentially male *mosâferin* ("travellers") who are constantly on the move. Although in daily contact with the more settled Hazara population (among whom they have relatives, friends and former neighbors), they continue to gear their plans to Hazarajat and the families still living there. They come and go as work opportunities and their own preferences dictate, staying for a time in Quetta, leaving for Iran or returning to Hazarajat. The social categories among the Hazaras are not clear-cut but form a continuum, so that a migrant may gradually extend his stays in Quetta until he finally brings his family there (which, in turn, does not preclude a further eventual move). At one extreme are descendants of the first Hazaras to settle in Quetta; at the other are the *mosâferin*. In addition to travelling salesmen and money-changers, those who work in the nearby coal mines also belong to this category; they gravitate around the inns or *mosâfer-xâna* (literally "travellers' homes"), which, as we shall see, play a central role in the Hazara migratory circuits by organizing the crossing of frontiers (chapter 6) and providing a place for money-changers and *hawâladâr* to gather (chapter 7). The *mosâfer-xâna* also serve as employment centers, as foremen know they will find men there who are looking for work.

Afghan refugees are to be found all over Pakistan as unskilled workers. In the urban centers, crowds of able-bodied men gather at certain road junctions in the hope that someone will hire them for some menial task (Development Alternatives 1990; Morton 1991, 1994). In Quetta, for example, Shiites go to Sar-e Maidani and Sunnis to New Ada. Whereas Afghan

Pashtuns are happy to take work in agriculture or construction, the social connections among Hazaras incline them more towards the coal mines.

In the early-twentieth century, the miners were mostly Makranis from southern Baluchistan, but local Pashtuns and Hazaras are also mentioned in the records (*Imperial Gazetteer of India* 1991: 47). Some old miners say that they already came there in the time of the British, but that there were fewer Hazaras (and other Muslims) in the mines than Sikhs and Hindus. It was mainly after independence (1947), and especially in the 1970s, that their numbers began to increase; many were farmer heads of large families who took advantage of the slack winter months to make a little money in Pakistan. Today three communities are represented among the miners in the region: Swatis (Pashtuns from northern Pakistan), Wardakis (Pashtu-speakers from Afghanistan), and Hazaras from Ghazni (Afghanistan). Few local Baluch or Pashtuns work in the mines, except as lorry drivers.

Coal-mining as such is not seasonally dependent, but the September almond harvest that ends the agricultural year in Hazarajat releases labor for migration until the following March. Those who work in the mines in summer are more integrated into the urban social fabric, usually having close relatives in Quetta or even a family and home of their own.

The mines near Quetta play an important economic role for the Hazaras. At the Marwad site, for example, 60 kms north-east of the city, there are ten landowners (Baluch tribal chiefs) and twenty to thirty directors (mostly Pashtuns and Pakistani Hazaras), while fifty Hazara contractors run approximately two hundred mines and employ several thousand workers. The latter figure varies a great deal from season to season: several thousand men come each winter from southern Hazarajat, representing dozens from each *manteqa* in the district of Jaghori.[12]

Work in the mines brings these migrants into contact with local society through the Pakistani Hazaras who employ them. The way in which things are organized encourages the formation of groups by place of origin; a functional hierarchy imposes relations of solidarity. The mining vocabulary is a veritable hodgepodge of English, Urdu and Persian. One hears the words *kontraktor, tekadâr* or *ejâradâr* (contractor, director or manager), *jamadâr* (the foreman, who hires labor and organizes the work and supplies), *jorisar* or *sarjori* (the team leader responsible for actual work in the mines), *kârgar, muzdurkâr, muzdur* or *leyberz* (ordinary miners), as well as *manajer* (the man in charge of security), *bâbu* or *munši* (secretary or bookkeeper), *deriwâr* (lorry drivers) and *kelinar* (drivers' assistants). There are also experts in charge of the water pump, the small truck, the electrical generator, and so on.[13] The permanent staff (managers, bookkeepers, drivers), who often live with their families in Quetta and receive a fixed basic salary, are called *molâzem* (or more rarely *employi*); whereas most of the miners come from Afghanistan and are paid in accordance with their output.

The employer provides food and docks it from the miners' pay. Two different criteria are used in wage calculations: when little or no coal is actually being produced, the work is measured by the speed at which galleries are dug and the difficulty of the terrain, usually giving a wage of about 300 rupees (or $9) per foot; when normal production is under way, the pay is output-related. One sack of coal sells for 110 to 150 rupees ($3.3 to $4.5), depending on its quality and the state of the market. The foreman takes a cut of 2 rupees for each sack, in addition to a fixed wage of 2,000 rupees per month and per mine (he may work for several at the same time). In 1995 Mardan Ali, for example, earned a total of 80,000 rupees (nearly $2,500). The team leader receives a commission of one rupee, in addition to the 12 to 16 rupees per sack that he shares among the ten to fifteen members of his team. On average, then, a miner's pay comes to $3 to $4 a day. If a team is working on a high-quality seam, the monthly wage may rise as high as 4,000 rupees ($120), which is a considerable sum in Quetta for manual labor.[14] A team leader may earn more than $30 a month in commission.

There is no rule against special arrangements within each team of miners: an especially hard worker may even receive an extra pay with his colleagues' agreement, and a team may decide to continue paying one of its members who is off sick. The system encourages a kind of internal solidarity, but also mutual checking. It tends to make workers aware of their responsibilities, leading them to form small and highly interdependent groups. But, in the event of a dispute or rising tension, these groups tend to break up, as it is in nobody's interest to work in an atmosphere of suspicion. There is an overlapping of responsibilities: the *jamadâr* hires people he trusts, and the *jorisar* has considerable leeway in running his team. The output-related pay means that everyone has an interest in developing cordial and cooperative relations.

The bookkeepers earn 2,000 rupees (approx. $60) a month, with no extra commission but an occasional extra payment for medical care, weddings, and so on. Drivers are paid a low basic wage (1,500 rupees), but for each return trip to Quetta (an average of twenty a month) they receive two sacks of coal that they can sell on the market for 200 to 300 rupees. Apprentices receive a basic wage of 600 rupees, plus 30 rupees per trip, making a total of 1,200 rupees a month.

Once the miners' wages have been subtracted, the contractor uses the remaining money (90 to 130 rupees per sack) to cover his electricity, diesel and other costs, staff salaries, the landowner's cut (8 rupees per sack), government taxes (2 rupees per sack), and the depreciation of equipment (generators, pumps, small trucks, lorries, etc.). That leaves him with a profit of 15 to 20 rupees per sack.

Let us take the example of Haji Sarwar (see above). He had been running coal mines since the early 1980s. His foreman was Mardan Ali, who hired people only if he already knew them (relatives or neighbors in Afghanistan) or if they were introduced by someone he trusted. This explains why nearly all the workers were Hazaras from Jaghori.[15] There were a few Pakistani Hazaras in positions of responsibility. In 1995 and 1996 Haji Sarwar had two concessions in Marwad. Two teams of a dozen men worked by turns, from 7.00 A.M. to 5.00 P.M. and from 7.00 P.M. to approximately 5.00 A.M., doing eight to nine hours of actual work. (They had meal breaks down below and, at the end of their shift, had to wait quite a long time to be taken back up.) Haji Sarwar also ran a mine on the outskirts of Mach. Altogether, he employed a minimum of sixty people—more in winter because of the arrivals from Hazarajat.

The coal miners went into town on Thursday afternoons and returned on Friday evenings (this corresponded to a weekend).[16] On Thursday afternoon each miner queued patiently at the office to be paid, and on Friday morning plans were made for the following week. They took advantage of these moments to exchange a few words, to catch up on the latest gossip. Haji Sarwar's office had concrete walls decorated with old picture calendars and an artistically written prayer; there was a television in a cupboard, and a desk studded with coins from various countries. Everything had a modern and well-kept appearance. The furniture seemed very unusual to the miners from Hazarajat; the fact that they were expected to sit on benches (in fact mini-van seats) instead of on the ground made them feel a little intimidated and helped to reinforce the prestige of their Pakistani employer. The sequence was always the same: a miner would enter the office, say a respectful word of greeting, sit down and silently await his turn; he would take the opportunity to watch was happening around him and to take in the atmosphere. The presence of a foreigner always aroused intense curiosity, as well as further enhancing the boss's reputation. Only when Haji Sarwar asked them did they explain the reason for their visit and make their request. That never happened quickly—there was a time for everything; people were not in a hurry. Besides, this was proof of caution or even suspicion: a miner did not speak out rashly, but first sized up the other person while making polite gestures. Sometimes an intermediary was asked to say something on his behalf. The rules of politeness operated as a subtle language expressing the degree of proximity and hierarchy between the actors.

Coal-mining is hard work, and many are unable to endure it. Although the workforce is highly mobile, it forms a small world where everyone knows everyone else. Recruitment takes place on the basis of individual networks, and the pegging of pay to work and output compels each team to maintain a high degree of cohesion.

QUETTA: LAST REFUGE OF THE HAZARAS?

In 1984, during *moharram*, more than ten people were killed in violent clashes in Quetta between Hazaras and the forces of order. In the late 1990s, when relations between religious groups took a turn for the worse in Pakistan, a number of leading Shiite figures (journalists, intellectuals, businessmen) were killed by members of small Sunni organizations. Early in July 2003, a commando group attacked the main Shiite mosque in Quetta during Friday prayers and killed dozens of people, most of them Hazaras.

Despite these dramatic events and a progressive deterioration of the social and political climate due to the action of some Sunni Islamist groups, the situation of the Hazaras in Pakistan remains generally good, and in a sense Quetta was for long years the only place that offered them satisfactory security. They can lead a reasonably unfettered existence there and have little difficulty obtaining Pakistani papers. On the other hand, the labor market offers scarcely any outlets other than the coal mines and the retail trade (for those with the capital to open a shop). In Afghanistan, where all the economic infrastructure has been destroyed, there is great insecurity. In Iran, Hazaras face numerous restrictions and do not have the option of settling down permanently; they live in fear of arrest and expulsion, although they can find little jobs easily enough.[17] Despite the difficulties facing migrants, the Afghan Shiite parties, especially the Hezb-e wahdat, continue to base themselves in Iran.

Hazaras have never lived in great numbers in the official Afghan Refugee Villages (ARVs). As the name suggests, these are not enclosed areas and at first sight there is little to distinguish them from Pakistani villages in the surrounding area. According to official figures, the number of Afghan refugees peaked in 1990 at 6.2 million; 3,272,000 were then in Pakistan alone, three-quarters of them women and children (Hatch Dupree 1990: 121). Only a quarter were adult males, therefore, and many of those were old or sick. In 1987 Pashtuns formed by far the largest group (87%), followed by Tajiks (6%), Baluch (3.6%), Nuristanis (2.9%), Turkmens (1%), Uzbeks (under 1%), Hazaras (under 1%) and others (approximately 1%) (Sliwinski 1989: 46; Shahrani 1995: 193–194). As one would expect from these figures, the Pashtun proportion of the population in Afghanistan had fallen from 39 percent in 1978 to 22 percent in 1987 (Sliwinski 1989: 45, 46).

Afghans living outside the ARVs, for whom the term "self-settled refugees" is often used (Connor 1987, 1989), are not in UNHCR care and do not always appear in the statistics. Yet this is a large group, whose relative weight has been continually increasing, and it covers the great majority of Hazaras in Quetta and elsewhere. In fact, the only camps in Pakistani Baluchistan that have held any Hazaras are those at Mohammad Khel and Surkhab: at most, two to three hundred families at the latter and roughly double that number at Mohammad Khel in 1989, or a maximum of 6000 persons. Soon after 1989, the Hazaras left Surkhab because of safety problems associated with certain Pashtun groups, and those at Mohammad Khel left not long afterwards. Thus, the few Hazara families in the camps preferred to leave in search of work in Quetta, mostly settling in Brewery between 1989 and 1992. By 1995, when it had to interrupt the distribution of rations, the UNHCR estimated that there no longer any Hazaras living in the camps in Pakistan.

Many Hazaras took refuge in Pakistan during the terrible fighting of 1992–1995 in Kabul between factions of the former resistance. Like their predecessors, the refugees who left Afghanistan after the fall of Kabul (September 1996), the escalation of fighting between Hezb-e wahdat and the Taliban (summer 1997), or the fall of Mazar-e Sharif and Bamyan (August-September 1998) did not pass through the camps on their way to Quetta. Moreover, unlike in the 1980s, refugees from urban areas outnumbered those from the countryside.

The war evidently intensified the Hazara migration to Quetta but did not fundamentally alter its nature (except in the sense that the journey became more difficult, as migrants had to use smugglers' routes that presented a number of dangers). Historically, the Pakistani-Afghan frontier has never marked a real separation. Like the Pashtuns, the Hazaras in Quetta have well-developed solidarity networks and long-established communities defined by place of origin. By contrast, Tajiks, Uzbeks or Turkmens from northern Afghanistan had no links with Pakistan before the war and did not benefit from a welcoming milieu there. They found themselves a long way from their homelands and remained relatively marginal, even if there were occasional examples of great economic success. They were the first to return to Afghanistan in the course of the 1990s, and only those who were engaged in some profitable activity (such as the carpet or pelt trade) decided to stay on.

Movement back and forth between Afghanistan and Pakistan is much more common among the Hazaras and Pashtuns, for whom the very notion of return or repatriation appears to lose its meaning. The Hazaras have suffered as much from poverty as from war, and they have a long history of connections with Quetta that is reflected in constant migratory flows. Despite their small numbers, many Hazaras have risen to high positions in the Pakistani army and civil service. In Quetta they invest a great deal in education, which they see as a means of improving their lot. These efforts to overcome a tradition of disdain towards them are often combined with political demands.

Economically, the influence of Quetta has mainly been felt in southern Hazarajat: Jaghori, Qarabagh and the areas around Ghazni and Behsud are alive with commercial activity, but the many traders have a limited field of action. In 1995 and 1996 Mazar-e Sharif, in northern Afghanistan, might have appeared to play a more important economic role, but, as we shall see (chapter 7), activities there scarcely had any impact on Hazarajat. And political-military developments in Mazar-e Sharif in 1997 and 1998 dramatically showed that Hazaras could not find security there. In more than one way, then, Quetta has occupied a quite special place in the social, cultural, political and economic life of the Hazaras, as well as being a necessary point in every migratory network.

Chapter Five
Asylum and Labor Migration to Iran

MIGRANT WORKERS AND MONEY REMITTANCES

Unlike in Pakistan, where Afghans have benefited from international aid and great freedom of movement, the Iranian authorities have always restricted the activity of outside bodies (UN, ICRC, NGOs) and allowed very few refugees camps to be created. But, while watching their every move, they have integrated them into the labor market. Already before the war, many Afghans were going to Iran in search of work, and the Afghan community there largely consisted of young unmarried men working in the large urban centers. All kinds of activity were forbidden to them, however, so that they were essentially left with unskilled and poorly paid manual labor (Centlivres 1989). Forced to spread out in search of work, Hazaras did not establish forms of sociability and solidarity comparable to those in Quetta. They often stayed for several years—the period required to make the initial effort worthwhile—and sent any spare money back to their family in Afghanistan. They might gather together temporarily, depending on the employment situation, but only in very few cases did they think of settling in Iran for good.

The situation of the Hazaras in Iran perfectly illustrates the difficulty of distinguishing between economic migrants and political refugees. Hazarajat is one of the poorest regions in Afghanistan, and none of the governments in Kabul has been able or willing to make the necessary effort to improve its economic situation. It was relatively spared by the Soviet occupying forces, but the partial severing of migratory routes to the urban centers of Afghanistan made life even worse for its inhabitants. War and poverty have been mutually reinforcing factors propelling hundreds of thousands of Hazaras abroad. Once again we should stress that, although economic and personal insecurity due to the ravages of war partly explain these population movements, they were never unidirectional and scarcely corresponded to the usual image of refugees.

Money-transfers from Iran to Hazarajat are one of the most striking features of the Hazara migratory networks, and more generally of their social practices. Migration has gradually expanded the area of activity of the Hazaras: from their village and home district in Afghanistan (Damarda, Jaghori) through a big city in Pakistan (Quetta) to the whole country in Iran (especially the large urban centers of Tehran, Qom and Mashad).

A BRIEF HISTORY OF THE HAZARA PRESENCE IN IRAN

The presence of the Hazara in Iran goes back a long way, but the documentary sources are incomplete. It is not out of the question that Hazaras were involved in the massive population transfers of the eighteenth century, especially in the reign of Nader Shah Afshar (1736–1747). Captain Napier, a British intelligence officer who travelled in North-East Iran in 1874, noted a Hazara presence in Khorasan before the subjugation of Hazarajat by Abdur Rahman, but the population movement mainly concerned Sunnis from Herat and Badghis whose relations with the people of Hazarajat are unclear. According to Napier:

> the tribes of Herat are Eimak and Hazara; the term Eimak is confined to the four tribes: Jamshidi, Firozkohi, Taimuni, and Hazara; but some of the Shiah Hazara tribes and the Taimuris are also called by that name, especially in Persia, where the distinction is little known. [. . .]
>
> The Hazara reckoned among the Char Eimak are a section of the great tribe, holding the line of the Hindoo Koosh, from the valley of the Oxus to that of the Helmund. They have, however, been long separated from the main body and subject to Afghan influence through their location at Kala Now to the north-east of Herat, and have accepted the Sunni creed. They were entirely dispersed by Yar Mahomed Khan, and are now to be found principally in Persian territory.
>
> Two thousand families were brought to Mashad, and granted lands in Isferayeen after the last siege of Herat [. . .] There are also some families in the town of Mashad, and in Jam and Bakharz. They may be put down at 3,000 families in all (Napier 1876: 229, 231).

The fourth edition of the *Gazetteer of Afghanistan* (1910: 145–157) mentions quite a large number of Hazaras—as well as Timuris, Taymanis and others—in Iranian Khorasan (1910: 261, 282–284). But it is unclear about the links between the (Sunni) Hazaras of Qala-ye Naw and the (mainly

Shiite) Hazaras of Hazarajat. Some thirty years before Napier, a French officer and traveller by the name of Ferrier wrote that the Sunni Hazaras of north-eastern Herat claimed to be of Afghan descent (that is, Pashtuns). In his view, although they were Persian-speaking, their origin was Turko-Mongol (1976: 191–194).

The name "Hazara" is therefore far from univocal in Khorasan. Two distinct groups are to be found there: Those who settled in the region under Nader Shah Afshar (in the first half of the eighteenth century) were mostly Sunnis from the Herat and Badghis regions. Many returned to Afghanistan after the death of Nader Shah, but some remained where they were; one small group was moved to the Rafsanjan area by the future Reza Shah, around the year 1920 (Perry 1975). Those who fled to Iran from the onslaught of Abdur Rahman (late-nineteenth to early-twentieth century) were mainly Shiites from Hazarajat. Since the reign of Reza Shah (1925–1941), they have been called Berberis (Mousavi 1998: 148–153)[1] or Khawaris (from *xâwar,* "east"). A Soviet author, Aliyev, put the number of "Berber (Hazara)" at just 2,700 in 1956 (1966: 64).[2]

We do not have a clear picture of the historical relations between Shiites fleeing Hazarajat and Persian-speaking Sunnis such as the Timuri (usually classified among the Aymaq) (Dupree 1980: 58, 60). Khorasan received population groups from various origins. One finds Kurds and Turkmens in the north-east, mainly Persian-speaking Sunnis (Baluchi, Timuri) near the Afghan frontier, and Berberi in the areas around Fariman and Sang Bast and as far as Torbat-e Jam and Torbat-e Hedariyeh, south and south-east of Mashad (they live in various parts of the urban area of Mashad itself, especially in Koh-ye Tollâb and semi-rural Gulshahr in the north).

Thus, although people called Hazara have long been present in Iran, it is only since the subjugation of Hazarajat that the population of interest to us here has been going to Khorasan. In 1996, during a stay in Mashad, I got to know a young man who described himself as Berberi; he did not seem to think that this implied the slightest link with Afghanistan and the Hazaras. According to him, his family, which originally came from somewhere in Afghanistan (he did not know precisely where) at a time when it was part of Iran, had been living in the region for at least three generations. That was a way of saying that his family had always been Iranian.

The fate of the Hazaras in Iran and in British India (later Pakistan) was very different. As we saw in the last chapter, those who went to British India mostly came from southern Hazarajat and were well received by the British; they formed quite a prosperous urban community, while continuing to maintain a distinct identity. Those who fled to Qajar Persia, with their origins in western Hazarajat, have not maintained close relations with Afghanistan; the distances are too great and there is not the same kind of back and forth movement as exists between Quetta and Hazarajat. Nor have the descendants of Hazara settlers in the rural areas around Mashad known the same kind of social and economic advancement as in Pakistan. They try to keep their distance from new Afghan arrivals, not wishing to suffer the disdain with which most Iranians treat the latter. Without a marked identity of their own, they soon merged into a local population whose language and religion they shared (unlike the Hazaras of Quetta, who were Shiites among Sunnis and Persian-speakers among people who spoke Pashtu or Baluchi). The Hazara community of Mashad is more "Iranianized" that the Quetta community is "Pakistanized." Whereas, in Quetta, there is constant interpenetration of the Pakistani and Afghan communities (which does not rule out certain hierarchical relations), a new identity has been created in Iran that conjures away the links with Afghanistan. Descendants of the late-nineteenth-century Hazara immigrants have even abandoned their ethnonym, in favor of the name Berberi or, less often, Khawari. Nevertheless, Afghan Hazaras are particularly numerous in parts of Mashad inhabited by Iranian Berberis.

FROM ONE REVOLUTION TO ANOTHER: THE AFGHANS IN IRAN

Afghanistan and Iran went through revolutions and ensuing problems at almost the same time, yet they have developed in very different ways. Despite an endemic crisis, the Iranian economy offers an attractive labor market and numerous employment opportunities; Afghans began to migrate to Iran before the Communist coup of 1978, and many (essentially male) Hazaras had been going there since the 1960s (a movement that intensified after the terrible famine of 1971–1972).

It is interesting to note that until recently the number of Afghans in Iran was more stable than in Pakistan, being less dependent upon the political-military situation in Afghanistan. In 1990 Pakistan had 3.27 million Afghans (compared with 2.94 million in Iran), whereas in 1996 UNHCR figures (UNHCR 1998)[3] show more in Iran than in Pakistan (1.4 million and 1.2 million respectively). These figures involve a certain distortion, however, since all Afghans registered in Iran count as refugees, whereas only those who live in camps are so recorded in Pakistan. In addition, several hundred thousand Afghans are living in Iran illegally, working without social protection for wages 30 percent below the average (Khosrokhavar and Roy 1999: 251). This makes them attractive to employers, especially in low-status jobs at the bottom of the economic ladder (construction, road maintenance, excavation and canalization, quarrying, brick production, abattoirs, tanning, caretaking and security, agricultural labor, and so on).

Few Afghans can ever hope to settle in the Islamic Republic with their family. Rather, there is a to-and-fro movement of individuals in search of work opportunities that the war closed to them in Afghanistan. The Afghan migration to Iran therefore has many elements of work migration, but it cannot be explained without reference to the insecurity prevailing in Afghanistan since the late 1970s.

Isolated on the international stage, Iran has been neither as able nor as willing as Pakistan to accept refugee aid (HCR 1997; Colville 1998). There are a few official camps that the UNHCR can visit (containing not only Afghan refugees but also Iraqi Kurds, for example), as well as expulsion centers for people who have been arrested and convicted. According to UNHCR estimates, only one per cent of Afghans in Iran live in camps (HCR 1997: 4); most are scattered through Iranian society, often in small teams of workers who move around from one building site to another. Three scenarios may be distinguished:

Persons who arrived before 1992 have been given prima facie recognition as refugees (approximately 850,000): they have a permit entitling them to move around without special permission, to live in Iran as a family, to work and to use the health and education services.

After the fall of Najibullah (1992), Afghans no longer received refugee status (the reasons for their departure being then seen as mainly economic). Eventually, the Iranian authorities agreed with the UNHCR to issue some 550,000 temporary permits with a validity up to 1995. (They are now invalid, therefore, and the individuals in question have to be careful moving around the country.)

Some 300,000 to 400,000 Afghans have come to Iran officially—whether to visit relatives, to carry out a pilgrimage, or to receive medical care—and remained after their visa expired. This is a highly mobile group about which the UNHCR has little information, similar to the numerous Afghans who enter Iran illegally.[4]

Most of my informants had none of the papers just mentioned. Like other Afghans, the majority of Hazaras from Jaghori use special networks to enter Iran illegally (see chapter 6) and then stay a few years before returning to Afghanistan. It is not uncommon for them to make a series of trips. The only papers they have are refugee identity cards issued by the Hezb-e wahdat or another of the Afghan resistance parties, which often prove sufficient when they are checked by the Iranian police.

An issue of the Iranian magazine *Goft-o-gu*[5] gave the following breakdown for Afghans living in Iranian cities: Zahedan: 33%; Yazd: 14%; Kerman: 10%; Bandar Abbas: 9%; Tehran: 3% (Goft-o-gu 1996: 44–45). Men are in a clear majority: 71.2% against 28.8% for women (Goft-o-gu 1996: 26).[6] According to Khosrokhavar and Roy, "68% of the Afghan workers are aged between 15 and 35 [. . .] the great majority are illiterate (81%) and 75% [. . .] have laboring jobs" (1999: 250; see Goft-o-gu 1996: 26). The age distribution is skewed towards people between 20 and 40, and 65% of Afghans in Iran are unmarried.[7]

According to one of the articles in this magazine, Afghans have a bad reputation among Iranians and only 20% of people interviewed in Tehran knew that Afghans spoke the same language as themselves; 65% said that they came across Afghans only in public areas (Goft-o-gu 1996: 25–31). Another survey reported that, despite their difficult living conditions, Afghan women used their time in Iran to broaden their horizons. The Iranian model helped them to emancipate themselves (Goft-o-gu 1996: 33–40; HCR 1997: 15). Nowhere in this issue of *Goft-o-gu* is there mention of any difference between Shiites and Sunnis among Afghans. Iranians do not seem make a clear distinction between Hazaras who share their religious affiliation and other Afghans.

Contrary to Sliwinski's assumption (1989: 46), Pashtuns appear to be a minority among Afghans living in Iran, with Tajiks, and especially Hazaras, proportionately more numerous than in Pakistan or even Afghanistan (Centlivres 1994a: 15, 16). According to some unofficial estimates by UNHCR workers, a third to a half of all Afghans in Iran are Hazaras. In summer 1996, nearly five hundred people from Dahmarda were in the Islamic Republic—that is, roughly 10% of the total population of the *qawm*, but a sixth to a seventh of the *manteqa*. They formed only twenty complete households, so that approximately 350 workers were there without their family. Forty members of the Dawran lineage were living in Tehran at that time.

It is necessary to situate Iran's Afghan policy in relation to the string of collapses and modest upturns that have marked the evolution of its economy. The informal sector has continued to blossom in spite of, or thanks to, all these crises, and it is often there that Afghans manage to find a place for themselves. For, despite the high unemployment, the Iranian economy needs the help of these immigrant workers, who put up with low wages and have a reputation for hard work. In 1994–95, their labor contributed 4.4% to an Iranian GNP of $161 billion (Goft-o-gu 1996)—or, in other words, a sum greater than $7 billion.

At a political level, the Islamic Republic has not been as involved as Pakistan in the Afghan crisis. In the 1980s, the special geopolitical context of war with Iraq and a US embargo meant that its leaders did not want to make the situation worse by alienating the Soviet Union as well; their political support to Shiite factions was therefore discreet and varied with the international circumstances. During the 1990s, however, Hezb-e wahdat enjoyed excellent relations with Tehran and received from it both financial and military support. It had offices in the main cities, such as Tehran and Mashad, issued membership cards and periodically intervened with the authorities to halt an expulsion order.

Iran's attitude to Afghan refugees has been much more repressive than Pakistan's. In an attempt to control the situation, the Iranian police and army keep close watch along the Pakistani frontier for illegal immigrants, drug traffickers and assorted smugglers. Even though it is true that the frontier has historically been less porous than the Durand Line between Afghanistan and Pakistan, theirs is certainly a difficult task. The desert and mountainous terrain of Baluchistan and Khorasan favor the illegal networks run by local people (see chapter 6).

However serious the Iranian efforts to control illegal activity, one sometimes has the impression that the authorities are playing a game of cat and mouse. On the one hand, the country has needed Afghan manpower (especially during the Iran-Iraq war and the ensuing reconstruction), but the government also wants to avoid a Pakistani-style situation and takes various steps to discourage integration and long-term residence. This complicated policy, whose frequent shifts are not directly linked to Iran's relations with Afghanistan, leads to a degree of arbitrariness that is ruinous to the morale of the Afghans. Repression alternates with periods of much greater tolerance. Although Afghans can easily find a job, and are accepted as workers, they generally do not feel secure enough to settle down with their families in Iran. "The state and the general population see the Afghans as strange and disturbing neighbors, ignoring everything they have in common with them as regards language and religion" (Khosrokhavar and Roy 1999: 254). Afghans are exposed to the disdain, open hostility or even racism of the Iranians.

Some populist forces in Iran try to make it appear that there is a link between the number of unemployed and the number of Afghans. This may make expulsions more likely, although a new outbreak of fighting inside Afghanistan has sometimes caused moves in that direction to be halted. Take the situation in spring 1996, for example. Rumors began to spread among the Quetta Hazaras that the Iranian authorities had announced their intention to send back 200,000 to 250,000 Afghans. Tensions mounted as it became more and more difficult to enter Iran illegally; police checks grew tighter and many Afghans who lacked the necessary papers were expelled. In June, Tehran responded to UNHCR pressure by agreeing to relax its position on Afghan refugees and to halt the expulsions. But in summer 1998 a new hardening of policy led to a wave of arrests, especially in the capital. It may be that this shift was due to irritation among Iranian leaders at political and military events inside Afghanistan (the fighting around Maymana, then the fall of Mazar-e Sharif and the killing of Iranian diplomats by the Taliban). In the winter of 1999–2000, the authorities of the Islamic Republic announced that they intended to regularize the position of illegal immigrants, while also beginning a program of voluntary repatriation. This did not work, and a toughening of policy followed on several occasions.

The climate of suspicion and police controls makes any ethnographic work especially delicate, as Afghans are constantly on their guard and feel even more cautious in the presence of a Westerner. On several occasions, a person with whom I had made contact refused to see me, on the spurious grounds that I had been given the wrong address or telephone number.

The close relations between Hezb-e wahdat and the Iranian government scarcely help to improve the daily lives of Hazara migrants. The authorities pose a real threat to illegal immigrants. Thus, the uncle of one of my informants was arrested in Zahedan and is thought to have died soon afterwards as a result of abuse in prison. Rumors fly around, and not everything that is said is necessarily true, but this itself illustrates the atmosphere of tension and mistrust between Afghans and Iranians and the fear that the authorities inspire among migrants and refugees.

Since the international coalition led by American forces intervened in Afghanistan causing the fall of the Taliban in late 2001, life conditions of Afghans in Iran further deteriorate. The authorities have increasingly been implementing a policy to limit their number in the Islamic Republic and to push them back, arguing that their home country is now peaceful. Regulation of the labor market became stricter. Police controls building sites and factories, and employers hiring illegal Afghan workers are severely fined. Welfare facilities (in education and health sectors) are progressively withdrawn. Under pressure, several hundred thousands Afghan refugees and migrants decided to repatriate.

EMPLOYMENT STRUCTURES

In Iran, by contrast to Pakistan, people originating in the same part of Afghanistan cannot appoint a representative to intercede on their behalf with the local authorities; nor can there be neighborhood associations of

Afghan workers who are constantly moving around from one building site to the next. In such a context, employment networks play a key role, as certain enterprising and competent individuals are promoted to take charge of a work team. As in the coal mines of Quetta, the foreman is usually an Afghan himself and has responsibility for the hiring of workers. The Iranian employer allows him considerable leeway and, so long as things are running smoothly, does little to intervene in the everyday organization of work. The workers form temporary groups around a central personality, and it is the relations of each individual with that figure which are decisive. The members of the team do not necessarily know one another, since the sources of the relationship with the foreman may be sociologically diverse: paternal kinship (*qawm, kâkâxel*), maternal kinship (*mâmâxel*), kinship through marriage (*xeš*), neighborhood circle in the village of origin, and so on.

Families always try to have one of their members in Iran as a means of financial support. Whenever an Afghan goes there, he has good chances of finding a job through a relative or neighbor; he can also be sure that someone will pay the debt he contracted to fund his journey to Iran (see chapter 6). As this is much more expensive than the trip from Hazarajat to Quetta, ordinary laborers, unlike traders, spend much longer periods in the Islamic Republic—rarely less than a year, often much more. But migration is not due only to economic need; it is also a kind of rite of passage to adulthood through which young men spread their wings and prove themselves. The men in Dahmarda usually go to Iran once before they marry, so that they can save something for wedding expenses and gain some experience of living away from the parental home.

The case of Mohammad Ali, brother of Mardan Ali, may serve to illustrate the structures of employment in Iran. He is the foreman in a Tehran construction company that specializes in the production of friezes, window-frames and stucco doors. He hires the workers, while the Iranian boss is happy to confirm his choice and to pay him a lump sum for the work. Mohammad Ali then distributes this sum among the members of his team. During my stay in spring 1996, the team consisted of a group of six Hazara workers: Mohammad Ali himself, Mohammad Husayn, his cousin (FBS), Mohammad Jawad, Ghulam Ali, Ahmad and Sakhi. The first four were from Dahmarda, the last two from Dawud. It was late April and the summer months were approaching—the high season for construction work. A lot of people were coming and going. Mohammad Ali's team was recomposed several times in less than a month, as he successively took on two new workers: Mohammadullah and Ali Mohammad (the latter being the younger brother of Mohammad Jawad, who was already employed there).

It was a complicated chain of relations, as everyone was related to at least one other member of the team.

Mohammad Ali was 27 or 28 years of age. He left Dahmarda for the first time in 1982, before his fifteenth birthday, and spent two and a half years in Quetta and one year in Iran. Between 1986 and 1987 he again spent a year in Iran with his father. Then, after a year back in Dahmarda, he travelled a third time to Iran for a period of eleven months (1989), before returning to Dahmarda for another three years. He married in the mid-1980s, between his first and second trips abroad. When I met him in Tehran, he had been there since 1993. He had not yet seen his three-year-old daughter, who was born shortly after his departure.

Mohammad Husayn is the 20-year-old *bace kâkâ* (FBS) of Mohammad Ali. Being younger, as well as lower in the hierarchy, he says *kâkâ* (FB) to Mohammad Ali, who answers by calling him *bace kâkâ;* the terms they use to address each other are therefore not symmetrical. Still unmarried, Mohammad Husayn has been living in Tehran for a year and a half, having previously spent a year and a half there with his elder brother Mohammad Hasan.

Mohammad Jawad is also a Dawran, but he does not come from the hamlet of Chaghl-e Sang. One of his sisters is married to Mohammad Yusuf, the *bace kâkâ* (FBS) of Mohammad Ali and Mohammad Husayn. He is 25 years old, and this is his third time in Iran. He first went there in 1989 and stayed for four years; then he returned for eight months to Dahmarda, before spending another two years in Iran. There followed six more months in Dahmarda, during which his wedding took place. He returned to Iran in the late winter of 1995–96, but he no longer thought of staying for more than one year. His periods there have tended to grow shorter with age.

Ahmed is 21 and was born in Dawud. At the age of ten he went to Iran with his elder brothers, and since then he has only been back to Jaghori for one nine-month period. He has found work with his relative Mohammad Ali, being from the same lineage as his paternal grandmother, mother and wife—quite a typical case of repetitive marital unions over several generations. (He addresses Mohammad Ali as *xwâr-zâda,* ZS/FZS.) Ahmad's father is also the *bace kâkâ* (FBS) of the paternal grandfather of Mohammad Ali's wife; they themselves skirt round the women's role by explaining that *padar-e Ahmad bace kâkâ-ye padar-e xosur-e Mohammad Ali* ("Ahmad's father is the paternal cousin of the father of Mohammad Ali's father-in-law").

Sakhi is 20 and also from Dawud. His mother comes from the same lineage as Ahmad, and therefore the same as Mohammad Ali's mother and wife. He is also the *bace mâmâ* (MBS) of the wife of Aziz Azizi, Mohammad Ali's younger brother. Curiously, given the difference in age and status,

Mohammad Ali and Sakhi address each other as *bola* (MZS)—a symmetrical term for the sons of two sisters—and justify this by saying that their respective mothers come from the same lineage. On the other hand, since Sakhi's mother is from Ahmad's lineage and Ahmad is slightly older, Sakhi addresses her as *mâma* (MB). Sakhi has been in Iran for more than six years and plans on returning to Jaghori to marry. Throughout these years he has sent his savings back to his family in Afghanistan, through the *hawâladâr* services in his village (see chapter 7). He has been working with Mohammad Ali only for the last two weeks, having previously lived in Arak, 250 kms south-east of Tehran. He telephoned various relatives, friends and neighbors to ask if they could find him a job, and it was because of kinship links that Mohammad Ali agreed to employ him in his team without really knowing him in advance.

Ghulam Ali is the son of a fellow-worker of Mardan Ali's in the coal mines of Quetta. He is twenty-one and has been living in Tehran for three years. He originally comes from the hamlet of Chaghl-e Sang, like Mohammad Ali, but belongs to the lineage of the Basmanay. Mohammadullah, aged 23, is also a Basmanay from Chaghl-e Sang, the *bace kâkâ* (FBS) of Ghulam Ali's father. When I met him in April 1996, he had just arrived on his third trip to Tehran. Ali Mohammad, only just 15, is the younger brother of Mohammad Jawad; he had traveled with Mohammadullah and was in Iran for the first time.

Other people, such as Asef and Mohammad Yusuf from the Dawran lineage, regularly come on visits and occasionally even lend a hand. Asef, a 17-year-old Dawran from Dahmarda, is the *xosur-bura* (BW) of Mohammad Jawad; his father is the *bace mâmâ* (MBS) of Mohammad Husayn's father. He has been in Tehran for seven months, having spent three summer months in Dahmrada and two previous years in Tehran. He works in a private school, as caretaker, security guard and general handyman, earning 30,000 tomans ($75) a month. He has three brothers and four sisters: his two elder brothers have already been to work in Iran. At this moment, many relatives of his are in Tehran: one *kâkâ* (FB), three *bace kâkâ* (FBS), two *dâmâd* (ZH) and a number of more distant ones such as Mohammad Ali and Mohammad Husayn.

In the late winter of 1995–1996 Mohammad Yusuf, the *bace kâkâ* (FBS) of Mohammad Ali and Mohammad Husayn, came to Tehran with Mohammad Husayn's mother. She stayed a month and then returned to Quetta to live with her daughter and son-in-law, Husayn Bakhsh. Mohammad Yusuf remained in Tehran and found work in a building firm with a cousin of Asef's. Being also a *hawâladâr,* he makes use of his time there to visit workers from Dahmarda and collect the money they have saved (see chapter 7).

Safdar Khan, the *kâkâ* (FB) of Asef, is also the *bace mâmâ* (MBS) of Mohammad Husayn's father. Although they belong to the same lineage, Mohammad Husayn addresses him as *mâmâ* (MB) and not *kâkâ* (FB). In this particular case, the relationship through the women is not covered up. Safdar Khan has been in Tehran for two years, and, if the situation in Dahmarda returns to normal after the violent winter of 1995–96, he intends to return there soon. He is foreman in an Iranian building firm that employs

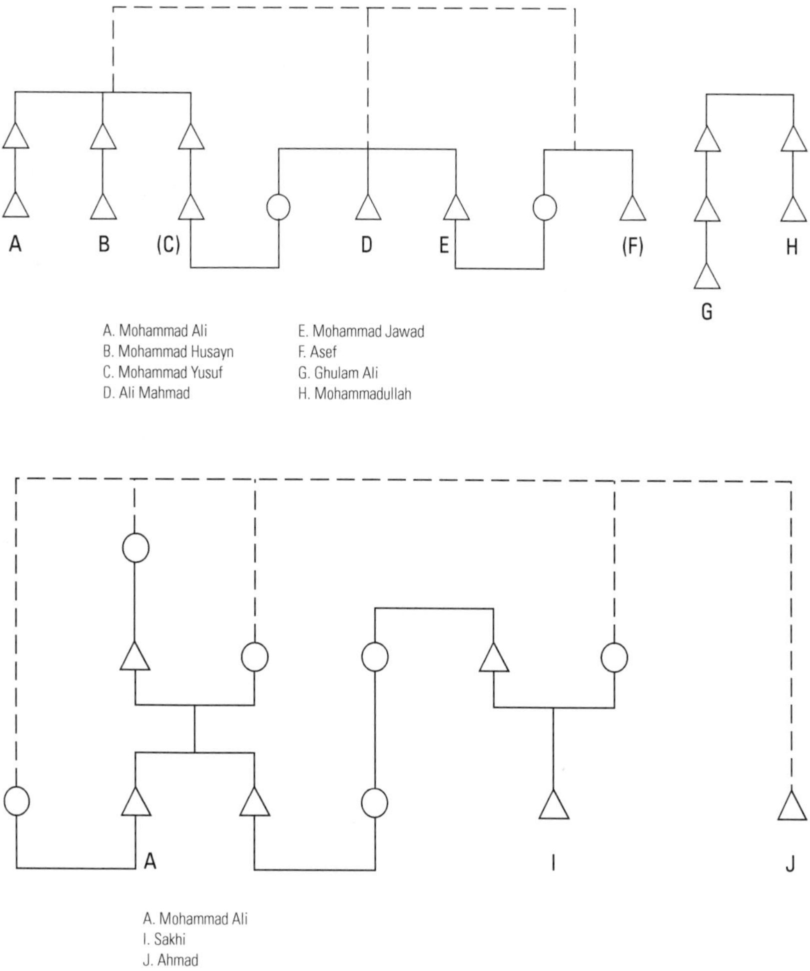

Figure 7: Kinship relations among the members of Mohammad Ali's work team

twenty Hazara workers (mainly from Dahmarda and Anguri, but also from Jaghori and Malistan), as well as a few Tajiks. Rather symptomatically, all the Hazara workers sleep in the same large room, while the Tajiks have a bedroom of their own. Safdar Khan has a refugee card that is no longer valid. All it mentions are his first name, his family name (Afghans create these ad hoc, as they usually do not have one), his date of birth (also often invented, as Afghans only have a vague idea of their age), the date and place of issue, a number and the administrative stamps.

Safdar Khan first came to Iran on a pilgrimage in the 1970s, in the time of Mohammad Reza Shah. He worked for a long time in Kandahar for an American electricity company, and was there at the moment of the Communist coup in April 1978, while his family was living in Dahmarda. He fled to Iran through Nimruz province, and since then has divided his time between Iran and brief visits to Dahmarda (he has never spent a long period in Quetta).

This team of workers has two sub-groups, each linked to the person of Mohammad Ali, the foreman and person responsible for the hiring of labor: (1) people from Dahmarda who are members of his lineage (Dawran) or who live in the same hamlet as himself (Chagl-e Sang); and (2) people originally from Dawud who are related to his mother in one way or another. In other words, the groupings around Mohammad Ali are on the basis of patrilineage, kinship through the mother (or women more generally) and residential proximity.

Afghans abroad form groups together, and the employment networks anyway make this a necessary strategy. In the case in question, it is Mohammad Ali who, as team leader, is responsible for the quality of work, hires workers as they are needed, keeps attendance lists and communicates with the Iranian boss. The latter hands over to him all the wage money, which he then distributes among the members of his team. His responsibilities mean that he earns 2,300 tomans (roughly $5.75) a day, compared with 2,000 tomans ($5) for a skilled mason and 1,200 tomans ($3) for an unskilled worker. All members of the team have agreed that Mohammad Husayn—who spent two months in hospital and is unfit to work after a bad fall from the sixth floor of a building—should continue to receive his wage. As they live on site, sleeping and eating in simple accommodation provided by the company, they spend little and have no bills for rent, water or electricity. During my stay in 1996, I shared their spartan accommodation—less than 10 sq. meters—on the second floor of a building under construction; the room contained nothing other than four metal boxes, a few suitcases, mattresses and blankets, a small black-and-white television, a few photographs on the walls (I could recognize Mohammad Hasan, Akram Ali and Mohammad Husayn; Mohammad Ali; and so on), and some nails on which to hang their clothes. My informants preferred this crowding to isolation (they did not like to sleep alone in a room). The only water point, a pipe jutting out from a bare brick wall, was in the basement; the toilets consisted of a hole in the basement, curtained off with pieces of hessian. The team members took it in turns to cook. A team of Iranian Lurs were living on the ground floor of the same building. But the two teams did not sleep or eat together, and did not seem to be on very friendly terms. The Hazaras looked down on the others, considering that their own work (the making of friezes for the facade) was artistically superior to the building work performed by the Iranians; while the Iranians thought of the Afghan workers as a bunch of peasants. People from different backgrounds did not tend to mix, even when they were fellow-Afghans.

Practical links among members of the work team (not necessarily known to one another before) were organized around the foreman and remained dependent on that context. On the other hand, festivities gave rise to meetings of a more official nature, when the *qawm* functioned as the significant level. Bourdieu's distinction between official kinship and practical kinship was in evidence here: the former, based on an abstract geographical definition of groups that legitimated a social order, came to the fore at certain highpoints of social life; the latter, arising out of everyday strategies, consisted in the relations actually deployed for the ordinary needs of existence (Bourdieu 1972: 78, 83, 1980: 279, 282–284). The *id-e qorbân* meal that I attended in Tehran in 1996 provided striking testimony of this distinction. Sakhi and Ahmad did not join the group but went off to find other people from Dawud. As to Mohammadullah and Ghulam Ali, the only members of their lineage in Tehran, they took part in the festivities of their neighbors from Dahmarda. Despite this exception, however, the great feast of *id-e qorbân* is a real opportunity to express the symbolic primacy of the lineage over the work relationships. On that day, eighteen people gathered in a room measuring 6 to 7 sq. meters: there were fifteen Dawran, two Basmanay from Chaghl-e Sang and a foreign ethnolographer.

Unlike work relationships and employment structures, such festivities bring paternal kinship to center stage. Another highpoint comes with *moharram,* which provides an opportunity for everyone from Dahmarda to meet one another on a wider basis, to catch up on the latest news from the "homeland," but also to keep informed about work opportunities in Iran, dangers on the migratory routes and the general situation in Afghanistan.

HAZARA FAMILIES BETWEEN IRAN AND AFGHANISTAN

Available figures are not very reliable but, as we have seen, only a third of the Afghan immigrant population in Iran live in a family situation in the mid-nineties—a proportion that also seems to apply among the Hazaras. In 1996 there were approximately 350 workers from Dahmarda in Iran but only twenty families (between 120 and 150 individuals, or 25–30% of the Dahmarda immigrant population). Only two or three such families were living in Tehran; there were more in Qom, a holy city and university center on the edge of the desert, 150 kilometers south of the capital, which houses the tomb of Masumeh, sister of Imam Reza (the eighth Shiite imam, who is himself buried in Mashad).

Let us take the example of Ali Husayni, a 30-year-old Dawran from Dahmarda. He has been living in Qom with his family for a number of years, in a stylishly converted house. As a student of theology and calligraphy, he was able to obtain a residence permit and a grant of 20,000 tomans (approx. $50) a month. Despite these privileges, however, Husayni admits that he has very few relations with Iranians. A brother in Kuwait sends him money, as he cannot manage on his grant alone. At the time of my visit, seven people were living with him: his mother, his wife, their little daughter, a sister, a nephew (the son of his elder brother, who lives in Quetta), and the wife and daughter of the brother in Kuwait. Although he cannot cope financially with all the related expenses, his official status in Iran allows him to house several close relatives in good conditions and to ensure that the boys and girls receive an education.

Mohammad Husayn's *mâmâ* (MB), Hamid, also lives in Qom. A Wafa from Dahmarda now into his fifties, he has been living in Iran since the mid-1980s. Unlike Ali Husayni, he does not have official residence papers, but he brought his family over in 1989 and was able to move into a house with a deposit equivalent to $1,500. Eleven people live under the one roof: Hamid and his wife, their eldest son, his wife and baby, two younger sons and four unmarried daughters. Hamid admits that it is fairly easy to make a living in Iran: he works for a building firm and receives a wage of 50,000 tomans (approx. $125) a month. But he complains of the insecurity and the constant risk of expulsion.

Afghans in Iran are like a society under siege; their relations with Iranians are very limited. Most migrants get used to this, as their reason for being there is to work and send money to Afghanistan. But the families feel the pressure more acutely, as the precariousness of the situation places an obstacle in the way of any future plans in Iran.

Most of the Hazara families living in the Islamic Republic come from the humblest sections of the population. Often landless farmers, they saw their lives deteriorate under the impact of a war that made them particularly vulnerable both socially and economically. With nothing much to lose, they made the decision to migrate en bloc to Iran—but the numerous irritations and the impossibility of settling down persuaded many families to return to Afghanistan, though not to their home district where they would be unable to buy any land. Their meagre savings from the time abroad enabled some to purchase a piece of land and build a house around one of the urban centers (especially in Herat and sometimes Mazar-e Sharif, but not in the uncertain Kabul of the 1990s). Thus, one comes across many Hazara settlements around Herat, in Jibra'il, Noqra or Baba Ji, as well as towards Kolâb and Gozârgâh.

In September 1996 I visited the village of Jibra'il, north-west of Herat City. Its appearance reminded me of Brewery in Quetta: gently sloping ground above the city, more or less cultivated plots between houses with thick high walls, an occasional shop side by side with its owner's home. The area underwent major development in the early 1990s and now houses nearly a thousand Hazara families.

Ahmad Jaffari, an important mullah in the village, originally came from Behsud. He spent eight years in Iraq during the time of Zaher Shah (before 1973), settled in Kabul and then, shortly after the Communist coup of 1978, left for Mashad and spent the next sixteen years in Iran. In 1995, when fifty Hazara families from various backgrounds with whom he had been in contact were issued with expulsion orders, he grew tired of the endless difficulties and accompanied them back to Afghanistan. This group of several hundred people eventually settled in Jibra'il.

Jalal Alemi followed a similar trajectory. Originally from Day Kundi, he settled in Herat in 1994 after spending fifteen years with his family in Iran. The family heads in Jibra'il named him *kalân-e qawm*, in the belief that, despite his poverty, the professional skills he had acquired in Iran stood him in good stead to deal with international organizations and NGOs over any local development issues (especially the construction of wells).

The population of Jibra'il mainly consists of landless families who have spent a long time in Iran. Their diverse origins (Ghor, Behsud, Jaghori, Malistan, Day Kundi, Shahristan, etc.) favored the emergence of new forms of power and a certain degree of politicization; the most distinguished members of the community, such as Jaffari or Alemi, are members of Sheykh Asef Mohseni's organization, the Harakat-e islami.

Baba Ji is inhabited by three hundred families of Hazara *mohâjerin* originally from all parts of Hazarajat, including a dozen families from Jaghori. Only a few of these own any land in Hazarajat. The *kalân-e qawm* of this community, 38-year-old Safar Maqsudi, comes from Baba (Jaghori); he has only been in Herat for one year, having bought a little land to build a house there. He spent fourteen years in Iran (Mashad) with his family, which now consists of two wives, eight sons and one daughter. He also owns 15 *jerib* in Jaghori, looked after by *dehqân* who, as is the custom, keep a quarter of the harvest. Maqsudi goes there quite regularly to sell his share of the agricultural produce. Thus, unlike most of the Hazaras who settled in Herat after leaving Iran, he is a fairly well-off man with various sources of income: his family lands in Jaghori; the carpet-making trade that his children learned in Iran; a little commerce (he has set up a shop next to his house and sells goods there that he has bought in town); day-laboring jobs; and his *kalân-e qawm* activities which, though unpaid, bring him some benefits.

In 1996, the Taliban were causing few problems for the Hazaras in Herat, who for their part were trying to keep relations with the Taliban to a minimum. Among the families who left Iran, there was a fortunate minority who did not want to return to the harsh living conditions in Hazarajat and were hoping to diversify their sources of income, and a landless majority who had no means of subsistence or economic prospects of any kind in Hazarajat. In both cases, their migratory circuits set them apart from most of the Hazaras bound for Iran.

Since the end of 2001, the families are the first victims of the deterioration in the situation of Afghans in Iran. More vulnerable than simple workers who move from one labor site to another, they strongly feel the pressure of authorities and many have decided to repatriate benefiting from a modest UNHCR assistance. Often landless, they face the difficult choice to settle down in the Afghan countryside, where the drought and the demographic growth render every return problematic, or in urban centers, where economic perspectives are gloomy. Their massive repatriation may not be a sustainable solution and they will possibly undertake further displacements in the following years.

AN OVERVIEW OF THE HAZARA MIGRATION

My travels from Quetta to Hazarajat and Iran allowed me to study at both ends the migratory networks used by my informants. In spring 1996, I met in Tehran many people I had first encountered in Dahmarda in the autumn of 1995 or come across in Quetta (for example, Mohammad Yusuf and Mohammad Jawad). By following the itineraries of several individuals, I could reconstitute the migratory contacts and multilocal family networks of people from Dahmarda, especially those of Mardan Ali's close relatives—I met his two brothers and three living *bace kâkâ* (FBS)—and other kin. The fragmented settlement of members of the group had its corollary in a fragmentation of my research locations. My trips gave me a clear idea of living and working conditions in the various places where the members of an enlarged kinship group had settled. I was therefore able to see for myself the respective advantages and disadvantages of Hazarajat, Quetta and Iran.

Afghanistan is a devastated country. War, poverty and the lack of schools and hospitals are all major handicaps. Yet the cost of living is low, even though all manufactured goods have to be imported from Pakistan or elsewhere. My informants have their family ties and lands in Afghanistan; the women, children and old people remain there. People live there among their own; the women are not isolated. This makes it possible for a lot of men to leave their family in Hazarajat when they go to Pakistan or Iran; women such as Mardan Ali's wife often actually prefer rural life, which leaves them greater freedom and means that they do not have to stay indoors all the time.

Disorganization and corruption are widespread in Pakistan, but by the same token there is great freedom of movement. Hazaras can easily obtain a Pakistani identity card or even a passport. Quetta is a central location for the migratory networks of the Hazaras. In a sense, it is the capital of the Hazaras—or, at any rate, of those originating in Ghazni province and elsewhere in southern Hazarajat with whom I mainly worked. The town serves as a stopover, an assembly point and a place of refuge. If expulsions are under way in Iran, or if there is major fighting in Hazarajat, people know that there will always be a relative to welcome them in Quetta. Trade flows and human movement in both directions add up to an intense migratory continuum. On the other hand, the capital of Pakistani Baluchistan offers scarcely any occupational outlets other than the coal mines and retail trade. As the Hazara have spent very little time in refugee camps, humanitarian aid has been much less important for them than for the other Afghan communities.

Iran presents a striking contrast with Pakistan. Indeed, one might almost say that the situation there is the opposite. Many Hazaras have an ambivalent perception of the country—a mixture of love, admiration, frustration and even hatred. On the one hand, they complain of the contempt in which Iranians hold them, and seek cold comfort by endlessly criticizing the bread in Iran as opposed to Quetta or Hazarajat. On the other hand, they admire the great Shiite neighbor for its cleanliness, organization and development, both technological and social (the roads are good, women work outside the home, etc.). Despite the veil, Iranian women have a freedom of movement that is lacking in Quetta or Hazarajat; they go out alone in the towns, have access to jobs and education, and are entitled to vote and to stand in elections. Many Hazaras admire these progressive aspects and are aware of their importance.

In Iran, it is easy to find a relatively well-paid job by drawing upon family or tribal networks, but Afghans are mainly employed as unskilled workers and find that many activities are forbidden to them, while the constant danger of expulsion, harassment and police violence means that it is difficult for them to settle with their family on a permanent basis. They do not monopolize any sector of the local economy, nor is there the same continuum between immigrants and the locally born population that one finds among Hazaras in Pakistan. In Mashad, where the community is as old as Quetta's, Hazaras have not kept in touch with Afghanistan nor done much to welcome refugees.

Since Iran was unwilling to accept the kind of international aid that Pakistan allowed to be channelled to refugees, proper camps have been very thin on the ground. Countless stories circulate, however, about widespread physical abuse at the two infamous internment camps of Tal-e Syâh (near Zahedan) and Sang-e Safid (near Tahebat).[8] This is where Afghans are held prior to expulsion, after trying to cross the frontier illegally or being picked up without valid papers.

In Pakistan, then, there is great freedom of movement but limited economic activities, while in Iran the labor market offers numerous possibilities but living conditions generally remain precarious. The following table summarizes the respective advantages for Hazaras of Afghanistan, Pakistan and Iran:

Table 8: The locations of Hazara migration

	disadvantages	advantages
Afghanistan	war; insecurity; poverty	kinship and neighborhood relations, property, homeland
Pakistan	little stable employment	security; freedom of movement; seasonal jobs (mining); host community
Iran	official controls; repression; hostility	employment; wages

Although the Afghan migratory networks have acquired a transnational dimension, they seem to divide along ethnic lines: Pashtuns, Tajiks, Hazaras, Uzbeks and others rarely rub shoulders along the way. Too great a stress on the ethnic dimension does, however, mask the reality of the solidarity networks, which are usually organized around infra-ethnic aspects such as lineage, marital ties or residential proximity. Regional origin also often carries greater weight than ethnic affiliation. People from Logar or Herat, for example, may spend time together whether they are Pashtuns or Tajiks—and the same is true of Uzbeks, Turkmens and Tajiks from the north of Afghanistan. At the macrosocial level, three faultlines are especially visible: the gap between urban and rural populations; the tense relations between Sunnis and Shiites; and the mistrust with which minority groups view Pashtuns (the example of Logaris and Heratis would seem to be exceptional in this respect). At the microsocial level, the really operational solidarity groups are based on a set of overlapping criteria (kinship and residential proximity, but also religious affiliation, educational level, and so on), which cannot be simply reduced to the dimension of ethnicity, tribe or lineage.

PART THREE

THE FLOWS

Chapter Six

Forms and Strategies of Population Movement

MIGRATION AS AN EXISTENTIAL PRINCIPLE

Now that we have examined the social organization, solidarity structures and forms of cooperation among people from Jaghori in Hazarajat, Quetta and the urban centers of Iran, we must turn to consider the flows linking these places with one another. Here it is useful to distinguish: (1) the movement of persons and its cross-border organization; (2) the transfer of money and goods by workers to their country of origin; and (3) the circulation of information and the various methods of communication. These three complementary aspects will be analysed in successive chapters.

Since 1978, the political and military conditions in Afghanistan have made all movement difficult. The persistent insecurity, together with the destruction of most of the infrastructure, means that travel is a long and perilous undertaking. Numerous obstacles stand in the way of anyone wishing to go to Iran or the Arab Gulf states, while the West—a magnet for many city-dwellers and intellectuals (Centlivres 1995b)—is too remote a horizon for the rural population of southern Hazarajat. Nevertheless, the Hazaras and Afghans in general have established large-scale transnational circuits which barely call upon the services of international agencies or NGOs (Centlivres and Centlivres-Demont 1999b: 954).

Because of the war and the insecurity, it is usually small support groups which have been relied upon to organize the often large-scale relocation. As far as possible, Hazara *mosâferin* travel in groups of relatives and neighbors, and enter into relations with "strangers" (*begâna*) only when this is absolutely necessary to cross what some call the "Pashtun Belt" or the frontier between Pakistan and Iran. A study of how these population movements are organized will therefore throw light on certain cooperative structures and relationships of trust—and hence on the organization of social relations. For neither extended kinship nor ethnic affiliation alone can explain the ties of solidarity to be found among Afghans today.

Although migratory movements acquired an unprecedented scale during the war, they have existed for a long time in one form or another—and have remained in the memory of the Hazaras, as of other Afghan communities. Nor do they necessarily have the traumatic significance that is often attributed to them; individual mobility and the dispersion of families or mutual support groups are not experienced as destructuring phenomena in and of themselves. Today the lineage of the Dawran, for example, is spread around Dahmarda, Quetta and Iran, but has not for all that lost its cohesiveness. Seen through this migratory prism, the concepts of "economic migrant," "political refugee," "country of origin," "host country," "voluntary" or "forced" migration, or even "return," appear singularly reductionist. The fact is that all these categories overlap in the Afghan context, with its combined presence of political, cultural, economic and ecological factors.

A study of individual trajectories and family strategies shows that very few Afghans have not left their country at some point in the last twenty years, and also that very few have never returned for at least a short visit. The leaving and coming back (*raft o âmad*) has been constant. We are a long way from the figure of the refugee compelled to leave his or her homeland in the face of a towering threat, with the vague hope of one day being able to return. Afghans give different and usually plural reasons for their decision to migrate: perhaps an outbreak of fighting, a threat from a personal enemy, the danger of bombing or compulsory conscription; perhaps the search for work or opportunities to trade, the need for medical treatment, or the undertaking of a pilgrimage. My main aim here, however, is not to demonstrate these motives but to focus on the migratory circuits and the strategies developed by individuals and families. The movement in question, which provides an opportunity to see friends and relatives again, expresses the transnational character of the networks woven by people originating in Jaghori. Visits and personal favors create mutual obligations and permit the reproduction of social ties.

THE IMPACT OF THE POLITICAL-MILITARY SITUATION ON MIGRATORY ROUTES

During the years of war, population movements did not always take the same forms. A first period, from the coup of April 1978 to the Soviet withdrawal in 1989, was marked by repression at the hands of the Kabul regime and the Soviets but also by a degree of collaboration among resistance groups. People on the move could count on reliable places to stop over inside Afghanistan itself. Between 1989 and the fall of the Communist regime in April 1992, a wait-and-see period in which the various parties reorganized their relations with one another witnessed a rampant ethnicization of Afghan political life (Centlivres 1991; Glatzer 1998; Harpviken 1996; Roy 1993). Thus, shortly after the Soviet pull-out, violent conflicts pitted Hazara and Pashtun fighters against one another for several months in the areas bordering on Uruzgan, Zabul and Ghazni provinces; the fighting spread as far as the district of Jaghori, and caused a dozen of victims among the population of Dahmarda. In general, however, the inhabitants of Jaghori kept a *modus vivendi* with their Pashtun neighbors. Despite the hostilities between different factions, lorries and travellers continued to move between areas in the hands of the resistance, whereas they were unable to take the government-controlled road via Ghazni between Kabul and Kandahar.

Until the victory of the resistance, then, smaller roads served as the main communication routes for individuals and traders. People were able to reach Pakistan along tracks perpendicular to the highway that crossed the provinces of Paktika, Ghazni and Zabul. After the Soviet withdrawal and then the capture of the capital by the *mujâhedin* (April 1992), the alliance game grew more complicated and national and local processes did not always follow the same logic. Commanders belonging to parties opposed to each other in Kabul might cooperate at provincial level. In the region of Ghazni, there was a long history of conflicts but also of close relations between Hazaras and Pashtuns. For someone living in Dahmarda, Pashtun neighbors were potential enemies who could not be trusted, but who were nevertheless more familiar than the distant inhabitants of the Shomali or Panjshir valley.

In 1993 Hazaras could cross the Pashtun Belt thanks to an alliance between Gulbuddin Hekmatyar's Hezb-e islami and the Hezb-e wahdat, but it was dangerous to pass through Kandahar, where many commanders ran a veritable racket at the expense of travellers. The old Badini road (through the frontier district of Shamulzay, in Zabul province) was still widely used. Then the appearance of the Taliban in late 1994 considerably changed the situation, as their first action was to eliminate (often physically) local commanders in the Kandahar region—an initiative which benefited the Hazaras and helped to boost the popularity of the Taliban.

By 1995–96 the frontier and the through route were in the hands of the Taliban, who were in open conflict with the Wahdat, yet the Hazaras, by keeping a low profile, were still able to cross areas under Taliban control. The situation grew worse as the conflict intensified in 1997 and the Taliban imposed a blockade on Hazarajat.[1] After the fleeting Taliban occupation of Mazar-e Sharif, in May 1997, many of their fighters were trapped and slaughtered, and their systematic vengeance in August 1998 was directed especially at Hazaras living in the city.

The fall of Bamyan (apart from some pockets of resistance) to the Taliban in September 1998 further altered relations in the local area and region. Hazaras were again able to move around quite freely, although tension with Pashtuns remained high because of the massacres on either side. In Jaghori district, people adapted to the relatively discreet Taliban rule, a long history of interaction and compromise having made it easier to accept the military defeat. A few *mujâhedin* groups there had previously affiliated to the Hezb-e islami, a largely Pashtun-dominated party, and when the Wahdat had driven out these junior Hazara commanders in 1995 many of them had moved closer to the Taliban and acted as a screen for the local population.[2]

In Quetta, there were fewer travellers in 1995 than in 1993. People on the ground give different reasons for this. Some put it down to military events in Afghanistan, arguing that in 1993 the fighting was mainly concentrated in Kabul but that the opposite was the case in 1995; the capital was for a short time relatively peaceful following Massoud's victory (Dostum and the Wahdat had to abandon their positions there and the Taliban had also been driven back), whereas fighting flared up again in the rest of the country, especially in Hazarajat between the dominant section of the Wahdat and forces allied to Massoud. Others maintain that the change was due to difficulties experienced by Afghans in Iran and to the opening of a new road through Nimruz. Curiously, however, all my Hazara informants considered that in 1995 and 1996 (that is, before the major conflicts of 1997 between the Taliban and the newly formed Northern Alliance[3]) the Taliban made the roads safer between the Pakistani frontier and Hazarajat. It is therefore difficult to give a satisfactory explanation for the fall-off in the number of *mosâferin*.

According to the pattern of alliance and conflict among the various political and military factions, commercial and migratory routes cut a way through for themselves or, where necessary, made long detours around obstacles. In 1995, for instance, when the Salang road was closed because of conflict between Dostum and the Rabbani government, it was necessary to take the Shibar pass and later the Do-Ab-e Mikh Zarrin route to Doshi. In summer 1994, the week-long journey via Dara-ye Suf became the only way to get from Bamyan to Mazar-e Sharif, as the road through Doshi and Pul-e Khumri was closed because of fighting between the "government" (Rabbani and

Massoud) and the Shura-ye hamahangi (the Junbesh of Dostum and the Wahdat). The situation was then fairly calm in Hazarajat, and Bamyan was governed by an assembly drawn from parties opposed to one another at national level. In summer 1996, however, things turned around as the Wahdat sought to extend its control over pro-government pockets in Hazarajat (Akbari faction and Harakat-e islami); numerous skirmishes throughout the region led to the closure of both the Dara-ye Suf and the Balkhab route. The road through Shibar, Dara-ye Shekari and Doshi and on to Pul-e Khumri and Mazar-e Sharif became the only link between the north of the country and Kabul, although even that was blocked occasionally at Tala-wa-Barfak because of the high tolls demanded by local commanders. On one such occasion, in July 1996, an agreement was reached when I happened to be in the region; on July 29 I could see dozens upon dozens of lorries from Mazar-e Sharif resume their slow but steady course, mostly towards Ghazni via the Hajigak and Unay passes, and on July 31, as I was making my way back to Bamyan, I saw a line of at least fifty lorries coming in the other direction. It is always a hazardous and time-consuming business for them to pass each other on those mountain roads, and yet they are few and far between away from those main routes.

Squeezed by the Taliban, the Rabbani government and the Shura-e hamahangi eventually drew closer to each other. The Salang was then briefly reopened on August 29, 1996, but when the Taliban took Kabul the following September it again became impassable until the autumn of 2001. These repeated changes led to a multiplication of trade routes across highly uneven terrain. Large bazaars opened up in formerly isolated regions, whereas the towns underwent commercial and economic stagnation.

SEASONAL MIGRATORY CYCLES

In addition to these phases linked to political-military events, a seasonal migratory cycle means that the movement of people and goods is most intense in spring and autumn. Summer is the agricultural season in Afghanistan, as well as the time of the year when construction work reaches its peak in Iran. In winter, fewer jobs are available in Iran and many men take advantage of the slackening of agricultural activity to seek employment in the mines of Pakistan. Thus, in both summer and winter, most people remain where their plans have taken them, while spring and autumn are transitional periods in which the temperature is more agreeable. September is always a month of great calm, when the guests in the inns of Quetta are mostly traders from Hazarajat who have come to buy goods for their shops back home. October is the time when migrants throng the roads and wayside inns.

Migratory movements involve different sections of the Hazara population, depending on whether they are in the direction of Pakistan or Iran. As we have seen, the great majority of men heading for Iran are young and unmarried; they will stay there for a number of years. In the case of the mature heads of families who go to work in the mines of Quetta, we are speaking of recurrent migratory flows linked to the agricultural calendar: they leave Hazarajat after the September almond harvest and return in early spring to work in the fields. Apart from the special characteristics of the labor market, the relative proximity of Quetta explains why married men prefer to go there. They can keep in touch with events back home and, since they are responsible for their family's protection, can quickly return in case of necessity.

At the time of the Soviet occupation there was also another type of seasonal migration. Following the example of Mardan Ali from the Hezb-e islami, many Hazara *mujâhedin* spent the summer fighting in Afghanistan and the winter working in the coal mines of Pakistani Baluchistan.

Women keep in the background in the small world of the *mosâferin*, and never travel anywhere without a male companion. But, although they receive little public recognition, this does not mean that they play no role in the shaping of Hazara migratory strategies. Moreover, the reduced presence of men in their home villages allows women to overturn the usual division of tasks and, in many cases, to engage in normally forbidden agricultural labor.

MIGRATORY ROUTES WITHIN AFGHANISTAN

In addition to aspects of timing and traveller profile, the specific problems and dangers also lead to differences in how people actually move between Hazarajat and Quetta on the one hand, and Quetta and Iran on the other. Several routes are possible between Hazarajat and Iran.[4]

(1) In 1995 and 1996 most of my informants who left Hazarajat joined the Kabul-Kandahar road at Ghazni or in the vicinity of Jaghori and continued on to the Pakistani frontier (Spin Boldak, Wesh and Chaman); from Quetta they then made their way to Iran via Taftan, Mirjawa and Zahedan.

It was impossible to reach Kabul from the south between March 1995 (military defeat of the Wahdat and the Taliban setback at the hands of Massoud) and September 1996; the frontline cut the capital from the rest of the country. It was fairly easy to join the main road to Kandahar from the districts of Markaz-e Behsud, Behsud-Gardandiwal, Jalrez, Day Mirdad (Wardak province), Nawur, Jighatu, Qarabagh, Malistan and Jaghori (Ghazni province), or, further on, from the districts of Shahristan and Day Kundi (Uruzgan province) or Waras and Punjab (Bamyan province). Approach roads crossed the passes of Hajigak (between Bamyan and Behsud), Unay (between Behsud and Jalrez), Shatu (between Yakawlang and Punjab), Kirmu (between Lal-wa-Sarjangal and Punjab), or else via the Nawur highland plateau. Thus, three roads led to the southern fringes of Hazarajat: one via Jalrez to Maydan-Shahr, one between Dasht-e Nawur and Ghazni, and one through the district of Jaghori. It was along these routes that one found the most active bazaars, especially those of Anguri (Jaghori district, Ghazni province) and Syakhak-Sarcheshma (Jalrez district, Wardak province).

Once you were on the main highway linking Kabul to Kandahar, you were never very far from Hazarajat. Hazara *mosâferin* could eat and sleep at well-run Hazara inns along the way, where they felt safe in a region they saw as generally hostile. Quetta itself offered a welcome break in a long and perilous journey: there was always a relative to visit there, or some business to conduct.

Traffic was considerably lighter on other through-routes. People from Uruzgan, for instance (especially the districts of Kajran and Gezab), could pass down the valleys of the Helmand or its tributaries and then turn off towards Kandahar. But communal tensions were particularly high in that region,[5] and it had limited facilities for travellers, so that many preferred to make a detour to reach a busier road at Nawur or Jaghori.

(2) The route through Herat and Islam Qala to Mashad may seem the most direct (on the way to Tehran, for example). But, although some Hazaras took it in the opposite direction after being expelled from Iran, there are several reasons why it has never played as important a role as the Quetta route. Not only have the authorities of the Islamic Republic made it difficult for people to cross the Afghan-Iranian frontier; there are no good roads directly linking Hazarajat to Herat: Ghor province is generally undeveloped in this respect, while the route via Mazar-e Sharif becomes almost impassable west of Shibirghan. The road between Herat and Kandahar is certainly good in Afghan terms, but it does not have the facilities or the proximity to Hazarajat that the Kandahar–Ghazni route can offer.[6]

(3) The way from Delaram, which crosses Nimruz province and ends at Zabul in Iran, seems never to have been used by large numbers of Hazaras. The state of the road makes the going difficult, and no stopovers are considered safe in these regions inhabited by Pashtuns and Baluch.

(4) Another route to Iran passes through the Central Asian republics, either from Herat (via Torghundi) or from Mazar-e Sharif (via Hairatan and Termez), but Turkmenistan and Uzbekistan have tightly controlled frontiers that only businessmen, smugglers and political leaders are able to cross.
(5) The cross-country Badini route linking southern Hazarajat to Pakistani Baluchistan (through Shamuzlay district, Zabul province) used to be the most popular when the Soviet Army controlled the main roads, the trickiest moment coming when it was necessary to cross the Kabul-Kandahar highway that physically marked off the territory held by the resistance and the pro-Soviet government. But, after the fall of the Najibullah regime in April 1992 and the arrival of the Taliban in the winter of 1994–95, very few Hazara migrants continued to use it.

The most important of the other routes to Pakistan was the one from Kabul to Peshawar via Jalalabad and the Khyber Pass; further possibilities were to travel through Paktya province or to cross from Badakhshan or Kunar to Chitral. Kabul was linked to the north of the country by two main roads: one through Salang (mostly closed after 1992 because of conflict between Dostum and Masssoud, and then between Massoud and the Taliban), and the road through Shibar. Essential though these may have been for Afghanistan in general, they were of only marginal significance for the population at issue in this study.

It is hard to quantify the use of the various migratory routes, but the stories told by *mosâferin* as well as the large number of wayside *mosâferxâna* suggest that, beginning in the winter of 1994–1995, the great majority of Hazaras chose to travel via Ghazni or Jaghori and on through Kandahar to reach Quetta and the Iranian frontier. To the north, apart from the highway linking Ghorband to Doshi via Shibar and Dara-ye Shekari, there was only the long and bad road from Yakawlang to Herat via Lal-wa-Sarjangal, and another one from Yakawlang to Balkhab. A more recent route from the Bamyan valley to Dara-ye Suf appears mainly to have served the strategic purpose of directly linking the centers of the Junbesh and the Wahdat.

In the 1980s and 1990s, travel in Afghanistan was both difficult and dangerous. In Hazarajat, in particular,[7] the terrain was highly uneven and fighting was endemic among the various Shiite factions. Moreover, unlike Pashtuns, the Hazaras were cut off in the center of Afghanistan and had no direct access to an international frontier.

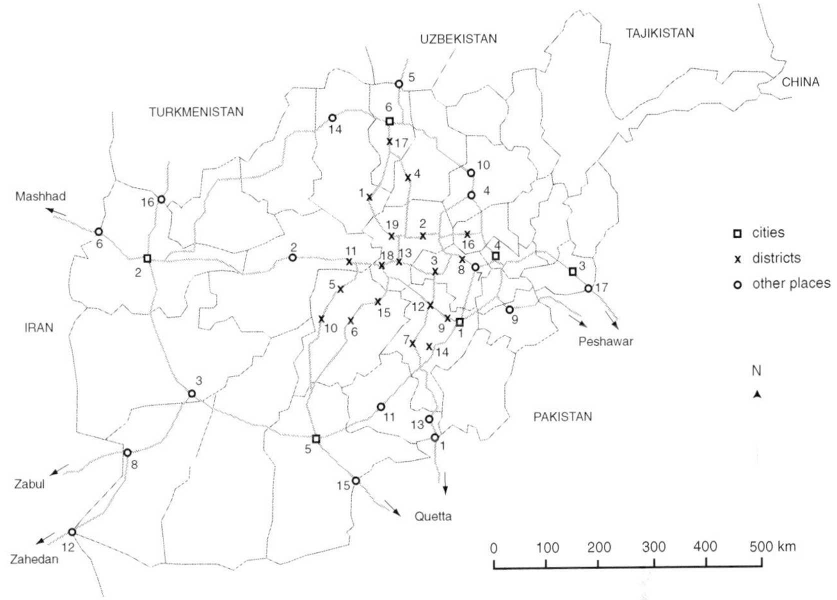

Key:

□ Towns:

1. Ghazni
2. Hérat
3. Jalalabad
4. Kaboul
5. Kandahar
6. Mazar-e Sharif

x Districts of Hazarajat:

1. Balkhab
2. Bamyan
3. Behsud (Gardandiwal, Markaz, Day Mirdad)
4. Dara-ye Suf
5. Day Kundi
6. Gezab
7. Jaghori; Malistan
8. Jalrez
9. Jighatu; Khwaja Omri
10. Kajran
11. Lal-wa-Sarjangal
12. Nawur
13. Panjab
14. Qarabagh
15. Shahristan
16. Sheykh Ali; Surkh Parsa
17. Sholgara; Char Kent
18. Waras
19. Yakawlang

o Other places:

1. Badini
2. Chaghcharan
3. Delaram
4. Doshi
5. Hairatan
6. Islam Qala
7. Maydan-Shahr
8. Nimruz (Zaranj)
9. Paktya (Gardez
10. Pul-e Khumri
11. Qalat
12. Robat
13. Shamulzay
14. Shibirghan
15. Spin Boldak/Wesh and Chaman
16. Torghundi
17. Torkham

Figure 8. Migratory routes in Afghanistan & Key to map of migratory routes in Afghanistan

The Hazaras feel ill at ease in the south of the country; the Pashtun Belt is more than a metaphor as far as they are concerned. Physical and other stereotypes abound there,[8] and a veritable 'popular anthropology' (Centlivres and Centlivres-Demont 1988a: 31–44) refers to countless little signs that are supposed to mark off members of the different communities. Shiites, for example, pray with their arms by their sides, whereas Hanafi Sunnis cross them on their chest—a difference that makes the religious affiliation of passengers visible when the vehicle on which they are travelling stops for prayer. Of course, a Shiite who feels threatened is allowed to practise *taqiya* ("dissimulation"), but others things such as his accent, headgear, attitude or general appearance may give him away.[9] This climate of mistrust encourages people to travel with others of the same origin, and to stay in the same places at stopover points on the journey.

Two political events, which both served to improve safety on Afghan roads, played a role in defining the migratory circuits: the fall of Najibullah in April 1992, and the emergence of the Taliban in October-November 1994.[10] In a first stage, both the Hezb-e wahdat and Hezb-e islami agreed jointly to open up the routes under their control, so that in summer 1993 Hazaras were able to cross the Pashtun Belt. There were then five intermediaries on the long route from Hazarajat to Iran. (1) The Wahdat representative in Ghazni, himself a Hazara; a *mosâfer,* by registering at the Party office, could benefit from the political agreements and the provision of infrastructure. (2) The lorry or mini-van driver, a Pashtun, who was personally responsible to the Wahdat and Hezb-e islami for ensuring that his passengers arrived safely in Quetta. (3) The Hazara manager (*ejâradâr*) of the *mosâfer-xâna* in Quetta, where migrants put up and planned the next stage of their journey. (4) The Hazara guide (*râhbalat*), a compulsory intermediary, who accompanied the groups of *mosâferin* to their journey's end in Iran. (5) The Baluch people-smuggler (*qâcâqbar*), who organized the crossing of the Pakistani-Iranian frontier and the last stage of the trip in Iran.

At that time the journey cost 45,000 afghanis (approx. $50) between Ghazni and Quetta, and 14,000 tomans (approx. $120)[11] between Quetta and Tehran. Usually those seeking to make the trip could not produce the whole sum: they might advance 20,000 afghanis, for example, and owe the remaining 25,000 afghanis. This debt was passed on from intermediary (1) to (5): the Wahdat representative would receive money from the driver for supplying him with customers; the driver would be paid by the manager of the *mosâfer-xâna,* who would in turn "sell"[12] the migrants to the *râhbalat* and the *qâcâqbar;* and, once the latter reached the final destination in Iran, the relatives of the *mosâferin* would become liable for the debts incurred at the beginning and for the stretch between Quetta and Tehran: that is, in our example, 25,000 afghanis and 14,000 tomans.

The migration specialists soon came into conflict with the Wahdat representative in Quetta, who wanted to make the procedure more official and to place it under Party control. In autumn 1993, however, he had to abandon his office in the *mosâfer-xâna,* and the following November the whole situation fundamentally changed. The attempted centralization through representatives from the different resistance groups lost its reason for existence, less than two years after the Wahdat had introduced it, as the Taliban arrival on the scene began to make roads more secure for travellers. In 1995 and 1996, Hazara migrants were bargaining directly with drivers of taxis, lorries and mini-vans over the journey between Afghanistan and Quetta. Despite the improvement brought by the Taliban, however, the constant threat of renewed fighting remained a problem for secure travel.

In autumn 1995, in the company of Mardan Ali who was going to join his family in Dahmarda, I covered in the opposite direction a route that the inhabitants of Jaghori had been taking to reach Quetta. For me it felt almost like an initiation: my first trip to Afghanistan, at last. The region was safer than in 1993 because of the Pax Talibana. And, despite the assassination of the charismatic Wahdat leader Abdul Ali Mazari in March of the same year, the Hazaras were benefiting from the improved security. The old Badini route was barely used, and *mosâferin* were taking the road through Kandahar.

Here is an extract from my field diary, dated October 9 and 10, 1995:

> *The crossing of the Pakistani-Afghan frontier at Chaman passed without incident. People were not even stopping as they came and went. Once inside Afghanistan, the only tangible sign of change is the driving on the right and a few white (Taliban) flags by the side of the road; there are no checks (I am almost disappointed). Everything seems quiet.*
>
> *Quite regularly between Spin Boldak and Kandahar, you see abandoned mud-brick houses: these are the checkpoints of former local commanders, who used to hold travellers for ransom and who have now been eliminated by the Taliban. Sometimes the carcass of a Soviet tank reminds you that it has not always been so peaceful here—and when we stop to eat a little before Kandahar the ground is strewn with cartridge cases from heavy machine-guns.*
>
> *In the period of the Soviets and the Communist government, the refugee streams used to flow across the sands of Registan, to the west of the road I am taking today, or else through the Katawaz mountains to Badini.*

[. . .]

In Kandahar there are no women in the streets and the men's heads are covered (white turbans, surely a recent Taliban-inspired fashion, are in abundance)—but things are scarcely different in Quetta. On the other hand, all the buildings bear signs of past fighting: virtually no windows are intact (they have been replaced with sheets of transparent plastic), and the walls are riddled from the impact of rockets and bullets. Yet the bazaar seems quite active and the shops sell all kinds of goods: plastic household items, bars of soap, shoes (a lot), packets of tissues, torches, padlocks, etc.

There are some vehicles: Toyota pick-ups, a few rickshaws and Volgas (old-fashioned Russian cars, taxis painted yellow and white), bicycles and, above all, Soviet-made lorries (Kamaz) as well as German ones (Mercedes-Benz, often still with their original insignia). A few men are in the streets, carrying a kalashnikov or a rocket-launcher—but the atmosphere is calm, almost sleepy.

Of course, the town has neither running water nor electricity: people use oil lamps for lighting. Mardan Ali and I spend the night at the Mirwais Hotel, near the Herat Gate in the west of town; its luxury surprises me—I think Mardan Ali chose a high-class establishment for Afghan standards—and there are even some iron beds as well as benches in the dining-room. A meal (a palao*) costs 3,000 afghanis (about $0.68) and a room for three people 2,500 afghanis (about $0.57). There are twenty-five rooms and sixty to eighty guests, two-thirds of them Pashtuns and a third Hazaras in transit.*

Neamatullah, the manager, is a Hazara from Sang-e Shanda (Maska, Jaghori). He pays a rent of 1,000,000 afghanis (around $230) to the Pashtun landlord. He keeps the room payment tally on a bit of cardboard torn from a carton of Seven Star cigarettes. Apart from managing the mosâfer-xâna*, he does a little dealing in petrol: it comes from Pakistan in metal barrels, and he takes it from there to Jaghori. He goes to Jaghori three or four times a year to see his family (he's afraid to bring them to live in Kandahar, although he says that for the time being the Taliban are not subjecting the Hazara to harassment).*

[. . .]

Apart from the Mirwais Hotel, the mosâfer-xâna *are concentrated around the Edgâh Gate (in the north of town) and are less luxurious. I count a total of four: the Anguri, Ettefâq, Jâghori and Pamir. The Anguri* mosâfer-xâna*, for example, can accommodate as many as a hundred travellers a night, sleeping rolled in their* patu *(blanket) on the ground; they do not pay for the night if they eat there (2,800 afghanis for a full meal, or roughly $0.64).*

Mardan Ali has a little difficulty organizing our journey to Jaghori. He approaches several people around these mosâfer-xâna; *they all seem to be Hazaras. Eventually he agrees with a certain Qodratullah (who has a Volga) for us to go from Kandahar to Anguri for a price of 40,000 afghanis (roughly $9) each. If I understand right, he comes from the same lineage as Mardan Ali's mother (from Dawud); Mardan Ali says to him* bace mâmâ *(MBS) (but I have a feeling that they did not know each other before). Qodratullah tells me that the journey will last around twelve hours . . .* inshâllâh!

[. . .]

We will have breakfast at the Pamir Hotel. The people and the faces are the same as in Quetta, but the setting is different. First of all, the teapots—like many other objects—are Russian-made. And then, the dining-room overlooks a wide avenue in a bad state of neglect: the lack of care for the green spaces, the decaying facades, all gives an impression of decrepitude. The room is huge. At the end, a fanciful mural painting depicts a landscape of lake and forest, as well as a Bavarian-Romantic castle (in the style of Neuschwanstein); there are pillars and cement platforms covered with carpets on which the guests sit cross-legged. A large, almost intact plate-glass window carries the inscription Pamir Hotel in several calligraphic styles. The owner's desk is turned away from the window to face the room.

The people pay no heed to my presence. Apparently, several of them take me for a Sayyed (presumably because of my fair complexion and my non-slanting eyes). Most of the guests here are Hazaras. They freely shout out to one another, exchanging pieces of information and personal impressions. The military situation is at the center of all the discussions: "Rabbani has announced that he's ready for war . . . It is said that Akbari is near Khalili and that the Hazaras have formed a united front . . . At last! Thank God!" The voices are not so loud when they talk of job opportunities and the quality of life in one place or another: "Where are you from?—From Quetta.—What do you do?—I'm in the coal mines.—Is it okay there?—Not bad!" Someone else says that there is no work in Pakistan . . . Mardan Ali, with his usual verve, retorts that there is a lot for those who are willing to get their shirt dirty, and then he asks the assembled company "ki kaldâr mexara?" *("who will buy some rupees?"). The* ejâradâr *offers him 112 afghanis per rupee, but Mardan Ali rejects this out of hand (he will get 138 in the street).*

Two Pashtuns are seated on the right, a little way off. Another arrives, sweeps the room with his eyes, then automatically walks towards them. People from the different ethnic groups do mix, it is true, but you can feel the mistrust. Mardan Ali's habit in the street is to make a very clear selection: when he asks for information, he goes up to people with "a

> *Hazara face." Afghans from the same region or the same ethnic group often address each other as* berâdar *(brother)—otherwise they will say* watandâr *(compatriot).*
>
> *The places where the* mosâferin *sleep and eat are also meeting-places where they can get all kinds of practical information about future migratory strategies as well as their immediate journey. When Hazara drivers come across each other on the road (whether they are driving a lorry, a small van, a jeep or a car), they readily stop to exchange a few quick words: "Is the Luman road open? Last week I heard there was fighting around there.—No, everything's calm now, but there's fighting higher up towards Nawur . . . it's best to take another way round."*

Whereas, in summer 1993, it took two nights and three days to travel from Quetta to Jaghori via Badini, in 1995 the same trip via Kandahar was taking less than two days. It would cost them roughly 60,000 afghanis ($14): 35,000 (approx. $8) between Kandahar and Hazarajat,[13] 10,000 (approx. $2.3) from Kandahar to the frontier, and 100 rupees ($3) from the frontier to Quetta. Most travellers spent the night in Qalat if they were coming from Quetta, and in Kandahar if they were coming from Hazardjat. They paid 3,000 afghanis ($0.68) for an evening meal and floor space for sleeping, and in addition there was the expense of anything they ate or drank along the way (a tea cost 500 afghanis, or $0.10).[14]

There were Hazara-run inns in all the main places along the way: that is (coming from Kandahar), Shahr-e Safa, Jaldak, Qalat, Gelan, then Moqur and Ghazni. Nearly all the bridges had been destroyed, and asphalt cover was usually no more than a memory on the terrible roads. Yet a lot of people were on the move—by lorry, mini-van, pick-up, jeep or car, or even bicycle—and there were also huge numbers of goods vehicles. Lorries heading for Pakistan carried crates of fruit, animal hides or old iron (originating in the former USSR), while in the opposite direction they brought wheat, flour, rice, tea, sugar and various manufactured items (fabrics, pots, plastic goods, etc.).

When the main roads were in the hands of the pro-Soviet government, a whole alternative world of communication routes and commercial centers took shape in formerly isolated regions. With its mountainous terrain and scant strategic importance, Hazarajat was relatively untouched by Soviet army incursions; it became criss-crossed with new roads, in a kind of late and temporary revenge for a region that had throughout history been geographically and economically marginal.

Anguri, the main southern gateway to Hazarajat, has a number of special advantages: it has mountain protection yet is close to the country's main communication routes, being the place where many secondary roads converge from Malistan or Nawur and, further afield, from Day Kundi, Day Zangi or even Behsud. Its bazaar grew through the long years of war into the one of the largest in Hazarajat, with several hundred shops in 1995. Anguri had seven *mosâfer-xâna* in October 1995, but the figure was constantly fluctuating as new establishments opened and others closed. The largest among them even had a generator that allowed them to generate electricity and to connect a television. Guests paid for their meal (3,000 or 3,500 afghanis for a *palao,* 300 or 500 for a tea), but not for the night's lodging as such. With all its equipment, the price of a large establishment might be as high as 20 million afghanis (a little over $4,500), while the annual rent on a small *mosâfer-xâna* hovered around 1,100,000 afghanis (approx. $250). As we have seen, the main trade was in spring and autumn: the relatively small Bâqowat Hotel, for instance, had between fifteen and forty guests a night in October 1995 and, according to the manager, a similar number in spring; but in mid-winter it was often empty and in summer there were rarely more than ten people staying there.

The bazaar at Sang-e Masha, the capital of Jaghori district situated a little to the north, had almost as many shops and *mosâfer-xâna* as Anguri, and many other bazaars were active in the region (Hutqol, Dawud-e Asiab, Dawud-e Ashia, Ghujur, Sang-e Shanda, etc.).[15]

Steeped in history, the former imperial city of Ghazni is today a dusty provincial capital, whose population of 35,000 includes a large number of traders who are constantly travelling around. The main Hazara commercial area was Ada-ye Qarabagh to the south-west of the city (in 1995 and 1996 it was held by Harakat-e islami which, though allied to the Rabbani national government, had no problem coexisting with the Taliban at local level), and here there were just under ten *mosâfer xâna*. Most of them had a good appearance, usually above a shop, and consisted of one huge room divided by pillars, simple floor carpets, posters of modern cities or green landscapes, a few holy images, the manager's desk, a window to communicate with the kitchen, separate partitions for families, and so on. At mealtime a long cloth was unrolled on the floor, which was also where the guests slept at night.

FROM QUETTA TO IRAN: THE SMUGGLING NETWORKS

Whereas the situation in Afghanistan made one think of a latent Hobbesian war of all against all, Iran presented the picture of a relatively strong state that did not hesitate to employ repressive means. Accordingly, the ways in which trips were organized between Pakistan and Iran were very different from those between Hazarajat and Quetta, where the role of smugglers was fading quite rapidly from the winter of 1994–1995 onward. Between

Afghanistan and Pakistan, the state of lawlessness paradoxically enabled a certain freedom of movement (when no fighting was taking place); between Pakistan and Iran, the main difficulties stemmed from the attitude of the Iranian authorities. It was the border crossing to Taftan that was the trickiest moment for *mosâferin,* and it was here that they turned to the services of professional smugglers. They swam in an illegality that was tolerated to a greater or lesser extent according to the period: the administrative and legal framework certainly allowed some special arrangements to be made, but a sudden crackdown was always to be feared.

The Islamic Republic has taken a much harder line than the Pakistani regime towards Afghan refugees, not to prevent them from coming to work but to maintain a degree of control over the clandestine immigration. An Afghan who wishes to work in Iran has two options:

(1) The official route is often long and tortuous. First, he has to obtain an Afghan passport if he does not already have one. Since, in 1995 and 1996, Kabul was hard to reach for someone living in Jaghori district, the only possibility then was to apply to the Afghan Consulate in Quetta (which was loyal to the Rabbani government rather than the Taliban), to hand over a fee of 1,000 to 1,500 rupees ($35 to $40), and to wait a month for the passport to be issued. The next stage was to ask for a visa at the Iranian Consulate—which took at least one to two months and cost a few dozen dollars more. Logically enough, the holder of an Afghan passport cannot obtain an Iranian visa in Pakistan unless he already has a valid Pakistani visa. (In reality, this condition—which was the cause of further delays—was fulfilled by almost no one apart from the few Afghans living in Pakistan who travelled from there on an Afghan passport.) The administrative costs in themselves may not be so great, but the long period of waiting involves considerable expenditure on food and lodging and, above all, a lack of income from work. Furthermore, an Iranian visa obtained in this way has limited validity, and since an Afghan going to Iran usually wants to stay a long time there he will eventually be forced into illegality.

(2) Many Afghans prefer the alternative, clandestine route, which is riskier and more expensive (around $150 in 1995 and 1996) but much faster and therefore less of a drain on financial resources. It would be wrong, however, to draw a rigid separation between a perfectly official system and total illegality; the two aspects are actually intertwined and give great flexibility to the whole. Thus, shortly after the fall of Najibullah (April 1992), blank Afghan passports arrived in large number on the black market in Pakistan, via Jalalabad or Khost, or even Kandahar. All that was necessary was to fill in the details, and it was the professional counterfeiters who undertook the

delicate task of attaching a customer's photograph and forging the Afghan seals and Iranian visa. In Quetta in 1995, the price of such a passport was 500 rupees (or just under $15): 300 rupees for the blank and 200 rupees for the forger's labor. There were also false Pakistani passports and false Iranian documents allowing refugees to travel around the country. The Baluch smugglers were frontiersmen[16] who had relations with Iranian customs officers or policemen involved in the registration of foreigners. For 2,000 tomans ($5) a head, travel permits could be drawn up for Afghan *mosâferin*.

Most Afghans, then, travelled to Iran with false (*ja'li* or *qollâbi*[17]) papers, entering into the familiar debt that was then passed on at each stage of the journey until it was finally cleared by a relative at the final destination, in accordance with the system previously described.

The *mosâfer-xâna* of Quetta were the key migration hubs, where it was possible to find specialists in money-transfers and the clandestine crossing of frontiers. Here the *mosâferin* came into contact with the shady world of forgers and people-smugglers; the latter, indispensable though they were, aroused strong moral repulsion at what was seen as human trafficking, a system of exploitation that went beyond the limits of cooperation. The word *râhbalat* means "guide" (literally, "he who knows the road") and has a less negative connotation than *qâcâqbar* ("smuggler" or "dealer in contraband"). Although the two terms are often interchangeable in current parlance, there is a tendency to use *râhbalat* for the Hazara intermediary and *qâcâqbar* for the Baluch accompanying them on the trip.

The Hazara *mosâfer-xâna* are concentrated on Alamadar Road. Between 1995 and 1996 I counted a total of fourteen, most of them at Saray-e Namak and others further up at Sar-e Maidani. In 2001 three or four new establishments opened their doors, while several others closed down. Let us take the example of the Husain-e Kohna Mosafer-khana, at Saray-e Namak. In 1993 it had three managers (*ejâradâr,* literally "lease-takers"): Abdul Naser, who was also the owner, Haji Mohammadullah and Ghulam Sakhi. The brother of the last of these was married to the sister of Haji Mohammadullah's wife, so that they had family links without belonging to the same lineage. All originally came from the province of Ghazni, the first being a Bayat and the other two Hazaras (Chahar Dasta from Qarabagh). Each had contributed the equivalent of $2000 to a joint fund. In 1995 and 1996 the team changed a little: Haji Mohammadullah was dealing with some business in Mazar-e Sharif and was replaced in Quetta by his younger brother Enayatullah; Ghulam Sakhi left and Akbar Ali, the brother of Abdul Naser, came to lend a hand in the running of the business. Their office was a simple room near the entrance, with a safe, an ever-ringing telephone, one portrait each of Khomeini and Khamenei (they vanished in 1995), but no furnishings except for carpets and a few cushions. The hostelry comprised nine rooms, each of which could accommodate two to five people.

In September 1995 there were barely a dozen guests—but there were two to three times more in October. Most were going to or returning from Iran: coal miners coming to town for the weekend (on Thursday or Friday); men without a family who would find petty jobs in Quetta and remain there for a few months or more; or traders from Hazarajat on a business trip. *Râhbalat* and drivers also often spent the night there (whereas the *ejâradâr* generally lived with their family in a home of their own). A large majority of the guests were Hazaras from Qarabagh, Chahar Dasta or Mohammad Khoja, or else Sayyeds or Bayats from the vicinity of Ghazni. They chose this *mosâfer-xâna* because it was run by *ejâradâr* from the same background.

In 1993 a room cost a thousand rupees ($50) a month or 40 rupees ($2) a night; a single person paid 10 rupees ($0.5) a night. By 1995 the prices had slightly increased in rupees (20 for a single person, or 60 per night for a whole room rented for a long period and shared among four or five persons), but the dollar equivalents had remained approximately the same. Together with food, this amounted to roughly 50 rupees ($1.5) per person per night. An average *palao* cost between 15 and 20 rupees. Not all the *mosâfer-xâna* offered cooked dishes, however, and many *mosâferin* prepared their own food. In such cases the *mosâfer-xâna* supplied the mattresses, blankets and pillows, but not the glasses, teapots, cooking pots, and so on.

Apart from running the *mosâfer-xâna,* the managers also functioned as *hawâladâr* (the yard was often blocked by large packages containing clothes that migrants had bought with their savings to send to Afghanistan). This activity, plus commissions from people-smugglers operating on their premises, accounted for the greater part of their profits. As a rule, however, the men specializing in border-crossing and in financial networks were sociologically distinct: the *hawâladâr* from Jaghori were mostly small traders who did most of their business with people they knew (see chapter 7); the *râhbalat* were younger men, often with a *mujâhed* past, who lived dangerously but made a good living. Together with the drivers and the Saray-e Namak innkeepers, they formed a small world with its own subculture that gravitated around the *mosâfer-xâna;* they paid no heed to the Ramadan fast and went on smoking, playing cards and (discreetly) drinking alcohol. Their easy spending, loose morals and crude language set them apart as a kind of bad-boy fraternity. And yet, the distinctions remained fairly fluid, so that in summer, when few people were on the move, many *râhbalat* went themselves to Iran to work as laborers.

For each customer that they recruited in an inn, the *râhbalat* paid a "person price" (*bahâ-ye nafar*) that could be as high as 200 or 300 rupees (roughly \$6 to \$10), or sometimes even 500 rupees (\$15). The group of *mosâferin* would leave Quetta by bus for Taftan (200 rupees), where the Hazara guide passed them on to a Baluch smuggler who took them across the frontier on foot and on to the outskirts of Mirjawa, where vehicles were waiting to take them to Zahedan. For this dangerous part of the journey, during which a patrol could always intercept the convoy and begin a shoot-out, the Hazara *râhbalat* paid some 10,000 tomans (approx. \$25) to the Baluch *qâcâqbar;* the latter never dealt directly with *mosâferin* on money matters.

At Zahedan, the *mosâferin* were hidden in a special place fitted out for them by the local population, paying an extra 3,000 tomans per night (roughly \$7.5) that was not included in the fee for the trip. Here they were given false Afghan passports and Iranian visas. The group of migrants, still accompanied by the *râhbalat* (or his partner) and a *qâcâqbar* (generally another individual connected to the previous one), then took a specially hired bus for the night-time journey to their destination. The price of this final leg was 15,000 tomans (approx. \$37.5) per person. The Baluch smuggling networks thus received income from three sources: the trip from Taftan to Zahedan; the lodging in Zahedan; and the bus journey from Zahedan to the end-point.

The Baluch smuggler handled the tricky relations with the Iranian police. The risks were high, and although the checkpoints thinned out as they moved west there were an average of ten on the way from the frontier to the final destination. Each time it was necessary to pay from 10,000 to 100,000 tomans (\$25 to \$250) in bribes—as much as 400,000 tomans (\$1,000) for a busload of forty Afghans—and it was always possible that the Iranian police or army would refuse the money and intern everyone in a camp before expelling them from the country. One *râhbalat* showed me his right hand, its thumb missing as a result of a bullet fired at point-blank range by a guard at Tal-e Syâ. Another said he had been thrown into jail eight times during the eight years he had been engaged in this activity; several of his clients had been killed while crossing the frontier.

The two main routes from Zahedan to Tehran are via Mashad and via Kerman and Yazd. Once they arrive, they have to pay their debt to the *râhbalat* for the journey: if they are relatives, or people from the same village, he may agree to be paid later; but usually the migrants phone a relative or friend to come and pay for them. Sometimes, if they have been in Iran before and their former employer agrees to take them back, he may repay the debt and dock the sum from their wages. As long as they have not paid the smuggler, the *mosâferin* are kept locked up, each day being charged a further

2,000 tomans($5) for board and lodging. But, in general, a system of family support is organized in advance, so that one member is always working in Iran and able to prepare the ground for his "successor."

In 1996, then, the trip to Iran from Quetta cost between 50,000 and 60,000 tomans ($125 to $150), made up as follows:

- the commission paid by the *râhbalat* to the *ejâradâr* of the *mosâfer-xâna*: 200 to 500 rupees ($6 to $15);
- the Quetta-Taftan bus journey: 200 rupees ($6);
- Taftan-Zahedan: 10,000 tomans ($25) to the Baluch *qâcâqbar* (roughly five hours on foot between Taftan and Mirjawa, then from Mirjawa to Zahedan in a pick-up);
- the journey from Zahedan to Tehran in a hired bus: 15,000 tomans ($37.5) to the Baluch;
- bribes at various checkpoints along the way, averaging a total of 10,000 tomans ($25) per head.

The Hazara guide made a net profit between 5,000 and 15,000 tomans ($12.5-$37.5) per traveller on the whole trip, a sizeable sum given that he took some thirty to fifty people each time. It certainly had its dangers, but he could pocket as much as a thousand dollars at the end. The *râhbalat* worked in teams of two, one operating between Quetta and Zahedan, the other between Zahedan and the final destination in Iran; the man accompanying the *mosâferin* would collect the money at the journey's end. In a single inn in Quetta, I counted ten such teams.

The Hazara guides were essential intermediaries between the migrants and the Baluch people-smugglers; the former turned to them because they were from the same *qawm,* while the latter had known them for a long time because of their common interest. Without the help of the *râhbalat,* the *mosâferin* would have had no idea how to go about things or whom to contact. The *râhbalat* knew well both ends of the link of which they were the key middle. The system was able to function because of their relations with the migrants (despite the bad reputation they had among them) and their frequent contact with the Baluch smugglers.

When the Afghans left Iran, they usually travelled freely as far as Zahedan, where they made contact with a smuggler and paid between 7,000 and 10,000 tomans ($17.5 to $25) for the riskier border-crossing to Taftan. Then they continued on public transport to Quetta.

Asef, the young Dawran from Dahmarda whom I met in Tehran (see chapter 5), told me that on his first trip to Iran, in 1993, he and 350 others had crossed the frontier with a man from Day Zangi whom they had met in a Quetta inn. He had stayed three nights in Taftan, then another three in Zahedan and four en route for Tehran (the whole journey from Quetta to Tehran thus lasting ten days). The group had travelled by night, taking minor roads that allowed them to bypass certain checkpoints. He himself had then spent two nights in a hidden location in Tehran, until his brother finally came to pay off his debt and obtain his "release." (As he had not been given advance notice, it took the brother several days to collect the 24,000 tomans, or $60, that Asef owed to the smuggler.) In the spring of 1995, when Asef temporarily returned to Afghanistan, some people with connections helped him obtain a permit so that he could travel by public bus through Mashhed, Islam Qala, Herat and Kandahar to Jaghori.

In September 1995, after spending three months in Dahmarda, Asef travelled back to Tehran, this time with a forged Pakistani passport bearing a one-month Iranian pilgrimage visa. Out of fear that a police check would spot the forgery, he turned to a Baluch smuggler in Taftan to take him across the border, and then made his own way by public transport. Once in Tehran, Asef went to see his *kâkâ* (FB) and worked a couple of months with him for a construction firm. After he found a job as a guard in an Iranian private school, caution led him to throw away his false passport; he then carried around a simple certificate issued by his employer which, though not an official document, was usually enough to satisfy the police. During one large campaign of expulsions, however, when he was on a trip to the holy places in Qom, he was stopped by the police, detained for eighteen days in the Sang-e Safid camp, and forced to leave the country. At Islam Qala, in Afghanistan, he immediately got in touch with a Pashtun smuggler who took him back to the outskirts of Tehran. There he spent two nights in a basement and, without delivering payment, eventually escaped with three other Hazaras.

By sticking together, migrants of the same origin find it easier to look for work and to pay back the smuggler for the costs of the trip. Hazara migrants, who in this respect are no different from other Afghans, have many people to whom they can turn in their final destination in Iran, as well as along the way in places such as Quetta. Young Asef, for instance, found his job as a guard at a private school in Tehran through his brother Jalal, who was working in a similar institution at the time of his arrival. Jalal's own return to Afghanistan shortly afterwards is a good illustration of the rotation between brothers or close relatives to which reference has already been made; migration flows should therefore be located among the strategies worked out by family groups.

On their way out, having no money and no contacts, *mosâferin* are forced to rely upon the *râhbalat*. But, on their way back from Iran, the fact that they do not travel in groups means that they attract less attention and have fewer problems using public transport. They are also freer, in the sense that they have saved some money and are no longer in the grip of debt. Nevertheless, as they still have no official papers, they prefer to cross the Iranian-Pakistani frontier by clandestine means.

THE GULF STATES AND THE WEST

Whereas, in the West, some Pakistanis pass themselves off as Afghans in the hope of obtaining refugee status, many Afghans go to the Gulf States with Pakistani papers. In 1995 at Saray-e Namak, I met Ali Madad, an Alawdini from Nawur, who wanted to go to Saudi Arabia; it would cost him 150,000 rupees (nearly $4,700) but he would have the chance to set himself up as a baker (a long-established occupation among Hazaras in Kabul and in the Afghan emigration), and in Saudi Arabia even an unskilled worker can earn more than $500 a month. Ali Madad hoped that, with his own shop, he would be able to make as much as $2,500 a month—an income well worth the sacrifice of the initial outlay.

Abdullah, a young Hazara from Dahmarda, obtained a Pakistani passport through the *kalân-e qawm* of Dahmarda in Quetta. One of Abdullah's friends from Dahmarda put him in touch with a Pakistani Pashtun called Haji Ghulam, to whom he paid an initial sum of 60,000 rupees (roughly $1,875). This Haji Ghulam then informed some agents in Karachi or Islamabad, and got his brother in Saudi Arabia to send a letter of invitation that Abdullah could use to apply for a visa, with the idea that Abdullah would then pay a further commission of 55,000 rupees (a little more than $1,700) to Haji Ghulam and his brother. Numerous problems arose, however, and Abdullah never made it to Saudi Arabia; nor did he recover the sum he had advanced to Haji Ghulam.

This case shows that abuses of trust do take place. Haji Ghulam's behavior would have been unacceptable if the victim had been a relative of his, but it is difficult to put pressure on someone who belongs to a different group. Indeed, non-cooperation can be advantageous if the networks of the two parties are sufficiently distinct from each other. Most interactions, of course, take place within a fairly restricted group—a quality which offers some guarantees, as the people in question know the others well and how they are likely to behave. But sometimes it is necessary to rely upon individuals outside one's own group, whether specialists of various kinds (forgers, guides or people-smugglers, intermediaries or drivers, and so on), or else people holding a certain monopoly (as Baluch do in the area of the Iranian-Pakistani frontier). The example of Abdullah also shows the great difficulties that Hazaras have to face to reach the countries of the Arabian Peninsula—not because the dangers of the trip are so great, but because they arise outside their own social context and networks of relations. Pashtuns control the channels of migration towards Arabia.

The West is a distant but highly desirable horizon for some sections of the Afghan population. There are reckoned to be 250,000 Afghans settled there, including 100,000 to 150,000 in Europe, mostly with urban origins and often stemming from the former dominant classes or the bourgeoisie (Centlivres-Demont 1999). Very few Hazaras from the Jaghori region have managed to reach the West. In the mid-1990s, fewer than twenty people from Dahmarda were settled in Europe,[18] whereas more than a thousand were living in Quetta and several hundred in Iran and the countries of the Arabian Peninsula.

Mohammed Ibrahim, one of the rare exceptions, has been living in Germany since 1992. Two of his *bace kâkâ* (FBS) are also there with their families. He first went officially to Iran and then travelled on illegally to Turkey. After less than a year there, he went to work for five months as a travelling salesman in Syria, where he eventually obtained a Swiss visa and flew to Switzerland. A people-smuggler took him across into Germany for a fee of 800 deutschemarks, and there he obtained refugee status after claiming to be a former official under Najibullah who had been threatened since the fall of the Communist regime. Mohammed Ibrahim's presence in Germany was of benefit to his whole family: he worked in a hotel and in the space of five years sent home remittances totalling nearly $10,000. His case well illustrates the combination of luck and perseverance that is necessary to get somewhere in the West. He arrived shortly after the capture of Kabul by resistance forces, at a time when the authorities in various European countries were showing a certain indulgence towards Afghans.

Not everyone has been so successful. Another young Hazara, whom I met in Saray-e Namak, told me of his ill-starred attempt to settle in Sweden. With a Pakistani passport and an official visa, he first went to China and stayed there for two months; for a thousand dollars he bought the passport of a young Czech he met there, and for another $900 a one-way ticket to Sweden. He destroyed his passport on arrival and applied for political asylum as an Afghan citizen, but after less than a week he was sent back to Pakistan. All in all, the little adventure cost him $5,000, but he did not lose heart and in fact had devised a plan to go to Australia via China.

Another entrance to the West is the Visa Lottery—a number of Green Cards issued through the simple drawing of lots—that the US government organizes from time to time. Many try their luck but very few succeed. Abdul Ali, the younger brother of Ali Madad (the baker who wanted to go to Saudi Arabia), asked me to fill in a number of forms for him. The first was in his own name: Abdul Ali Jawadi (the Jawadi being invented on the spot); he asked me to knock a couple of years off his age. The next was in the name of his brother Aziz, to whom he gave the name Ahmadi and for whom he invented two children; their dates of birth also came off the top of his head. Moreover, although Abdul Ali said he was a Pakistani born in Quetta, he told me to put his brother down as an Afghan born in Ghazni. Unmarried or head of a family, Pakistani or Afghan: the family members were pursuing a rational strategy of diversifying their sociological profile, in the hope that this would improve the chances that one of them would be selected. Another not uncommon ploy is for the same person to send in several forms, with small changes in his name, age, civil status, and so on. In 2001 I learned that neither of the brothers had obtained American residence, but since then Aziz has managed to emigrate to Australia, leaving his wife and children behind in Quetta.

THE FORMS OF MIGRATION

On the basis of the 1951 Convention Relating to the Status of Refugees and the 1967 Protocol, international law distinguishes refugees and internally displaced persons from migrants. This juridical and normative approach is necessary for the action of aid agencies and host country governments, but it scarcely corresponds to the experience of most Afghans and makes it impossible to account for social strategies and practices. The Hazaras do not appeal for international agencies to help them return to Afghanistan and have not benefited from any repatriation measures. As we have seen, very few have settled into the refugee camps of Pakistan. Though exposed to the hostility of Pashtun refugees and the indifference of Pakistani officialdom, strategies of social advancement have led them to cluster almost exclusively in an urban setting, In Quetta they have had the advantages of a welcoming milieu, outside the main circuits of refugee aid.

The Hazara illustrate the fact that no hard and fast distinction can be drawn between the categories of political refugee and economic migrant. We can distinguish four main cases: (i) families that permanently settle in Quetta or (more rarely) Iran; (ii) young people who go to work in Iran (construction, quarries, factories) for long periods of usually more than a year; (iii) mostly mature men who work a few months of the year in the coal mines near Quetta; (iv) traders who are constantly on the move between Afghanistan, Pakistan and Iran. Women are represented only in the first of these categories.

Let us take the case of Husayn Bakhsh, born in 1959. He went to Quetta for the time when he was only 14 or 15 years old (in 1973 or 1974), on a brief visit to his sister who had been living there for a number of years. He again left Afghanistan in 1978, a few months after the Communist coup, then spent four years in Iran before settling in Quetta, where his mother and wife joined him. (He had married shortly before leaving Dahmarda, but the couple had no children.) He had made three long trips to Iran, and also been there several times on a pilgrimage. He had returned to Afghanistan only twice: in 1993, for the wedding of Mohammad Hasan, his *xosur-bura* (WB), and in spring 1996 to settle some matters connected with the ownership of a small plot of land.

This case illustrates what we may call the migratory continuum of the Hazaras. Before the war, the young Husayn Bakhsh went off to find his sister in Quetta, where she had long been living with her husband. This kept up the link with geographically distant relatives and familiarized him with a new place. He left Afghanistan at the beginning of the war, although no definite correlation can be established between the two events. He did not immediately settle in Quetta and remained highly mobile.

Although Mohammad Husayn moved around more than Husayn Bakhsh, the chronology in his case too leads us to look more critically at the concept of refugee. He was born in 1975 or 1976. In the early 1990s he went to Iran for the first time, together with his elder brother Mohammad Hasan. They encountered a number of problems on their journey back to Afghanistan (1993). At that time Hazaras were avoiding Kandahar, where they did not feel secure, and so the two brothers decided to take the considerably longer route through the north of Afghanistan. They left Tehran for Mashad, but there the police detained them for being without papers and took them to the camp at Sang-e Safid. Four days later, the police escorted them to the frontier at Islam Qala, where they found a lorry going to Herat. They stayed two days in a Hazara-run *mosâfer-xâna* in Herat, then travelled by bus to Mazar-e Sharif. The journey lasted eight days. They passed through Qala-ye Naw, Maymana, Dawlatabad, Shibirghan and finally Mazar. After a two-day break, they pressed on to Pul-e Khumri, then got a ride on a lorry carrying old iron to Ghazni via Doshi, the Hajigak Pass, Behsud and Dasht-e Nawur. Here, Hasan and Husayn took another lorry bound for Jaghori. It took them six days to get from Mazar to Dahmarda, but the whole journey lasted a full twenty-three! In a familiar pattern Mohammed Hasan, the elder of the two, married soon after his return—using the money saved in Iran to start a family.

As to Mohammad Husayn, he ran away three months later from the family home after a quarrel with his brother. They were working in the fields with Husayn Bakhsh, and it seems that Mohammad Husayn made fun of Husayn Bakhsh for having no children and that Hasan severely rebuked him. Husayn felt offended and decided to leave without asking his family's approval. For his travelling expenses he was forced to borrow 100,000 afghanis (roughly $115 at that time), on extremely unfavorable terms that meant he would have to repay 150,000 afghanis. He went to Quetta, stayed no more than three days, and then moved on to Taftan. Here he found a Baluch people-smuggler to organize the trip to Tehran, agreeing to pay the equivalent of $150 dollars on arrival. The group of *mosâferin* (more than a hundred people in four Toyota vans) was stopped by the police near Mirjawa. He was taken to Tal-e Sya and held for a fortnight, before being escorted to Robat (the point where Iran, Pakistan and Afghanistan meet). Husayn spent twenty-five days there, running up a debt to a Hazara hotel-keeper who originally came from Uruzgan. He had hoped to acquire an Iranian travel document, but nothing came of this as his Baluch contact fell out with the relevant Iranian official over a sudden increase in his financial demands. Husayn then decamped to Quetta, leaving the hotel bill unpaid, and in that winter of 1993–94 worked for a while in the coal mines along with his *bace kâkâ* (FBS), Mardan Ali. Mohammad Yusuf, another *bace kâkâ,* was returning from Iran and persuaded him to accompany him to Dahmarda via Badini. (They did not use a *râhbalat* but directly contacted a Pashtun driver from Gelan district, adjacent to Jaghori, who took them from Quetta to Anguri for 50,000 afghanis each, a little less than $60) Husayn made it up with his brother Hasan and helped with the construction of the family home. He thus stayed about ten months in Dahmarda before returning to Quetta. This time he travelled via Kandahar, as the roads had become safer since the emergence of the Taliban. The trip cost him no more than 25,000 afghanis.

In Quetta he again worked in the coal mines along with Mardan Ali. A month later, however, he developed a large cyst on the neck and decided to go back to Iran. He borrowed 20,000 tomans from Husayn Bakhsh (who had forgiven his jibes) and for the umpteenth time secretly crossed the frontier between Taftan and Zahedan. In Zahedan he was able to sleep a couple of nights at the Hezb-e wahdat office. Then he really chanced his luck by going to the bus station and buying a ticket for Mashad, without documents of any kind. He ran into an army checkpoint, but used the spectacular appearance of the cyst to persuade the soldiers to let him through. Encouraged by this success, he continued in similar vein all the way to Tehran, where he finally arrived at the end of 1994. He went to see Mohammad Ali, the brother of Mardan Ali, who recruited him to his team of workers. He also had his cyst treated, but in December 1995 there was a fresh setback when he fell backwards from the sixth level of some scaffolding. Fortunately the fall was softened by a pile of sand, so that he escaped with multiple fractures in one leg, a few back problems and an open wound on the elbow. Although he had no official documents or social security cover, his Iranian employer took care of the costs of hospital treatment.

Mohammad Husayn and Husayn Bakhsh have opposite temperaments, but their trajectories both show how remote the international conception of a refugee is from the reality experienced by Afghans. The back-and-forth movement for various purposes never comes to an end, and the problems to be solved are not the same in Afghanistan, Pakistan and Iran. Nor do the solutions found by the people of Jaghori rely upon the humanitarian aid of international agencies or NGOs. In the course of their migrations, the Hazaras have opened up new territories for themselves; they develop within a space which, though broken up, derives its coherence both from strong links of communal support and from individual initiative.

The Afghan migratory networks are transnational and far-flung, taking in Afghanistan, Pakistan, Iran, Saudi Arabia, the United Arab Emirates and Kuwait, but also the countries of Western and Eastern Europe, North America and Australasia. Nevertheless, one can observe a clear line of separation among groups that by no means perfectly corresponds to ethnic divisions.

It seems to be a constant of Afghan history (Canfield 1986: 99) that the first dividing-line is religious, with Sunni on one side and Shia on the other. In Quetta the Sunnis are generally gathered around New Ada, the Shiites on Alamdar Road and at Saray-e Namak. Within these concentrations, however, more sophisticated groupings and cooperative foundations emerge in accordance with a schema that is more geographical than ethnic. The numerous *mosâfer-xâna* of New Ada are organized according to the place of origin of the guests: Panjshiri and Kohistani use the same establishments, while Persian-speaking Logari rub shoulders with Pashtuns from the same region with whom even intermarriage is not a rare occurrence. The peoples of the North, for their part, are constantly interacting with one another: even in daily life in exile, an Ishaqzay Pashtun from Sar-e Pul might have more contact with a former Uzbek neighbor than with an Ishaqzay from Kandahar.

The same tendency is visible on the Alamdar Road. Hazara are certainly the main presence in the neighborhood, but one also finds Sayyeds,

Bayats from around Ghazni, as well as plenty of Kandahari and Pakistani Shiites (Gilgitis, Baltis, Pashtun Turis and Punjabis, in particular). Each regional group has, at least nominally, its distinct places of worship—and this basis of segregation is again found in the *mosâfer-xâna*. People from Jaghori do not frequent the same places as people from Shahristan. The Mohammad Khodja from Qarabagh interact more with the Chahar Dasta from their region than with individuals of the same tribal affiliation who come from Jighatu or Nawur.

With few exceptions, Shiites and Sunnis do not readily mix with each other. But, apart from this polarization, we should speak more of local groupings than of ethnic segregation as the basis of migratory networks. Of course, the destinations often differ from one community to another. Shiites tend to go more to Iran than to countries with a Sunni majority (the Arabian Peninsula, for example). When Hazaras travel, they prefer to be with other Hazaras. But, as these networks are based upon trust, the only real cooperation is with permanent contacts whose origin is known—that is to say, with relatives or neighbors.

Chapter Seven
Transfers of Money and Goods

MIGRATION AND CAPITAL FLOWS

The endemic insecurity of war and the resulting lack of economic prospects drove large numbers of Afghans to leave their country. After more than twenty years, the migratory movements are highly organized; and the networks created for this purpose seem not so much a response to war as a major, even constitutive, element in the social-cultural and economic life of Afghans. One of the most striking aspects of this migration is the huge flow of capital that it draws towards Afghanistan.

For the Hazaras, Pakistan is mainly a place of transit and refuge. Iran, whose religion and language they share, is the principal goal of migration; much fewer go to the Sunni Arabic-speaking countries of the Gulf. Once they are in Iran or elsewhere, Afghan migrants have to solve the technical problem of sending money they have saved to their family in Afghanistan—an especially acute problem in the 1980s and 1990s, when no banks were operational there. This is where the figure of the *hawâladâr*[1] comes in (from the Arabic *hawâla,* "transfer" and by extension "letter of credit, cheque"). Half-merchant, half-banker, his expertise in the transfer of funds has kept money and goods flowing without interruption between Iran, Pakistan and Afghanistan—a role that goes back a long way but acquired unprecedented dimensions during the war. Indeed, these remittances have become a key factor in the Afghan economy, especially in Hazarajat, which is too far from Pakistan, too isolated and too inaccessible to benefit from sizeable humanitarian aid. The Hazaras have had to count on their own resources to confront poverty, war and exile. And, within the limits of their means and circumstances, they have shown remarkable inventiveness and ingenuity in tackling that task.

Apart from serving the particular needs of migrants, these huge money-transfer networks structure Afghan transnational society and make it possible to reproduce the ties among scattered members of each solidarity group. Their importance thus goes well beyond their economic dimension. The remittance system cannot be reduced to an economic phenomenon embedded in social relations, as would say Polanyi (1945, 1957). It is not only a response to violence and war, or even to poverty. Rather, it is a planned strategy by which the Hazaras widen their social and cultural horizon. Money-transfers are a social event that affects all aspects of the life of Afghans, whether in their homeland or in a migratory context.

MONEY-TRANSFERS AND LETTERS OF CREDIT

During my first stay in Quetta, in 1993, a chance remark in a conversation made me aware of the existence of money-transfers to Afghanistan. I then came to realize, in the course of various interviews, how widespread and important this practice is among all sections of the Afghan population; tens of thousands of Hazaras go to Pakistan or Iran mainly in order to remit money back home through the offices of a *hawâladâr.* Yet the whole process—such a common routine for the Hazara—is not directly visible to an external observer. My informants took it all so much for granted that their first explanations were extremely schematic: you give money to a dealer in Iran and get it back in Afghanistan; the dealer buys some goods and has them sent to his shop in Afghanistan, then repays the families. In some cases, a secret code is used—what could be simpler! Afghans do not understand why a foreign ethnologist should find it so puzzling. The idea of money-transfers has long been known in the Middle East, and letters of credit are first mentioned in the eighth century in the Muslim world (Labib 1969). Bills of exchange, which were unknown in Roman law, underwent a lengthy evolution in Europe; they were introduced by Italian merchants at the Champagne fair, where they had the simple form of written promises to pay a sum of money in a place other than the one at which an agreement was made. The instrument was gradually refined in the late-thirteenth and early-fourteenth centuries, then entered widespread use in the late-sixteenth century and played an essential role in the economic and commercial development of Europe (de Roover 1953: 17–18). Since then, a bill of exchange has been not only a payment order but a combined instrument of exchange and credit (Goody 1996). "As a rule, the medieval banker was at once a lender and a dealer" (Pirenne 1963: 104). This is the twin principle on which Afghan still base themselves.[2]

The following characters featured in one of the first *hawâla* transfers that I was able to collect:

- A: Abdullah Jan, an ordinary worker living in Isfahan, wants to send some money to his family in Hazarajat (Qarabagh).
- B: Ramazan Ali (my interlocutor) goes back and forth between Iran and Quetta.
- C: Abdul Jaffar has a shop in Qarabagh.
- D: The *bace mâmâ* (MBS) of Ramazan Ali, Mohammad Taqi, is a *hawâladâr* in Qarabagh.
- E: Qodratullah, the brother of Abdullah Jan, lives in Qarabagh. Their families share a house.

A entrusts his savings to B in return for a *hawâla* (a half-ticket torn from a book with a stamp cut in two). B entrusts the money to some large merchants with import-export licences who effect a bank transfer between Iran and Pakistan. He keeps the other half of the *hawâla* and goes to Quetta. He gets D to take on the *hawâla,* recovers the money and lends it to C, who is known to him as a shopkeeper from his village of origin. C buys various goods (rice, wheat, clothes, etc.) and rents a lorry to take them to Afghanistan. Once in Qarabagh, C checks and signs for the goods, sells them and repays to D the money entrusted by B. D in turn pays E. Meanwhile, E has received the half of the *hawâla* note that A in Iran gave to an acquaintance returning to Qarabagh.

Sajad, another *hawâladâr* from Qarabagh, has a shop in the Quetta bazaar. He works with his two brothers: Sakhi, who is in Isfahan, and Jalal, who has a shop in Hazarajat. Sakhi collects money from Afghan workers in Iran with the help of three partners (*šarik*): Ahmad Ali (who belongs to his lineage, their fathers being *bace kâkâ:* FBS), Mohammad Jan (their *bace amma:* FZS) and Akhtar (their *bace mâmâ:* MBS). Their collaboration with one another means that they have more customers and therefore increases their capital. Sakhi telephones Sajad to tell him the workers' names and the relevant amounts, then effects a bank transfer from the Bank-e Sepa (Iran) to the Habib Bank (Pakistan). Sajid picks up the money in Quetta and buys some goods for his own shop in Pakistan and his brother's in Afghanistan. He also sends his brother a list of the customers and the respective sums of money (it is not possible to communicate by telephone with Qarabagh). Jalal sells these goods and reimburses the workers' families, who have meanwhile been kept informed by relatives or neighbors just back from Iran. This example, slightly different from the previous one, represents an interesting case of family multilocality: the three brothers complement one other by virtue of their geographical dispersion, while their wives and children remain in Qarabagh.

We can see that the *hawâla* is not only an instrument for the transfer of money but also an instrument of credit and exchange. In the first example, the *hawâladâr* lend the money in their care to a third party; in the second example, the *hawâladâr* themselves engage in trading activity. Another example will help us understand better the accounting side of the money-transfers. Latif, a young *hawâladâr* from Pashi (Jaghori) who now operates in the Sang-e Masha bazaar, explained his activities to me in detail and showed me the documentation. There are nine brothers and four sisters (one of whom has married and has left home); the father is old and sick; Hasan, the eldest son, is looking after some land in Pashi; the next, Karim, is a *hawâladâr* in Quetta; my interlocutor, Latif, takes delivery of the *hawâla* that Karim sends to his shop in Sang-e Masha; the fourth brother, Sharif, produces sweets in his workshop in Anguri. The other brothers are still children. The extended family, which has twenty members, lives in one house in Pashi and collects the proceeds from the business activity of Karim and Latif, as well as of Sharif. They share all the household expenses.

Karim is posted in Quetta. He has no business premises, but visits the main areas of Hazara commercial activity: Sar-e Maidani, Alamdar Road and Saray-e Namak. He collects the savings of various Hazara workers in Quetta, buys some goods ("everything Afghanistan needs") and hires the services of Pashtun carriers. He deals with no more than five or six individuals, always the same and known to him for a long time, who also come originally from Ghazni province. In 1995 the haulage price was 9000 afghanis per 100 kg. Latif's shop in Sang-e Masha takes some of the goods, and the rest is sold to various shopkeepers in Anguri, Sang-e Masha and elsewhere. At the same time, Karim hands over *hawâla* to his customers in Quetta and sends a detailed list to Latif of their names and places of residence in Afghanistan, and of the sum to be reimbursed. Latif copies this list in a notebook, page one of which contains an index of all the names and places as well as the numbers of the pages on which the respective dealings are recorded. Those pages show the name, place, *hawâla* number (sometimes the actual ticket is stuck there with sellotape), the total sum entrusted to the *hawâladâr* (in afghanis), and details of the reimbursement (which often takes place in stages). Once the full sum has been reimbursed, Latif puts an easily visible mark on the page. When someone presents himself, he compares the *hawâla* that is given to him (in this case, a small printed ticket containing a space to be filled in) with the information from his brother:

Name	Place	N° of *hawâla*	Sum received (in figures)	
			Sum received (in words)	
First payment			Amount	
Second payment			Amount	
Third payment			Amount	
			———	
Payment			Total amount	N° of page

Box 1

As a rule, no commission is deducted; Latif and Karim make their profit from the selling of the goods and from speculation on the rate of exchange. Here is a translation of the kind of *hawâla* issued by Karim to his clients in Quetta:

Shop of Abdul Latif and Abdul Karim	
Address: Upper Sang-e Masha Bazar	
Date	
Name of *hawâladâr*	Name of beneficiary
Resident at	Residence
Son of	Son of
Amount of *hawâla* in words	Afghanis
Scheduled date for payment	Date of payment
Signature	Signature of beneficiary

Box 2

This is a particularly elaborate specimen. More often, a *hawâla* is just a page torn from a notebook mentioning the name of the *hawâladâr,* the name of the customer transferring the money, his origin, the date, the amount and the scheduled date for repayment. The document generally contains a secret code (*ramz*) that enables the partners to be sure of its authenticity. Sometimes they will also ask for personal identification marks. A number of (not mutually exclusive) techniques may be employed: a deliberate spelling mistake; a mark at a particular place (for example, a disguised mark within the *hawâladâr*'s signature; a stamp or banknote torn in two, with the issue number on each half (one for the *hawâladâr,* the other for the customer, who send them to Afghanistan by separate routes); an object that the customer has to point out in the *hawâladâr*'s shop, or a story that he has to tell (see also chapter 8). Periphrases are also often used: such as "600 kilos of wheat" for 6 million afghanis. It is difficult to know how useful these techniques are, given that the real guarantee is that the different players are already known to one another (see also chapter 9).

Some *hawâladâr* work alone. This is the case with Mohsen, a 37-year-old man from Dawud (Jaghori), who periodically travels to Iran (Isfahan, Shiraz and Tehran) to collect money from migrant workers whom he already knows from Dawud. His shop in Jaghori remains closed while he is away. He says that he contacts twenty to thirty people on each trip, who place an average of $100 to $200 each in his care. He then hands over the total sum ($2,000 to $6,000) to big merchants in Iran, who deduct a commission of 2.5%. In Quetta, Mohsen recovers the money and converts it into afghanis. Sometimes, if security conditions allow it, he takes the money with him to Afghanistan and repays the families directly, but more often he buys some goods and has them sent to Jaghori.

Mohsen's profit is mainly bound up with the exchange-rates. From Iran, he telephones Quetta to ask the prevailing rate between the Iranian and Afghan currencies, then agrees with his client the sum to be reimbursed in afghanis at the final destination in Jaghori, usually based on the day's rate in Quetta minus 10 percent. For instance, if the day's rate in Quetta is one toman for 40 afghanis,[3] he agrees to pay the sum of 36 afghanis per toman in Jaghori. For every 1,000 tomans collected in Iran, Mohsen therefore receives 975 tomans in Quetta. He immediately changes them into afghanis at the rate of 1:40 and receives a total of 39,000 afghanis. In other words, for each 1,000 tomans that he collects in Iran, he makes a profit of 3,000 afghanis (equivalent to 75 tomans) on arrival, or 7.5 percent.

Here is a specimen letter of credit issued by Mohsen:

> I the undersigned, Mohsen, from Dawud, village of Bedak, recognize that I have received the sum of one hundred thousand tomans at the fixed rate of 36, which represents in afghanis the sum of three million six hundred thousand afghanis, from Mr Mahmud, Dawud, village of Wakilkhel, as a loan for a period of one month, and hereby undertake to remain honest.
>
> Respectfully, Mohsen, 1375/9/19

The said Mahmud would entrust this document to an acquaintance due to return to Jaghori and ask him to hand it over to his family, one of whose members would present himself to Mohsen. Apart from its practical function, the letter of credit is therefore a genuine symbol (from the Greek *sumbolon,* "sign of recognition"), which allows two people to recognize each other and thereby helps to reproduce the social bond (see chapter 8). There is no guarantee against devaluation of the afghani, but in this case the period for repayment is only one month. In the event of a longer period, the *hawâladâr* invests the money and makes it work—for example, by buying goods. This extra profit means that he will offer his customer a more favorable rate of exchange between tomans and afghanis.

You don't give your money to someone you don't know well; the only guarantee comes from the relationship of mutual acquaintance. Acting as he does within a realm where future encounters are highly probable, or even unavoidable, the *hawâladâr* has no interest in cheating his customers (see chapter 9). Someone who made off with the money of people close to him would ruin his reputation and therefore his future as a *hawâladâr.*

Let us take a final example from the Dawran lineage in Dahmarda. Mohammad Yusuf, the *bace kâkâ* (FBS) of Mardan Ali, offers a typical example of the economic and social strategies of an itinerant businessman whose trading and money-transfer activities are inseparably linked to each other. Having pooled his capital with Mohammad Jawad, his *xosur-bura* (WB), to open a shop in the Dahmarda bazaar, Yusuf is constantly travelling between Jaghori, Quetta and Tehran. In Quetta he stays with Husayn Bakhsh, his *bace amma* (FZS). Yusuf, Mohammad Jawad and Husayn Bakhsh are all members of the Awlad-e Atay branch of the Dawran lineage, but their most direct relations are mediated by the women. In April 1996, when I came across Yusuf in Tehran (having previously met him in Dahmarda and Quetta), he was living with a distant member of his lineage, Juma Khan. He would stay several weeks in Tehran to collect the savings of people from Dahmarda, but also to work as an ordinary laborer on a building site. He would use the money to buy some Iranian-made shirts and sandals and arrange for a Baluch he had known for some years to smuggle them into Pakistan. Then he would take possession of them again, sell them in Quetta (his first source of profit) and buy some food products (flour, wheat, oil, sugar, tea, etc.) to take back with a Pashtun driver for his shop in Dahmarda. With the money obtained through sales, he would finally reimburse the families of the migrants in Iran who had left their savings in his care. Mohammad Jawad, younger and less experienced than Yusuf, has spent long periods in Iran and has not invested a lot of himself in commercial activity. Apart from the capital he contributed, his role

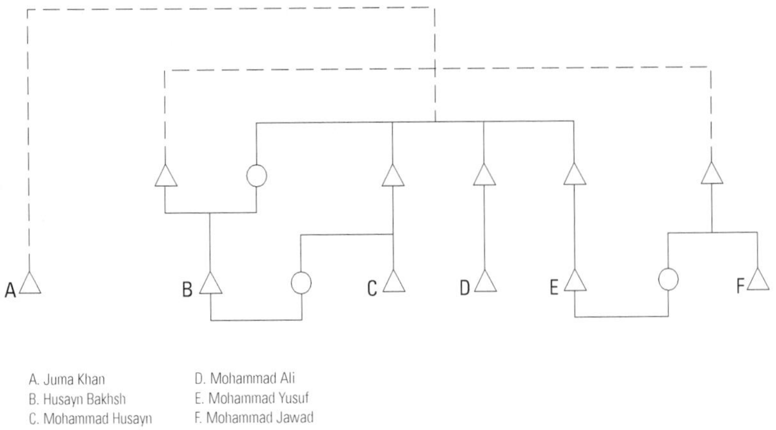

Figure 9: The migratory network of Mohammad Yusuf

is limited to running the jointly owned shop when he is Dahmarda. When both partners are away, it remains closed.

These examples show that many different scenarios are possible. Ramazan Ali and Mohammad Taqi are not engaged in commerce themselves; they lend to merchants the money they have collected from Hazara migrants in Iran. Karim and Latif, by contrast, though owning a shop in Jaghori, sell some of their products wholesale. Others combine the two functions. Mohsen and Yusuf work alone—which means that they have to keep moving back and forth between Afghanistan, Pakistan and Iran—whereas Sakhi, Sajad and Jalal, as well as Karim and Latif (whose activities do not extend to Iran), each remain in a single place. Between the itinerant and stationary extremes are intermediate cases such as Ramazan Ali and Mohammad Taqi, where only one of the two associates travels. But, whatever the degree of mobility, all these individuals gamble on currency differences, in a system in which money-transfers, commercial credit and exchange mechanisms are inextricably intertwined. Multilocation, together with *hawâla* transfers, take quite spectacular forms among people from southern Hazarajat (Ghazni province: Jaghori, Qarabagh, etc.). It would be no exaggeration to say that, in one way or another, the whole population of the region is involved in the phenomenon.

THE ACTORS IN THE FIELD

The money-transfer networks of Afghan workers are certainly transnational, but the relations they involve are ultimately based on proximity. In Dahmarda one finds both ordinary workers (*kârgar*) and, sometimes overlapping with them, people who specialize in the transfer of money and goods (*hawâladâr*). In both cases, the family networks are multilocal: the former rotate family members, so that each in turn looks for paid work abroad that will be of benefit to all; the latter establish businesses involving a commercial partnership in more than one place. Furthermore, the two categories are interdependent: ordinary workers need the *hawâladâr*'s services to remit their savings back to their family, as well as to have manufactured goods in the locality; the *hawâladâr* need the migrants' money to have enough capital for their own economic activities.

Among the Hazaras there are several categories of *hawâladâr:*

(1) Small shopkeepers (*dokândâr*) who regularly travel to Pakistan or Iran to collect the savings of migrants from the same place as themselves and to purchase goods for their shops in Hazarajat. For this, they rely essentially on locally based acquaintance networks. As they have no stable associates in Pakistan or Iran, they are constantly on the move between their home region (Jaghori or Qarabagh, for example) and Quetta, Tehran, Isfahan or Mashad. It is truly "wandering trade," to use Pirenne's expression (1963: 79). Mohsen and Yusuf are good examples of this model.

(2) The main traders, whose associates (*šarik*) have settled shops in several places. Usually it is question of close relatives. On the one hand, ownership of a shop in Quetta enables them to widen their networks a little; their visibility in a place where people with different origins tend to meet gives them the possibility of extending and diversifying their customer base. On the other hand, the service they offer is different from that of the first type of shopkeeper since they are always there on the spot; migrants do not have to wait for them to appear before sending money to Hazarajat. With associates in various places, these traders do not need to be on the move all the time. Abdul Karim and Abdul Latif are examples of this kind.

(3) The large merchants (*tâjer*, pl. *tujâr*), who have business connections in many countries, outside the circle of their relatives and acquaintances. Their networks are international, involving large-scale import and export between Pakistan, Iran and Afghanistan, but also with the republics of Central Asia, the Arabian Peninsula, Azerbaijan and Turkey, or even Singapore, Thailand and Indonesia. Having commercial licences and partners in the countries in question, they rarely travel but use all the modern

means of communication to handle their business. A large proportion of carpet dealers in the United Arab Emirates and Kuwait are Afghans. Money-transfers are only one part of their activities, and sometimes a marginal one at that.

The first two categories are sometimes clients of the third. Thus, as we saw in the example of Ramazan Ali, a small shopkeeper who deals in *hawâla* between Iran and Hazarajat may use an important businessman to send money between Iran and Pakistan. It is possible to make a transfer from an Iranian to a Pakistani bank, but it is a slow, pernickety and expensive process that people prefer to avoid. The *hawâladâr* is faster, more discreet and less expensive. Iran, like Pakistan, places all kinds of restriction on trade and prohibits the export of certain goods—a practice which, paradoxically, pushes many merchants towards the informal networks. When a large merchant is interested at all in dealing with ordinary workers, he uses the services of an intermediary (*dallâl*) to collect the money. On a modest scale, Sajad and his brothers come close to this scenario.

(4) There are also pure *hawâladâr,* who concern themselves with nothing other than the transfer and lending of money—not even with other banking services such as a deposit or investment account. The two largest and best-known Hazara *hawâladâr* in Quetta, who came there from Jaghori before the Communist coup of 1978, have a fabric shop on Alamdar Road that is only a cover for their main (illegal) activity, the exchange of *hawâla.* They have five main partners, in Ghazni, Tashkent, Mashad, Tehran and Dubai. All are Hazaras, but they are not related by kin. They make scarcely any profit from transactions with Ghazni, but keep links there to maintain credibility with their Hazara clients. On the other hand, they have no dealings with the Jaghori bazaars such as Anguri or Sang-e Masha, which remain the favorite area of activity for the small *hawâladâr-dokândâr* in the first two categories. It should be stressed again that these are all ideal types, and that the models usually overlap.

There is a feeling that you can only trust someone with whom you have close ties. For merchants as for *hawâladâr,* it is often profitable to use an intermediary (*dallâl*) to enlarge their customer base. Often the intermediary is closely linked to the *hawâladâr* (as in the case of Sajad and his cousins); he then receives a fixed share of the proceeds. In other cases, the intermediary takes a commission equivalent to one per cent of the transaction, chargeable half to the migrant worker and half to the *hawâladâr.*

The greater the social distance between the players, the higher are the risks of a swindle. Nevertheless, kinship relations are not always a sufficient guarantee against fraud. Alidad (a young man from Dahmarda working in Tehran) learned this to his cost in 1995, when he handed over 50,000 tomans to a member of his lineage, Abdul Khadim, who had a shop in Jaghori and acted as a *hawâladâr.* Since the latter disappeared to North America with the money he had collected, Alidad has relied entirely on his *bace kaka* (FBS) to send funds to his family. Once he is back in Jaghori, where he is familiar with the house and family lands of the swindler, he intends to demand a settling of accounts with Abdul Khalil, the brother of Abdul Khadim. An expression in widespread use among Afghans—*e'tebâr nist,* "there is no trust"—is therefore not without foundation. Abuses certain do exist, even among kith and kin.

Are small *hawâladâr,* from the same village as oneself, more trustworthy than large merchants connected to international networks? In both cases, it is possible that money will not arrive at its destination. It is reassuring if the family of the *hawâladâr* who organizes the smuggling of goods from Iran to Pakistan, and from there to Afghanistan, owns land in a familiar place in Hazarajat; that means he would be extremely unlikely to vanish into thin air. There are many other dangers connected both with the illegal nature of the trade—the goods might be intercepted by brigands or seized by the authorities, for example—but the risks of a swindle remain low. Large-scale operators have official permits and business connections in the different countries, as well as large financial reserves that enable them to offer more flexible repayment schedules. In dealings with them, however, the financial risks are higher, the social bond weaker and the likelihood of abuse greater.

THE CIRCULATION OF GOODS

Money-transfers are inseparable from the circulation of goods. Like the little streams that pass round a rock and eventually wear it down, trade routes clear a way for themselves even in the face of terrible security conditions, countless tolls, transport difficulties and inexorable devaluations of the Afghan currency. The costs of long journeys soon make themselves felt. All trade is based on sequential buying and selling: the further one is from the source, the higher the price becomes. The transport of goods is a separate branch of activity run by specialists. In general, a lorry team consists of three men: the driver, the driver's mate and an assistant. A number of scenarios are possible: the vehicle may belong to the driver himself or, more often, to a well-off relative or the larger kinship group; sometimes the driver is employed for a wage by an influential commander or a large merchant. Between Iran and Pakistan, goods may circulate either officially (with a payment of government taxes) or illegally through the Baluch who have a veritable monopoly over cross-border smuggling. Between Pakistan and Afghanistan, the situation is so confused that, in order to lower the risk of theft and racketeering, it is preferable to use a carrier from one of the Pashtun tribes in the region.

Trade flows with Pakistan, many of them through Iran, are particularly important (World Bank 2001). Afghanistan is thus the scene of intense activity, but this mainly involves transit operations or, to put it more crudely, re-exporting by means of smuggling. Apart from drugs, the only significant Afghan exports are woven rugs and carpets, animal skins, a little wool and cotton, and fresh and dried fruits (especially grapes and mulberries). Afghanistan imports from Pakistan food, fabrics, petrol, etc.; from Iran plastic goods, manufactures and clothing; from Uzbekistan and Turkmenistan scrap iron and petrol. Goods produced in Japan, Taiwan, Hong Kong and South-East Asia (e.g. cameras, televisions, VCRs, stereo systems, cassette-players and electrical household goods) are flown in to Kandahar directly from the United Arab Emirates or shipped in by sea and road. Many cars and mini-vans also reach Afghanistan via Iran, often ending up in Pakistan. Quetta, located close to both Afghanistan and Iran, is a hub for the carpet trade, which is largely controlled by Afghan refugees (with the Hazaras in only a secondary role). The main customers are Pakistani traders in Karachi, Lahore or Islamabad.

Like the avenues of migration, the trade routes have been constantly changing in accordance with the political-military situation. In 1993 people rarely used the Kandahar option because of systematic pillaging by local commanders, but it was possible to take the longer route through Badini. In 1995 and 1996 the Taliban opened the Kandahar road but the Kabul route was impassable as the frontline between the Taliban and Massoud's forces. The Taliban capture of Herat in autumn 1995 made it easier to conduct trade between Pakistan and Central Asia, but hostility between Tehran and the Taliban made it difficult to cross the Iran-Afghanistan frontier.

Between 1995 and 1996, the war meant that Kabul could not play a central role in trade. At that time the most important cities were Mazar-e Sharif and Herat, where numerous merchants were engaged in wholesale trade with neighboring countries. Kandahar and Jalalabad were also active centers, and Ghazni had become a major crossroads between the South (Kandahar and Pakistan) and the North (Mazar).

The difference between the transit trade and the activities of Hazara *dokândâr-hawâladâr* may be seen in the choice of routes and goods. Ghazni province is teeming with small traders, who keep their village shops stocked out of the money they collect abroad from relatives and neighbors. Their main purchases are of food products in Pakistan: wheat, rice, flour, cooking oil, tea, sugar in powder and pieces, sweets. Manufactured goods such as shoes, sandals, slippers, clothes, jackets, fabrics, turbans, detergents, shampoos, soap, pots and pans, industrial carpets, cassette-players, cassettes and televisions also occupy an important place in these networks. Plastic goods—plates, dishes, etc.—and vests come from Iran, while glasses, teapots and petrol lamps come from the former USSR. The bazaars of Jaghori are certainly well stocked, and it is possible to find there batteries, cigarettes, notebooks, pens, guns and ammunition, marriage necklaces decorated with rupee notes, and so on. The many pharmacies are also well supplied.[4]

Migrants working in Pakistan and Iran are therefore the source of the money used to buy the goods on display in Hazarajat shops—all the goods, in fact, that local people need and do not produce themselves. Hazarajat has few products to offer in return, almonds being the only export crop of any size that brings in some cash to the peasantry of Jaghori or Qarabagh. Other local products, such as poplar wood, broad beans, chickpeas, cumin or *qrut* (dried buttermilk), play only a minor role. The production of felt and carpets is only gradually picking up again, usually with the support and encouragement of NGOs. Overall, then, the asymmetry between imports and exports is quite spectacular; a balance of trade is maintained only through the large-scale emigration of labor.

The Hazara drivers who dominate the transport between Ghazni and Mazar-e Sharif mostly use Soviet-made military lorries, the four-wheel-drive Kamaz. Between Ghazni, Kandahar and the Pakistani frontier, it is Pashtun drivers who have a virtual monopoly. For this unavoidable stretch, Hazara merchants strike a deal with Pashtuns they have known for a long time, either because they live in Quetta (often the case with Achekzay, Nurzay and members of other Durrani tribes from the frontier region) or because they come from Shah Joy, Gelan, Moqur, Andar or another area close to Hazarajat (which is the case mainly with the Taraki, Kharuti, Naser, Andar and other components of the Ghilzay).

To illustrate the social and economic strategies of the Hazara merchants and *hawâladâr,* let us take the case of Mahmad Nur from Qarabagh. In 1993 he had two associates: Khodanazar, his *mâmâ* (MB), in Isfahan, and Haji Ahmad, his father's *bace mâmâ* (MBS), in Ghazni. They represent a perfect example of multilocation. Mahmad Nur uses the services of no more than three drivers, Kharuti from a region in Afghanistan close to his own with whom he has been dealing since the beginning of the war. He describes them as his *âšnâ* (that is, "acquaintances" or "connections"), but not as his *dust* ("friends"). Mahmad Nur gives one letter for his partner in Afghanistan to the driver and another letter to a friend who is going to Afghanistan: they both mention the names of his customers, the amounts in question, and a list of the goods sent, for he prefers to send the same information twice. In 1993 the cost of transport was roughly 1,200 afghanis or 30 rupees ($1.5) per *ser* (7 kg), although the price might be higher if the goods were exceptionally bulky. Between Quetta and southern Hazarajat, it was also necessary to tip the *mujâhedin* the exorbitant sum of $200 to $300 for each lorry. In 1995 these figures declined because of the improved security, and under the Taliban there was a sharp decrease in improper toll charges. Drivers were then charging 20 rupees ($0.60) per *ser* for heavy goods, and 25 rupees ($0.75) for light goods.

Some shopkeepers in Jaghori and Qarabagh also stocked up in Herat or Mazar-e Sharif, or even Ghazni. Let us take the case of Mohammad Hanif, a young shopkeeper from the Dawlatjam lineage in Dahmarda (introduced in chapter 2). There are four brothers: Abdul Hamid (48), who is studying in Mashad, and three others—Qader Ali (55), Abdul Aziz (38) and Hanif (32)—who are in business together. With the help of Qader Ali's youngest son, they take it in turns to look after their two shops (in Dahmarda and Anguri). Their father is 78 and scarcely works any longer. They all live in the same *awli* and run a single household: "we cook together, eat together," Hanif explains. The family has some land in Dahmarda, 72 hours of water rights and approximately 12 *jerib* (3 for each brother) cultivated by sharecroppers. It also owns land in the Herat region (approx. 60 *jerib*), which it bought before the war but had to stop cultivating several times because of fighting and the great distance.

Depending on the political-military situation and the security situation on the roads, Hanif and his brothers go to one place or another to buy the goods they sell in their shops in Jaghori. Before the war, he and his older brothers used to buy mainly in Kabul, but then they kept switching between Mazar-e Sharif, Ghazni, Herat and Kandahar, and finally—after the emergence of the Taliban—did more and more business outside the country, in Quetta and Iran.

It is a dynamic family that has known how to enrich itself: the three associated brothers are not really multilocal but travel a lot between Jaghori, Herat, Mazar-e Sharif, Quetta and Iran. Abdul Aziz goes to Mazar, mainly to buy imported products from Central Asia and various fruits. Mohammad

Hanif, for his part, regularly goes to Kandahar and Quetta to buy medicines and manufactured items or to sell a few products from Afghanistan (almonds, broad beans and chickpeas, in particular). In Quetta he also buys dollars, which his brother then changes in Mazar at a substantial profit. Less often, Hanif goes to Iran to buy fabrics and clothing. He might perhaps use the services of a leading *hawâladâr* in Quetta to send money to Iran for his business. When he does not have enough cash, he turns himself into a *hawâladâr,* collects the savings of Hazaras working in Quetta and Iran, and uses the money to buy various goods.

As we have seen, almonds are Jaghori's only marketed product, whose autumn harvest marks the end of the agricultural year. Many farmers then leave for the Quetta mines and take their almonds with them to sell in Kandahar, Spin Boldak or Wesh, at a greater profit than in the Anguri or Sang-e Masha bazaar. In 1995 I had the opportunity to take part in such a trip, in a lorry rented in Jaghori. The driver, who had just bought the vehicle for 45 million afghanis (approx. $10,000), loaded a few barrels with almonds, with the idea of later buying tea and petrol in Wesh to make the return journey worthwhile. He charged 4,000 afghanis ($0.85) per *ser* of goods and 20,000 afghanis ($4.25) for an inside seat or 12,000 afghanis ($2.55) for a place on the back of the lorry, although those who accompanied their goods did not have to pay for themselves. Fifteen people were making the trip, all more or less related to one another by several links. Some went only to Wesh to sell their almond crop, while others continued to Quetta to spend the winter there. The people on board included Mardan Ali, Mohammad Hasan, his *bace kâkâ* (FBS), Bostan, the father-in-law (*xosur,* HF) of one of Hasan's sisters, Hasan's brother-in-law (*dâmâd,* ZH) Hazrat Ali, and Khodadad, the young son of Mohammad Reza (who was both Mardan Ali's *xosur-bura,* WB, and Hasan's *dâmâd,* ZH).

Mardan Ali had fourteen sacks of almonds and Hasan had thirty—that is, approximately 980 and 2,100 kg respectively. In Kandahar, the Taliban imposed a levy of 135 afghanis per *ser* (a little under $4 for the first and $8.6 for the second). They went on to Wesh, where the wholesale price was 965 rupees for 40 kg, so that Mardan Ali made a total of 24,000 rupees (approx. $740). With this he bought various items for his son's shop in Dahmarda: 900 kg of wheat; six sacks of sugar; ten 17 kg containers and twenty 5 kg containers of cooking oil; two large sacks of granulated sugar; four crates of Iranian soap; and one 50 kg package of tea. That left him with just 300 rupees (less than $10). As to Hasan, he received 7.5 million afghanis (approx. $1,600) for his almonds; he then bought forty-five sacks of wheat at 90,000 afghanis each, and handed over what was left (3.45 million afghanis, or approx. $740) to a companion who was returning to Dahmarda. Mardan Ali (who worked in Pakistan) conducted his dealings in rupees, while Hasan (who was living in Afghanistan) bought and sold in afghanis. Although both were illiterate, they had no problem juggling with different currencies and exchange-rates.

Dahmarda exported two things, labor and almonds, and imported all manner of supplies from Quetta or the frontier area. The money for these purchases came from the profits on the sale of almonds and from the savings of people working abroad.

A few little examples will illustrate the vast commercial network operating around Afghanistan. As the war destroyed all official infrastructure, traders could count only on themselves to obtain from source the goods they would sell in their shops. Buying and selling were superimposed on each another, and not even small shopkeepers could specialize in only one activity. Everyone saw diversification as a guarantee in the event of a sudden worsening of the situation in the region.

OUTLINE OF THE *HAWÂLA* SYSTEM

These examples illustrate the way in which the *hawâla* system combines letters of credit, money-transfers, exchange mechanisms and the transport of goods. Money-transfers involve broad commercial transactions among the following figures:

In Iran: A, the migrant worker or *kârgar;* B, the intermediary or *dallâl* who collects money from A and delivers it to C; C the *hawâladâr,* both businessman and broker, who executes the money-transfer. In Pakistan: D a merchant (*tâjer*) associated with C, who recovers the money and buys goods with it, or who may invest it in other financial operations, especially if he is a money-changer (*sarrâf*) or money-lender. In Afghanistan: E, the shopkeeper (*dokândâr*), collects the goods, which he sells in his shop, and reimburses the family of A. The latter is informed of the transaction by a migrant just back from Iran in whose care A left the *hawâla.*

All these players occupy logically distinct functions, although C, D and E are inevitably close to one another and it is even possible that B, C, D and E are one and the same person. If the ties between A and C are loose, the intervention of an intermediary is necessary; the larger the sums of money, the more the functions tend to be differentiated. Sometimes C works with Iranian import-export dealers or Baluch smugglers. In all cases, D and E call on the services of a Pashtun to ship the goods between Quetta and Hazarajat.

Among the Hazara *hawâladâr* from Ghazni province, there are two ideal types who represent the poles of a continuum within which all kinds of intermediary are possible: (1) the *hawâladâr* who works alone, runs a shop and regularly travels to Iran and Pakistan to collect money (his shop remaining closed while he is away); and (2) three associates who organize a division of labor, one gathering money in Iran, one picking it up in Quetta and buying goods, and one running the jointly owned shop in Hazarajat and paying the sum of money to the relevant families. This trilocal schema, involving Iran, Pakistan and Afghanistan, is quite common. The commercial partners are always related to one another, but they are not always brothers and do not necessarily belong to the same lineage. In fact, there is a tendency to favor partnerships with members of the maternal lineage, or even with relations by marriage. Each household group seeks to diversify its investments, so that brothers usually try to spread the risks by keeping their economic activities separate. Different types of strategy may coexist as a feature of particular situations.

The system is partly determined by the available infrastructure. Between Iran and Pakistan it is possible to make bank transfers, to mail letters and to telephone, but between Pakistan and Afghanistan it is necessary to travel personally. Quetta serves as an essential stopover between Iran and Afghanistan. Modern technology is used for communication between Iran and Pakistan, while a lack of state control is exploited for communications between Pakistan and Afghanistan. There are two ways of moving capital between Iran and Pakistan: bank transfers in cash and cross-border smuggling in goods. In the case of Afghanistan, however, it is almost exclusively goods that are moved into the country. In Quetta, money can be invested in various business activities—especially speculation on exchange-rate variations among the rial, rupee and afghani and, to a lesser extent, the US dollar and other currencies. According to the size of their business, Hazara *hawâladâr* might transfer as much as several thousand dollars in one operation. Figure 10 resumes their activities. As a rule, the *hawâladâr* is both a merchant and a money-changer, although some do not trade in goods but specialize only in money-transfers and credit operations. A *hawâladâr* should not be thought of as a real banker, because a customer cannot deposit money with him and earn interest. His banking operations are, in fact, a means of employing his capital reserves.

Figure 11 depicts the activities of these pure *hawâladâr* and the system of commercial credit.[5] The *hawâla* system links many other countries besides Afghanistan and Pakistan and may function without any personal movement (if there is also someone who wishes to send money in the opposite direction). The *hawâladâr* is the middle term through whom money can be sent in both directions without any real circulation of liquidity (figure 12).

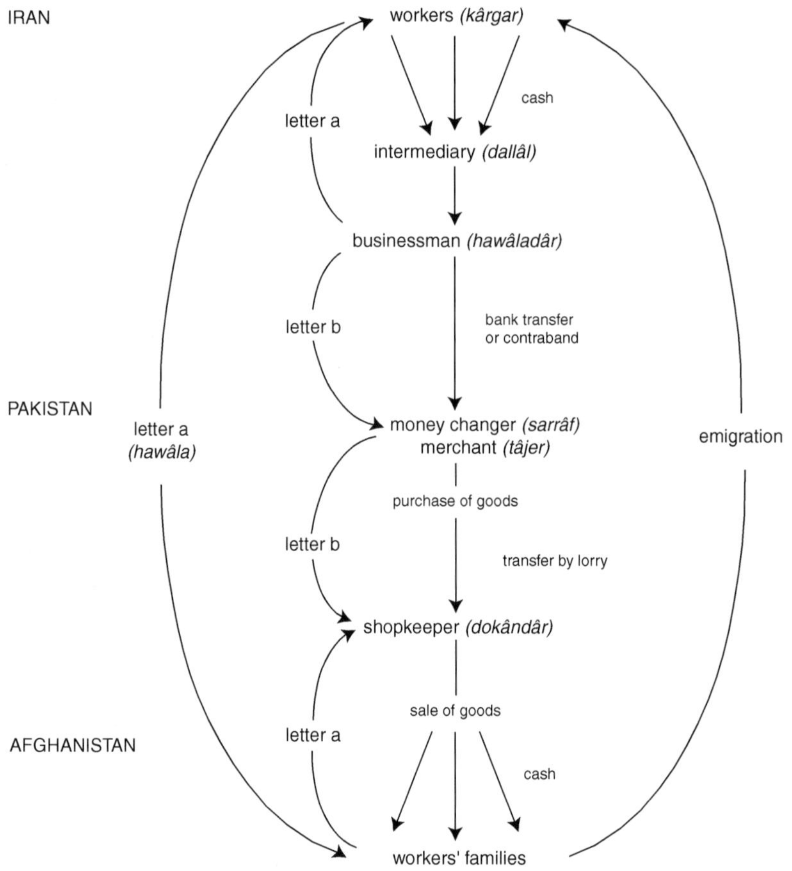

Figure 10. Money-transfers between Iran, Pakistan and Afghanistan

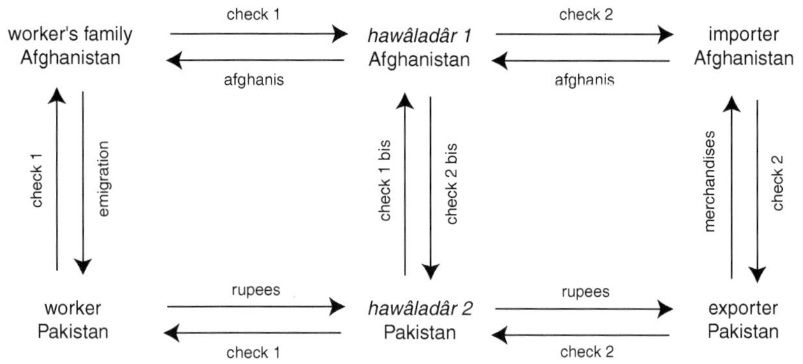

Figure 11. The *hawâla* system between Afghanistan and Pakistan

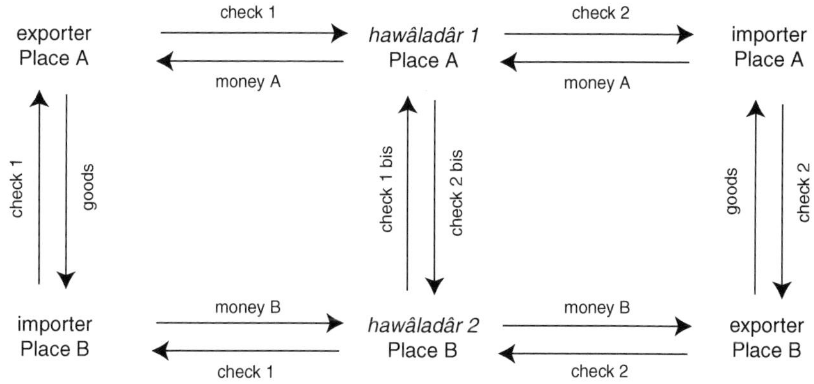

Figure 12. General sketch of the *hawâla* system

SOURCES OF PROFIT, ACCOUNTING AND EXCHANGE MECHANISMS

By issuing letters of credit, the *hawâladâr* create capital through which they conduct their trading activity. As we have seen, they have several sources of profit: (1) a transaction commission; (2) speculation on exchange-rates; and (3) the value-added of goods shipped to Afghanistan. From time to time, the partners meet to do the accounts and make a balance-sheet of their activities, as well as to share out the profit and loss. The mutual trust among them is again evident in the lack of strict checking or precise calculation at the time of the transactions. Income and expenditure are usually noted down on loose sheets of paper. The traders do not keep double-entry books, but this does not mean that their transnational financial networks are not highly efficient.

In the case of the large *hawâladâr*, the sums paid and received tend to balance out (see the general sketch of the *hawâla* system). The sums actually transferred from one place to another are in no way comparable to the size of the transactions.[6] Only very rarely does a cash payment conclude an accounting period between partners in different places. In 1993 (at a time, moreover, when the roads in southern Afghanistan were insecure), I witnessed the handing over of 8 million afghanis (approx. $8,000) in a shop in Quetta; the huge wads of notes had been sent from Ghazni inside bales of cotton, in payment for a shipment of sugar in the opposite direction. In the case of Hazara *hawâladâr* and *dokândâr* from Ghazni province, the partners are usually related to one another or from the same place of origin. Since the proceeds of their activity are used up by their own families, they do not need to be distributed outside the village of origin.

In principle, the money trade is prohibited: it is illegal to charge interest on a loan or an investment. But commercial and financial transactions do not exclude the payment of a fixed commission, which is considered not as usury but as a fair reward for services rendered. In general, the commission is rarely set above 5% of the transfer, and often around 2% or 3%. Afghans do not use an abstract term to refer to it; instead of saying "he takes 3% commission," they say "he takes 3,000 rupees for a *lak* (100,000)." Such sums are charged for money-transfers between Iran and Pakistan (to defray banking charges), but more rarely between Pakistan and Afghanistan. The practice is often disguised by financial techniques, such as the indirect commission that many *hawâladâr* build into the currency exchange-rate.

In the business hub of Quetta, the Pashtun money-changers (*sarrâf*) are concentrated in the Kandahari bazaar, while the Hazaras have established themselves at Saray-e Namak. Their activity sometimes brings sizeable profits, but it can also end in spectacular losses. Usually there are forty or so money-changers at Saray-e Namak; many of them are small shopkeepers from Ghazni who have come to Quetta for part of the year before returning to Afghanistan. They sit on the kerb in front of inns and shops, discussing business or exchanging the latest news as they wait for customers to show up. They do not compete with one another, because they know that people who want to change money go first of all to someone they know. The atmosphere in the Kandahari Bazaar is different: it is a large central street where the money-changers have shops of their own and display the currencies they accept; most of them also operate as wholesalers, and various packages litter the side of the road. The exchange-rates on offer vary remarkably little, and there is little or no scope for bargaining. Huge piles of notes change hands, in transactions that allow an observer to detect the degree of proximity or distance between the parties. If relations are close, it is a point of honour not to count the wads; if it is merely a business relationship, the money-changer himself will ask the customer to check the amount (which may take several minutes).

The two kinds of afghani note, which people refer to as *dawlati* ("the government's") and *dostumi* ("Dostum's"), are printed in different places and passed down through different networks. They may look similar, but a moment's attention is enough to tell which is which. The *dostumi* currency does not have a good reputation in the market and attracts a less favorable rate of exchange; sometimes people simply refuse to accept it outside the areas under Junbesh or Wahdat control. The smaller denominations (500 afghanis or less), which date from the time of President Daud (1973–1978) or even King Zaher (1933–1973), have lost nearly all their value over the years and are difficult to pass on. This is why, unlike in the case of the dollar,[7] money-changers offer a better rate for the sale of smaller notes. Again, people do not use the expression "one dollar is worth 32 rupees" but say "you get 3,200 rupees for 100 dollars" (and, in fact, they would not receive 32 rupees for a one-dollar note).

Money-changers earn a living by offering different rates for the sale and purchase of currencies. If, for example, someone arrives from Afghanistan and buys Pakistani currency from a Quetta dealer at the rate of one rupee to 150 afghanis, that same dealer might, the next day, buy a rupee for 135 afghanis from someone leaving Pakistan for Afghanistan. The difference of 15 afghanis is his profit. Were he to buy dollars at the 36.8 rate and sell them at 37, he would make 20 rupees per 100 dollars.

Risks are involved in such dealings, but most of the money-changers at Saray-e Namak are too small to do anything foolish. Let us take the example of Mohammad Taher, from the Dawlatjam lineage in Dahmarda. Towards the end of 1995, after the violence that divided his village (see chapter 3), he fled to Afghanistan with his sick wife and mute daughter. He rented a shop in the Anguri bazaar. He sold everything and went to Quetta with 2 million afghanis (approx. $450) in his pocket. His younger brother joined him there a few months later, while their father remained in Dahmarda. Taher's savings were soon used up and he had to borrow 8,000 rupees from his *xosur-bura* (WB), who works in Saudi Arabia, and 17,000 rupees from his *bace mâmâ* (MBS). With this money, he paid the medical costs for his wife and daughter and was able to start up as a money-changer at Saray-e Namuk. He said that he made an average of 50 to 100 rupees a day in profit ($1.5 to $3). He would repay his debts to his relatives when his situation improved (they asked no interest of him and did not set a repayment schedule). The big problem is the rapid devaluation of the afghani, since the profits that businessmen make by changing money or buying goods is not always enough to offset the decline in value. The small size of Mohammad Taher's capital, however, as well as the short period of his exchange transactions, mean that he does not lose money. If he played safe by hoarding dollars, his money would not make a profit.

In the absence of state regulation of the currency, money-changers follow political and military developments for signs of anything that might directly affect the exchange-rate. The prospect of a settlement boosts the value of the afghani (for example, when the *mujâhedin* captured Kabul in April 1992). In March 1995, there were doubts about the future of the Taliban after their defeat at the hands of Massoud in Kabul, but the market was favorably impressed by the Taliban capacity for resistance and counter-attack. At the end of 1995, when the afghani was strengthening with each Taliban victory, money-changers were making the following predictions: if the Taliban took Kabul, the rate would move from 1 rupee for 140 afghanis to 1 rupee for 100 afghanis; if the Rabbani government gained the upper hand, the afghani would be present in greater amounts on the market and its value would decline (perhaps 1 rupee for 200 afghanis).

On August 29, 1996, the Salang announcement concerning an agreement between the Rabbani government and the Shura-ye hamahangi caused a rise in the value of the afghani—from 28,000 to 24,000 to the dollar—and a fall in prices in Kabul. (The afghani rate remained lower in Mazar than Kabul, because *dostumi* notes were less highly valued than *dawlati.*) The Taliban capture of the capital on 26 September 1996, which suggested to the markets that a military solution to the conflict might be on the cards, led to a further strengthening of the afghani, but the growing international isolation of the Taliban regime soon sent the currency plummeting. This trend was reversed only after the American intervention in autumn 2001 and the establishment of a new interim administration in December of the same year.

THE HOUSEHOLD ECONOMY AND BUSINESS PARTNERSHIP

The household economy and business partnership are often intertwined in Afghan society, but it is important to retain the conceptual distinction between the two. As a rule, only the male descendants of a male ancestor, together with their spouses and unmarried offspring, live under the same roof. That leaves many possible scenarios, depending upon life strategies, preferences and personal affinities. The family legacy may be shared during the father's lifetime or remain intact even after the death of the father or grandfather. As long as their interests do not conflict, brothers hesitate to go their separate ways economically during their father's lifetime. Nevertheless, many cases do not conform to this model. Such situations need to be understood in terms of strategies and negotiations, interests and conflicts—in other words, in terms of practical reason and not the application of hard and fast rules. For example, Mardan Ali asked for his share of the legacy and struck out separately from his father and two brothers—behavior that was criticized as maverick and lacking in family solidarity, but also respected for its dynamism and enterprise. It is hard to identify clear rules among the various practices. Those which the interested parties formulate themselves certainly provide an official legitimation. But, as Bourdieu writes: "The ethnologist would doubtless gain if he assumed, as a general rule, that people obey rules (when they exist as such) only in so far as the interest in obeying them is significantly stronger than the interest in disobeying them" (1972: 90).

Let us take a few more examples to illustrate these points. Abdul Rauf is from Dahmarda and has a shop there. He belongs to the Dawran lineage and has two younger brothers. They preferred not to set up in business together and embarked upon separate activities: shopkeeping for the eldest, family agriculture for the second, and unskilled labor for the third in Tehran (where the second initially helped him find his feet). In winter, Abdul Rauf closes his shop and spends a few months in Quetta; sometimes he also goes there for short periods in the summer, staying either with his paternal cousin (FBS) or with his sister. He buys goods in Quetta and sends them to Hazarajat. He is associated with Reza Ali, his *bace mâmâ* (MBS), who has been working as a baker in Saudi Arabia for the last two years and sends money home every four or five months. By pooling their money, Abdul Rauf and Reza Ali increase their capital and expand their economic and commercial possibilities; the former does most of the work, but he would not have enough capital without the latter's contribution. Abdul Rauf chose Reza Ali as his partner because they get on well together and because he wanted someone from his mother's lineage rather than his own household or patrilineage; when he is in Quetta they speak on the telephone once a month; otherwise, they write ten or so letters a year to each other.

In 1995, I met Juma Ali in an inn at Saray-e Namak. He is a Chahar Dasta from Tamaki (district of Qarabagh), 42 years old, with two sons and three daughters. The family lands, which his eldest brother looks after, produce only 500 *ser* (3,500 kg) of wheat. Juma Ali uses trade as a second source of income, and he had brought some cumin with him. He and his partner Mahmad Nur, mentioned previously in this chapter, faced two problems: on the one hand, the Pakistani rupee was too low and it would not be in their favor to buy afghanis with the rupees they obtained from sales (they eventually hoped to receive 170 afghanis per rupee, instead of the current 148 afghanis); on the other hand, serious political tensions blocked commercial transactions in Karachi, from where the cumin would have to be exported to India. They would therefore have to wait several months before concluding the deal, which would then give them money to buy oil, flour, rice and sugar.

Juma Ali goes to Quetta once or twice a year, in addition to two or three trips to Mazar-e Sharif. He and Mahmad Nur travel with other traders like Gulistan from the same region as themselves. In Quetta eight or nine people rent a room in an inn by the year, and there are always two or three occupying it who share the costs of food. They conduct their transactions in parallel with each other: this gives them greater confidence, as well as greater bargaining power.

Gulistan lives in Qarabagh with his two brothers and two *bace kâkâ* (FBS) who are also his *bace xâla* (MZS).[8] Since their grandfather's death, they have preferred to keep an integrated household unit. Gulistan makes trips back and forth between Ghazni, Quetta and Mazar-e Sharif. He used to be in partnership with Mahmad Nur (and they have remained friends), but since 1995 he has been working with Ahmad Ali, his *bace kâkâ, bace xâla* and *dâmâd* (ZH) in one, who runs their shop in Ghazni. Gulistan's elder brother is in Iran, while the other brother looks after the family's undivided lands in Qarabagh.

There are many different types of flexible financial agreement, often limited in time and external to the circles of kin and neighbors. One such form in use among the Hazara is a kind of limited partnership called *commenda,* which has been known for centuries throughout the area from the Mediterranean to the Indian subcontinent. In the Islamic Middle East, it is based on the model of the Prophet Mohammad and his wife Khadija.

> The principle of *commenda* was that within the association the partners were equal, and one furnished the capital while the other managed the business [. . .] The *commenda* was intended to be a form of capital investment wherein the profits were distributed according to what the partners had agreed upon. Here we have a capitalistic calculation of accounts. The original capital invested is compared with the final sum and the surplus is marked profit to be distributed (Labib 1969: 91).

The Italian trading cities introduced the system to Europe. It first appeared in the ninth century in Venice, which took it from the practices acceptable under customary law in the Byzantine world (Pirenne 1963: 15). The *commenda,* based on a separation between capital and labor, played a decisive role in the economic rise of both Europe and the Middle East (Pirenne 1969; de Roover 1948). In the Islamic Republic of Iran, where this type of association is known as *mozârebeh* or *mozârebat,* it went through unprecedented development and institutionalization, but was then prohibited in 1990 (Adelkhah 1998: 81–116):

> To put it schematically, this contract involves an agreement between two persons, one of whom (the *mâlek*) holds money capital and the other (the *mozâreb*) has certain capacities for work. The *mozâreb* undertakes to conduct commercial activities (*tejârat*) with the help of the *mâlek*'s funds, to the exclusion of all other economic or social activity. On pain of rendering the contract null and void, the sharing of profits must be set in advance at 1/2–1/2, 1/3–2/3, 1/4–3/4, etc. [. . .] the *mozâreb* cannot be held responsible for loss of capital, unless the contract includes a clear provision for him to compensate the *mâlek* for such loss (1998: 86).

More modestly, and less formally, the *mozârebat* play a major economic role among the Hazaras. Agreement is often reached between close relatives—for example, a rich man and his young nephew. The profits are usually shared on a fifty-fifty basis. It is a way of investing one's money profitably, while circumventing the ban on interest-bearing loans. The consecrated formula for loans without interest is *qarz ul-hasana*, literally "good loan" (Adelkhah 1998: 87; Center for Afghanistan Studies 1993: 297). Islam resembles medieval Christianity in its ban on usury. We should bear in mind, however, that the commercial revival of Europe in the eleventh and twelfth centuries went together with a growing trade in money: usury was widespread in the West by the twelfth century (Pirenne 1963: 100), commercial credit and the *commenda* were flourishing in Italy, and letters of credit were in current use. As in the *hawâla* system, banking activities were a way of using reserves of capital. And traders have always been able to devise strategies to circumvent the ban on usury:

> Usually the borrower undertook to pay on the due date a sum higher than the one he had actually received; the difference constituted the interest. In *ad manaium* loans, [. . .] it was understood that the lender would not discharge the debt on the fixed day, so that the collection of usury was masked by a penalty for late repayment (Pirenne 1963: 107).

The examples given above illustrate the financial strategies and division of tasks within families. Many small traders associate with one or more partners while keeping separate accounts (this is also the case of the *râhbalat*); this allows them to increase the capital and spread the financial risks, to expand the customer base (each partner attracts members of his family circle), and to make better use of time (for example, one partner can go to Iran while the other is buying goods in Quetta). Trust is an indispensable element in such a relationship, but the underlying basis may also be kinship, friendship or a shared neighborhood, as well as a common interest and shared contributions. A business partnership does not necessarily entail a shared household budget. A number of strategies are possible, but often a household group—like Abdul Rauf and his brothers—prefers to diversify its economic activities through geographical dispersion. A rich man may invest money and at the same time help a less well-off relative by lending him money in the form of *mozârebat*. Mutual support, cooperation and partnership are distinct yet constantly overlap with one another. In some circumstances, one person may associate with a second person for a single business deal, then with a third for another deal. We may thus distinguish two tendencies in commercial and economic strategies:

(1) A highly integrated family, which manages its possessions as one, may combine several generations under a recognized head: the grandfather, the father or one of his brothers (the most capable but not necessarily the eldest). Sometimes there may be a division of tasks, so that one concerns himself with external "political" relations and another with economic matters. In such cases, the migratory and economic strategies are planned within the household unit; very often, the family members are also business partners.

(2) The business partners are close relatives but not members of the same household unit or lineage. The main emphasis is then on relations through the women, either within the lineage of the maternal uncle (that is, the mother) or his wife's kin. On the one hand, this means that there is less at stake—and fewer sources of conflict with maternal relatives, kin through marriage or neighbors. On the other hand, the degree of proximity is sufficiently great for a relationship of trust to develop. In such cases, people associate with others as the circumstances dictate, by sharing the financial risks inherent in any business venture. Tensions do not result in grave conflicts, as it is relatively easy to work out a way of sharing the joint capital and the profits. This is why brothers belonging to the same household unit often prefer to divide up the tasks: some look after the land, others engage in trade, still others go to work or study in Iran. The diversification of economic activity—and also of political affiliation—provides a guarantee for the family.

Social and economic cooperation may also take many different forms—from a single household unit to a limited trading partnership, from mutual support to the pooling of capital. In situations of war and migration, the dominant strategy among the Hazara tends to involve the separation of business partnership from the household economy.

THE SIZE OF MONEY-TRANSFERS

Some estimates suggest that in the 1970s Afghans working in Iran or the Gulf states sent home $100 to $300 million a year (Etienne 1982: 47). This flow of money, already far from insignificant, sharply increased in both absolute and relative terms during more than twenty years of war (World Bank 2001).

In a report for the UN, Johnson (2000: 77–81) set a very low figure for the number of families in Hazarajat who received funds from abroad: 2.5% in Yakawlang; 6.2% in Lal; 9.4% in Panjao; 23.0% in Shahristan; 32.2% in Day Kundi and Waras. Unfortunately she does not make any comment on the wide variations; nor does she take into account the strategies of multilocation and multipolar movement. My own data appear to show a much higher number of Hazara families who had one member abroad and benefited from transfers of funds. Indeed, in my eighty-nine completed interviews (more than 75% with people originating in Hazarajat), it is hard to find a single household unaffected in one way or another by this phenomenon.

In September 1995, a large merchant on Alamdar Road estimated that each day some 600 million afghanis ($140,000) circulated between Quetta and Jaghori—which would make an annual total of more than $50 million, mostly in the form of goods. These figures, which do not seem exaggerated, rest mainly upon the work of Hazaras abroad. Mardan Ali, from his job as a foreman in the coal mines, earned 32,000 rupees ($1,000) in three spring months of 1995. When he returned to Dahmarda, he took with him 1.5 million afghanis ($340–350), 10,000 rupees ($310) and two blankets worth 500 and 600 rupees ($35 together)—a spread that helped to minimize the risk. He thus saved 70% of his wages, or approximately $700. If this was extrapolated on an annual basis, it would give a transfer to Dahmarda of $2,800 out of wages totalling $4,000. It is true that, in the following summer, his earnings were slightly lower, and he was able to save only 2 million afghanis (approx. $450). These variations, due to the seasonal rhythm of work in the mines, correspond to the fact that Mardan Ali was paid by output in addition to a fixed wage. According to his own calculations, he transferred $2,000-$2,500 a year to his family. In any event, his is rather a special case, since his employer delegates to him the responsibility for many tasks. Few of the Hazaras working in Quetta can earn such a good living. Let us take the example of an ordinary miner, Abdullah.

(1) In spring 1995 Abdullah entrusts 7,000 rupees to Qorban Ali, the brother of his *dâmâd* (ZH), who has a shop in Baba (Jaghori). Qorban Ali hands over one million afghanis (approx. $250) to Abdullah's brother. The kinship relation is close, trust prevails and no *hawâla* changes hands; nor is any commission deducted. The benefit for Qorban Ali is that he is able to buy goods and take them to Jaghori from Quetta.

(2) In summer 1995 Abdullah hands over 3,000 rupees to Enayatullah, another trader in Baba, with whom he does not have a kinship relation. No commission is deducted, but Abdullah receives a *hawâla* and gives it to a friend from Baba together with a letter telling his brother to go and pick up 800,000 afghanis (which, because of the rapid devaluation of the afghani, is no longer worth $100).

(3) In the late autumn of 1995, Abdullah entrusts 4,000 rupees to a neighbor who is returning to Baba. As in the previous case, he gives to another migrant on his way back to Baba a letter telling his brother to pick up 800,000 afghanis (whose value has now risen to nearly $120).

(4) In spring 1996, after a year in Quetta, Abdullah returns to Baba with his winter savings of approximately $200 (winter is the time when the mines are most active and miners are paid the most).

This example is typical of the financial strategies of a coal miner. He earns and sends home less that Mardan Ali (who is a foreman), but over the year it adds up to the tidy sum of approximately $670.

Let us now turn to the Hazara workers in Iran. Mohammad Dawud, a 19-year-old from Chahar Dasta of Ahin (Qarabagh), works in Tehran as a caretaker for an Iranian family and earns 30,000 tomans a month. He sends 20% of his earnings—72,000 tomans (or approx. $180) a year—to Afghanistan. His elder brother Ishaq, aged 35, is also in Tehran, where he works for a construction company and earns 100,000 tomans a month. He sends roughly 60% of this back to Qarabagh: that is, 720,000 tomans (approx. $1,800) a year. In one year, then, the two brothers send a total of approximately $2,000 to their family in Hazarajat, through *hawâladâr* intermediaries who, like them, are originally from Ahin. A man from Dahmarda, 32-year-old Liaqat Ali, also works for a Tehran construction company, and regularly sends money to his family in Jaghori. Between spring 1995 and late winter 1995–96, he made three transfers for a total of 600,000 tomans (between $1,400 and $1,500).

Let us summarize the situation. In one year, a foreman at the Quetta mines sends between $2,000 and $2,500 to his family in Hazarajat, an ordinary miner transfers nearly $700, and workers in Iran send home an average of more than $1,000. The range of these cases makes them fairly representative of the work possibilities open to Hazaras in Pakistan and Iran. Let us now try to estimate the flow of funds into Hazarajat.

The population of Dahmarda consists of approximately 450 households, or more than 3,000 persons. Some 500 persons from the *manteqa* were in Iran in 1996, including 350 single male workers who were sending their savings to Afghanistan. If we consider that migrants put aside an average of $1,000 a year, the annual sum transferred to Iran from Dahmarda comes to $350,000. By extrapolating, as a mental exercise, these figures to the two million or so inhabitants of Hazarajat, we would obtain a figure of 10 percent employed in Iran as unskilled workers—that is, some 200,000 persons who regularly send their savings to Afghanistan (considerably lower than UNHCR estimates).[9] If we keep to the figure of $1,000 per person per year, we then arrive at a total of $200 million just for Hazaras working in Iran, and perhaps billions of dollars for the whole of the Afghan emigration. That is a considerable sum of money. The *hawâla* system is therefore not an epiphenomenon but an essential element in the Afghan economy, all too often neglected by analysts.

These estimates at least give some idea of the scale of remittances to Afghanistan, but it is unfortunately impossible to corroborate them with official figures. No government statistics have been available since the fall of the Najibullah government in 1992, nor any estimate of GNP (World Bank 2001: 3, 35). International Monetary Fund statistics give no indication of the Afghan balance of payments for the years in which we are interested, and the estimates in the annual French publication *L'état du monde* are too summary to be of real use. In 1993 Afghan GDP was supposed to have been a little more than $14 billion, and in 1998 twice as high (more than $28 billion). Figures for the balance of trade are not very reliable because of the large smuggling networks. In 1994 imports were estimated at $602 million (industrial and transport equipment: 37.7%; basic manufactures: 18.3%; minerals and fuels: 10.9%), and exports at $296 million (dried fruit and nuts: 51.3%; carpets: 13.1%; wool and animal skins: 4.9%; cotton: 1.4%). In 1996 these had fallen to $496 million and $125 million respectively.[10] Imports therefore exceed exports by $300 to $400 million—a sum that might be made up from the money-transferred by migrants.

The World Bank has put these figures higher: in the year 2000, $1.2 billion (300 millions) for total imports, with exports and re-exports also around $1.2 billion (300 millions) (World Bank 2001: 11). However, according to a survey at the various frontier points and the main trading centers, only a third of the imported products are destined for domestic consumption; the remainder are re-exported.

Imports for domestic use were mainly financed by money-transfers from Afghans abroad. As we saw in chapter 5, the contribution of Afghans to Iran's GNP was in excess of $7 billion, and an American journalist writes that, in the view of Pakistani bankers, the annual sum sent to Pakistan through the *hawâla* system is between $2.5 billion and $3 billion (whereas only $1 billion passes through the banks).[11] The contrast must be even more striking inside Afghanistan, where no bank was operational in the mid-1990s. Of course, from a macroeconomic point of view, the sums transferred by Hazaras from Iran to Afghanistan may not seem so huge, but in an Afghan context they are highly significant. By comparison, a Swiss daily reported that in 2001 the ICRC launched “a new appeal for 10 million (Swiss) francs, on top of an appeal for 50 million francs launched at the beginning of the year. The combined total represents 8 percent of the ICRC’s operational budget of around 850 million francs.”[12] And yet Afghanistan and the Balkans were the ICRC’s main areas of operation. As to the UN, in 2001 it asked for 250 million Swiss francs in aid to feed displaced persons in the camps in Afghanistan, but all it had received by April from the donor states was 85 million francs.

These figures, when compared with what is sent home by Afghans working abroad, put humanitarian aid into a sober perspective and underline the capacity of Afghans themselves to find solutions to their dramatic plight. Nevertheless, we should not neglect the role played by humanitarian organizations in Afghanistan. As Dorronsoro notes, “NGOs spend roughly $100 million a year in Afghanistan, a derisory amount for a population of twenty million. But their influence is much greater than these figures suggest, especially because they make it possible to maintain social services and provide jobs for thousands of Afghan executives.”[13] The food and health situation is alarming for large sections of the population, and the infrastructure is virtually in ruins. The country urgently needs massive aid to avert a humanitarian disaster. The formulation of a long-term strategy, however, requires us to look back at what went before.

In the 1980s, and more especially in the following decade, humanitarian organizations played a positive role in some respects and a pernicious one in others. They certainly saved many lives—which is enough to justify their activity—and they helped to stem the brain drain by providing jobs for many educated Afghans. Paradoxically, however, this very aid to the population often allowed local commanders to devote all available funds to the war effort without risking a loss of support among their community. The fact that the aid was not concerted also meant that the various NGOs accentuated the fragmentation of the country; they were often forced to get on close terms with a warlord in order to gain access to a particular valley, with the result that to a considerable extent the distribution of the NGOs matched the distribution of the warring factions. Finally, an obsession with the need to prove their efficacy to possible donors often led NGOs to establish themselves in the most accessible areas where the need was not necessarily the greatest. For NGO operations never evenly covered the whole of Afghanistan. The reproduction of old inequalities of treatment is well illustrated by the case of Hazarajat, which everyone recognized as one of the most economically vulnerable regions yet which never received really large amounts of aid.

Not only do Hazara migrants send a large part of their income back to Afghanistan (several hundred million dollars a year); many commercial activities in Hazarajat depend upon these remittances. All the shops there—from Yakawalang to Behsud, from Panjab to Qarabagh—are supplied by this system. It is thus a major social-economic phenomenon, which also has political implications. The war accelerated and intensified the movement of people and goods, as Hazaras developed new activities, became aware of their rights and gained confidence in their capacities. Migration is not simply a response to violence and arbitrariness, nor even to poverty; it is a planned strategy, which has enabled the populations of Hazarajat to survive while also broadening their social-cultural horizon.

THE *HAWÂLA* SYSTEM AND INTERNATIONAL SMUGGLING NETWORKS

Since the attacks of September 11, 2001 the media have taken a new interest in the *hawâla* system, but all too often they have stressed the uses that terrorist networks have been able to make of it.[14] Although the boundaries may not be too clear, the money-transfer system established by Afghan migrants must not be simply equated with international smuggling and money-laundering networks. Such an attitude is indeed dangerous, because it tends to discredit a practice that has helped to limit the humanitarian disaster in Afghanistan.

In 1995 and 1996, the trade networks between Hazarajat and Quetta were very different from those in the north of the country; the former, running parallel to the migratory routes to Iran via Quetta, mainly specialized in food and a few manufactured items of current consumption, whereas the latter involved economic activities that were little geared to the interior of Afghanistan. Herat and Mazar-e Sharif, for instance, were the domain of large merchants whose international networks scarcely touched the villages of Hazarajat.

The large international networks have some points of contact with those used by ordinary migrants. For it may happen that the smaller *hawâladâr-dokândâr* function as intermediaries, collecting money in Iran from workers they know and entrusting it to large-scale businessmen. Despite the overlapping or interlocking, however, there is a striking contrast between the activities of leading merchants in Herat or Mazar-e Sharif, or indeed Kabul, Peshawar or Quetta, and those of small Hazarajat shopkeepers.

The Taliban encouraged the development of Afghanistan as a special place of transit that was hugely profitable to them. Ahmed Rashid (2000), a

Pakistani journalist who has followed Afghanistan for many years, paints a vivid though alarming picture of the smuggling networks. In his estimation, the informal economy and the black market account for 30 to 50 percent of Pakistan's entire economy, with a large part covered by the drugs traffic with Afghanistan (2000: 121–122). In 1995 the UNDCP (United Nations Drugs Control Programme) put the export of drugs from Pakistan and Afghanistan at $1.35 billion a year, and by 1998 that figure had more than doubled to $3 billion (Rashid 2000: 124).

These activities also take in consumption goods. Since 1950 an international agreement on "Afghan Transit Trade" (or ATT) with Pakistan has allowed land-locked Afghanistan to import goods tax-free through the port of Karachi (Rashid 2000: 189–194; see also World Bank 2001). From the beginning, this gave rise to smuggling activities: convoys from Karachi would officially cross the border with Afghanistan, then part of their load would be shipped straight back to Pakistan through the tribal areas and sold at a large profit. The war gave this practice a huge boost, and it expanded on a quite extraordinary scale under the Taliban regime. Thus Afghanistan experienced intense levels of activity, despite the deplorable state of the roads and the transport difficulties, the lack of electricity and the rudimentary facilities (illustrated by the lorry containers that serve as shops in Kandahar, Ghazni, Kabul, Mazar-e Sharif, Herat and elsewhere). All kinds of consumption items, from household electrical goods through televisions and computers to motor vehicles, flood the markets of the countries bordering on Afghanistan. Wesh, on the Afghan side between Kandahar and Quetta, presents a quite surreal spectacle: hundreds of vehicles (most often Toyotas from Dubai, such as the Corolla, pick-ups and vans) are parked in the middle of the desert waiting for Pakistani customers to show up;[15] heaps of petrol barrels complete the picture. In Chaman, on the Pakistani side, the shops are crammed with televisions, video recorders and other luxury goods from Japan or South-East Asia. The Pakistani police turn a blind eye as three hundred lorries a day pass along this route, and two hundred along the route from Peshawar to Kabul through Khyber and Jalalabad (Rashid 2000: 124).

These smuggling activities represent a considerable loss for the countries bordering Afghanistan: in 1995 the ATT is thought to have cut 30 percent from Pakistan's potential customs revenue (a loss equivalent to $600 million by 1997–1998), and organized smuggling around Afghanistan to have reached the figure of $10 billion. In both Pakistan and Afghanistan, those who promoted such activities were the most enthusiastic supporters of the Taliban. For, by eliminating the highway racketeering of Pashtun Belt commanders (the effects of which were especially acute in Kandahar) and by establishing control over the Herat region in 1995, the Taliban reopened the trade routes between the Indian Ocean and Central Asia. The modest taxes they levied on trade were enough to bring them in considerable revenue. Then, in autumn 2001, the fall of the Taliban brought a partial return to the anarchy that had prevailed in the southern parts of Afghanistan between 1992 and 1994. It is not certain that the government which has been established in Kabul will be capable of guaranteeing security.

As the smuggling networks are based on transit trade, they greatly enrich a handful of individuals but are of scarcely any benefit to the country as a whole. They should be distinguished from the commercial activities and money remittances of Afghans in Iran, Pakistan and the Persian Gulf, whose main aim is to support their close relatives inside Afghanistan. As long as the country does not resume truly productive activity, such transfers from the emigration will remain the principal resource in rural areas. For the international community and the renascent Afghan state, a normalization of the geopolitical situation throughout the region must involve stricter control over the smuggling networks and a vigorous struggle against corruption. But large sections of the population would be harmed by a criminalization of the *hawâla* system, without which they could not have survived the terrible years of war.

Chapter Eight
Ways of Communicating

COMMUNICATION, PERSONAL MOVEMENT AND SOCIAL RELATIONS

Migrants operate in a context of mistrust and insecurity and do not always have access to modern means of communication. In studying how information circulates among them, we may therefore uncover other ties of solidarity and forms of cooperation than those considered up to now. For, despite the separation, Hazaras in Afghanistan, Pakistan and Iran do communicate intensely with one another by telephone and letter.

The Hazaras move around in well-signposted territory; they always know where they can make contact with other Hazaras who will enable them to receive news from home or track down a relative. The very lack of a postal service, like the insecurity of many regions through which they pass, forces them to band together with others for mutual support (for example, one will carry a message and ask a similar favour in return); otherwise they would not be able to keep up with the comings and goings of family, friends and acquaintances, or know where to meet and which *mosâfer-xâna* to stay at. The fact that a migrant has a message to pass on to someone else gives him a pretext to get in touch with others; it also allows him to obtain food and accommodation for two or three days at a time.

Hazara migrants prefer to use the telephone when that is a possibility. Since it is not available in Hazarajat itself, that makes Quetta an indispensable stopover. Contacts and exchanges of information can then be organized through relatives, friends or simple acquaintances who are on the move. The density of movement means that communication can be quick and effective even in the absence of telephonic and postal services. Migrants visit one another, discuss and pass on news; information is not private but has a marked oral dimension. Most of the individuals in question are illiterate and therefore have to find a third party to write or read messages. Communication takes place more through the messenger's tales than through the actual content of letters, whose main function is to give legitimacy to the oral discourse and to provide physical testimony of the cohesion of a scattered social group. People compare different accounts of an event, and in this way are to form a clearer picture of what actually happened.

By carrying a letter, friends and neighbors make it possible for relatives to keep in touch. The general exchange of help and support serves to strengthen social bonds across space. But it also illustrates *a contrario* the relative effacement of women, who are less spatially mobile than men and whose essential social-cultural contribution is not given any prominence in the public sphere. As we have seen, the migrant world is mainly a male world. But the fact that I was scarcely ever able to have a long discussion with women prevented me from studying their role more deeply.

THE ORAL AND THE WRITTEN

The oral and the written are related to each other in complex ways. Goody, who has devoted several works to this theme (1977, 1987), argues that the use of writing brings about profound changes in how people reason; it made possible the development of abstract thought and led in particular to the distinction between myth and history. Street, however, has disputed this (1984, 1987). Basing himself on a study of Iran, and especially its village school system in the reign of Mohammad Reza Shah (1941–1979), he maintains that stereotyped education led large sections of the Iranian population to swallow uncritically the belief in progress and the benefits of science, thereby reproducing an apprenticeship model imported from the West and causing a break with references to Islam and classical Persian literature. Schooling gave city-dwellers arguments to justify a sense of superiority over country people, who were supposedly incapable of distinguishing between fact and legend. Worse still, it was placed in the service of the dominant ideology, which rewrote the country's history by emphasizing a supposed continuity between the Achaemenid and Pahlavi dynasties.

Street's analyses should put us on our guard against clear-cut oppositions between the oral and the written. Afghanistan, like other Middle Eastern countries, has experienced a paradoxical but in the end fairly common situation: it is a land of ancient civilization, where poetry and philosophy have flourished for many centuries, but it also has an extremely low rate of literacy. According to some rather tenuously based figures, 88.5 percent of the population had no school education in 1980, but 31.5 percent of those aged above 15 were literate by 1995 (47.2% of men, against 15.0%

of women). It is more likely that only a little over 10 percent of the Afghan population knows how to read and write.[1] Moreover, as Eickelman noted with reference to Morocco, "Islamic education [. . .] was in some ways intermediate between oral and written systems of transmission of knowledge" (1978: 487). Eickelman's interest was in the mosque-universities of Fez and Marrakesh and their decline in the colonial era, but some of his remarks may be applied to the Afghan context and the village education system. In Morocco as in Afghanistan, the high intellectual tradition and popular conceptions of Islam presented religious knowledge as fixed and definitive. Eickelman speaks of the "art of memory" for which education involved the transmission of a closed body of texts that pupils had to memorize without any real process of reflection. Neither the teacher nor the pupils made any comment on the educational material.

In pre–1978 Afghanistan, school education rested upon a small list of works (Centlivres 1970: 59–62). The war then had paradoxical effects: on the one hand, all the infrastructure collapsed and government schools soon ceased to function in the countryside; on the other hand, whole sections of the population began to have access to new services provided by NGOs. But the NGOs did not have much of a presence in the remote valleys of Hazarajat. Although the Hazaras valued education as a means of social advancement, few children were actually able to attend school.[2] Still today, they mostly learn to read and write from a mullah, who is rarely well educated himself and teaches them religious dogmas in the form of stock refrains.[3] It is a long way from the speculative tradition of the great Shiite centers of Iraq and Iran.

This pedagogic method favours oral communication and repetition over writing and reflection. A person may even know from classes with a village mullah how to read the Koran in Arabic without understanding the words; what counts is not to understand the message but to be in touch with the word of God, to be impregnated with it. Those who had such an education as a child often have difficulty in writing or reading a letter in Persian, their mother tongue. Others may be able to decipher some signs or newspaper headlines, but not actually to read a text. There is a very subtle gradation in literacy, a constant interpenetration of the written and the oral.

Even the non-religious educational system remains marked by this vision of knowledge, and very often it does not impart an ability to read and write. Thus, at the school in Dahmarda—which makes use of UNESCO course material—boys come in the morning and girls in the afternoon. The teacher reads out a sentence from the blackboard and makes all the children repeat it together, swinging their torsos in rhythm with the words as they almost shout them out. The young voices can be heard far into the open countryside nearby. It is understandable why Afghans are so sensitive to the harmony of numbers and sounds.

One might think that this system develops visual and aural memory at the expense of powers of abstraction and judgement. It is certainly true that, in learning by heart the dogmas of religion or mathematics, children scarcely exercise their critical sense and forego any historical perspective. Yet there are certain areas where such memorized knowledge can be put to creative use: everyday conversations, discussions prior to a decision, legal debates designed to resolve a dispute, and so on. A quotation from the religious or poetic corpus may then sweep people along and end the debate. As Eickelman pointed out, the intellectual vivacity of pupils is expressed in their use of Koranic texts in appropriate contexts (1978: 494).

Inability to read and write is not an insurmountable social handicap. Mardan Ali, for example, is illiterate yet has a good sixty people working under him. He always carries around a little notebook in which he gets people to jot down all the information necessary to his work, especially the mine accounts. If he borrows some money, he has a third party enter his acceptance of the debt. Among the Hazaras, an illiterate person may be thought of as educated if he can wisely insert a Koranic quotation, a couplet from Hafez, or a proverb from another of the great Persian classics. A good memory and sense of context form a cultural capital more important than advanced schooling as such.

This relationship between the oral and the written, as well as the low rate of literacy, give a distinctive shape to communications between people. They impose a certain primacy of the oral over the written, and of the public over the private, since every letter has to be read aloud.

THE MEDIA AND HUMANITARIAN ORGANIZATIONS

The BBC and Voice of America broadcasts in Persian and Pashtu are religiously followed every day as sources of immediate information about political and military events in Afghanistan. But, although Afghans are generally well informed and discuss current affairs at length, they distrust the media on the grounds that "journalists are paid to say such or such a thing." Besides, the radio cannot replace the news that travellers bring about a particular region or particular individuals in Afghanistan. In 1995 and 1996, for example, Hazarajat was the scene of numerous local conflicts, sufficiently serious to close a road and change the lives of people in the area, yet minor in terms of national politics and therefore unreported in the media.

Television, which was anyway not available in Hazarajat during my fieldwork, is not a useful source of information, as the finer points of events are lost on the Pakistani and Iranian stations. On the other hand, there is a lively market in videos, with a preference for Indian musical comedies.[4] The middle classes greatly appreciate films of family marriages and pass them around their relatives. The press, too, scarcely fulfils the function of providing information. There is no distribution network in Afghanistan, and all that circulates among the Hazaras are the irregular publications of political parties that are of interest only to intellectuals. The media, then, play little role in the news and communication channels developed by Afghans. In 1995 and 1996, the post was partly functioning in Kabul: it was possible to receive letters there from abroad, but not really to send any. Once again, such facilities were completely lacking in Hazarajat.

As to the humanitarian organizations, their role in communications is not very important for the Hazaras. It is true that the ICRC developed a way of transmitting messages, but it was intended mainly for prisoners of war. The organization intervened when front lines separated people, in places where any way through was impossible. In 1995, in Mazar-e Sharif, letters were handed out on market day. As many people came to town then from the surrounding country, it was an opportunity for someone to send a message for a relative, a neighbor or a simple acquaintance. This system, though important at the time, always remained modest in comparison with the dense communications that took place through the Afghans' own informal networks.

As White (1999) points out in the case of Turkey (a largely literate country, moreover), communication takes place mainly through interpersonal relations, direct encounters and oral expression. The media and various technologies can certainly enter the picture—especially the telephone, which assumes an existing relationship and reproduces the simultaneity of everyday communication. "The telephone, in other words, is used to connect existing circles and amplify communal ties based on trust and oral communication" (White 1999: 173). Neither the written press nor television programs can play such a role.

THE TELEPHONE

The predominance of oral communication is expressed in the fact that people prefer to speak on the telephone rather than correspond by letter. In 1995 and 1996 there was no electricity or telephone network in Hazarajat (as in most of Afghanistan);[5] the closest place with these facilities was Quetta. The capital of Pakistani Baluchistan was therefore an indispensable stopover between Jaghori and the outside world, whether to communicate with Iran, the Arabian Peninsula or the West. Even in Quetta, however, few families had a private telephone, and Afghan workers in Iran had no direct access to an international line. To arrange a conversation with someone, it was therefore necessary to take preliminary steps such as the sending of a letter to fix a time days or even weeks ahead.

Certain shops in Quetta, especially the *mosâfer-xâna,* served the function of communication centers. The manager's telephone would be constantly ringing, and names or room numbers were called out. Everyone knew where their close one would be staying or working along the migratory route, and where it would be possible to ring and ask to speak with them. There were always many Afghans queuing at the central post office in Tehran to telephone abroad—Pashtuns and Tajiks, Uzbeks and Hazaras, as well as numbers of Pakistanis. They left a deposit of 5,000 tomans and, when the connection was made, went to the allotted booth. At the end, they went to another counter and paid or received the difference between the deposit and the actual cost of the call.

Let us take an example of how Afghans use the telephone and of the difficulties they face. During a stay of one and a half years in Iran in the early 1990s, Mohammad Hasan had four telephone conversations with his *dâmâd* (ZH), Husayn Bakhsh, then living in Quetta, who passed on the news to Dahmarda through a *mosâfer.* There were never any calls in the other direction.

Late in 1995, Mohammad Hasan went to Quetta from Jaghori and wanted to take advantage of his time there to catch up on the news from his younger brother Mohammad Husayn, who was then in Iran. First he had to arrange a time to telephone his brother, who did not know he was in Pakistan. The ideal sequence of events was as follows:

(1) Mohammad Hasan meets Abdul Qader, also originally from Dahmarda, who is due to telephone his nephew Abdul Aziz in Tehran. Hasan asks him to pass on a message for the attention of Mohammad Husayn, telling him to call on a certain day, at a certain time and place.
(2) Abdul Qader speaks with Abdul Aziz and tells him the message to be passed on.
(3) Abdul Aziz contacts Mohammad Husayn and gives him the message.
(4) Mohammad Husayn calls Mohammad Hasan from a post office in Tehran, at the given time and number.

Two places were involve—Tehran (post office) and Quetta (Mirza Husayn's house, a relative and neighbor of Husayn Bakhsh)—and four persons (Mohammad Hasan and Abdul Qader in Quetta, Mohammad Husayn and Abdul Aziz in Tehran). This appointment system was possible only because people from Dahmarda gathered in the same places abroad and therefore had many opportunities to meet, intentionally or not; they always knew how to trace a particular individual, whether in Quetta or in Tehran. But the procedure involved several stages and the information was passed on quite slowly. Hitches were always possible, and in fact, in the example just given, a fault with Mirza Husayn's telephone prevented the communication at the agreed time. But this did not worry Mohammad Hasan unduly.

Nearly two weeks after the failed appointment, Mohammad Hasan learned that a month earlier his brother had had quite a serious work accident in Tehran. He heard of this quite by chance, when he bumped into someone from Dahmarda who had just returned from Tehran. This man gave him information about people he knew in Tehran and passed on the telephone number of the Iranian employer of Khodadad, a relative who seems to have been his father's *nose kâkâ*.[6] Hasan telephoned the employer from the shop of Haji Ramazan, also a member of his lineage; he spoke with Khodadad and asked him to pass on a message to Mohammad Ali (his *bace kâkâ*), with whom Husayn lived and worked, saying that he should ring him the next morning at Haji Ramazan's shop on Alamdar Road.

Again Hasan waited in vain. He still hoped to be contacted through Mirza Husayn, whose number in Tehran was known. And that is indeed what happened. From his employer's office in Tehran, Mohammad Ali first rang Mirza Husayn in the mid-afternoon to say that he would call back in the evening, giving him enough time to find Hasan and ask him to be there. In this way Hasan and Mohammad Ali finally managed to speak with each other.

Even in the best of cases, such telephone contact is established in two stages that increase the risk of failure. In the present example, the difficulties were due to tensions within the kinship group, as Mardan Ali had not been on "telephoning terms" with his brother Mohammad Ali for several years; they had not broken off relations altogether, but they generally avoided each other. In Quetta it was not Mardan Ali who served as the link between Iran and Hazarajat: his swashbuckling reputation made the less closely related Husayn Bakhsh seems preferable.

These rather tortuous explanations illustrate how an everyday event that is perfectly straightforward for his informants can seem impenetrable to an outside researcher. It was these very difficulties, and the ways of circumventing them, which made visible to me the networks used by my informants from Dahmarda. Relations of trust and cooperation were not mechanically determined by kinship. Of course, people thought that a "free rider" like Mardan Ali was breaking the codes of conduct, but the very logic of solidarity and mutual aid does not belong to the nature of lineage. Multiple bonds were at work.

We have seen that, although people preferred to use the telephone, it involved frequent hitches or even failures. Members of the same family members (a father and son or two brothers, for example) rarely spoke more than five or six times a year between Iran or a Gulf state and Quetta, and rarely more than once or twice if it was necessary to make the journey from Hazarajat. All the men who migrated had in their pocket a crumpled sheet of paper with a list of telephone numbers.[7] The most important of these were the numbers of shops or inns in Pakistan, and of companies in Iran, which alone had a telephone and an easily traceable address (bazaar name and shop number, for example). Communication networks were thus built around these public places, which served as links and stopover points.

LETTERS

Letters also play an important, though somewhat different, role. As a Persian proverb has it, *xat nesb-e didâr ast:* "a letter is half of a meeting." Many written messages circulate among Afghans, especially when it is a question of communicating with someone in Afghanistan.

I managed to collect a dozen letters, all given voluntarily by the recipients. I heard many more read aloud, and I myself transported, received and sent others. In most cases, they conveyed greetings and best wishes together with a brief account of the sender's recent life and state of health. The epistolary style of Persian is very different from that of French or English. The greetings appear at the beginning, and the writer expresses his attachment by complaining (sometimes bitterly) that he has not received any news from the other person. It is not usual to mention the details of a money-transfer (amount, people's names, etc.)—in fact, I only saw one letter containing financial instructions—but it can happen that precise and focused information is transmitted in writing, often after the main text, in a blank space in the corner, on the reverse side or in a little note scribbled on a piece of torn paper. The way of writing often corresponds to Hazaragi pronunciation rather than to literary Persian, and the letters always contain many mistakes of syntax and spelling. Yet their emotion and their sense of propriety make them poignant documents.

The sender is often illiterate and has to dictate the letter to someone else, usually in a room where other people are present; the recipient must often have the letter read aloud and will listen to what the messenger has to say and question him at some length. All of this contributes to the strikingly public character of the communication. Whereas, in other contexts, Afghans like to surround themselves with secrets, and whereas mistrust appears to dominate most social interactions, the delivery of letters is an occasion for long and animated discussions during which a lot of news is imparted in both directions. Letters are the basis for oral exchange through people travelling between Hazarajat, Quetta and Iranian cities. They are never posted but are carried by an acquaintance. A man you know is setting off on a journey; you give him the letter, but above all you discuss with him over a cup of tea. Once the *mosâfer* reaches his destination, he communicates the personal messages and the letters you entrusted to his care. The scene is always the same: after the customary greetings, the new arrival speaks at length to an attentive audience, then an element of dialogue appears as each person asks him questions concerning certain people or places. The same questions are put several times, and consistent answers reassure the audience that they are accurate. In fact, everyone tries to diversify their sources of information about the political and military situation in Afghanistan.

The letters are simple sheets of paper from a notebook, folded many times until they become no more than a tiny square; they are usually without an envelope and are not sealed in any way. As they are passed from hand to hand, and read before they reach the final recipient, people never discuss their problems in them: any news is snappy, most things are not mentioned at all, no one wants to reveal their secrets or weaknesses. Information directly conveyed by the messenger partly makes up for the triviality of the information contained in the letter.

Despite their sense of propriety, the letters are still an opportunity for the communication of important information at two levels: the news in the main body of text (health, family, work, greetings and polite formulas); and the news conveyed by the messenger (who has recently met the sender and can add supplementary information about certain events). Only someone well inserted into the social network can play the latter role. This system of communication therefore relies upon mutual acquaintance.

When Mardan Ali is in Quetta, he writes—or has someone else write—a letter nearly once a month to his family in Jaghori, and he receives one from them at the same intervals. Another informant living in Quetta told me that he writes eight to ten times a year and receives six to eight messages a year from his family in Hazarajat. Once I witnessed Mardan Ali dictate a letter for his family in Dahmarda to the secretary of the coal mine where he works; as usual, it contained a long list of names of people he wished to greet. Then, having suddenly remembered it, he added instructions for the repayment of a debt of 500,000 afghanis that he had borrowed to buy soap from a man who had travelled with him between Jaghori and Kandahar (he would send the money through a friend who was returning to Dahmarda). The secretary, a former colonel in the pro-Soviet government army, was an educated man who suffered because of his drop in status; he took his revenge by later mocking Mardan Ali, the illiterate ex-resistance fighter, about a sentence he had added to the letter which allegedly said that Mardan Ali had found a new wife in Quetta. Such jesting, familiar though it may be, serves the social function of demarcating friendly ties from more formal relations, but also of publicly signifying complicity, indifference or hostility.

During a stay in Tehran in 1996, I was able to observe the "Afghan post" on a daily basis. I was living with Mohammad Ali's team of workers when a member of his mother's lineage from Dawud came on a visit; he was a *hawâladâr* and constantly travelled on business between Quetta, Iran, Karachi and Islamabad. He brought a number of letters from Jaghori and took the opportunity to collect some money, which he then used to buy some goods to take back to Jaghori. It was also around this time that I shared the *id-e qorbân* meal with a group of workers from Dahmarda. One of the guests there had arrived from Quetta the day before with four letters. One was from Husayn Bakhsh and bore the following address: *xat-e hazâ az taraf-e Husayn Baxš dar Tehrân be dast-e Mohammad Husayn wa Mohammad Yusuf wa Mohammad Ali berasad,* "this letter from Husayn Bakhsh is meant for Mohammad Husayn and Mohammad Yusuf and Mohammad Ali in Tehran." The messenger's arrival was the occasion to hear some news from the "fatherland": he was asked about the political situation in Dahmarda, about his relatives, about the shops that had recently opened or closed, and so on. The letters passed from hand to hand. An educated person read them out and everyone learned of their contents.

As I was myself familiar to the people from Dahmarda, and as my closer relations with certain individuals were known, they often asked me to take letters with me on my journeys. Similarly, when someone known to me was about to leave, he called on me to ask whether I wanted him to take a message or a letter.[8] Here is the translation of a letter that an informant from Jaghori gave me in Quetta, in spring 1996, to take to his younger brother in Tehran:

> From Moheb Ali for my brother Mohammad Juma in Tehran
>
> In the name of God the merciful and compassionate
>
> Best greetings from your dear considerate mother who kisses your eyes and from Neamatullah's father and Neamtullah himself and from

> Ruhullah and Besmellah for the light of our eyes Mohammad Juma the pilgrim and Qorban Ali and Ewaz Ali and Naser for each of the friends with whom you share your room, all our best wishes. First of all, I wish that God who is great, merciful and compassionate should give you health and honour. May you be happy and meet with success. I inform you, Mohammad Juma the pilgrim, light of my eyes and fruit of my heart, that it is a very long time since we received a letter or telephone call from you; my dear, we are very worried. I ask you to send us a letter through the bearer, blessed by God; that would be really very good. If it is expensive to telephone, it is not to write a letter; reassure us by sending us a letter. We will be waiting until a letter from the light of our eyes reaches us. Also keep us informed about Mohammad Jan, did he arrive or not? If he arrived, you should receive the sum of seven thousand two hundred tomans.
>
> As for myself, I am busy with my work and have begun to learn English, if God is willing I shall make rapid progress. For the moment, I shall not take up any more of your time, may God protect you.
>
> Sincerely,
>
> Moheb Ali, 15/1/1375
>
> Can you send back some size-eight plastic shoes to the Swiss brother, his name is Sekander

When I was about to leave Tehran (1996), Mohammad Husayn gave me three letters to give to Husayn Bakhsh in Quetta: one for Husayn Bakhsh himself, another from Mohammad Yusuf for Husayn Bakhsh, and one from a Dawran friend working in Tehran for a relative in Quetta. Mohammad Ali also gave me two letters, one for his eldest brother Mardan Ali (but he insisted that it was really meant for the latter's son, Abdul Karim) and one for Husayn Bakhsh. The latter played a major role in communication between members of his family circle, being much appreciated for his kindness and readiness to help. Mohammad Ali made it clear that I should deliver the letters to him in person. Another young worker gave me a letter for his father, whom I had met in the Quetta mines.

When I delivered Mohammad Ali's note to Mardan Ali, it became quite clear to me how information circulates among Afghans. Mardan Ali, who is completely illiterate, asked his employer to read it aloud; he did not appear to be greatly interested in the contents, but the insistence with which he questioned me made me realize just how important were discussions with the message-bearer. The letters may contain little news, but they say a lot about relations between people: who greets whom, and on what terms? Mardan Ali's relative indifference was thus an expression of tensions between him and his brother. The importance of letters in communication between Afghans is largely due to the fact they are a pretext for discussion and for a strengthening of social bonds. One of the roles of the courier is to legitimate the oral testimony that comes with him.

During my stay in Dahmarda in autumn 1995, Akram Ali received a letter from his son Husayn, who was with his cousin Mohammad Ali in Tehran. It was first read aloud and then handed over to me. Here is the translation:

> On behalf of your servant Mohammad Husayn Jahangir[9] for my father and/or Mohammad Hasan at Chaghl-e Sang with all my respect 24/9/1995
>
> In the name of God
>
> In the name of God the merciful and compassionate, from your servants Mohammad Husayn and Mohammad Ali, to first of all my respected father and my compassionate mother and my dear brother, Abdul Ali's father and Abdul Ali's mother and Abdul Ali himself and my dear Mariam and my dear Maleka and my uncle, the father of Mardan Ali and Mohammad Aziz Azizi, and my dear Abdul Karim and Mohammad Juma and Mohammad Jan and Husayn Ali Jan and the remaining members of the family and for my uncle Mohammad Mehdi's father and for Mohammad Mehdi himself and Abdul Khaleq Jan and Nawruz Ali Jan and Morteza Jan and Mohammad Dust Jan and my uncle Mohammad Jawad Amiri's father and Mohammad Jawad Amiri himself and Mohammad Ali Amiri and Sakhidad Amiri and the rest of the kin and for friends who have been forgotten in this letter by my pen I send them also my best greetings. If you wish to be informed of the situation, thanks to God the merciful and compassionate, I have until now been in the clothes of health. May God grant that you be well too my dear ones. I wish to tell my dear and fortunate brother Abdul Ali's father that your servant has sent a ball and a net through Mohammad Jawad Amiri, have you received them or not. Let me know and keep me informed about yourselves.
>
> Respectfully
>
> Mohammad Husayn Jahangir
>
> If I be far away, my spirit is with you
> The water's hundred parts will recognize one another,
> What is life if not suffering
> In the beginning was pain and in the end will be death
> The salt in my eyes is gentler than morning sleep
> What sadness before a son becomes as his father

This letter consists of a long list of greetings and compliments, the main aim being to bring relationships up to date and to provide an opportunity for an exchange of words. It is impermissible to write or utter in address the name of an elder or a woman (unless she is a girl below marriageable age). This explains the ubiquitous teknonyms: to refer to his elder brother Mohammad Hasan, for example, Mohammad Husayn writes "Abdul Ali's father." The text contains scarcely any factual information as such, yet the messenger was questioned at length about the situation in Tehran. Furthermore, it would be wrong to think that letters are without content: the greetings themselves reaffirm ties of solidarity and render them public. Omissions are also highly significant. Thus, in a letter to his elder brother Mardan Ali, Mohammad Ali explicitly states that he informs Abdul Karim (Mardan Ali's son) of Husayn's state of health—which is an indirect but clear way of emphasizing that Mardan Ali has not asked after him. The letters also have a strong emotional charge, as the poem ending Husayn's missive illustrates.

In Tehran, the already elderly Safdar Khan from Dahmarda showed me a letter dictated by his wife, in which she related the family's life in fairly neutral fashion. On the back, however, were the tiny footprints of her two sons and four daughters. These physical traces, which enabled him to follow at a distance the growth of his children, were what moved Safdar Khan the most. The letter, passed from hand to hand, embodied the ties of solidarity; it drew a man closer to his wife and children, a migrant closer to his native village.

RAMZ AND *NEŠÂNI*

When I was in Jaghori in autumn 1995, Mardan Ali made me write a brief letter informing his employer, Haji Sarwar, that we had reached our destination safely and giving him some news about the situation in Dahmarda. A shopkeeper in the bazaar folded it neatly, wrote Haji Sarwar's name and address on the outside, and signed and scribbled on the blank spaces so that nothing could be added. Mardan Ali then countersigned it in a complicated manner (he could not read or write, but he had learned to sign his name) and asked a relative who was leaving for Quetta to deliver it to Haji Sarwar. The fact that the shopkeeper (who was known to Haji Sarwar) had appended a few lines was a further guarantee of authenticity. I actually wrote it in English, because I was incapable of composing a text in Persian, and for Mardan Ali this use of a foreign language lessened the risk that it would be read before reaching its destination. (In fact, I heard a few weeks after my return to Quetta that the message-bearer had photocopied it before delivering it to Haji Sarwar, then had the copy translated in order to find out what I thought about the tensions in Dahmarda (see chapter 3).

Lack of discretion is therefore a possibility, even among close relatives. Although, as we have seen, letters generally contain little concrete information and the bearer is usually known to the recipient, my informants were always afraid that they would be intercepted by someone with bad intentions. When Afghans want to send private or delicate information, they have recourse to a *ramz* or secret code. And when the messenger is not known to the recipient, a *nešâni* or sign of recognition is used. The meanings of these two words partially overlap, but a *ramz* is a coded term or hidden sign within a text, whereas a *nešâni* may be a pre-arranged object that the messenger brings or a sentence he has to utter or a story known only to the persons involved. Another possibility is that a *nešâni* such as a ring, mat or half-banknote has to be returned as confirmation that a journey has gone well, and so on. Mohammad Ali gave a demonstration of some other techniques in Tehran. For example, he wrote a brief message on an intricately folded strip of paper, in such a way that when he opened out the sheet and gave it to me I was unable to reconstitute the text.

Partners agree on secret codes for business correspondence more than for private letters. A *ramz* may also be used as a coded indication of the security situation in a region: 14 for war, 12 for insecurity, and so on down to 0 for peace. In a letter that Ghulam Ali, a young worker in Tehran (see chapter 5), wrote to his father in Quetta, he used two *ramz* of this kind: *awzâ'-ye Irân qermez ast,* "conditions in Iran are red," meant that things were acceptable there; while the lack of a signature was an agreed indication of the letter's authenticity. Another migrant told me that he used a *ramz* in his signature: the letters S and R in Cyrillic characters (that is, C and P). Another informant told me that he signed in the reverse direction, from left to right, but only when he was sending business instructions. That made me wonder about the usefulness of secret codes that were divulged so readily.

It is not always easy to understand the function of the *ramz* and *nešâni*. Perhaps they express the limitations of the group and the general mistrust that characterizes social relations. It is true that Afghans have a marked taste for secrecy and for conspiracy theories, but this only underlines the openness that prevails in the circulation of letters. Various little tricks can provide further guarantees of the authenticity of a message, but they also signal the relations of trust that are so vital in the midst of general insecurity. In this sense, the *ramz* and *nešâni* are veritable symbols. The Greek verb *sumballo* means "to put together, to unite, to bring closer together"—hence the noun *sumbolon,* "sign of recognition," which for the ancient Greeks referred to any object divided between two persons which, when put together again, served to identify the bearers and to confirm the previously contracted relations of hospitality and friendship. Among Afghans, the use of secret codes and agreed objects helps to reproduce social bonds, and to express a more than imagined community of fate, despite a high degree of geographical dispersion.[10] At the same time, it is a symbolic expression of the fragility of social relations, in a transient world where "we are all only travellers."

PART FOUR

RESULTS AND ANALYSIS

Chapter Nine

Trust and Cooperation amid Conflict and Migration

THE FAULTLINES OF AFGHAN SOCIETY

Before the war, some observers of Afghanistan had already pointed to the weakness of the national bond outside the capital and stressed two more salient levels of identity: the supranational *umma* (the Islamic community of believers) and the subnational *qawm* (Centlivres, Centlivres-Demont 1988a: 34–35). The multiformity of the latter term well expresses the complexity of Afghan social reality, in which the ethnic group is only one register of identity. Besides, in the course of the history of Afghanistan, political coalitions have rarely been of an ethnic order. Religious distinctions have been highly significant and sometimes encompassed ethnic appellations (Canfield 1973a: 4–5, 12; 1986: 99). The correlation of these two levels is particularly strong among the Hazaras, whose history has been marked by religious heterodoxy and political, economic and social marginalization.

As in the epoch of monarchical government and the Daud presidency, ethnic realities have long been obscured by the factions present on the ground. It cannot be denied, however, that the country underwent a progressive strengthening of the ethnic identity reference after the Soviet withdrawal of 1989 (Roy 1989). This may have been originally induced by the Soviet-style nationalities policy of the Communist government (Centlivres 1991),[1] and it became most evident after the fall of Najibullah in 1992 (Centlivres 1994b; Roy 1993; Glatzer 1998). Because of their especially painful history and the Shiism that distinguishes them from the majority of the Afghan population, the Hazaras appear to have been the first to develop explicitly ethnic demands.

Ethnic differences are constantly objectified in popular discourse, which mixes together physical considerations with aspects relating to dress, food, behavior and so on ("the Hazaras are beardless and have slanting eyes; they are reserved with people they don't know"; "Pashtuns have large noses, speak loudly and are haughty" . . .).[2] But the differences are the result of a historical and social-political process, not a cultural given as such. For Barth, "ethnic groups are categories of ascription and identification by the actors themselves, and thus have the characteristic of organizing interaction between people" (1981a: 199). They should not be defined in terms of a set of objective cultural traits, for they involve a "form of social organization" in which the decisive element is not any objective difference but what the actors themselves consider to be significant (Barth 1981a: 202–203). Representations of identity are being constantly renewed and renegotiated (by local actors and political leaders, but also by researchers and aid workers). The boundaries are maintained by a number of emblems (or stereotypes) which make inclusion or exclusion manifest in various registers such as religious affiliation, social-occupational group, physical appearance, dress and food preferences.

Situations of conflict and migration are especially favorable to the emergence and strengthening of ethnic distinctions. Ancient social-economic complementarities blur and fade as the logic of confrontation over natural and economic resources becomes paramount. A certain division of labor, with its separate ecological and economic niches, ceases to be visible. Old elites exploit ethnic divisions to prevent the erosion of their power, while aspiring new leaders (Barth's "agents of change" (1981a: 222) do the same to base their ascent on a particular segment of society. It must be stressed, however, that these trends are more the result of war than its cause. Unfortunately, events often take a dramatic turn. The civil war that followed the fall of the pro-Soviet government in 1992 caused the destruction of Kabul and, in the second half of the nineties, large-scale civilian massacres. In exile, too, coexistence among ethnic groups has often been difficult. The refugee camps in Pakistan have been the scene of hidden rivalry to gain access to humanitarian aid (Janata 1990: 69).

In both Afghanistan and the host countries, tensions among the various components of society have become more pronounced in spite of the emergence of a certain national consciousness. A return to the situation that prevailed before the coup of 1978, or even the coup of 1973, is unthinkable in view of the new political and economic prospects that opened up for Hazaras, Tajiks and Uzbeks in the course of the war. The old Pashtun hegemony cannot provide a viable foundation on which to rebuild the country. The bones of contention are profound on all sides, and Pashtuns have often been the victims of atrocities in regions where they are a minority.

Other faultlines in Afghan society bode ill for the future of the country: the opposition between cities (especially the capital) and countryside, relations between the Sunni majority and the Shiite minority, the widening gap between Afghans living in the West and those who have remained in Afghanistan or neighboring countries, the conflicts of interest between diaspora elites and internal commanders or between royalists and Islamists. No single analytic key can do justice to the complexities of the situation.

BEYOND KINSHIP: TRUST AND FRIENDSHIP

Anthropologists with an interest in the Middle East and North Africa have much debated the importance of kinship and lineage, as well as the relevance of the segmentary model for an understanding of social structures.[3] Our aim here cannot be to take up this vast problem, but only to explore the bases of cooperation and mutual aid in a situation of war and migration.

The segmentary system, based on an interlocking of structural oppositions, does not exhaust the play of alliances and conflicts. For there is a fundamental ambiguity in Afghan and, more generally, Middle Eastern society: an undeniable solidarity of family and community coexists with an extreme degree of internal competition. The societies of the Middle East and North Africa are shot through with tendencies to fusion and fission that depend upon the relationship between the group in question and the outside world; "insecurity furnish(es) a negative principle of cohesion that can make up for the deficiency in positive principles: 'I hate my brother but I hate those who hate him'" (Bourdieu 1972: 123). We should be wary of tautological theories that claim to explain solidarity while presupposing it, or of determinist accounts which claim that kinship ties entail solidarity. The example of Hazara migratory strategies should lead us to be more cautious about the supposed primacy of kinship, and to take account of other aspects such as neighborly relations and friendship.

In Afghanistan, the moral obligations and respect stemming from kinship often go hand in hand with a hierarchical relationship and a certain formalism. As Richard Tapper (1979: 126) notes with regard to the Shahsevans of north-west Iran, status may be quite strictly distributed within families. Hostility between brothers is seldom openly declared and more often deflected on to the relationship between their spouses. On the other hand, tensions between paternal first cousins are acute:

> Among male agnates, three different categories have been distinguished: full brothers who are bound by duty and authority patterns into a relation of cooperation; first cousins, equals and striving for independence

> from each other, the proto-typical rivals; and agnates in general who are linked into a lineage corporation by common interests in honour, responsibility and [. . .] control of marriages (R. Tapper 1979: 131).

The terms of paternal kinship imply respect, but the idea of competition and jealousy is never very distant within the same generational level. Thus, in Pashtu (but the term is also used by people in Jaghori district), *tarbor* means both "paternal cousin" and "rival" (Atayee 1979: 95). For it is the descendants of the same ancestor who have to resolve the most decisive issues concerning land ownership, water rights, the enlistment of military support or outside humanitarian aid, and so on. Major obligations entail major tensions. In a way that is only seemingly paradoxical, the circle of solidarity is also the one in which violence is most common.

A person's attitude is often less affectionate and relaxed towards his close patrilateral relatives than towards his distant agnates, matrilateral relatives and family by marriage. The vocabulary of maternal kinship does not involve the same degree of constraint and formalism. And, more generally, relations through the women are characterized by greater freedom and bonding. The terms *bâja* (WZH) and *bola* (MZS) are both symmetrical: they refer respectively to the husbands and sons of two sisters. In many respects these are privileged relations, since they are devoid of the obligations and precedence inherent in blood ties. They are closer to the idea of friendship, even if the terms *dust, yâr* or *rafiq* ("friend"),[4] *andiwâl* ("pal" or "buddy") and *âšnâ* ("acquaintance") are used mainly for persons to whom the speaker is not related. We might risk drawing a parallel here between kinship and ethnicity: although Afghan society is characterized by the intensity of relations within the paternal kin and the various ethnic groups (which Afghans think of genealogically as large kinship groups), the weight of transversal relations should not be neglected.

Recognizing the importance of ties among individuals who do not belong to the same kinship circle, several authors have emphasized the role of friendship in the tribal societies of the Middle East. Thus, nomads often entertain dyadic relations with individuals belonging to sedentary society, relations that have a marked pragmatic and economic dimension. At first ambivalent and fluid, they may become friendly over time (Barth 1961: 93–100; R. Tapper 1979: 147–152). Giddens, for his part (1990), stresses the role of friendship in what he calls "premodern" societies. Friendship is certainly a complex notion. Born out of shared experiences of joy or suffering, it is experienced as free and disinterested—even if it also imposes certain obligations. Ideally, it is a relationship that no source of rivalry, jealousy or resentment can disturb, although in reality not every element of hierarchy or instrumentality is excluded from it. Often formalized and ritualized (blood kinship, foster kinship, etc.) and consolidated by a code of honor, it enables a man (but also a woman) to create more or less stable alliances with persons outside his or her group. Gifts and return gifts sustain the social bond; commodities become culturally invested and objectify social relations. Women play a major role in this system of invitations and favors, thereby exerting considerable influence over social life and intervening in decision-making processes that affect the household unit.[5]

In some of the cases described in the anthropological literature, friendship is institutionalized through pseudo-kinship relations. Most studies of this practice have focused on Christian regions in the Mediterranean (Andalusia, southern Italy, Serbia, Greece). Often mentioned under the Spanish term *compadrazgo,* it has its origin in the ritual relationship between parents and godparents of a baptised child. It is a complex system, which makes it possible either to strengthen family cohesion or to create a (vertical or horizontal) network of solidarity external to kinship. Spiritual kinship is sometimes used to resolve conflicts between groups and to avert the cycle of vendetta (Herzfeld 1985). According to the social-cultural context, the *compadres* may be chosen from within or outside the kin (Mintz and Wolf 1950; Pitt-Rivers 1973, 1976, 1977).

Pitt-Rivers (1977) has shown that in rural Andalusia the spiritual dimension of *compadrazgo* serves more to exorcise the jealousy and tensions inherent in kinship relations than to constitute a social network outside the circle of collaterals. The godfather and godmother are usually chosen from within the kin; it is sometimes a question of a close friend or an influential person who has agreed to support the family. In all cases, the godfathers and godmothers are treated as if they were part of the family—a practice made easier by the ban on marriage between *compadres,* that is, between the child's godfather and mother or godmother and father, as well as between the godfather and goddaughter or godmother and godson. Even if the *compadrazgo* often encompasses a kinship relation, it is still the result of a choice. It is a close and irrevocable personal relationship in its own right, which excludes competition and entails reciprocity, trust, obligations and formal marks of respect on both sides. It does not always unite persons of similar status (it may be the occasion of an alliance between members of different classes), but the moral equality that it implies makes social inequality acceptable. It cannot be reduced to a utilitarian contractual relationship, although it may serve practical ends. In an agonistic society, *compadrazgo* creates a protected sector where peace prevails (Pitt-River 1977).

In the Afghan context, there are two possible ways of consolidating friendship. First, it may be converted into a relationship through marriage (for example, two friends marry off their children, or a man marries his friend's sister). But this carries a risk, as tensions can arise during premarital negotiations or from the proximity of cohabitation. Some therefore prefer pseudo-kinship, where friendship can be seen as a kinship relation that usually (but not always) unites men of the same age and a similar social-economic status (sometimes, a relationship of this kind will have existed between their fathers): then people talk of *berâdar-xânda* ("sworn brothers"). Among the Shiites this relationship may be formalized before a mullah, who declares two men *berâdar-e dini* ("brothers in religion").[6] Like foster brothers (*berâdar-e širi, berâdar-e rezâ'i*), *berâdar-xânda* enter into the private family circle, the *mahram*. This term refers to forbidden degrees of kinship, or, in other words, to persons among whom marriage is not allowed. From that point on, each can see the other's *nâmus* unveiled—that is, the women for whom a man is responsible and whose conduct is decisive for his own honor: his wife, daughter, sister and mother (Spooner 1965). In some cases, a man may receive some property from the father of his *berâdar-xânda,* who thereby recognizes that he has a symbolic right to a share of the inheritance.

There are thus a number of similarities between *compadrazgo* and the formalized friendship found among Afghans. The two institutions may be used to give concrete expression to a relation of friendship. Like marriage, they may also serve to assuage the hostility between two families.[7] The close friends are treated as if they were part of the family, and any marital union is prohibited. Much more than an agnate, the *compadre* or friend is the person par excellence from whom money is borrowed. But there are important differences, since Afghan friendship—unlike *compadrazgo*—entails familiarity and a great freedom of tone.[8] It is not buttressed by such a strong religious dimension, and it does not unite men who are close agnates (whereas in Andalusia one can ask an elder brother to be the godfather of one's son, in Afghanistan one's brother cannot be considered a friend).

Trust, then, does not stem only from kinship—especially in a migratory context, where relations of trust are at once more necessary and more difficult to establish and maintain than in the case of a local residence group. For such relations imply respect for the dignity, honor and autonomy of the other person. As Shahrani remarks (1995: 197), this is not an easy condition to fulfil in exile. Persian has a rich terminology, often of Arabic origin, to express trust:

- *bâwar:* belief, credit (in the sense of believing someone, of giving credit to his words); *bâwar kardan* or *dâštan:* to believe (to consider true), to give credit;
- *e'tebâr:* trust, credit (that which a trustworthy person enjoys); credibility; consideration; value, validity; *e'tebâr dâštan* ou *dâdan:* to show confidence (in);
- *etminân:* trust; assurance, certainty; *etminân dâdan* or *kardan:* assure, guarantee; to trust, to have confidence (in);
- *e'temâd:* trust (in the strongest sense); *e'temâd kardan* ou *dâštan:* to count on, to have confidence (in).

This subtle vocabulary makes it possible to express different levels of interaction. There is a fruitful parallel here with Pouillon's reflections on the verb "to believe" (1979). "To believe something" does not exclude doubt and the existence of contradictory ways of seeing; "to believe *in* something" implies that there is no longer any room for debate. "To show confidence in" is limited to a particular situation. Hazrat Ali shows confidence in Mardan Ali to help him find work in the coal mines. It is the term *e'tebâr* that will be used here, as it does not eliminate all distance; the service rendered is a one-off matter. By contrast, Mohammad Husayn trusts or *has* confidence in Husayn Bakhsh: he can entrust his affairs to him and instruct him to be his representative in all circumstances. The relationship is profoundly symbiotic, since the relationship is long-lasting and profitable while the two persons experience it as disinterested. They will then speak of *e'temâd.*

Rules governing politeness and respect impose a constant raising of the verbal tone. In the case of a man whose origin is not known but whose age and status appear equivalent to those of the speaker, it is permissible to address him as *watandâr* ("fellow-countryman") or to draw upon the vocabulary of kinship. A person of slightly inferior status is often called *berâdar* or *brâr* ("brother"), whereas equality may entail a term such as *lâlâ* ("elder brother"). The degree of proximity is almost systematically overdetermined: a man calls his paternal cousin *brâr* (F), any male member of his lineage *kâkâ* (FB) or *bace kâkâ* (FBS), and any person with whom he is on familiar terms *mâmâ* (MB) or *bace mâmâ* (MBS). The point is not to conjure away the genuine genealogical link, but to characterize the relationship by degree of proximity.

Hazaras have a relatively flexible kinship system with a cognatic inflection, together with multiple registers of solidarity that are brought into service during the course of migration. Political unity and joint ownership are symbolically valued, but separation is often more profitable from an economic point of view.[9] Relations between agnates may display solidarity and competition by turns. The weight of lineages and tribal segments is hard to overestimate, as they are the locus both of maximum solidarity and of intense conflicts. In other words, relations of trust and distrust usually overlap and are deeper than in societies where the state acts as guarantor of contracts and maintains a certain level of security.

Relations are therefore always ambivalent and open to change: hostility can die down and closeness can degenerate into conflict. Lindholm (1982) emphasizes the strong tensions among Pashtuns in the Swat valley in Pakistan. In such a context individuals feel a deep affective need, and often this is invested in someone outside the social hierarchies and the competition for land, women and prestige. This impulse towards the outside world is inevitably frustrated, however, since it focuses upon someone external to the actual ties of solidarity. Friendship remains a difficult ideal to achieve. Afghan society also displays this ambivalence of interpersonal feelings (J. Anderson 1985): on the one hand, a complex mixture of internal competition and solidarity; on the other hand, a human warmth that has not failed to charm travellers but is insufficient to balance the weight of family ties. While remaining open to the outside world, Afghans are caught up in mutual obligations that tie them to members of their kin.

Kinship relations are not chosen. They are formal relations (excluding any reference to sexuality, for example) and are marked by rivalry, whereas friendship is free and disinterested, permits (or even prescribes) great freedom of tone, and theoretically involves no competition. Pitt-Rivers (1973: 93–94) remarks that friendship tends to reproduce the consubstantiality of kinship relations, consecrated by a ritual involving the direct exchange of solid or liquid food, blood or even saliva or sperm. Yet the relationship is never completely equated with a kinship bond, as it has a complementary and, in some respects, more important function.

There is a proverb which deserves a few comments: *az dust-e nâdân dušman-e dânâ behtar ast,* "it is preferable to have a knowledgeable enemy than an ignorant friend."[10] Someone with a stupid friend risks being dragged into pointless quarrels that he might otherwise have avoided. On the other hand, someone with an intelligent enemy is forced to rise to the same level in order to compete. The adversary or rival (*syâl:* another Pashtu term used by the Hazaras of Jaghori and Quetta) is a person one respects who is in principle recognized as one's equal; he is not denied an exchange of honor (Atayee 1979: 92). What is paramount here is the intensity of the social relation, whether it is characterized by solidarity or by rivalry.

Quarrels between relatives are common and potentially serious, but they follow an explicit logic that is known to all (Pitt-Rivers 1973: 101). On the one hand, patrilateral kinship is structurally opposed to ties of friendship (and, to a lesser extent, to matrilateral kinship and family relations through marriage), which are conceived in the mode of equality and affection. On the other hand, the intensity of these two types of relation distinguishes them from the diffuse and unpredictable hostility that is the main feature of relations with strangers.

THE SOURCES OF COOPERATION

In the Afghan context, the state does not have a monopoly of legitimate violence, nor is there a structure comparable to the Sicilian Mafia that produces a kind of trust and private protection (Gambetta 1994). Before the Soviet invasion, relations between the Afghan government and the rural population were tense and typically involved a "politics of mistrust" (Shahrani 1995: 196) and avoidance. Local populations had developed effective networks of cooperation and sought to minimize contact with the central administration (Dupree 1980: 248–251; Shahrani 1986). The legitimacy of rule was based on the preservation of a certain order and a claim to be defending Islam against foreign forces. But this modest basis vanished at the moment of the Red Army intervention (Centlivres and Centlivres-Demont 1981–82, 1988a).

In Afghanistan, the trust that may exist at the level of the family, neighborhood or dyadic friendship is therefore the corollary of the prevailing mistrust towards the outside. Afghan society scarcely corresponds to the theses of "trust theorists" such as Fukuyama (1995), who counterpoises "low-trust societies" to "high-trust societies," or Peyrefitte (1998), who insists that there is an "ethos of trust" peculiar to Western Christianity. This approach appears to be too simplistic. Trust and mistrust are measured on one and the same scale, which is much more decisive in Afghanistan (in its positive as well as negative values) than in the societies of Western Europe and North America.[11]

Giddens (1990) also supports a "discontinuity" thesis, on the grounds that modernity—that is, the modes of life and social organization which developed in Europe from the seventeenth century on—brought about fundamental changes. In his view, however, it is not the intensity of trust which is decisive but its institutional insertion. Trust is no longer a relation between precise individuals inserted into particular social contexts, but rather a diffuse feeling that the uninitiated have towards various specialists (bankers, lawyers, doctors, architects, technicians, and so on) who are not known to them personally. Giddens thus distinguishes between "facework commitments" and "faceless commitments": the former refer to trust relations which are sustained by or expressed in social connections established in circumstances of copresence; the latter concern the development of faith in symbolic tokens or expert systems, which he groups together in the term "abstract systems."

In the modern world, everyone has regular contact with unknown persons without feeling suspicious of them. Institutions act as guarantors of trust, which is thus detached from mere relations of proximity. In Afghanistan, by contrast, a stranger is potentially dangerous and a relation of trust can come about only through long interaction. The main risks stem from human violence: bombing, pillage and the exactions of local commanders or brigands. Trust is therefore a personalized relationship inscribed within four social contexts (Giddens 1990): the kinship group; the local community; religious beliefs and ritual practices; and tradition. In each case the point is to create opportunities for interpersonal encounter and to increase the frequency of interaction.

The political theorist Axelrod (1990) asks how cooperation can develop and maintain itself in a society of egoists that lacks a central authority. Three questions arise in this connection. How can a cooperative strategy spread in an environment dominated by non-cooperation? What type of strategy can develop in an environment made up of individuals using a wide range of more or less sophisticated strategies? Once cooperation has been established among a group of individuals, under what conditions will it be able to resist a different strategy?

Axelrod bases his approach on the prisoner's dilemma, a classical problem of game theory. This may be presented as follows (Hargreaves Heap et al. 1992: 99): the police are holding separately two accomplices whom they suspect of a serious crime; each can either admit or deny any involvement; if both refuse to talk, they will be charged with a lesser offence; if both admit responsibility, they will receive medium sentences; if one confesses and the other does not, the former will be acquitted and the latter condemned to the maximum term of imprisonment. This situation corresponds, at an intuitive level, to the more theoretical case where two gamblers, A and B, can choose either to cooperate or not to cooperate with each other. Each makes his choice without knowing what the other will decide. The interests of A and B are not totally contradictory: like most everyday transactions, it is not a zero-sum game. The following table sets out the four possible outcomes (the totalled figures in each box, where the scores obtained by A and B are indicated successively, do not have to be equal):

Table 9: The prisoner's dilemma

	B: Cooperation	B: Defection
A: Cooperation	3. 3	0. 5
A: Defection	5. 0	1. 1

If B cooperates, A obtains 3 by also cooperating and 5 by not cooperating; if B does not cooperate, A obtains 0 by cooperating and 1 by not cooperating either. In such a scenario, defection always makes it possible to achieve a higher result than could have been obtained through cooperation. Each gambler therefore has an advantage in not cooperating, whatever the other may decide. As each pursues the same maximization of his own interests, individual rationality leads to a poor result (both A and B score 1). Each gambler scores best when he defects but the other cooperates; yet mutual cooperation is more profitable than mutual non-cooperation. The dilemma is that both gamblers have an interest in defection, but would thereby obtain a worse result than if they cooperated.

According to this analysis, then, non-cooperation is the dominant strategy in any single encounter. Axelrod (1990: 115) remarks that this poses problems for population groups such as gypsies, who move from one place to another. Hazara migrants also face this difficulty. But the terms of the problem are different when some sanction is possible. The question of whether a person should or should not cooperate with another is transformed if there is a high probability of future encounters—in other words, if the prisoner's dilemma is made repetitive. By analysing the results of an information technology contest, Axelrod shows that a tit for tat strategy is more profitable in the long term: you start by cooperating, then respond to cooperation with cooperation and to defection with defection. The gambler who observes this rule is never the first to defect and is prepared to cooperate again even if the other party defected on a previous occasion. This strategy has the advantage of being clearly understandable to both parties; it is well-intentioned and indulgent, while not excluding the possibility of revenge.

When the number of encounters is indeterminate, or when the gamblers think that they will interact again, the future influences their perception of what is at stake and hence their eventual decision. Cooperation may develop on the basis of a small group of persons who practise reciprocity;[12] it becomes a profitable strategy that will grow progressively stronger. To promote cooperation, it is therefore necessary to "enlarge the shadow of the future" (Axelrod 1990: 129), either by lengthening the time spent together or by increasing the frequency of interaction. This may result in a certain social exclusiveness, so that interaction takes place with members of a given social group among whom reciprocity is the rule, and not with outside persons with whom relations of mistrust prevail. The aim is precisely to restrict the number of people with whom one has dealings, in order to increase the likelihood of meeting them again.

Having started from a hypothesis seemingly incompatible with all forms of cooperation, Axelrod arrives at an important conclusion: cooperation between two persons is possible even if one thinks that they are pursuing their individual interests; it arises from the likelihood of future encounters and entails a relationship based upon reciprocity. Axelrod's approach does not rest upon the sociobiological view that much of human behavior is determined by genetic inheritance, nor does he even assert that people make rational choices in their everyday practice or that they are truly egoistic. His only assumption is that people pursue individual interests—which allows him to study cases where cooperation is not based on altruism or a wish to promote the common good.

These remarks may be extended to the Afghan context, with its high level of violence and insecurity and its intense cooperation. What kind of solidarity is possible in a situation of conflict and uncertainty, when no institution guarantees that interpersonal commitments will be respected? The latent war of all against all, and the fact that one can never know whom to trust (*e'tebâr nist*), are close to the world of egoists on which Axelrod bases his argument. The crucial issue, however, is not whether individuals actually do seek to promote their own personal interests, but whether, even if that is so, it would advantageous for them to defect in a one-off encounter but to cooperate in a longer-term perspective. The greater the likelihood of future encounters, the lower is the risk of defection.

Axelrod scarcely considers the role of kinship and does not employ the concepts of trust and friendship (1990: 182, 187–188); he thinks it enough that relations should have a lasting and repetitive character. But the likelihood of future encounters cannot explain everything, and it would be wrong to attach the same significance to all encounters. Nor is it sufficient to know who interacts with whom and how often. We must supplement the foregoing analysis by giving some thought to cultural norms and the role of moral values. Thus Maurice Bloch (1973: 76) argues that the game theory approach (in which individuals seek to maximize their advantage and the main motive for action is its expected benefits) confuses the causes with the effects of action.

As Mauss (1985) already pointed out, a return gift must be delayed to be properly appreciated; the passage of time is the measure of trust (see also

Bourdieu 1980: 178–183). Basing himself on research in Madagascar, Bloch maintains that immediate reciprocity actually negates the moral dimension of the relationship, whereas kinship is based upon moral principles that guarantee long-term reciprocity. For, in order to widen the potential group of persons with whom they cooperate, Merina farmers ask neighbors and acquaintances more often than kin to help them with work in the fields. Members of their kinship group would come in any event, whereas the relationship with neighbors and acquaintances has to be kept alive through frequent mutual favors. The task is to find a balance between short-term and medium-term relations with immediate economic utility and the lasting solidarity involved in kinship ties. In other words, relatively unstable relations have to be repeatedly activated if they are not to disappear, whereas kinship imposes moral obligations that no one can shake off without incurring social sanctions.

Bloch's thesis that the most lasting relations are not necessarily the most frequent may seem flatly to contradict Axelrod's view that stable cooperation is based upon a high probability of future encounters. In reality, however, their levels of analysis are different. In the Afghan case, kinship (whether paternal, maternal or through marriage) constitutes a reservoir of diverse relations more than an undifferentiated solidarity group. The logic at work cannot be exhaustively reduced either to kinship structures or to the frequency and future likelihood of interaction. Trust, like cooperation, eludes any attempt at exclusive formalization.

The world of the Afghans is charged with symbols and values, obligations and codes. Honor (*âbru, ezzat*), hospitality (*mehmân-nawâzi, melmastia*), reputation (*šohrat*), name or renown (*nâm; neknâm* or *badnâm* according to whether it is god or bad) and vengeance (*enteqâm*) occupy a large place in their lives. These concepts acquire their full significance when one is moving in a world where everyone knows everyone else. *Badal,* a word of Arabic origin, means "exchange, replacement or substitution" in Persian, and by extension "vengeance." It is also used to denote the custom of giving a woman to ask pardon after an offence.[13] Similarly, one of the Pashtu words commonly used by the Hazara of Jaghori and Quetta is *por,* whose primary meaning is "debt" but which refers to the reparation necessary after an offence (Atayee 1979: 78). The spheres of reciprocity, exchange and vengeance are therefore superimposed on one another. Cooperation and rivalry are not mutually exclusive concepts.

Trust, like friendship, is a wager on future interaction. It represents a counterpart of reputation, which in the end is nothing other than information concerning the past behavior of an individual. This is an essential social capital, especially for people involved in trade, because it influences the relations they have with their clients and widens the circle of people who can be mobilized in their home village or in a migratory context. Only people whose social relations partially overlap can gather information about their respective reputations. To know someone's reputation is to know his name and therefore his identity. Close relatives are not so much people one can trust as people one knows; this makes it possible to predict their reactions and to take vengeance in case of defection (either by locating them and resorting to physical violence, or by ruining their reputation in a shared social milieu). Reputation is the shadow of the past; the possibility of vengeance is the shadow of the future.

Such considerations help to explain many of the phenomena in the ethnographic part of this work (chapters 3 to 8). In the absence of a genuine rule of law, illegal border-crossing as well as successful financial transactions depend upon trust and therefore great closeness among the people involved in them. Many Afghan social networks with an international dimension remain compartmentalized along social, regional, religious or ethnic lines—a fragmentation accentuated by the disappearance of old agri-pastoral complementarities. This is indeed the paradox of the migratory networks established by Afghans: they cover huge geographical areas yet rest upon narrowly defined solidarity groups. In a sense, we might say that closure is transferred from a territorial expanse to a multilocal group.

This statement needs to be qualified, however. On the one hand, trust does not spring automatically from any particular social relation, not even that which exists between brothers. On the other hand, it is necessary to maintain stable relations with people outside one's own solidarity group. The remittance networks, in particular, involve three types of actor. First, there are the core partners linked by close kinship ties, although this space of greatest relational intensity is not free from grave tensions and competition that can occasionally lead as far as murder. Second, there are the workers who use the *hawâladâr*'s services, always of the same ethnic and regional origin. And finally there are the key contacts in the host society (smugglers, people with "connections," and so on), without whom the network would remain a closed and ineffectual structure.

In a well-known article, Sahlins (1965) developed a model to account for the social dimensions of exchange and solidarity. He drew a distinction between three forms: "generalized reciprocity," where the social dimension of the transaction is more important than the material aspect, and the relationship is not broken if the beneficiary finds it impossible to perform a return service; "balanced reciprocity," a direct and immediate exchange of equivalent goods and services that is not without an instrumental dimension; and "negative reciprocity," involving an attempt to obtain something without giving in return (Sahlins 1965: 148).

> Here is one possible model for analyzing reciprocity: a tribal plan can be viewed as a series of more and more inclusive kinship-residential sectors, and reciprocity seen then to vary in character by sectoral position [. . .] Kinship-residential groupings from this perspective comprise ever-widening comembership spheres: the household, the local lineage, perhaps the village, the subtribe, tribe, other tribes [. . .] The structure is a hierarchy of levels of integration, but from the inside and on the ground it is a series of concentric circles [. . .] Reciprocity accordingly inclines toward balance and chicane in proportion to sectoral distance. In each sector, certain modes of reciprocity are characteristic or dominant: generalized modes are dominant in the narrowest spheres and play out in wider spheres, balanced reciprocity is characteristic of intermediate sectors, chicane of the most peripheral spheres (Sahlins 1965: 151–152).

In such a model, the social relations of an individual consist of several concentric zones: there is a gradation in intimacy from an existential core (where business partners are identical with close kin and form a genuine solidarity group with a common activity and purpose) through to an outer margin of essentially utilitarian and fluctuating relations that have to be continually renegotiated. Although Sahlins recognizes that kinship is significant but not necessarily decisive (1965: 158), he considers that the different levels of reciprocity are parallel to the degrees of kinship: strangers are very often the enemy (1965: 150).

Now, this view is not entirely consistent with the Afghan ethnographic data. As we have seen, interaction only within a clearly defined group lessens the risk of fraud and abuse, and only long experience of good neighborly or personal relations can convince someone to work with people outside his own *qawm*. Nevertheless, Afghans move in a number of social spaces that overlap but do not fit exactly together. On the one hand, the relations that involve the most compelling duties are also those which can lead to the most serious conflicts. On the other hand, there are more or less permanent bonds of trust, cooperation and solidarity that transcend the limits of social groups and state frontiers. Afghan migrants can and must contact members of other social groups, Pakistanis, Iranians or even Westerners. Sometimes they must ask for favors from local officials or employees of international organizations or NGOs.

For Sahlins morality, like reciprocity, is organized in concentric circles; norms are relative to circumstances and persons (1965: 153). In the Middle

East and North Africa, such a contextual morality based on proximity[14] is counterbalanced by the universal values of Islam. Moreover, Islam and the tribal code see eye to eye in the value they attach to hospitality. A man of honor must know how to appear aggressive towards his equals, who are also his rivals. The *sayyed* are mediators who obey different norms of conduct geared to moderation and equanimity (they play an essential social role among the Hazaras, even if they have a reputation for being lazy and smug). In all cases, however, the perfect man must protect the weak and display generosity and hospitality. A host may be assert his prestige when he entertains many guests, but this undeniably leads to a social and affective openness to the outside. It is said in Afghanistan that travellers have rights and that "a house without a guest is a house without God."

Writing in 1980, Bourdieu already warned that practical logic cannot be reduced to abstract models: "the genealogical relation never completely predetermines the relationship between the individuals whom it unites" (1980: 285). In other words kinship—but also neighborhood proximity—does not necessarily imply trust, even if it remains the principal ground on which trust develops. Among cousins, for example, both hostility and strong attachment are always possible. Yet any conflicts between them will not be of the same nature as those which may break out with a person outside the kinship circle. When hostility exists among fellow-kinsmen, it must be openly declared and free of deceit. (According to the tribal code, you must show yourself to the person you kill in an act of vengeance.)

Two strategies coexist among the Hazaras: (1) diversification of activity among members of the same family and cooperation with persons outside the lineage; and (2) withdrawal into highly integrated domestic groups. As we saw in chapter 7, some prefer to diversify by establishing permanent relations outside the circle of close agnates, while others mainly seek to strengthen the cohesion of the group of brothers (or even paternal cousins) by promoting the integration of the domestic and economic spheres. There is a tension between the two poles. For, "within families in the wider sense, political choices were diversified either deliberately or by force of circumstance"; whereas "community and family ties, resting on a strong descent principle and a strong sense of belonging, prove to be extremely solid and stable" (Centlivres and Centlivres-Demont 1998: 223). In other words, the fact that members of the same kinship group have opposing political allegiances does not prevent the continuation of strong ties of solidarity. Indeed, members of the group see such diversification as a kind of guarantee in the event of a worsening of the security situation. As one Hazara friend put it with reference to himself and his brothers, "whichever faction gets the upper hand, one of us will be part of it." At the same time, the mere fact of kinship does not always entail mutual support or cooperation. Behavior must therefore be contextualized if it is to be properly understood.

MIGRATION, MONEY-TRANSFERS AND REPRODUCTION OF THE SOCIAL TIES

Money-transfers are a matter of interest for at least four reasons: (1) they reveal the existence of social networks linking faraway places; (2) they are economically important for the areas from which the migrants originate; (3) they sustain migration as a strategy of domestic groups; and (4) they stimulate and orient future movement, since migrants pass on information about the possibilities in various regions.

The migration of Afghans is neither definitive nor temporary; it is more appropriate to speak of recurrent multidirectional movement. Few Afghan refugees never return after their initial departure, but there are few family groups without at least one member abroad. Migration and exile are therefore not usually followed by integration into a host country or definitive return to Afghanistan; movement is continual and eventually leads to the constitution of a genuinely transnational community. The Hazaras have established a "circulatory territory," to borrow an expression from Tarrius (1995). By maintaining a certain dispersion of family members, they take advantage of spatial and economic diversification at the same time that they diminish the risks associated with insecurity.

Although money-transfers can involve large sums and are a key economic factor in the Third World,[15] they are often viewed negatively. Some authors and many aid or development workers accuse them of causing price rises and of contributing neither to job creation nor to economic growth in the region from which the migrants originate. Outside the commercial sector as such, it is claimed, the inflow of money does little to promote local investment, as it is often spent on consumption or prestige goods or lavish wedding celebrations, and the skills acquired abroad are of little use in the national economic context. In fact, one of the only positive effects of the migrant remittances would be that they make it easier for children to attend school (see, for example, Kearney 1986: 346–347; Pérouse de Montclos 2000: 114–115).

What such considerations fail to appreciate is that the money-transfers play a crucial role in producing and reproducing social relations despite the context of dispersion and (very often) war. It is true that, in the Afghan case, the *hawâla* system would be better if it included banking facilities to convert money into loan and investment funds that could be used to rebuild infrastructure. Although the emigration of young men may pose long-term problems for the reconstruction of Afghanistan, it is still a survival strategy that has proved its effectiveness. The *hawâla* system has enabled many families to feed themselves, whereas humanitarian aid mainly focused on refugees during the Soviet occupation, then gradually dried up during the 1990s before making a chaotic reappearance after the fall of the Taliban in 2001. International aid has certainly helped many Afghans to cope with periods of acute crisis, but the multiplication of rival NGOs means that the overall results have been very poor. As we have seen, remittances through the *hawâla* system are considerably larger, and much better distributed, than the sum total of humanitarian aid. Afghans themselves say with bitter irony that the transfers are their "drip."

It should also be stressed that the exchange involved in the *hawâla* system, together with the circulation of letters and other documents, symbolize society in the original sense of "putting together." According to Mauss, the gift is a social fact expressed through all kinds of institutions: religious, juridical, political, economic, and so on. He underlines "the so to speak voluntary character, seemingly free and disinterested yet compulsory and interested," of the gift, before adding that it is one of "the human rocks on which our societies are built" (Mauss 1985: 147, 148). For the gift cycle—which rests on a triple foundation of giving, receiving and returning—creates the social ties. Presents should not cost a lot (so that they can be easily returned), but they must be frequent. Obligatory for the very constitution of society, the gift is experienced subjectively as something spontaneous. The uncertainty that always remains about the return gift makes it possible to reintroduce the importance of time (Bourdieu 1980: 168, 170). The time interval separating gift and return gift masks the obligatory dimension of this form of exchange.

> What one sees in every society is that, on pain of constituting an offence, the return gift must be both delayed and different; the immediate giving back of an identical object would quite evidently be tantamount to rejection. The exchange of gifts is therefore contrasted to giving-giving [. . .] it is also contrasted to a loan, whose repayment (is) explicitly guaranteed by a legally binding agreement (Bourdieu 1980: 179).

For Polanyi (1945, 1957), the economy is embedded in social relations. Many different transactions escape the classical and neoclassical model,[16] which is too formal and narrow for the study of other systems than the one that has prevailed in the West since the Industrial Revolution. The market cannot serve as the basis for a general theory of the economy. Polanyi therefore proposes a more open approach that takes account of interpersonal relations and the social environment. He thus defines the empirical economy as an institutionalized process of interaction between man and his environment (Polanyi 1957: 248):

> The outstanding discovery of recent historical and anthropological research is that man's economy, as a rule, is submerged in his social relationships. He does not act so as to safeguard his individual interest in the possession of material goods; he acts so as to safeguard his social standing, his social claims, his social assets. He values material goods only in so far as they serve this end (Polanyi 1945: 46).

Apart from the market, which is based on the quest for profit and relates back to the price system and the mechanism of supply and demand, Polanyi (1945: 47–49, 53–55) identifies three principles of behavior corresponding to forms of economic and social integration: *reciprocity,* most clearly exemplified in the gift cycle; *redistribution,* based on the existence of a public authority (chieftainship or state) that collects and redistributes goods and services outside the price system; and *householding,* involving production for direct use by the household and to cover its own needs.[17] These principles find their application through the institutional models of symmetry, centricity and autarky.

For Sahlins (1965: 225–226), who takes his inspiration from Polanyi, the social component of economic phenomena is decisive, since this is how social relations are maintained beyond the satisfaction of material needs. Moreover, there is a two-way relationship between material flows and social ties: "If friends make gifts, gifts make friends" (Sahlins 1965: 139). Rist (1998), for his part, adds the logic of prestige to Polanyi's four principles—reciprocity, redistribution, domestic economy and market exchange—and notes that it may result in waste or even in the massive ostentatious destruction of previously accumulated wealth (the classical example of this being the potlatch, where destruction is carried out in exchange for prestige and honor).

The *hawâla* system, a complex interlace of solidarity and competition, trust and mistrust, is certainly a total social fact whose study enables us to understand why Afghan society in exile has not sunk into Hobbesian chaos. The five principles identified above are found in it. Reciprocity appears through a plethora of gifts and favors, but also reprisals and acts of revenge. Redistribution is visible in the clientelist relations woven by political parties, commanders and certain large merchants. Domestic economy expresses the quest for autonomy on the part of households that can often count only on their own means to satisfy their needs. And market economy intervenes at many levels, through the purchase, circulation and consumption of various products, through brokerage and currency speculation. As to the logic of prestige, it is the constant quest for honor and the acute sense of hospitality which make Afghan society so beautiful and so difficult.

Conclusion and Epilogue

In the course of my field research and my work on this text, I tried to avoid the pitfall of looking at migration with an essentially external focus on the reasons for departure and the problems for the host society. I therefore took an interest in the strategies of individuals and households, without becoming involved in the debatable theory of rational choice. I did not set any a priori limits to a community but concentrated on what a small group of persons did and said, as the basis for a gradual reconstitution of the actual social relations. The results point beyond the few cases that were examined. War and exile have profoundly shaken Afghan society, but the people themselves have maintained, while also adjusting, most of their cultural references. Because of the research conditions and the cultural context, it was not possible for me to go more deeply into role and viewpoint of Afghan women. But, despite this serious lacuna, the study of Hazara social networks and economic strategies proved fruitful. Thanks to their dynamism, the Hazaras have been able to find answers to a dramatic situation by drawing upon social structures that already existed before. They have thus established large commercial and migratory networks on the basis of diverse social ties, the most prominent of which are kinship and neighborly proximity.

The inhabitants of Jaghori district face their various constraints with courage and ingenuity, and constant travelling between Afghanistan, Pakistan and Iran has opened up for them new social, economic and political horizons. Theirs is far from being an isolated case, however, and similar studies could have been conducted among other population groups in Afghanistan or elsewhere. The distinctiveness of the Hazaras lies in other areas. First, being Shiites, they limit their contacts with Sunni groups; their status as a disparaged minority, whose place of origin is a long way from any international frontier, means that they have to face especially difficult obstacles in the course of migration. Second, being from a poor mountainous region, they have been emigrating for a long time to towns and other countries; the war that ravaged Afghanistan after 1978 only intensified an ancient phenomenon. In fact, the Hazaras themselves see spatial mobility as an existential principle, not as a traumatic experience per se.

Analysis of the situation of the Hazaras shows that migration and war do not inevitably destructure societies. Nor should mobility be seen as an anomaly; social-cultural groups do not have clear boundaries and are not permanently tied to particular territories. In many cases, the social relations between faraway places may be intense.

These points suggest a new conception of the methods of anthropology that will enable us to understand better the world of today as well as the world of yesterday. Field practice—in the sense of work in a clearly defined distant geographical setting—needs to be rethought. Only a fluid and peripatetic ethnography is capable of showing the existence of multilocal families and the transnational networks created by the Hazaras.

The study of migration leads us to abandon the idea that societies are on principle integrated territorial entities. As Amselle points out (2000), whether one takes a positive or negative view of hybridity and cultural cross-fertilization, they are primeval phenomena; they have not made their debut in recent times or disturbed a mosaic of clearly demarcated cultures and societies. A settled way of life is no more normal than mobility, and a single residence is not always preferred to dispersion. It is therefore important that we do not think of the phenomenon of migrants and refugees as transitory or temporary. The model in which refugees are merely victims of events over which they have no control is one-sided and inadequate. Beyond the problems they allegedly pose for host societies, it is essential to study the actual strategies of migrants and refugees while remaining sensitive to the complexity and multipolarity of the migratory experience. Displacement, violence and suffering are part of everyday life for large numbers of people, and anthropology must develop conceptual tools to take account of them. Various theories of social change offer fertile perspectives that go beyond concepts of integration, assimilation or exclusion. The three lasting solutions contemplated by aid organizations—voluntary repatriation, integration into the host country and settlement in a third country—do not fully correspond to the realities of life for the Hazaras or for Afghan refugees in general.

The Hazaras today form a transnational community that has developed strong bonds of solidarity in the course of migration, but the places between which it moves have not thereby become "virtual"; each has a particular meaning within a complex multilocal system. Nor is it the case that all local groups have dissolved. As Mintz (1998: 120) shows in his work on the Caribbean, the dispersion of people who maintain social relations with one another does not mean that "unilocal communities" have ceased to exist or that "multilocal communities" have no historical precedent.

The population groups of Afghanistan—an ancient crossroads between Central Asia, the Indian subcontinent, the Middle East and even China—have undergone periods of expansion and withdrawal. The Hazaras, in the course of migration, travel to Pakistan and Iran and even to the Persian Gulf and the West. The movement is multiple not unilateral; the coming and going is continual. Nevertheless, the international dimension of these networks does not rule out the emergence of an ethnicist discourse of political emancipation in Afghanistan (Grevemeyer 1985, 1988; Harpviken 1996; Monsutti 1999). These two aspects—transnational networks and identity spasms—are far from contradictory and indeed go together in the evolution of national states. In the same way that globalization does not dissolve particularisms (quite the contrary), transnationalism does not cause territorial spaces to disappear.

The study of migration is thus of decisive significance for the method and object of the social sciences, economic and political ethnography and ethnicity. We cannot disregard the new approaches to migration in the work of Malkki or Glick Schiller, Basch and Blanc-Szanton (even if they present a distorted picture of history and anthropology) and, more generally, the fruitful critical anthropology of Appadurai and especially Marcus or Clifford (even if the kind of ethnography to which their efforts are leading is not always clear).

The strategies and networks developed by Afghan refugees are also of practical import for the policies of international organizations and the whole area of development aid. They throw a new light on the lively debate among Afghans as well as foreign observers about which political structures would be best suited to Afghanistan: a strong central government or a more federal system.[1] Any proposal that does not take into account the evolution of society since 1978 is doomed to failure. For, over and above the resistance to the pro-Soviet regime and the Red Army, the people of Afghanistan showed proof of inventiveness and dynamism by establishing broad transnational migratory networks there were extraordinarily effective. No attempt to solve the Afghan crisis and rebuild the country on a lasting basis can ignore this fact. Paradoxically, the war opened up spaces of freedom, and large sections of the population (like the Hazaras) have acquired habits of autonomy that they are certainly not willing to abandon. The challenge would be to establish a strong central power that guaranteed the country's unity while respecting regional autonomy, in line with a subsdiarity principle still to be defined.

The definitions given in the international texts are heuristically unsatisfactory and cannot be easily applied to Afghanistan. For Afghans have taken responsibility for their own lives—through their capacity to take advantage of exile and dispersion, through their community-based strategies, and through their constant movement among the various countries in the region. The social ties underlying these strategies are not incompatible with a high degree of economic efficiency, and any development programme must support local initiatives and refrain from imposing preconceived ideas. In addition to urgent humanitarian aid and improvements to the security situation, the other main priorities appear to be restoration of the health system, rebuilding of roads and agricultural infrastructure, and the establishment of a credit system. If the international organizations active in Afghanistan want to understand the contribution of anthropologists and to take into account the know-how of Afghans themselves, they must be prepared to modify their vocabulary and their approach. It is necessary to regenerate the conceptual and institutional framework.

The strategies, stories and documents that we have presented in this work afford a more vivid picture of the Hazaras, one that does greater justice to their enterprising spirit and various initiatives. Their multiple affiliations and multidirectional migratory movements—what is now by common agreement called transnationalism—are a characteristic feature of Hazara and, more generally, Afghan society. Although the war following the Communist coup of 1978 considerably amplified them, the mobility and dispersion of solidarity groups are an experience that goes back a long way in time for all the population groups in Hazarajat. New social, economic and political horizons have opened up over the years, and developed through a multilocal management of space.

Despite the major obstacles and political-military vicissitudes of recent years (capture of Kabul by the Taliban in September 1996, blockade of Hazarajat in 1997 and 1998, fall of Mazar-e Sharif in August and Bamyan in September 1998, American bombing of Afghanistan after 9/11 and the fall of the Taliban regime), the movement of goods and persons among the Hazaras—as among other Afghan population groups—never came to an end but adapted to the changed circumstances. Nor is this likely to change with the normalization that is expected to follow the establishment of a new internationally supported government in Kabul in December 2001 and the return of hundreds of thousands of people in the wake of the *loya jirga* of June 2002.

* * *

I happened to be in Quetta on September 11, 2001, at the time of the attacks on New York and Washington. Hazaras perceived the American reaction in various ways: some appeared cautious about the likely political developments, but everyone rejoiced at the fall of the Taliban despite the improvements they had brought to the security situation on Afghan roads. In fact, everyday life had never been turned upside down for my Hazara friends. In Quetta, some inns had closed and others opened. The seasonal flow of Hazara farmers to the local coal mines had never ceased, and young people had continued to travel to Iran. The main change was that a growing number of people from Jaghori now had relatives in Europe, Australia or North America. Everyone was trying to expand their network, not only in Afghanistan, Pakistan and Iran but also in the Arabian peninsula and the West—a geographical expansion that might eventually weaken the networks. Independently of recent events, this tendency corresponds to a profound crisis of confidence in a future that remains difficult to predict. In Quetta, for instance, the mood is one of gloom and disappointment with how things have developed politically and economically. More and more people, and not only the city-dwellers and intellectuals of the later 1990s, feel that they can no longer live in Afghanistan, Pakistan or Iran and instead pin their hopes and aspirations on a *Drang nach Westen*—even if the number of those who make it to the West is still relatively small in comparison with those who plan or begin the attempt. Here, globalization is bound up not so much with the scale and speed of migratory and financial flows as with a relocation of the imagination.

A complex map of the obstacles and stopover points on the migratory routes would have to take in the policies and means adopted by various states. Often families diversify their strategies: for example, one son makes an official application to study in the West, while another tries one of the unofficial routes. Early in September 2001 an incident hit the headlines in Europe, when a Norwegian cargo ship, the *Tampa,* picked up 438 migrants without official papers south of Indonesia. Most of them were Afghans, including many Hazaras. Like many others, they had certainly taken a flight to Jakarta on a false visa and then paid a people-smuggler $3,000 or $4,000 each to find them a place on a ship. One young Hazara told me of his attempt to reach Australia with thirty-two other migrants, on a boat that eventually broke down and had to put in to Timor. He was repatriated to Pakistan by the United Nations.

Other Hazaras prefer the European way. When I met him again in 2001, Mardan Ali's son Abdul Karim told me of his travels since leaving for Iran in the winter of 1997–1998. After two and a half years there, he had tried to reach Europe via Turkey, in the hope of travelling on to Britain where a few dozen people from Dahmarda were apparently already living.

Unfortunately for him, the Turkish police stopped his little group of illegal immigrants near Lake Van and asked which of them could speak English. Abdul Karim, who had taken classes in Quetta and Iran, rather naively put himself forward, in the hope that the better-educated members of the group would be given a visa. But, in fact, the police were after the smuggler and beat him up. After twenty days in jail, Abdul Karim was taken to the Iranian frontier and handed over to the authorities, who expelled him to Afghanistan. Not wanting to return home without any money, he then set out to cross back into Iran as soon as possible, but the Taliban soon spotted him in his Western clothes, beardless and bare-headed. He was again thrown into prison and beaten up, then forced to join the troops of the students in religion. The only Shiite among hundreds, he was dressed, housed and fed, as well as being paid 18,000 afghanis a day (roughly $6 a month). After three months, a man from Dahmarda saw him in Kandahar and told his father. Mardan Ali then went to the Taliban and got them to agree to his son's discharge. In the spring of 2001 Abdul Karim accompanied his grandfather from Quetta (where he had received unsuccessful medical treatment) back to Dahmarda, where he died soon afterwards. Abdul Karim then became engaged to a girl from the valley. (This was not the sister of Mohammad Hanif, as the negotiations mentioned in chapter 2 had not borne fruit.)

After Mardan Ali brought his family to Quetta in the winter of 1995–1996, he went back to Dahmarda only once, at the end of 1996. The closure of Haji Sarwar's coal mines left him without a job for several months, but then he was taken on as a foreman. He and his wife had a third son in the winter of 2000–2001.

Mohammad Ali, the brother of Mardan Ali, returned to Iran after a period in Dahmarda. The youngest brother, Aziz Azizi, is still in Dahmarda. Together with his neighbors, he has become involved in the building of a new irrigation channel with the help of an NGO. He looks after Mardan Ali's lands in return for the entire crop. (Mardan Ali considers that his brother is doing him a favor.) Their cousins, Mohammad Hasan and Mohammad Husayn, are both in Tehran. Husayn married in Dahmarda in 1999. Mohammad Yusuf continues to travel between Afghanistan and Iran, where he collects the savings of people known to him. Husayn Bakhsh has not left Quetta. Still without a child, he married a second wife—but did still not succeed to have a child. In the end, he took in one of Mohammad Hasan's sons (born in 1998) and now takes care of his education.

Their relative Mohammad Jawad left in summer 2001 for Indonesia, where he hoped to travel on to Australia or New Zealand. According to rumors that I have been unable to confirm, he was one of the illegal immigrants picked up by the *Tampa*. Mohammad Hanif was more fortunate and succeeded in reaching Australia. Mohammad Reza is in Jaghori, but regularly comes to Quetta to work in the mines. Hazrat Ali has also continued his seasonal peregrinations: in September 2001 he was in Iran, having spent the previous winter working in the mines of Pakistani Baluchistan. As to the old people, we have already seen that Mardan Ali's father, the gentle Mohammad Akbar, died of cancer in the spring of 2001, after travelling to Quetta and back for treatment. Akram Ali is still in Dahmarda, where he looks after the family lands in the absence of his two sons.

Contact is intense between the migrants and those who stay in Dahmarda. Hazaras sometimes meet with great success outside Afghanistan, and most of them send money to their family in Hazarajat or Quetta. In this way, they contribute to the livelihood of their nearest and dearest and to the reconstruction of their native country. More generally, the system of migration and remittances makes it possible to reproduce social ties in spite of geographical dispersion. The intense and multipolar character of movement among my informants is such that geography does not prevent them from maintaining solid social ties. They are neither mere victims of events nor people who take pleasure in violence. They answered my questions with kindness and politeness, but also took an interest in my own life. In the cycle of exchange, it is pointless to try to determine who gives and who receives, because everyone gives all the time; and the greatest gift is the gift of trust. I hope that I have been worthy of it, because the people of Afghanistan deserve all our respect.

Appendix 1

The Transcription System

The transcription system used here is based on works by Lazard (1995) and Heslot (1984–85). In general, it follows pronunciation and sometimes departs from the standard Persian of Iran and Afghanistan. Pronunciation can vary from one region to another, but also from one context to another (indeed, a speaker may keep passing between Hazaragi, Kabuli and Tehrani). Except between â et a, no distinction has been made between short and long vowels.

ʿ	glottal occlusive (stop is scarcely noticed in Hazaragi)
â	similar to **a** in f**a**ther
c	as **ch** in **ch**eque
e	l**e**nd
g	always pronounced as in **g**et
gh	fricative **r** as in French ma**r**i
h	**h**ave
j	**j**elly
q	uvular occlusive
r	rolled **r** as in Italian **r**isotto
s	always pronounced as in **s**ee
š	**sh**ake
u	t**oo**
w	as in **w**ater and diphthongs (âw, aw, ew)
x	as in German a**ch**
y	as in **y**ellow and diphthongs (ây, ay, ey)
z	as in ra**z**e
zh	like **s** in mea**s**ure

Appendix 2

Glossary

âbru	honour, esteem, respect
afghâni	Afghan currency
âghel	hamlet
alaf	forage
âm	ordinary people, commoners, non-*sayyed*
amnyat	security
andiwâl	friend, buddy
ansar	inhabitants of Medina who welcomed the Prophet Mohammed
arbâb	head of lineage or village
âšnâ	acquaintance, relative
atay	father
awlâd-e . . .	children of. . . . (lineage)
awli (literary: *haweli*)	yard; large house with yard
âxund	person with higher religious education
aylâq	high mountain settlement (seasonal)
az xod	self- (expression indicating *inter alia* an endogamous marriage)
bâbu	secretaire (title)
bace amma	patrilateral cross-cousin (FZS)
bace kâkâ	patrilateral parallel cousin (FBS)
bace mâmâ	matrilateral cross-cousin (MBS)

bace xâla	matrilateral parallel cousin (MZS)
badal	exchange; vengeance
badnâm	bad reputation
bahâ-ye nafar	price of a person
bâja	brother-in-law, husband of two sisters (WZH, reciprocal term)
bâwar	belief, credit
begâna	stranger (often with sense of "outside the lineage")
berâdar, brâr	brother (B)
berâdar-e dini	brother in religion
berâdar-e rezâ'i/širi	foster-brother
berâdar-zâda, brâr-zâda	nephew, niece (son or daughter of brother, BS, BD)
bola	matrilateral parallel cousin, son of two sisters (MZS)
câdari	large veil covering the face with acloth mesh
câdor	large veil covering the whole body (literally: tent)
calma	cake of dung and straw (used as fuel)
canda	monthly dues to an association among the Hazara of Quetta
carâgâh	pasture
dallâl	intermediary, broker
dâmâd	son-in-law (daughter's husband: DH); brother-in-law (sister's wife: ZH)
dârugha	headman of a hamlet
dasta	group of people, sub-district
dawlati	governmental (currency)
dayma	non-irrigated land
dehqân	farmer, sharecropper
dehqâni	sharecropping
deriwâr	driver
dokân	shop

dokândâr	trader, shopkeeper
dostumi	of Dostum (currency)
doxtar-e amma	patrilateral cross-cousin (FZD)
doxtar-e kâkâ	patrilateral parallel cousin (FBD)
doxtar-e mâmâ	matrilateral cross-cousin (MBD)
doxtar-e xâla	matrilateral parallel cousin (MZD)
dust	friend
ejâra	lease, concession
ejâradâr	concessionaire, manager
ejâradâri	leasing
employi	employee
enteqâm	vengeance
e'tebâr	credit, credibility; trust; consideration; value, validity
e'temâd	trust, confidence
etminân	trust; assurance, certainty
ezzat	honour, glory
farâri	exiled, runaway
gala	brideprice
gandom-e bahâri	spring wheat
gandom-e termâhi	autumn wheat
gelim	carpet (woven)
gerawi	loan against security
hamsâya	neighbour; client, dependant
hawâla	letter of credit, cheque, money-transfer
hawâladâr	person executing money-transfer by *hawâla*
hazâr	thousand
hoseiniye	place where the maryrdom of Imam Husayn is enacted during the month of *moharam* (Iran)
id-e qorbân, id al-kebir	festival commemorating the sacrifice of Abraham (at the end of Mecca pilgrimage period)

id-e ramazân, id al-fitr	festival marking the end of Ramadan
idgâh	meeting place for the *id*
imâmbârgâ, imâmbâra	place (meeting room, place of prayer, etc.) where Shiites gather in the Indian subcontinent
ja'li	counterfeit, falsified
jamadâr	foreman
jerib	unit of surface measurement (approx. 0.2 hectares)
jeya	nephew (sister's son, ZS), any child of a woman from lineage of ego
jihâd	holy war, struggle against vice
jirga	tribal assembly
jorisar, sarjori	team leader
juy	stream, irrigation channel
kâfer	infidel
kâkâ	paternal uncle (FB)
kâkâxel	lineage of paternal uncle
kalân-e mahalla	head of neighborhood
kalân-e qawm	head of tribal segment
karbalâ'i	person who has completed pilgrimage to Kerbela (tomb of Imam Husayn)
kârez	underground irrigation channel capturing groundwater
kâr(i)gar	manual worker
kelinar	assistant to driver of lorry or bus (from English "cleaner")
kontraktor	contractor
lak	hundred thousand
lâlâ(y)	elder brother (B+)
leyberz	labourer
mâdar	mother (M)
madrasa	religious school (but also village school when instruction is given by a *mullâ*)

mahalla	local area, neighborhood group
mahram	close family circle where women can appear unveiled
malek	head of lineage or village
mâmâ	maternal uncle (MB)
mâmâxel	lineage of maternal uncle
manajer	manager
manteqa	region (group of hamlets forming a social-territorial unit)
masjid	mosque
mehmân-nawâzi	hospitality
mehtar	village head
melmastia	hospitality
membar	place (meeting room, place of prayer, etc.) where Shiites gather in Hazarajat
mir	tribal leader in Hazarajat
mohâjer(-in)	refugee(s) (religious connotation)
moharram	first month of Islamic lunar calendar when Shiites commemorate martyrdom of Imam Husayn
molâzem	employee
mosâfer(-in)	traveller(s) (often with sense of migrant)
mosâfer-xâna	hotel, inn
mozâreba(t)	*commenda* (type of trading partnership where one of the partners provides the capital and the other the labor)
mujâhed(-in)	fighter(s)
mullâ	mullah, person dispensing religious education (in a village school)
munši	secretary
muy-safid	old person, lineage elder (literally "white hairs")
muzdurkâr, muzdur	labourer, unskilled worker
nâm	name, reputation

nambar tu	counterfeit, falsified (from English "number two")
nâmus	women for whom a man is responsible (mother, sisters, wife, daughters); male honor
nazr	votive offering (usually a meal offered to the poor)
neknâm	good reputation
nešâni	sign of recognition, keepsake
nim-roz	midday; unit of time equivalent to six hours of irrigation
nosa (literary: *nawâsa*)	grandson (SS)
padar	father (F)
palao	dish of rice and meat
parda	female (literally: curtain)
paštunwali	Pashtun tribal code
q(u)rut,	dried and clotted buttermilk
qâcâq	contraband
qâcâqbar	smuggler (of goods or people)
qala (literary: *qal'a*)	large fortified farm
qaria	hamlet
qariadâr	village head, representing a region in dealings with state administration
qarz ul- hasana	good loan (without interest)
qawm	solidarity group (lineage, tribe, ethnic or occupational group)
qawm o xeš	whole kin (related by blood and by marriage)
qišlâq	permanent village
qollâbi	counterfeit, falsified
qomândân	commander (in resistance forces)
ra'is	head, leader, president
rafiq	friend, comrade
raft o âmad	coming and going
râhbalat (literary: *râhbalad*)	guide, people-smuggler

ramz	code, secret message
riš-safid	old man, lineage elder (literally "white beard")
roz	day; unit of time equivalent to twelve hours of irrigation
ruhâni (plural: *ruhâniyun*)	person with higher religious education, member of clergy (among Shiites)
sadr	president
sarrâf	money-changer
sayyed (plural: *sâdât*)	descendant of Prophet Mohammed through his daughter Fatima
ser	unit of weight (in Jaghori, the Kabul *ser* of approx. 7 kgs is in use)
syâl	rival
šab	night; unit of time equivalent to twenty-four hours of irrigation
šahed	martyr
šarik	partner, associate
šeyx	person with higher religious education
šohrat	reputation
šohar, šuy	husband (H)
tâjer (plural: *tujâr*)	merchant, businessman (import-export)
takya-xâna	gathering place among Shiites
taqiya	dissimulation (Shiites are permitted to conceal their religious affiliation if their life is in danger)
tarbor	patrilateral parallel cousin (FBS); rival, enemy
tejârat	trade
tekadâr	manager, entrepreneur
tomân	name in ordinary use for Iranian currency (= 10 rials)
uluswâli	district; district capital
umma	Islamic community of believers

waqf	religious foundation
watandâr	fellow-countryman
xân	tribal head, rich and influential man
xân(a)wâda	family, dynasty
xân(a)wâr	family, lineage
xâna	house, household
xâwar	east
xayrât	charitable act
xeš	kinship through marriage
xeši	relatives through marriage
xosur	father-in-law (father of husband or wife: HF, WF)
xosur-bura	brother-in-law (brother of husband or wife: HB, WB)
xums	fifth of income collected and managed by the *sayyed* for the community
xwâr (literary: *xâhar*)	sister (Z)
xwâr-zâda	nephew, niece (sister's son or daughter, ZD), any child of a woman from the lineage of ego
yâghi	honourable bandit
yâr	friend, companion
zakât	legal alms
zâker	person who recounts the martyrdom of Imam Husayn during *moharram*
zamin-e alafcar	pasture
zamin-e âbi	irrigated land
zamin-e ahiâi	developed land
zamin-e ersi	inherited land
zamin-e lalmi	non-irrigated land
zamin-e omumi	common land
zamin-e zarxarid/xaridari	bought land
zaxira	treasure; funds held in common

Appendix 3
Travel Narrative

This is the travel story of Abdul Ahmad from the Rabat valley (district of Shahristan, province of Uruzgan). At my request it was recorded and transcribed in Hazaragi by Mohammad Akbar Shahristani, on April 3, 1996 in Quetta, then translated into French by my good offices, revised by Roman Gehring, and finally translated into English by Patrick Camiller. I have tried to preserve the sometimes jerky style of the original. It relates events that took place between the fall of the Najibullah regime (April 1992) and the capture of Kandahar by the Taliban (November 1994). It perfectly illustrates the problems encountered by Hazara migrants as well as the solutions they devised.

> *In the name of God, he who shows mercy, the merciful. When I left home, I had a great desire to study. I arrived in the town of Ghazni where I tried to find out how to get to Pakistan. Well, I eventually went to the office of the [Shiite] Harakat Party. There was a representative there dealing with travellers and drawing up contracts with Pashtun carriers on behalf of migrants. From there they were sent to Quetta. I introduced myself by saying that I was going to Pakistan. He said to me "go, my brother, and find ten or a dozen passengers so that I could profit from it too"; it was also to my advantage to fill the car quickly and set off for Pakistan. He, the chief representative, was a Hazara; but the guy taking travellers to Pakistan was Pashtun. Well, we found twenty to thirty people in the bazaar and took them to the representative's office. Altogether there were thirty-two of us. There were one or two Toyota pick-ups with which he [the Harakat representative] had always dealt. One belonged to a Pashtun from northern Afghanistan, the other was from southern Afghanistan; both were Pashtuns. An agreement was reached for the travellers to be taken to Pakistan in these two Toyotas. And so the travellers were handed over to those Pashtuns. At the time it cost 60,000 [afghanis]: 10,000 or 20,000 for the representative himself and another 40,000 for the owner of the car that would take them there [to Pakistan]. He [the Harakat representative] wrote down the people's names and the price of the ticket so as to check how many arrived safely and how many were missing at the*

end. [. . .] One guy said he wouldn't go at that price. The representative told him he could go for 40,000. But, in fact, that concealed another truth: he had agreed a price of 60,000 with the carriers, but had said 40,000 to the traveller. The traveller gave him 40,000 there [in Afghanistan] to come here [to Pakistan], but when he arrived the Afghan [the Pashtun carrier] took another 20,000 from him by force. But at that time that was how they sent people, in two Toyotas, with eighteen people in each. Well, we set off for Kandahar. At that time the Kandahar road had only just been opened after an agreement between the Hazaras and the Pashtuns. The Hazaras were afraid of the Pashtuns, because the road had only just been opened. The first evening we reached Shah Joy and stayed there. The Pashtuns looked threateningly at the Hazaras. We spent the night there and then we reached Kandahar. Our driver told us: "Don't go walking in Kandahar, because the Pashtun people are very prejudiced against Hazaras, and you mustn't give them a chance to start problems. We'll take you straight from the Kandahar Gate to Quetta." We soon reached the Pakistani frontier. Here some Pakistanis questioned and searched us, at the frontier and at Chaman. The carriers gave them money to soften them up, and we didn't have to change Toyotas [. . .]. At the frontier they told the driver that he didn't have a permit, that he wasn't Pakistani. He replied that he was a refugee and gave them a bit of money; it was just a question of money! And so we reached Quetta that evening around midnight. I stayed here nearly a year. I even found some classes. But, because of money problems, because of other things . . . in short!

A lot of travellers were coming. They were taken to Iran by smugglers. These travellers told similar things to what I've just said; they came from Ghazni or other places in Afghanistan; there were a lot of Hazaras. When they come here, to Quetta, most of them get themselves sold. How do they get themselves sold? When the driver leaves, he takes them there, he brings them here; the travellers themselves don't have any information. He goes to a hotel and tells the manager he has a certain number of travellers "and you give me three hundred, four hundred or five hundred rupees." Well, the manager gives him the money and the driver sells the travellers to the hotel. The travellers then no longer have any power, because they are put in a room and locked up like prisoners until they are sold to a smuggler who takes them to Tehran. Well, these travellers come here, mainly to Saray-e Namak and the hotels of Sar-e Maidani. Here, in these two places, Hazaras are the majority. It's here, in the hotels, that the smugglers buy [the travellers]. They don't pick them up in the bazaar [. . .] I said that the commission is like this: some, especially the drivers, take from the hotels, while the hotels take from the smugglers. How much do the hotels take? The hotels take from four hundred to five or six hundred, or even seven hundred rupees for each traveller sold. They sell them to the smugglers; they hand over a hundred or seventy people and take the commission. Well, there's a rule: the smuggler won't take travellers without a certificate; there's got to be a document. The document can be of different kinds. Sometimes he gets false Pakistani passports made. He takes them with him, because [Pakistani passports] have a certain value in Iran. That is how they went there. But how many difficulties crop up for Afghan travellers! False Afghan passports are also put together. It used to cost two or three hundred to buy a passport, but now it's different. At that time it was very cheap, seventy or eighty rupees, but later it could be as much as five hundred. But once the passports are made they put photos in them. Then you can head for Iran.

Well, I found out about the travelling system. That is how I myself decided to take some travellers. I went to a hotel at a time when there were travellers and said that this time I wanted to take some travellers. I started working with another smuggler, because I didn't know the ropes. We bought ten or twenty passports, then we took pictures of the people we wanted to take with us and noted the names of their fathers. We did a good job on them [the passports], with the kind of people who know what to do. Then we got the travellers together at the hotel: they paid the bus fare and we loaded them up. Some were going to Taftan but still paid the hotel, to make the profit bigger. The bus fare is a hundred and fifty; you take three hundred from the traveller, for example, then give two hundred and fifty to the bus and pocket the other fifty. Well, there were around thirty travellers in all . . . We'd done a perfect job on their passports. We sent them in two groups, because if we'd done the journey together the Pakistani police might also have created problems. Some of them, fifteen people, left in ten or so little cars—what are they called? Wagons [that is, mini-vans], which belong to Baluch who take them to Taftan. And the other fifteen left with us. We went to the bus station, took the bus, sat down and went to Taftan. [. . .] If there are a lot of travellers, you can fill the whole bus; if there are not so many, you ring up and arrange to be given some of the seats. Well, that's how it is. If the Pakistani police ask questions on the way—for example, "have you got identity cards or not?"—we answer, "no, we're Afghan refugees." In Taftan, there are other special hotels that organize things for travellers. Many hotels there have connections with Iranian smugglers. They're the ones who give them a place. Well, we went to a hotel that opens the way for most of the travellers from Taftan. In the hotel where we went, the system was like this: whatever food the wretches brought with them, whether they had money or not, everyone obviously had to eat something. If you've got money you pay directly; if you haven't got any, they tot it up and it's the smuggler who pays. If you're ill, whether you want to or not, you have to eat the filthy food they cook—whether you eat or not, they count it up. Some of the smugglers are more decent. They give people carefully prepared meals and provide them with separate rooms.

Well, the hotels make contact with a smuggler in Iran. They ask him what the road's like at that moment, when they should leave. He gives them information: for example, right now it's good or not good. When he says the time is right, a special person—the hotelier—sends him the travellers. [. . .] Well, we stayed one night there. Most travellers stay ten nights if the road's not good; others stay maybe twenty days, four days.

The men aren't split up here, because difficulties can arise on the way. Only one road is still open, but some of the travellers are given to another smuggler. The smugglers take a lot of money—maybe five hundred or a thousand tomans [1 toman = 10 rials] per person. They take travellers separately through the mountains, through the smuggling route, with the help of a Baluch acquaintance.

We got going very early in the morning. Very early we were told it was the day to leave, that we had to set off. The smuggler brought a couple of Toyotas [. . .] It was six o'clock; each Toyota was crammed with twenty to twenty-five people. The roads were bad. The cars arrived at the foot of the mountain, then we continued on foot. It was close to the frontier; the mountain lies between the frontiers of Afghanistan, Pakistan and Iran. In fact, the mountain is the frontier. The Pakistani cars took us to the foot of the mountain; altogether there were a good hundred or hundred and fifty of us. Well, we went in two groups; we went with the people who had been waiting for us, and we got together around two o'clock. We had a bit of bread, but there wasn't any water on the mountain; some had brought a little water, but others hadn't. Then we headed off. There are always thieves in those mountains, because the Baluch themselves know that a certain number of people will be passing through that day. They wait there quietly and then seize the travellers' watches, rings, fine clothes and shoes; they take whatever they fancy. Good God! The traveller is left naked. Well, when we went there that day, half an hour earlier, we ourselves saw a lot of thieves waiting, but they thought the travellers weren't going to come and left. Really, they are always posted on the road used by travellers. The travellers leave off their Afghan country clothes and take a lot of winter clothing, so they won't be recognized in Iran. The road in the mountains was very long—three or four hours of walking. We came down to the frontier and arrived in Iran. Once in Iran, there's a permanent road in the direction of Pakistan. We couldn't stay there during the day, because there was a lot of traffic and vehicles. Well, there was a narrow valley where the travellers waited, then some smugglers left to see what the traffic was like and whether there were any Iranian soldiers around. They got the picture and when it was quite dark, after nightfall (always after nightfall), we set off. [. . .] How did we set off? There were three or four smugglers in all, surrounding the travellers on all sides, on all four sides, and ahead were the Baluch guides. They knew the situation. For example, when there was some danger, they told the travellers to sit down, then to start walking again, then to go faster or slower, not to make any noise, etc. So, they went on ahead. If the travellers made some noise, they beat them mercilessly, beat them with sticks. If a brother lagged behind, perhaps an old man who couldn't walk well, if that happened, he'd be shot at and killed. So, it was very dangerous. Well, how long was the way? Maybe two kilometers between the permanent road and the mountain. When we left the mountain we ran a lot. At night, when it was really dark, we slept before starting the journey again. This time we left very quickly; we crossed the frontier immediately. It was desert; the travellers went into the undergrowth. They stayed in the undergrowth because it was dark there and nothing could be clearly seen from outside. You could go on this side or the other and not be able to tell what was what. We stayed hidden there until the smuggler from Iran came to meet the travellers. We were sitting down and a couple of Toyotas pulled up. The smugglers arranged to meet at such and such a place. A couple of Toyotas arrived; there were a hundred and fifty of us. Fifty people left, in those two Toyotas; they set off for Zahedan . . . There were some Iranian cars that took them secretly. Well, as for us, we stayed there until one in the morning . . . it was seven in the evening when the first travellers were taken . . . the rest of us waited and we stayed there until one in the morning. It was very cold, there was no water, and we were very hungry. Sometimes people stayed a whole day in the undergrowth, and some died of hunger and thirst.

Well, the vehicles eventually came back and we left. We were taken close to Zahedan, close to the town. There were many other dangers on the journey, although we went well with the Toyota on the permanent road. [. . .] We passed close to a guard post. The driver went straight through the desert without any lights; he switched off the lights and drove very slowly. We lost our way. Sometimes we passed through mud, sometimes through dust. We arrived close to another mountain, near the town of Zahedan, near the outskirts of Zahedan. It was night, and we couldn't go into the town. It rained a lot during the night; it was very cold and we were very hungry and thirsty . . . And so we were taken from the mountain. [The Baluch smugglers] came back to the mountain and said, "you stay here while we take the others to the hotel, then we'll come back for you." They left and we remained in the rain and the cold until three in the morning. They left and then came back. [. . .] We got on the permanent road itself; we went past the outskirts of Zahedan, because the hotels where travellers stayed were not part of the town. They are not like other hotels; for example, they are shaped like a house—no one knows who is taken inside. We spent the night there; we stayed there and they brought us tea and we drank the tea . . . They handed out passports to everyone. You can find other things in those hotels; you can also find buses, because the travellers and smugglers can't go out and an agreement is made with someone from the buses, for example. He says he has two or three buses going to Tehran. They know the Iranian police and give them a commission. The travellers' journey continues. If the usual price for a whole bus to Tehran is fifty thousand tomans, it will be two hundred and fifty thousand tomans for the travellers.

Well, the evening we arrived, we drank tea and also had a meal there. What other rules do those hotels have? If you stay a night, or if you stay one hour, they add it up and charge five thousand tomans whether you stay one night or one hour. If you stay two nights, they take ten thousand tomans. Well, from there they put us on a bus; there are normally thirty-six people on a bus. Then we got going in the direction of Mashad—in one bus, thirty-six people . . . Well, the road police came and asked questions, "have you got passports or haven't you?" Usually they can't tell the passports are fake. We gave them the passports and said they were ours. They looked at them said it was okay . . . There were a lot of police checks on the way to Mashad. We didn't go into Mashad itself, because they were checking travellers carefully and discovering the false passports. So there, thirty kilometers from Mashad, we turned onto the road for Tehran; from there we headed for Tehran . . . Afghans go there to work, but also for their religious faith; they have a great desire [to go on a] pilgrimage to Mashad. In this case, [in addition to] the two hundred and fifty thousand, you have to give the bus driver thirty thousand to take you to the Mashad pilgrimage. For those who do this, there is another police control near Mashad where they carry out strict checks. But—I don't know—the driver had some connections. Anyway, we weren't searched a lot and were taken into Mashad. There we weren't taken to the terminal [bus station], because a lot of searches were being done there. They took us close to the sanctuary. There was a hotel opposite the sanctuary, which was mainly for the use of pilgrims. We went there on foot; we suddenly showed up at the hotel so that the police wouldn't notice us; we took refuge inside the hotel. We took a room there before making the pilgrimage. It was ten o'clock when we arrived in Mashad. We went quickly and made the pilgrimage and then returned to the hotel. The hotel charged five hundred rupees a night per person. It cost the travellers to stay there, but not the smugglers. The costs of the car, the hotel and the night were charged to the travellers themselves. The price of transport for the smuggler with a guarantee of reaching Tehran . . . [. . .] It was two in the afternoon when we left Mashad for Tehran. We got well on our way to Tehran. We weren't questioned much [any more] on the road. Things were very strict around the frontier. Afterwards, if we were questioned, we said we were going on a pilgrimage to Qom, to Shah Abdul Azim [at Shahr-e Rey, near Tehran], or to Behesht-e Zahra [the tomb of Imam Khomeini, near Tehran] . . . We reached the Tehran terminal at four in the morning. There were some travellers there who had the trust of the smugglers. The smugglers let them go at the terminal . . . they were relatives . . . they [the smugglers] were trustful and let them leave. They told them to go, and they knew where they were going, where they were working, who were their relatives. They said, "I'm going now, I'll give you the smuggling money at such and such a place; either I come myself or you come" . . . If there is not this trust, the smuggler himself goes to a special hotel. There are special hotels in Tehran. He takes the others to these secret hotels and locks them up. The travellers are locked up there; they are prisoners. And the hotel owner charges each traveller two thousand tomans a night. What does the smuggler do? Each traveller has addresses; he says that a relative will come or gives his work address where [the smuggler] can claim the money . . . if the traveller himself has money here, he [the smuggler] takes it off him; if he doesn't have any, he takes it from relatives. Anyway, without paying the smuggler, the relative cannot take him away. You've got to have kin or an exact address. The smuggler goes there and demands to be paid, then returns to the hotel. In this way he gradually gets his money back, either in Qom, in the area near Tehran, or somewhere else. [. . .] The Baluch who came from Zahedan had a partner, who locked up the traveller and contacted his relatives. He told them to bring the money to such and such a place . . . He said, "Bring the money to this place! If you don't come I'll keep your friend locked up." The traveller asks the money from his closest kin: from his brother if he's there, from his uncle [FB] if his brother isn't there, and from friends or fellow-villagers if his uncle isn't there.

What work do people get? There's a lot of work in Iran. You find it through your own kin. For example, someone has an address and goes to Karaj [a town 40 kms west of Tehran], or to a poultry-farmer in Mardabad. When he gets there the poultry-farmer knows that there is work in such and such a place, and no work somewhere else, so the traveller isn't left without work. Iranian employers never give money to smugglers; Iranians never give guarantees. If he's a good friend and has been working with the traveller several times or for a number of years and there really is a lot of trust, he might give something. But I never saw that myself, and it must be very rare. In general, it's relatives or [Afghan] friends who give. So, what work do refugees do? Only in building sites and factories, quarries, poultry or cattle farms, agriculture. Someone arriving in Iran from Afghanistan for the first time must have a companion or a very reliable address. Those who have already been once or twice know where to go, where to look for work, where to find their relatives, who can perhaps find them a job. Besides, all that means a lot of money. For example, when I went there, the trip cost forty-five thousand tomans, now it's sixty or seventy thousand tomans. And those who go to Iran, if they work very hard, can make thirty or thirty-five thousand a month, or twenty thousand in poultry-farming. You've got to work many months to pay back all the expenses of the trip; it's very difficult to make it all balance out.

Appendix 4

Chronology of Political-Military Events

- 1891–93: subjugation of Hazarajat by Abdur Rahman.
- 1929: the Tajik adventurer Habibullah, known as Bace Saqqao, takes power in Kabul for nine months. He is defeated by Nader Shah, who restores the Mohammadzay dynasty.
- 1946: revolt of Ibrahim Khan, known as Bace Gawsawar, in the region of Shahristan (Hazarajat).
- 14 August 1947: declaration of independence and partition of India and Pakistan.
- 1962: the Hazara acquire the status of a "native tribe" in Pakistani Baluchistan.
- 1971: terrible famine in the north-west and centre of Afghanistan; tens of thousands perish.
- July 1973: Mohammad Daud, cousin of King Zaher Shah, takes power following a coup d'état and establishes a Republic.
- April 27, 1978: Communist coup d'état (*Enqelâb-e sawr,* "April Revolution"); Daud is killed during the assault on the presidential palace. Nur Mohammad Taraki is appointed president of the Revolutionary Council.
- July 1978: first rebellions in the east of Afghanistan.
- January 17, 1979: exile of Shah of Iran (he takes refuge in Egypt).
- February 1979: uprising in Dara-ye Suf (northern region with a Hazara majority), then throughout Hazarajat. From autumn 1979, the whole region remains autonomous until the end of the war.
- February 1979: insurrection in Iran, fall of imperial regime.
- April 1, 1979: proclamation of the Islamic Republic of Iran.

- September 1979: assassination of Taraki and his replacement by Hafizullah Amin.
- September 1979: foundation at Waras (central Afghanistan) of the Shura-ye Ettefaq-e Islami ("Council of Islamic Unity"), a Shiite alliance headed by Sayyed Ali Beheshti.
- December 1979: Soviet intervention; Amin is killed and replaced with the more pro-Soviet Babrak Karmal.
- September 22, 1980: the Iraqi army invades Iran.
- Spring 1984: the power of the Shura-ye Ettefaq is demolished by two pro-Khomeini parties, the Sazman-e Nasr ("Victory Organization") and Sepa-ye Pasdaran ("Guards Army"), which take control of most of Hazarajat.
- 1984: confrontation between the Hazara and the forces of order in Quetta (Pakistan) during the month of Moharram.
- May 4, 1986: Babrak Karmal is replaced at the head of the Afghan Communist Party by Najibullah, who swiftly launches a policy of national reconciliation.
- February 1988: Gorbachev talks of withdrawing the Red Army if an agreement is signed.
- July-August 1988: ceasefire between Iran and Iraq.
- February 15, 1989: complete withdrawal of Soviet troops. Moscow continues to support the Kabul regime logistically and financially. The Sunni resistance parties establish an interim government in exile
- June 4, 1989: death of Ayatollah Khomeini (Ali Khamenei succeeds him in the position of guide of the Islamic Republic of Iran).
- July-August 1989: foundation at Bamyan of the Hezb-e wahdat ("Unity Party"), which brings together the main Shiite parties of Afghanistan (particularly the Shura-ye Ettefaq, the Nasr and the Sepah-ye Pasdaran). Abdul Ali Mazari (originally from the Nasr) assumes the leadership.
- July-October 1990: violent conflicts between Pashtun and Hazara fighters in the province of Uruzgan, overflowing into Jaghori district.
- March 1992: pro-government militias rise up, especially the Uzbek militia of General Abdul Rashid Dostum in northen Afghanistan.
- April 15–16, 1992: fall of Najibullah (he takes refuge in United Nations offices); the *mujâhedin* enter Kabul.

- June 28, 1992: Borhanuddin Rabbani (leader of the Jamiat-e islami) is appointed head of the interim government of the Resistance for one non-renewable term of four months (he subsequently takes power and extends his period of office).
- August 11, 1992: start of first battle of Kabul, between Ahmad Shah Massoud (Jamiat-e islami) and Hekmatyar (Hezb-e islami).
- January 20, 1993: fresh fighting in Kabul between "government" troops (led by Massoud) and the Hezb-e islami; the Wahdat sides with the latter while Dostum remains neutral.
- February 13, 1993: the forces of Sayyaf and Massoud enter the Shiite district of Afshar-Mina; hundreds of civilians are massacred.
- January 1, 1994: formation of an anti-government coalition grouping the Junbesh-e Melli (Dostum), Jabha-ye melli (Mojaddedi), Hezb-e wahdat (Mazari) and Hezb-e islami (Hekmatyar); violent battles in Kabul.
- May 27, 1994 and September 14, 1994: fighting between Shiite factions in Kabul (Mazari faces the opposition of Mohammad Akbari, who draws closer to Massoud).
- November 1994: the Taliban movement emerges in southern Afghanistan; it takes control of Kandahar.
- February 1995: the Taliban near Kabul after a series of successes.
- March 6, 1995: Massoud launches a major offensive against Wahdat forces (in Western areas of the capital), whose allies Dostum and Hekmatyar have been driven back by the Taliban advance. Caught in a pincer movement, the Wahdat surrenders its positions to the Taliban.
- March 13, 1995: Abdul Ali Mazari, head of the Hezb-e wahdat, is killed by the Taliban in unclear circumstances (M. Karim Khalili succeeds him). The Taliban are driven back by Massoud's offensive.
- September 5, 1995: the Taliban capture the city of Herat, in northeastern Afghanistan.
- October 1995: fighting at Bamyan between Massoud's troops allied to the Akbari faction of the Wahdat and the Khalili faction of the Hezb-e wahdat. The latter emerges victorious and extends its control over central Afghanistan.
- September 26, 1996: the Taliban take Kabul and hang former president Najibullah (who until then has remained in the refuge of UN offices). Massoud withdraws to the Panjshir.

- October 10, 1996: formation of a broad anti-Taliban front including the Jamiat-e islami (Rabbani, Massoud, Ismael Khan), the Hezb-e islami (Hekmatyar), the Junbesh-e Melli (Dostum) and the Hezb-e wahdat (Khalili).
- May 24, 1997: the Taliban enter Mazar-e Sharif; Dostum flees.
- May 26, 1997: the Taliban government is recognized by Pakistan.
- May 27–28, 1997: fighting in Mazar; the Taliban reportedly break into a Shiite area and clash with the Hezb-e wahdat militia, soon joined by troops from the Junbesh; they are forced to withdraw from the city.
- June 1997: the Taliban establish a blockade with the aim of starving Hazarajat into submission.
- September-October 1997: the Taliban approach Mazar several times but are driven back.
- November 13, 1997: the UN intervenes unsuccessfully to get the Taliban to lift their blockade of central Afghanistan; the risk of famine causes alarm.
- August 8, 1998: the Taliban capture Mazar-e Sharif and especially target the Hazaras in a massacre of the civilian population.
- August 20, 1998: American bombing of what are claimed to be terrorist training camps.
- September 13, 1998: the Taliban enter Bamyan.
- November 13, 1998: Mohammad Akbari, head of a Hazara faction, rallies to the Taliban.
- Between spring 1999 and the late winter of 2000–2001: the Taliban are unable to break the resistance of Wahdat, whose forces recapture Bamyan on several occasions. The Taliban carry out several massacres of Hazara civilian populations.
- February 26, 2001: Mullah Omar, the Taliban leader, decrees that all pre-Islamic monuments in Afghanistan, including the buddhas of Bamyan, should be destroyed.
- March 2, 2001: after recapturing Bamyan, the Taliban begin the destruction of the buddhas, which is confirmed on 12 March.
- September 9, 2001: a suicide squad assassinates Ahmad Shah Massoud.
- September 11, 2001: terrorist attacks in New York and Washington; the United States accuses Osama bin Laden and his Taliban hosts.
- October 7, 2001: start of American bombing of Afghanistan.

- November 2001: anti-Taliban forces successively capture Mazar-e Sharif, Bamyan, Kabul and Kunduz.
- from November 27 to December 5, 2001: UN-sponsored conference on Afghanistan held in Bonn.
- December 6, 2001: the Taliban surrender in Kandahar.
- December 22, 2001: an interim administration under Hamid Karzai takes office in Kabul.
- June 2002: the so-called emergency *loya jirga* in Kabul establishes a new government under Karzai's presidency; a number of Hazara occupy ministerial positions. But peace is far from being fully restored.
- December 2003—January 2004: the new *loya jirga* established the Afghan Constitution.
- October 9, 2004: presidential elections; Karzai is elected with about 55% of the votes.

Notes

NOTES TO THE INTRODUCTION

1. See the UNHCR site: http://www.unhcr.ch/, consulted on May 8, 2002 and September 18, 2002.
2. The organization Human Rights Watch published a report on these events on their site: www.hrw.org/reports98/afghan/, consulted on May 9, 2002.

NOTES TO CHAPTER ONE

1. In order to underline the multidimensionality of population movements, as well as to favor the viewpoint of the migrants over that of states, I have avoided use of the terms "emigration" and "immigration."
2. Afghanistan is not one of the signatories, nor is Pakistan, a country that accommodated the largest number of refugees in the 1980s and early 1990s. Iran, on the other hand, signed the two texts in 1976.
3. According to this criterion, many Afghans who went to live in Pakistan should not have been considered refugees.
4. The Palestinians, who come under the United Nations Relief and Works Agency for Palestine Refugees, are not included in these estimates. See the UNHCR site: http://www.unhcr.ch/cgi-bin/texis/vtx/home?page=statistics, consulted on May 1, 2002.
5. For example, Shami (1996: 6).
6. "Ecumene": transliteration of a word that the ancient Greeks used to denote the totality of the inhabited world.
7. Migration studies have also made considerable headway in the French-speaking world. See, for example, the works by Bruneau (1994), Ma Mung (1992) and Tarrius (1995, 2001).
8. "Rather it is the current moment of capitalism as a global mode of production that has necessitated the maintenance of family ties and political allegiances among persons spread across the globe. (. . .) We believe, however, that current transnationalism marks a new type of migrant experience, reflecting an increased and more pervasive global penetration of capital" (Basch et al. 1994: 24).

9. See, for example, Braudel (1979), J. Abu-Lughod (1989), Goody (1996), Wallerstein (1974, 1980, 1989) and Wolf (1982).
10. See also Conte, Giordano and Hertz (2002).
11. In his remorseless attack on postmodernism, Lindholm (1997) accuses L. Abu-Lughod of reproducing the moral and logical errors of romanticism.
12. See also Bright and Geyer (1987).

NOTES TO CHAPTER TWO

1. Both Marsden (1992) and Colville (1998) stress this capacity of refugees to become self-reliant.
2. See Ahmed (1986); Boesen (1986); Centlivres (1987, 1988a, 1988b, 1991, 1993, 1994a, 1994b); Centlivres and Centlivres-Demont (1987a, 1987b, 1988b, 1988c, 1988d, 1992, 1998, 1999a, 1999b, 2000); Centlivres, Centlivres-Demont and Gehrig (2000); Centlivres-Demont (1994, 1996); Colville (1998); Connor (1987a, 1987b, 1989); Edwards (1986b, 1990); Huld and Jansson (1988); Marsden (1992); Rizvi (1990); Shahrani (1995); Titus (1999), to mention only a few.
3. The humanitarian reports are mostly written by anthropologists or sociologists: Ashraf (1988); Centlivres (1993); Centlivres and Centlivres-Demont (1992); Christensen (1983, 1984); Christensen and Scott (1988); Development Alternatives (1990); Donini (1996); HCR (1997); Morton (1991, 1994); RAASTA (1992); Robert R. Nathan Associates (1989); RPG (1991, 1992); UNHCR (1993, 1995); Webster University (1987). This rather colorless literature is often rich in factual information, but it adopts the humanitarian vocabulary and does not question the paradigm in which the refugee is seen as a victim in need of assistance.
4. As one of the Pakistani contributors writes, "Repatriation and rehabilitation of the refugees can be the only durable solution to this problem" (Azhar 1990: 114).
5. One noteworthy exception is Donini (1996), who stresses the destabilizing impact of the humanitarian organizations in Afghanistan and draws a mixed balance-sheet of their role. By concentrating on material aspects and failing to promote genuine national reconciliation, they certainly bear some responsibility for the extreme fragmentation of the country and the never-ending culture of war.
6. See also Centlivres and Centlivres-Demont (1988b).
7. Relations between Sunnis and Shiites have always been tense in Afghanistan. In Pakistan, despite the fact that the country was constituted around the ideal of Muslim unity in opposition to the Hindu majority of the subcontinent, the 1980s and especially the 1990s were the scene of interreligious violence that tended to harden the positions of many Sunni and Shiite movements.
8. Centivres and Centlivres-Demont (1988c: 74–75) also review the motives for departure from Afghanistan and draw similar conclusions to Connor's.
9. See Baily (1999); Centlivres (1995b); Centlivres and Centlivres-Demont (1999b, 2000); Centlivres, Centlivres-Demont and Gehrig (2000); Edwards

(1994); Gehrig (1999); Omidian (1994); Omidian and Lipson (1992); Shalinsky (1996).

10. See Barnes (1954, 1969); Boissevain (1968, 1974, 1985); Boissevain and Mitchell (eds 1973); Granovetter (1973a, 1973b); Hannerz (1967); Mitchell (1974, ed 1969,); Scott (1991); Whitten and Wolfe (1973).
11. For Rodman (1992), the term "multilocality" is the pendant of "multivocality." It expresses the multiplicity of lived spaces and discourses within a social group, so that the latter can no longer be seen as homogeneous or as having univocal links with its environment.
12. See also Centlivres and Centlivres-Demont (1998: 220–221).
13. In this text, Marcus refines and explains previous remarks on such themes as "multi-issue ethnography" as opposed to "strategic single site ethnography" (1989: 18, and 1992: 316).
14. During a tourist trip to Istanbul in spring 2000, I happened to find myself face to face with a young Hazara whom I had first met in Quetta in 1993 and then again in 1995 and 1996. In the intervening period, he had managed to leave Pakistan and used various smuggling networks to establish himself in Turkey.
15. My research concerned particular networks on the basis of which it is possible to draw more general conclusions. While wishing to avoid the reification of ethnic groups, which are nothing but the result of social-cultural interactions and historical processes, I often found it more convenient to speak of "the Hazaras" as well as of Pashtuns, Pakistanis or Iranians in general. After all, it is difficult to avoid all collective names.
16. The principal published works are: Bacon (1951a, 1951b, 1958); Bindemann (1987); Canfield (1971, 1973a, 1973b, 1976, 1978, 1984, 1985, 1986); Davydov (1965); Dianous (1961); Dulling (1973); Emadi (1997); Ferdinand (1959, 1962, 1964); Gawecki (1980, 1986); Grevemeyer (1985, 1986, 1988); Harpviken (1996, 1997); Hudson and Bacon (1941); Iwamura (1959); Iwamura and Schurmann (1954); Kopecky (1982, 1986); Mousavi (1998); Poladi (1989); Schurmann (1962); Thesiger (1955, 1956, 2000); Timurkhanov (1980). There are also a number of works in Persian: Gharjestâni (1989); La'li (1993); Yazdâni (1993); Tanzim (1980).
17. The names have been changed to protect my informants.
18. In 1996, when I first met him in Tehran, he had never seen his daughter, who was born a few months after his departure.
19. A Shiite resistance party.
20. I attended his wedding during a period I spent in Dahmarda.
21. I learned Persian first with Micheline Centlivres-Demont in Switzerland, then through some classes during my period in the field, with a Hazara student, Ahmad Ali. People speak many local variants of Persian, but it is usually possible for them to understand one another. Hazaragi is certainly one of the most distinctive of these forms, but my informants constantly shifted from one level to another by employing turns of phrase typical of Kabuli, Hazaragi or the Persian of Tehran. The language of those who live in Quetta, or who stay there for long periods, is sprinkled with Urdu, Pashtu and English words.

22. The idea was given to me by Paul Titus.
23. A Shiite group that came from Iran in the eighteenth century.
24. The word *nâmus* (derived from the Greek *nomos*, "law," which served to designate the angel bearing divine revelation, Glassé 199: 298) refers in Afghanistan to the women of the house and their chastity, but also to male honor (Atayee 1979: 65), for a man's honor crucially depends upon the behavior of the women for whom he is responsible (wife, mother, sisters and daughters). This conception allows women to acquire what Nancy Tapper calls their "subversive power" (1991: 21–22). Thus, a counter-discourse or alternative vision of society has emerged among women, which is more often expressed in actions than formulated in words.
25. See, for example, Meyer (1976), who describes an abortive ethnographic experience in Afghanistan.
26. In his study of the Pashtuns of Swat (Pakistan), Lindholm (1982) speaks eloquently of the affective ties between a researcher and the people among whom he works. But his remarks cannot be simply extrapolated to contemporary Afghanistan, where a foreigner always runs the risk of being taken for an aid worker from whom some favor can be obtained.
27. On rare occasions I noticed that some people felt repelled at the thought of having to share the same plate with me, especially in the communities of eastern Hazarajat whose Shiite and Ismailian members avoid having a meal together (see Canfield 1973a, 1973b).

NOTES TO CHAPTER THREE

1. Pronounced locally as "Damurda."
2. Estimates of the number of Hazaras living in Afghanistan range from less than 10% to more than 25% of the total population. According to US State Department figures, which seem plausible, the ethnic distribution of the Afghan population was as follows in 1990: Pashtuns 38%; Tajiks 25%; Hazaras 19%; Uzbeks 6%; others 12% (http://www.state.gov/r/pa/ei/bgn/5380.htm, October 30, 2003).
3. A community of 126 persons in the Murghab valley, Turkmenistan and Bukhara shows up in the 1926 Soviet census and was probably later assimilated by the Turkmen majority or by the Shiite Irani population (of Iranian origin) in Central Asia (Mousavi 1998: 153–154).
4. Babur speaks not only of the Hazara but also of the Nikdîrî or Nikudârî, a term that appears to designate peoples of Mongol origin (1987: 200). On several occasions he uses the word *aymâq* to refer to Mongol tribes (1986: 196, 207, 221).
5. See also Ferdinand (1959, 1964).
6. I have kept his transliteration, even though it differs from the one adopted in this work.
7. Ridgway (1983: 228–229, recapitulated in Adamec 1991: 369) provides a different and less precise list of the Hazara tribes.
8. The dictionary of the Center for Afghanistan Studies defines *dasta* as "a group of people" (1993: 363).

9. "Chief, head, leader" (ibid. 1993: 715).
10. Gharjestani (1989) writes Day Marda.
11. Qalandar means "wandering dervish," according to the dictionary of the Center for Afghanistan Studies (1993: 574).
12. It should be noted, however, that the British travellers Moorcroft and Trebeck recorded the presence of Ghilzay nomads in the Behsud region as early as 1824 (Moorcroft and Trebeck 1979 II: 384). Some twenty years later, Ferrier mentioned that hostility between Hazaras and Pashtuns discouraged the latter from crossing Hazarajat (1976: 220–221).
13. During the same period, Pashtun nomads were exempt from taxes and military service.
14. He was a Hazara from the region of Ghazni who, although he collaborated with the Kabul government, is valued by today's Hazara intellectuals as a witness to the atrocities committed at that time. Unfortunately his great work, *Serâj al-tawârix* (1912–1914), has not been translated into any Western language.
15. In Pashtun-populated areas around Dahmarda (Taraki, but also Kakar, Kharuti and Andar), the housing is more concentrated, in real villages with streets separating the high-walled houses.
16. It cost around $400 to purchase a shop in the Dahmarda bazaar.
17. Pluvial agriculture is most prevalent in the highest regions of Hazarajat (Day Kundi, Lal-wa-Sarjangal, Yakawlang, Panjab, Waras, Behsud and Nawur).
18. Johnson estimates that in Behsud families have an average of only 1.7 jerib of irrigated land and 1.26 jerib of pluvial land (2000: 16).
19. On all agricultural matters, see Humlum (1959: 163–222).
20. These figures are generally little different from those reported in the 1960s (Etienne 1972: 278–279).
21. Literally: "rattling of stones."
22. These *kârez* have delightful names that deserve to be translated: Takht-e Sang-e Bâlâ and Takht-e Sang-e Pâyn mean respectively "upper flat stone" and "lower flat stone"; Qockâr-e Bâlâ and Qockâr-e Pâyn, "upper ram" and "lower ram." As to Peshbughundi-ye Bâlâ and Peshbughundi-ye Pâyn, their names derive from *bughund*, "round" or "rounded," and *peš*, "in front"-hence "in front of the upper round hill" and "in front of the lower round hill." *Lux* is the stem and *nula* the pourer of a teapot or any other recipient. (My thanks are due to M. Akbar Shahristani for the benefit of his knowledge.)
23. This is the Kabul *ser* used in Jaghori, roughly the equivalent of 7 kg.
24. Elsewhere the system is different: no shepherd is formally appointed, and each family takes it in turns to send one of its members to guard the flock.
25. Literally, the words *câdor*, *câdar* and *câder* mean "tent."
26. Bourdieu (1972: 72–80, 100, 129; and 1980: 273–279, 290) forcefully points out that the calculation of rates of endogamy is based on abstract divisions, which do not take actual practices into account. Genealogically similar unions may result from very different, or even opposite, strategies and negotiations. But statistics do make it possible to show that marriage between a man and his patrilateral parallel cousin (known as "Arab marriage"

in the ethnological literature) is a minority phenomenon among the Hazaras. R. Tapper (1979: 142) also notes that among the Shahsevan the proportion of unions between MBD/FZS is higher than between FBD/FBS.

27. If these two cases are excluded, then 31% of marriages were between a man and a woman from his mother's lineage, where that lineage was different from his own.
28. This kind of union does seem more frequent among the Sayyeds, however.
29. The Gazetteer of Afghanistan (1985: 185) counts a total of sixty-five villages in Jaghori, but this figure appears quite arbitrary and does not correspond to the divisions that the local population considers significant.
30. My thanks are again due to M. Akbar Shahristani, who was kind enough to share his linguistic knowledge with me.
31. I counted only three brothers and their two patrilinear cousins, or five households in all.
32. In Hazarajat people speak more often of *jây-namâz*, "place of prayer," than of mosque in the strict sense.
33. The use of this term may seem surprising, as *qaria* denotes a hamlet among the Hazara. It seems to have had a wider referent in the language of government administration.
34. Active in Afghanistan under the name Ettehadiya-ye mujâhedin-e islâm-e Afghânistân.
35. Khalili and Massoud drew closer to each other after the fall of Kabul. As to Akbari, he sided with the Taliban after their capture of Mazar-e Sharif and Bamyan and came out in opposition to the dominant faction in the Wahdat.
36. See Monsutti (1996a).

NOTES TO CHAPTER FOUR

1. Formerly known as Shal or Shalkot.
2. A town roughly 150 kilometers south of Quetta.
3. During these events, the great majority of Hazara refused to support the regime of the Tajik Habibullah, nicknamed Bace Saqqao ("Water carrier's son"), who had driven out King Amanullah.
4. The name of the city derives from the Pashtu word *kot*, which means "fort."
5. Called Cantonment, Cantt or Chawni (*câwni*).
6. Encyclopædia Britannica, CD-ROM 99.
7. There were 3,255,000 Afghan refugees registered in Pakistan in 1989, and only 1,477,000 in 1994. Their number stabilized around 1,200,000 in the following years (UNHCR 1998).
8. The spacious new housing in Gulistan Town gradually developed in the second half of the nineties, on demilitarized plots of land sold off to private individuals.
9. As we saw in chapter 3, these tribal segments sometimes coincide with a *manteqa*, as is the case in Dahmarda.
10. This is why the *kalân-e qawm* is also known as the *sarcanda* ("head of the *canda*").

11. His inspiration for this was Roger LeTourneau, *Fès avant le protectorat, les villes musulmanes d'Afrique du Nord* (Rabat: Institut des Hautes Etudes Marocaines, 1957).
12. According to one informant, more than ten per cent of adult males in Dahmarda are involved in this seasonal migration.
13. The English terms contractor, laborers, manager, driver and cleaner are transliterated in accordance with the local Persian-inspired pronunciation, as those who use them on a daily basis are not aware of their foreign origin.
14. By way of comparison, a large loaf of bread costs 2 rupees, a plate of rice and meat (*palao*) in a small bazaar restaurant 25 rupees. A rickshaw driver has an average monthly turnover of less than $200, but his income is rarely more than a third of that amount (as he must either rent or pay off his vehicle, which costs several thousand dollars to buy). An electrician takes home less than $100 a month. A local HCR worker receives between 5,000 and 8,000 rupees ($150–$240 dollars), and a ICRC field officer between 10,000 and 12,000 rupees ($300–$360 dollars). A driver for an international organization is paid 3,500 rupees (a little over $100).
15. Haji Sarwar, who was born in Quetta, had his origins not in Jaghori but in the Nawur region. The foreman's provenance is thus more of factor than that of the contractor.
16. The days are not divided up as in the West: they begin not at midnight but at sunset on the previous evening (so our Thursday evening corresponds to Friday evening for Afghans).
17. Whether in Afghanistan, Pakistan or Iran, very few Hazara women have a paid job. Their economic role is essential, but is usually limited to the domestic sphere.

NOTES TO CHAPTER FIVE

1. Neither Napier (1876) nor the Gazetteer of Afghanistan (1910) lists the Berberis among the peoples of Khorasan, but Ferrier (1976: 223) briefly mentions them in Afghanistan.
2. L'Ethnologue, a huge catalogue of the world's languages, mentions 283,000 Hazaragi-speakers and 113,000 Pashtu-speakers in Iran (1993). But it is not clear whether these are immigrants from Afghanistan or part of the Iranian population (http://www.ethnologue.com/show_country.asp?name=Iran, consulted on May 1, 2002).
3. Since then, the number of Afghan refugees has fallen.
4. According to the Iranian authorities, a total of 700,000 Afghans are in the country illegally (AFP dispatch, 13.08.00).
5. See, in particular, Bijan Khajehpour-Kouei, "Panâhande paziri-ye šahrvandân-e tehrâni," 25-31; Ziba Jalali Naini, "Xod âgâhi va panâhandegi: nazari bar vaz'iyat-e zanân-e panâhande-ye afghâni dar irân," 33–40; and Omid Farhang, "Kârigarân-e afghâni, sâzandegân-e binâm va nešân-e irân," 43–49.
6. Another passage sets the percentage of men as high as 92% (Goft-o-gu 1996: 47).

7. 0–10 years: 10.8%; 10–20 years: 12%; 20–30 years: 37%; 30–40 years: 20%; 40–50 years: 10%; over 50 years: 10% (Goft-o-gu 1996: 47).
8. By an irony of fate, these two names translate as "black hill" and "white stone."

NOTES TO CHAPTER SIX

1. The movement of persons never came to a complete halt, however, as the blockade mainly affected goods.
2. The violent anti-Shia positions of the Taliban leaders did not stand in the way of these local arrangements.
3. After the fall of Kabul, the former rival factions buried their differences. Dostum and the Wahdat drew closer to Massoud and Rabbani to form the Northern Alliance.
4. The large numbers of Hazaras in Kabul formed a special case that lies outside the bounds of the present study.
5. Uruzgan was the scene of violent clashes in the time of Abdur Rahman, when some parts were emptied of people and resettled by Pashtuns (Poladi 1989). The reverse occurred after 1978 and Pashtun nomads no longer dared to venture there (Centlivres 1991: 75). After the Taliban took control of the region in autumn 1998, land ownership disputes became especially acute.
6. It takes a day to travel from Herat to Delaram and another day from Delaram to Kandahar. In other words, three days are needed to get from Herat to Ghazni, whereas a day and a half or two days are enough from Quetta. (Some repairs were carried out in 2001 and have made the times shorter.)
7. Thus, in summer 1996 it took me two and a half days to travel by lorry from Ghazni to Bamyan: the first stage lasted ten hours (from Ghazni to the Syakhak bazaar), and the second nearly ten hours (the Unay and Hajigak passes).
8. One often hears it said that Hazaras have mongoloid features and little body hair. The shape and size of the nose is another common theme, as it is thought to be small among the Hazaras and large (a sign of virility) among the Pashtuns. In one cameo piece that I witnessed in 1996, a Taliban checking our bus took one look and told the passengers in Pashtu that they should wear a beard to be *mobarak* ("blessed"); one of his colleagues then told him to drop it, and added with a laugh that these were "people from China" (*mardom-e cin*).
9. One day a former colonel in the Communist army, a Shiite Bayat from Ghazni, explained to me that shortly after the fall of Najibullah he had passed himself off as a Kandahar mullah among a group of Pashtun *mujâhedin* from Hezb-e islami. This subterfuge saved his life as well as that of his family, but it could succeed only because he had spent many years in Kandahar and spoke perfect Pashtu.
10. It is not certain that the new process which began in late 2001 with the fall of the Taliban will bring an improvement of the situation, and the forms of migration to Iran and the Gulf states will probably not be fundamentally altered as a result.

11. In the summer of 1993, 1 rupee = 6 tomans (that is 60 rials) and 1,000 rupees = 46,000 afghanis.
12. The various parties themselves use the term "to sell" (*sawdâ kardan*).
13. In 1996 the prices in afghanis increased because of a devaluation of the currency, so that it was necessary to reckon on 6,000 to 8,000 afghanis for a *palao* and roughly 50,000 afghanis for the trip from Kandahar to Ghazni), but the prices converted into dollars remained fairly constant.
14. By way of comparison: at that time a Volga car cost $1,000, a Kamaz (a Soviet-made cross-country military lorry) between $10,000 and $35,000, a gallon of petrol 11,500–12,000 afghanis ($2.7) in Kandahar and 13,500–14,000 afghanis ($3.1) in Jaghori.
15. By contrast, there were considerably fewer large bazaars in the districts of Qarabagh and Jighatu, which were less sheltered and closer to Ghazni.
16. During my trip to Taftan I naively asked one Baluch if he was Iranian or Pakistani. His only answer was to burst out laughing at the incongruity of the question.
17. Sometimes people also use the expression *nambar tu*, from the English "number two."
18. This figure more than doubled in 2001.

NOTES TO CHAPTER SEVEN

1. The form *hawâlawâlâ* is also used, under Urdu influence.
2. My field data were clarified by my reading of work by many different anthropologists, historians and economists: Appadurai (ed. 1986); Braudel (1979); Goitein (1963; 1964); Goody (1996); Labib (1969); Pérouse de Montclos (2000); Pirenne (1963); de Roover (1948; 1953); Udovitch (1967; 1970; 1990; ed., 1981). Eichfeld's report (1995) was a particularly valuable source of inspiration.
3. One toman = 10 rials, the official currency of the Islamic Republic of Iran.
4. In summer 1996 the same container of throat pastilles cost 6 rupees in Quetta and 4,000 afghanis (a little more than 10 rupees) in Ghazni, a difference of 66%.
5. See also Monsutti (1997a, 2000a, 2000b). Eichfeld (1995) gives a slightly different schema.
6. This makes it especially difficult to trace and quantify money-transfers under the *hawâla* system.
7. The dollar exchange-rate may vary by 15% according to the face-value and date of issue of the note: it should be recent and in good condition, and have a value of $100 ($1, $5 and $10 notes elicit scornful or sarcastic looks).
8. In other words, in the previous generation, two brothers married two sisters.
9. We should remember that, according to UNHCR figures (1997), there were approximately 1.4 million Afghans in Iran in 1996. Although no official estimate exists, the proportion of Hazaras was higher in this migrant population than inside Afghanistan.
10. See *L'état du monde: Annuaire économique et géopolitique mondial* (Paris: La Découverte, 1997 to 2001).

11. Michelle Cottle, "Hawala v. the War on Terrorism," The New Republic, October 15, 2001 (http://www.thenewrepublic.com/101501/cottle101501.html, consulted on March 27, 2002).
12. Pierre Hazan, *Le Temps*, June 7, 2001.
13. Gilles Dorronsoro, "L'injustice faite aux Afghans," *Le monde diplomatique*, June 13, 2001.
14. A Google search on September 20, 2002 turned up 10,600 entries for the term *hawâla*. Although some authors stress its positive role in the transfer of money, most consider it to be a tool in the service of terrorism.
15. It seems that 2500 vehicles are parked in the desert (World Bank 2001: 27).

NOTES TO CHAPTER EIGHT

1. http://www.state.gov/r/pa/ei/bgn/5380.htm, October 30, 2003.
2. In this respect, Jaghori district was a noteworthy exception. Even under Taliban rule, thousands of children (girls as well as boys) were able to receive a good education through the offices of a local NGO, the Shuhada Organization.
3. It should be noted that the fall of the Taliban and the establishment of an interim government in Kabul, following American intervention in the wake of 9/11, have scarcely altered the situation of women or the educational system in the Afghan countryside.
4. In Afghanistan, televisions and VCRs are powered by car batteries.
5. During my periods in Afghanistan in 1995 and 1996, Kabul was said to be the only capital city in the world without electricity. The situation was somewhat better in Mazar-e Sharif. Since 2001, things have changed a little and it is possible to telephone Pakistan from Afghan towns such as Kabul, Ghazni, Kandahar and even Herat.
6. Literally his FBSS. It is a descriptive term usually serving to classify any somewhat remote member of his own lineage, whereas *bace kâkâ* (FBS) denotes a closer family relation.
7. Even those with contacts in the West often had only telephone numbers, and not complete addresses.
8. In such cases I found myself in the situation of an illiterate Hazara: my mastery of written Persian was quite poor, and so I preferred to dictate the general meaning to someone who could read and write and leave it to him to compose the actual text.
9. This is a surname that the person in question gave himself and which literally means "he who takes hold of the world."
10. It rests upon a high degree of mutual knowledge. Social relations are therefore different from those which, for Benedict Anderson, are predominant within the nation: "It (the nation) is imagined because the members of even the smallest nation will never know most of their fellow-members, meet them, or even hear of them" (1983: 6)

NOTES TO CHAPTER NINE

1. The pro-Soviet regime in Kabul designated nationality by the Arabic-Persian term *melliat* (Centlivres 1994b: 165).

2. For an analysis of popular ethnography in Afghanistan, see Centlivres and Centlivres-Demont (1988a: 31–44).
3. See Anderson (1975, 1983); Barth (1953, 1959, 1961, 1981a, 1981b, 1992); Black-Michaud (1975); Bourdieu (1972); Digard (1987); Dresch (1986, 1988); Eickelman (1998); Geertz (1971, 1979); Gellner (1969, 1981, 1995); Hart (1989); Jamous (1981); Lancaster (1997); Munson (1989, 1993, 1995); Peters (1990); Salzman (1978, 1995); Street (1990, 1992); Tapper N. (1991); Tapper R. (1979, 1983), to mention only a few of the authors.
4. The first two of these terms may also be used in amorous discourse (e.g. *dust dâštan* means "to love").
5. Werner's study of Pakistanis in Britain (1990) shows the role that women play in establishing relations of friendship and neighborliness. In their new context, immigrants from Panjab have developed wide networks that go beyond kinship. Although my investigative framework did not allow me to go more deeply into the question of women's social networks, it is undeniable that they also play an essential role among the Hazaras.
6. Other expressions exist, such as *qawl-e berâdari* ("promise of brotherhood") or *berâdar-e qorâni* ("Koranic brothers"), where the commitment is sometimes actually written down in a copy of the Koran.
7. This said, the relationship between two sworn brothers is more symmetrical than that which exists between two brothers-in-law, since the man who gives a woman acquires a certain precedence that is close to that of the father-in-law. Moreover, the Dari terminology of kinship distinguishes between the taker of a woman (*dâmâd*, brother-in-law, ZH, but also son-in-law, DH) and the giver (*xosur-bura*, WB, constructed on the basis of father-in-law, WF/HF, *xosur*).
8. As Werbner remarks in connection with Pakistanis (1990: 68), business partners often permit each other jokes that would be incongruous within the kinship circle. This is equally the case in an Afghan context.
9. See Bourdieu (1980: 317–318) for the Kabylie.
10. One already come across it at the end of La Fontaine's fable *L'ours et l'amateur des jardins*: Rien n'est si dangereux qu'un ignorant ami/ Mieux vaudrait un sage ennemi.
11. For a discussion of the concept of trust, see also Gambetta ed. (1989) and Revue du MAUSS (1994).
12. Axelrod's most striking example (1990: 73–87) is the "live-and-let-live system" in the trenches of the First World War, when forces deployed against each other for a long period eventually refrained from opening fire on each other.
13. *Sar-badal*, literally "exchange of heads," refers to the discredited practice whereby two men marry each other's sister at the same time. It scarcely exists any more except among poor people or to end a cycle of vengeance.
14. Bourdieu mentions the example of a man who was disavowed by his brother after a local quarrel in the Kabylie. Although he was manifestly in the wrong, public opinion did not understand that his brother violated

the rules of family solidarity in the name of an abstract sense of justice (1972: 15–16).

15. They may amount to 10 to 70 percent of the export income of certain countries in the South (Bruneau 1994: 12).
16. This model is constructed around different ideas: the individual has unlimited needs and seeks to maximize his interests; rational choice formalizes the relationship between an end and scarce means; the price system defined by market laws, and especially the law of supply and demand, is the economic fact par excellence.
17. The word œconomia meant domestic administration for the ancient Greeks, while Aristotle called chresmatics the quest for profit which is the market principle (Polanyi 1945: 53; see also Rist 1998: 27).

NOTES TO THE CONCLUSION AND EPILOGUE

1. See a special issue of Nouvelles d'Afghanistan on the unity of the Afghan nation, with contributions by Haquani (1997), Maley (1997), Roy (1997) and Reshtia (1997). See also Maley (ed., 1998).

Bibliography

Abu-Lughod, Janet (1989). *Before European Hegemony: The World System* A.D. *1250–1350*. New York, Oxford, etc.: Oxford University Press.

Abu-Lughod, Lila (1991). "Writing against Culture." In *Recapturing Anthropology: Working in the Present*, edited by Richard G. Fox. Santa Fe: School of American Research Press, 137–162.

Adamec, Ludwig W. (1991). *Historical Dictionary of Afghanistan*. Metuchen & London: Scarecrow Press.

Adelkhah, Fariba (1998). *Être moderne en Iran*. Paris: Karthala.

Ahmed, Akbar S. (1986). *Pakistan Society: Islam, Ethnicity and Leadership in South Asia*. Karachi: Oxford University Press.

Akram, Assem (1996). *Histoire de la guerre d'Afghanistan*. Paris: Balland.

Aliyev, S. M. (1966). "The Problem of Nationalities in Contemporary Persia." *Central Asian Review* 14(1): 62–70.

Amselle, Jean-Loup (2000). "La globalisation: 'Grand partage' ou mauvais cadrage?" *L'Homme* 156: 207–226.

Anderson, Benedict (1983). *Imagined Communities: Reflections on the Origin and Spread of Nationalism*. London; New York: Verso.

———. (1992). "The New World Disorder." *New Left Review* 193: 3–13.

Anderson, Ewan W., and Nancy Hatch Dupree, eds (1990). *The Cultural Basis of Afghan Nationalism*. London & New York: Pinter Publishers.

Anderson, Jon W. (1975). "Tribe and Community among the Ghilzai Pashtun." *Anthropos* 70: 575–601.

———. (1982). "Social Structure and the Veil: Comportment and the Composition of Interaction in Afghanistan." *Anthropos* 77: 397–420.

———. (1983). "Khan and Khel: Dialectics of Pakhtun Tribalism." In *The Conflict of Tribe and State in Iran and Afghanistan*, edited by Richard Tapper. London: Croom Helm, 119–149.

———. (1985). "Sentimental Ambivalence and the Exegesis of 'Self' in Afghanistan." *Anthropological Quarterly* 58(4): 203–211.

Antoun, Richard T. (1976). "Anthropology." In *The Study of the Middle East*, edited by Leonard Binder. New York: Wiley, 137–228. [Appendices by David M. Hart and Charles L. Redman]

Appadurai, Arjun (1988). "Putting Hierarchy in its Place." *Cultural Anthropology* 3(1): 36–49.

———. (1991). "Global Ethnoscapes: Notes and Queries for Transnational Anthropology." In *Recapturing Anthropology: Working in the Present*, edited by Richard G. Fox. Santa Fe: School of American Research Press, 191–210.

———. (1995). *Modernity at Large: Cultural Dimensions of Globalization.* Minneapolis: University of Minnesota Press.

———. (1999). "Disjuncture and Difference in the Global Cultural Economy." In *The Cultural Studies Reader*, edited by Simon During. London & New York: Routledge, 220–230. [1st ed.: 1990]

Appadurai, Arjun, ed. (1986) *The Social Life of Things: Commodities in Cultural Perspective.* Cambridge: Cambridge University Press.

Ashraf, Asif (1988). *Economic Impact of Afghan Refugees in NWFP.* Peshawar: Pakistan Academy for Rural Development.

Atayee, M. Ibrahim (1979). *A Dictionary of the Terminology of Pashtun's Tribal Customary Law and Usages.* Kabul: International Centre for Pashto Studies, Academy of Sciences of Afghanistan.

AVICEN (1990). *Hazarajat: The Development of the EPI Programme in the Central Provinces.* Peshawar: Afghanistan Vaccination and Immunisation Centre.

Axelrod, Robert (1990). *The Evolution of Cooperation.* London: Penguin Books. [1st ed.: 1984]

Azhar, Said (1990). "Afghan Refugees in Pakistan: The Pakistani View." In *The Cultural Basis of Afghan Nationalism*, edited by Ewan W. Anderson and Nancy Hatch Dupree. London & New York: Pinter Publishers, 105–114.

Babur, Zahirud-din Muhammad (1987). *Babur-nama.* Lahore: Sang-e-Meel Publications. [Translated by Annette S. Beveridge]

Bacon, Elizabeth E. (1951a). *The Hazara Mongols of Afghanistan. A Study in Social Organization.* Berkeley: University of California (PhD Thesis).

———. (1951b). "The Inquiry into the History of the Hazara Mongols of Afghanistan." *Southwestern Journal of Anthropology* 7(3): 230–247.

———. (1958). *Obok: A Study of Social Structure in Eurasia.* New York: Wenner-Gren Foundation/Viking Fund Publications.

———. (1963). "Review of H. F. Schurmann, *The Mongols of Afghanistan.*" *Central Asiatic Journal* 8(1): 62–67.

Baily, John (1999). "Music and Refugee Lives: Afghans in Eastern Iran and California." *Forced Migration Review* 6: 10–13.

Barnes, John A. (1954). "Class and Committee in a Norwegian Island Parish." *Human Relations* 7: 39–58.

———. (1969). "Networks and Political Process." In *Social Networks in Urban Situations: Analyses of Personal Relationships in Central Africa*, edited by J. Clyde Mitchell. Manchester: Manchester University Press, 51–76.

Barth, Fredrik (1953). *Principles of Social Organization in Southern Kurdistan.* Oslo: Brødrene Jørgensen.

———. (1959). *Political Leadership among the Swat Pathans.* London: Athlone Press.

———. (1961). *Nomads of South Persia: The Basseri Tribe of the Khamseh Confederacy.* Prospect Heights: Waveland.

———. (1981a). *Process and Form in Social Life.* London: Routledge & Kegan Paul. [Selected Essays of Fredrik Barth Volume 1]

———. (1981b). *Features of Person and Society in Swat: Collected Essays on Pathans*. London: Routledge & Kegan Paul. [Selected Essays of Fredrik Barth Volume 2]

———. (1992). "Method in our Critique of Anthropology." *Man* 27: 175–177.

Basch, Linda, Nina Glick Schiller, and Cristina Blanc-Szanton, eds (1994). *Nations Unbound: Transnational Projects, Postcolonial Predicaments and Deterritorialized Nations-States*. Langhorne: Gordon and Breach.

Bindemann, Rolf (1987). *Religion und Politik bei den schi'itischen Hazâra in Afghanistan, Iran und Pakistan*. Berlin: Ethnizität und Gesellschaft.

———. (1988). "Kunst und Widerstand: 'Revolutionäre' und 'nationale' Lieder der Hazara." In *Neue Beiträge zur Afghanistanforschung*. Liestal: Bibliotheca Afghanica, 85–100.

Black-Michaud, Jacob (1975). *Cohesive Force: Feud in the Mediterranean and the Middlbe East*. New York: St.Martin's Press.

Bloch, Maurice (1973). "The Long Term and the Short Term: the Economic and Political Significance of the Morality of Kinship." In *The Character of Kinship*, edited by Jack Goody. Cambridge, London, etc.: Cambridge University Press, 75–87.

Bocco, Riccardo (1994). "Migrations, démocratisation, médiations: enjeux locaux et internationaux au Moyen-Orient." In *Moyen-Orient: migrations, démocratisation, médiations*, edited by Riccardo Booco and Mohammad-Reza Djalili. Geneva: IUHEI; Paris: PUF, 9–29.

Boesen, Inger W. (1986). "Honour in Exile: Continuity and Change among Afghan Refugees." *Folk* 28: 109–124.

Boissevain, Jeremy (1968). "The Place of Non-Groups in the Social Sciences." *Man* 3(4): 542–556.

———. (1974). *Friends of Friends: Networks, Manipulators and Coalitions*. Oxford: Basil Blackwell.

———. (1985). "Networks." In *The Social Science Encyclopedia*, edited by Adam Kuper and Jessica Kuper. London: Routledge & Kegan Paul, 557–558.

Boissevain, Jeremy, and J. Clyde Mitchell (1973). *Network Analysis: Studies in Human Interaction*. Paris, The Hague: Mouton.

Bourdieu, Pierre (1972). *Esquisse d'une théorie de la pratique précédé de trois études d'ethnologie kabyle*. Geneva: Droz. [*Outline of a Theory of Practice*. Cambridge: Cambridge University Press, 1977]

———. (1980). *Le sens pratique*. Paris: Minuit. [*The Logic of Practice*. Cambridge: Polity Press, 1990].

Boyd, Monica (1989). "Family and Personal Networks in International Migration." *International Migration Review* 23: 638–670.

Braudel, Fernand (1979). *Civilisation matérielle, économie et capitalisme, XVe-XVIIIe siècle: Les jeux de l'échange*. Paris: Armand Colin. [*Civilization and Capitalism, 15–18th Century*. London: Collins, 1981].

Bright, Charles, and Michael Geyer (1987). "For a Unified History of the World in the Twentieth Century." *Radical History Review* 39: 69–91.

Brightman, Robert (1995). "Forget Culture: Replacement, Transcendence, Relexification." *Cultural Anthropology* 10(4): 509–546.

Bruneau, Michel (1994). "Espaces et territoires de diasporas." *L'Espace géographique* 1: 5–18.

Bunbury, N. L. St. Pierre (1949). *A Brief History of the Hazara Pioneers (Indian Army) 1904–1933*. Quetta: ms.

Burnes, Alexander (1986). *Cabool: A Personal Narrative of a Journey to, and Residence in that City*. Karachi: Indus Publications. [1st ed.: 1841]

———. (1992). *Travels into Bokhara . . .* New Delhi, Madras: Asian Educational Services, 3 vol. [1st ed.: 1834]

Canfield, Robert L. (1971). *Hazara Integration Into the Afghan Nation: Some Changing Relations Between Hazaras and Afghan Officials*. New York: Afghanistan Council of the Asia Society.

———. (1973a). *Faction and Conversion in a Plural Society: Religious Alignments in the Hindu Kush*. Ann Arbor: Museum of Anthropology/The University of Michigan.

———. (1973b). "The Ecology of Rural Ethnic Groups and the Spatial Dimensions of Power." *American Anthropologist* 75: 1511–1528.

———. (1976). "Suffering as a Religious Imperative in Afghanistan." In *The Realm of the Extra-Human: Ideas and Actions*, edited by Agehananda Bharati. Paris, The Hague: Mouton Publishers, 101–122.

———. (1978). "Religious Myth as Ethnic Boundary." In *Ethnic and Intergroup Relations in Contemporary Afghanistan*, edited by Jon W. Anderson and Richard F. Strand. New York: Afghanistan Council of the Asia Society, 35–46.

———. (1984). "Islamic Coalitions in Bamyan: A Problem in Translating Afghan Political Culture." In *Revolution and Rebellions in Afghanistan: Anthropological Perspectives*, edited by M. Nazif Shahrani and Robert L. Canfield. Berkeley: Institute of International Studies, 211–229.

———. (1985). "Hazaras." In *Muslim Peoples: A World Ethnographic Survey*, edited by Richard V. Weekes. Westport, London: Greenwood Press, 327–332. [1st ed.: 1978]

———. (1986). "Ethnic, Regional and Sectarian Alignments in Rural Afghanistan." In *The State, Religion, and Ethnic Politics: Afghanistan, Iran, and Pakistan*, edited by Ali Banuazizi and Myron Weiner. Syracuse: Syracuse University Press, 75–103.

Center for Afghanistan Studies (1993). *Dari-English Dictionary / Farhang-e fârsi wa englisi*. Omaha: Center for Afghanistan Studies.

Centlivres, Pierre (1970). *Un bazar d'Asie Centrale: forme et organisation du bazar de Tâshqurghân (Afghanistan)*. Wiesbaden: Ludwig Reichert.

———. (1987). "Dans les camps au Pakistan: gestion administratives et organisation politique des camps." *Les Nouvelles d'Afghanistan* 35–36: 18–23.

———. (1988a). "Les trois pôles de l'identité afghane au Pakistan." *L'Homme* 28(4): 134–146.

———. (1988b). "L'innocence en question: les enfants afghans dans la guerre et l'exil." *Nouvelle revue d'ethnopsychiatrie* 12: 127–142.

———. (1989). "L'Iran: l'autre pays d'accueil." *Afghanistan Info* 24: 12.

———. (1991). "Exil, relations interethniques et identité dans la crise afghane." *La Revue du Monde musulman et de la Méditerranée* 59–60: 70–82.

———. (1993). *A 'State of the Art' Review of Research on Internally Displaced, Refugees and Returnees from and in Afghanistan*. Neuchâtel: ms.

———. (1994a). "Le difficile retour des réfugiés afghans." *Les enfants du monde (Unicef)* 119: 14–16.

———. (1994b). "Les groupes ethniques et les 'nationalités' dans la crise afghane." In *Moyen-Orient: migrations, démocratisation, médiations*, edited by Riccardo Bocco and Mohammad-Reza Djalili. Geneva: IUHEI; Paris: PUF, 161–170.

———. (1995a). "Le Moyen-Orient et nous: Point de vue de l'anthropologue." *Synergies*, édition spéciale: 36–38.

———. (1995b). "Des absents d'importance: les Afghans de l'exil et de la diaspora." Geneva: IUHEI (ms).

———. (1997). "Violence légitime et violence illégitime: A propos des pratiques et des représentations dans la crise afghane." *L'Homme* 144: 51–67.

———. (2000). "Introduction: portée et limites de la notion de diaspora." *Cahiers d'études sur la Méditerranée orientale et le monde turco-iranien* 30: 5–12.

Centlivres, Pierre, and Micheline Centlivres-Demont (1981–82). "Village en Afghanistan." *Commentaire* 16: 516–525.

———. (1983). "Frontières et phénomènes migratoires en Asie centrale: le cas de l'Afghanistan de 1880 à nos jours." In *Migrations en Asie: Migrants, personnes déplacées et réfugiés*, edited by Micheline Centlivres-Demont. Berne: Société suisse d'ethnologie, 83–114.

———. (1987a). *Rapport: enquête ethnologique auprès des réfugiés afghans au Pakistan*. Neuchâtel: ms.

———. (1987b). "Sociopolitical Adjustment among Afghan Refugees in Pakistan." *Migration World* 15(4): 15–21.

———. (1988a). *Et si on parlait de l'Afghanistan? Terrains et textes 1964–1980*. Neuchâtel: Institut d'ethnologie; Paris: Maison des sciences de l'homme.

———. (1988b). "The Afghan Refugee in Pakistan: An Ambiguous Identity." *Journal of Refugee Studies* 1(2): 141–152.

———. (1988c). "The Afghan Refugees in Pakistan: A Nation in Exile." *Current Sociology* 36(2): 71–92.

———. (1988d). "Hommes d'influence et hommes de partis: l'organisation politique dans les villages de réfugiés afghans au Pakistan." In *Neue Beiträge zur Afghanistanforschung*, edited by Erwin Grötzbach. Liestal: Bibliotheca Afghanica, 29–46.

———. (1992). *Afghanistan: étude de cas*. Neuchâtel: ms.

———. (1998). "Exil, diaspora et changement social: le cas de l'Afghanistan." In *Islam et changement social*, edited by Mondher Kilani. Lausanne: Payot, 219–229.

———. (1999a). "Etat, islam et tribus face aux Organisations internationales: le cas de l'Afghanistan 1978–1998." *Annales* 54(4): 945–965.

———. (1999b). "La diaspora afghane en Europe." *Bulletin SSMOCI* 9: 9–10.

———. (2000). "Exil et diaspora afghane en Suisse et en Europe." *Cahiers d'études sur la Méditerranée orientale et le monde turco-iranien* 30: 151–171.

Centlivres, Pierre, Micheline Centlivres-Demont and Tina Gehrig (2000). "La diaspora afghane: le paradoxe apparent de l'identité et de l'intégration." In *Les défis migratoires: Actes du colloque CLUSE, Neuchâtel 1998,* edited by Pierre Centlivres and Isabelle Girod. Zurich: Seismo, 272–278.

Centlivres-Demont, Micheline (1994). "Les réfugiés afghans au Pakistan: gestion, enjeux, perspectives." In *Moyen-Orient: migrations, démocratisation, médiations,* edited by Riccardo Bocco and Mohammad-Reza Djalili. Geneva: IUHEI; Paris: PUF, 33–40.

———. (1996). "Les réfugiés afghans au Pakistan: situation d'exil et adaptation alimentaire." In *Cuisines reflets des sociétés,* edited by Marie-Claire Bataille-Benguigui and Françoise Cousin. Paris: Sépia–Musée de l'Homme, 243–255.

Christensen, Hanne (1983). *Sustaining Afghan Refugees in Pakistan: Report on the Food Situation and Related Social Aspects.* Geneva: United Nations Research Institute for Social Development.

———. (1984). *Réfugiés afghans au Pakistan: d'une situation d'urgence à une situation d'autosuffisance. Rapport sur l'aide alimentaire et les aspects socio-économiques connexes.* Geneva: Institut de Recherche des Nations Unies pour le Développement Social.

Christensen, Hanne, and Wolf Scott (1988). *Survey of the Social and Economic Conditions of Afghan Refugees in Pakistan.* Geneva: United Nations Research Institute for Social Development.

Clifford, James (1986). "Introduction: Partial Truths." In *Writing Culture: The Poetics and Politics of Ethnography,* edited by James Clifford and George E. Marcus. Berkeley, Los Angeles, London: University of California Press, 1–26.

———. (1988). *The Predicament of Culture: Twentieth-Century Ethnography, Literature, and Art.* Cambridge: Harvard University Press.

———. (1992). "Travelling Cultures." In *Cultural Studies,* edited by Lawrence Grossberg, Cary Nelson and Paul Treichler. New York: Routledge, 96–116.

———. (1994). "Diasporas." *Cultural Anthropology* 9(3): 302–338.

———. (1997). "Spatial Practices: Fieldwork, Travel, and the Disciplining of Anthropology." In *Anthropological Locations: Boundaries and Grounds of a Field Science,* edited by Akhil Gupta and James Ferguson. Berkeley: University of California Press, 185–222.

Clifford, James, and George E. Marcus, eds (1986). *Writing Culture: The Poetics and Politics of Ethnography.* Berkeley, Los Angeles, London: University of California Press.

Cohen, Abner (1965). *Arab Border-Villages in Israel: A Study of Continuity and Change in Social Organization.* Manchester: Manchester University Press.

———. (1970). "The Politics of Marriage in Changing Middle Eastern Stratification Systems." In *Essays in Comparative Social Stratification,* edited by Leonard Plotnicov and Arthur Tuden. Pittsburgh: University of Pittsburgh Press, 195–209.

Colville, Rupert (1998). "Afghan Refugees: Is International Support Draining Away After Two Decades in Exile?" *Refuge* 17(4): 6–11.

Connor, Kerry M. (1987a). *An Analysis of Residential Choice Among Self-settled Afghan Refugees in Peshawar, Pakistan.* Lincoln & Omaha: University of Nebraska.

———. (1987b). "Rationales for the Movement of Afghan Refugees to Peshawar." In *Afghan Resistance: The Politics of Survival,* edited by Grant M. Farr and John G. Merriam. Boulder and London: Westview Press, 151–190.

———. (1989). "Factors in the Residential Choices of Self-Settled Afghans Refugees in Peshawar, Pakistan." *International Migration Review* 23(1): 904–932.

Conte, Edouard, Christian Giordano and Ellen Hertz (2002). "La globalisation ambiguë." *Etudes rurales* 163–164: 9–24.

Darnell, Regna (1995). "Deux ou trois choses que je sais du postmodernisme: le 'moment experimental' dans l'anthropologie nord-américaine." *Gradhiva* 17: 3–15.

Davydov, A. D. (1965). "The Rural Community of the Hazaras of Central Afghanistan." *Central Asian Review* 14(1): 32–44.

de Roover, Raymond (1948). *Money, Banking, and Credit in Medieval Bruges. Italian Merchant-Bankers, Lombards and Money Changers: A Study in the Origins of Banking.* Cambridge, Mass: The Medieval Academy of America.

———. (1953). *L'évolution de la lettre de change: XIVe–XVIIIe siècles.* Paris: Armand Colin.

Development Alternatives (1990). *A Preliminary Analysis of Border Catchment Points.* Peshawar: Development Alternatives.

Dianous, Hugues J. de (1961). "Hazaras et Mongols en Afghanistan." *Orient* 5(19 & 20): 71–98 & 91–113.

Digard, Jean-Pierre (1987). "Jeux et structures: segmentarité et pouvoir chez les nomades Baxtyari." *L'Homme* 102(27/2): 12–53.

Donini, Antonio (1996). *The Policies of Mercy: UN Coordination in Afghanistan, Mozambique, and Rwanda.* Providence: Watson Institute for International Studies.

Dorronsoro, Gilles (2000). *La révolution afghane: des communistes aux tâlebân.* Paris: Karthala.

Dresch, Paul (1986). "The Significance of the Course Events Take in Segmentary Systems." *American Ethnologist* 13(2): 309–324.

———. (1988). "Segmentation: its Roots in Arabia and its Flowering Elsewhere." *Cultural Anthropology* 3(1): 50–67.

Droz, Yvan, and Beat Sottas (1997). "Partir ou rester? Partir et rester: Migrations des Kikuyu au Kenya." *L'Homme* 142: 69–88.

Dulling, G. K. (1973). *The Hazaragi Dialect of Afghan Persian: A Preliminary Study.* London: Central Asian Research Centre.

Dupree, Louis (1980). *Afghanistan.* Princeton: Princeton University Press. [1st ed.: 1973]

du Toit, Brian M. (1990). "People on the Move: Rural-urban Migration with Special Reference to the Third World: Theoretical and Empirical Perspectives." *Human Organization* 49(4): 305–319.

Edwards, David B. (1986a). "The Evolution of Shi'i Political Dissent in Afghanistan." In *Shi'ism and Social Protest,* edited by N. R. Keddie and J. R. I. Cole. New Haven: Yale University Press, 201–229.

———. (1986b). "Marginality and Migration: Cultural Dimensions of the Afghan Refugee Problem." *International Migration Review* 20(2): 313–325.

———. (1990). "Frontiers, Boundaries and Frames: The Marginal Identity of Afghan Refugees." In *Pakistan: The Social Sciences' Perspective*, edited by Akbar S. Ahmed. Karachi, Oxford, etc.: Oxford University Press, 61–99.

———. (1994). "Afghanistan, Ethnography, and the New World Order." *Cultural Anthropology* 9: 345–360.

Eichfeld, Andy (1995). *The* Hundi *System: A Model of the Informal Channel for Remittances in the Middle East and South Asia*. Chicago: The University of Chicago (ms).

Eickelman, Dale F. (1978). "The Art of Memory: Islamic Education and its Social Reproduction." *Comparative Studies in Society and History* 20: 485–516.

———. (1998). *The Middle East and Central Asia: An Anthropological Approach*. Upper Saddle River: Prentice Hall. [3rd ed.]

Elphinstone, Mountstuart (1992). *An Account of the Kingdom of Caubul*. Karachi: Indus Publications, 2 vol. [1st ed.: 1815]

Emadi, Hafizullah (1997). "The Hazaras and Their Role in the Process of Political Transformation in Afghanistan." *Central Asian Survey* 16(3): 363–387.

Etienne, Gilbert (1972). *L'Afghanistan ou les aléas de la coopération*. Paris: PUF.

———. (1982). *Développement rural en Asie: les hommes, le grain et l'outil*. Paris: PUF.

Fairchild, Henry Pratt (1925). *Immigration: A World Movement and its American Significance*. New York: Macmillan.

Ferdinand, Klaus (1959). "Preliminary Notes on Hazâra Culture (The Danish Scientific Mission to Afghanistan 1953–55)." *Historisk-filosofiske Meddelelser udgivet af Det Kongelige Danske Videnskabernes Selskab* 37(5): 1–51.

———. (1962). "Nomad Expansion and Commerce in Central Afghânistân: A Sketch of Some Modern Trends." *Folk* 4: 123–159.

———. (1964). "Ethnographical Notes on Chahâr Aimâq, Hazâra and Moghôl." *Acta Orientalia* 28(1–2): 175–203.

Ferrier, J. P. (1976). *Caravan Journeys and Wanderings in Persia, Afghanistan, Turkistan and Beloochistan*. Karachi: Oxford University Press. [1st ed.: 1857]

Friedman, Jonathan (1994). *Cultural Identity and Social Process*. London: Sage.

———. (2000). "Des racines et (dé)routes: Tropes pour trekkers." *L'Homme* 156: 187–206.

Fukuyama, Francis (1995). *Trust: The Social Virtues and the Creation of Prosperity*. New York, London, etc.: Free Press.

Gambetta, Diego (1994). *La mafia siciliana: un industria della protezione privata*. Torino: Einaudi.

Gambetta, Diego, ed (1988). *Trust: Making and Breaking Cooperative Relations*. Oxford: Basil Blackwell.

Gawecki, Marek (1980). "The Hazara Farmers of Central Afghanistan. Some Historical and Contemporary Problems." *Ethnologia Polana* 6: 163–175.

———. (1986). "Structure and Organization of the Rural Communities of Central and Northern Afghanistan." *Ethnologia Polana* 12: 7–35.

Gazetteer of Afghanistan (1910). *Gazeteer of Afghanistan: Herat*, vol. III. Calcutta: Superintendent Government Printing. [4th edition]

———. (1985). *Historical and Political Gazeteer of Afghanistan. Vol. 6: Kabul and Southeastern Afghanistan.* Edited by Ludwig W. Adamec. Graz: Akademische Druck-u. Verlangsanstalt.

Geertz, Hildred (1971). "Review of Ernest Gellner, *The Saint of the Atlas.*" *American Journal of Sociology* 76(4): 763–765.

———. (1979). "The Meanings of Family Ties." In *Meaning and Order in Moroccan Society,* edited by Clifford Geertz, Hildred Geertz and Lawrence Rosen. Cambridge: Cambridge University Press, 315–391

Gehrig, Tina (1999). "La diaspora afghane au Pakistan et en Europe: réseaux et stratégies des élites urbaines." *Tsantsa* 4: 183–188.

Gehrig, Tina, and Alessandro Monsutti (2003). "Territoires, flux et representations de l'exil afghan: le cas des Hazaras et des Kaboulis." *A Contrario* 1(1): 61–78.

Gellner, Ernest (1969). *The Saint of the Atlas.* London: Weidenfeld and Nicolson; Chicago: University of Chicago Press.

———. (1981). *Muslim Society.* Cambridge: Cambridge University Press.

———. (1983). *Nations and Nationalism.* Oxford: Basil Blackwell.

———. (1995). "Segmentation: Reality or Myth?" *Journal of the Royal Institute of Anthropology* 1(4): 821–829.

Geokart (1984). *National Atlas of the Democratic Republic of Afghanistan.* Warsaw: Geokart.

Gharjestâni, Mohammad Isâ (1989). *Târix-e Hazâra wa Hazâristân.* Quetta: Gharjestâni Publisher.

Giddens, Anthony (1990). *The Consequences of Modernity,* Cambridge: Polity.

Glassé, Cyril (1991). *The Concise Encyclopaedia of Islam.* London: Stacey International. [2nd ed.]

Glatzer, Bernt (1998). "Is Afghanistan on the Brink of Ethnic and Tribal Disintegration?" In *Fundamentalism Reborn? Afghanistan and the Taliban,* edited by William Maley. London: Hurst & Co., 167–181.

Glick Schiller, Nina, Linda Basch and Cristina Szanton Blanc (1992). "Towards a Definition of Transnationalism: Introductory Remarks and Research Questions" & "Transnationalism: A New Analytic Framework for Understanding Migration." In *Towards a Transnational Perspective on Migration: Race, Class, Ethnicity, and Nationalism Reconsidered,* edited by Glick Schiller, Nina, Linda Basch and Cristina Blanc-Szanton. New York: The New York Academy of Sciences, ix-xiv & 1–24.

———. (1995). "From Immigrant to Transmigrant: Theorizing Transnational Migration." *Anthropological Quarterly* 68(1): 48–63.

Goft-o-gu (1996). "Panâhandegi va mohâjerat." *Goft-o-gu* 11: 3–113.

Goitein, S. D. (1963). "Letters and Documents on the Indian Trade in Medieval Times." *Islamic Culture* 37: 188–205.

———. (1964). "Commercial and Family Partnerships in the Countries of Medieval Islam." *Islamic Studies* 3: 315–337.

Goody, Jack (1977). *The Domestication of the Savage Mind,* Cambridge: Cambridge University Press.

———. (1987). *The Interface Between the Written and the Oral.* Cambridge: Cambridge University Press.

———. (1996). *The East in the West.* Cambridge: Cambridge University Press.

Granovetter, Mark S. (1973a). "The Strength of Weak Ties." *American Journal of Sociology* 78(6): 1360–1380.

———. (1973b). "The Strength of Weak Ties: A Network Theory Revisited." In *Social Structure and Network Analysis,* edited by Peter V. Marsden and Nan Lin. Beverly Hills, London: Sage, 105–130.

Grevemeyer, Jan-Heeren (1985). *Ethnizität und Nationalismus: die afghanischen Hazaras zwischen Emanzipation, Widerstand gegen die sowjetischen Besatzer und Bürgerkrieg.* Berlin: Ethnizität und Gesellschaft.

———. (1986). "Widerstand und Emanzipation: die afghanischen Hazara." *Afghanistan Info* 16: 11–15.

———. (1988). "Ethnicity and National Liberation: the Afghan Hazara between Resistance and Civil War." In *Le fait ethnique en Iran et en Afghanistan,* edited by Jean-Pierre Digard. Paris: CNRS, 211–218.

GRSP (1996). *Report of Hazarajat Mini Survey on Jaghori District 1995.* Ghazni: Ghazni Rural Support Programme (GRSP).

Gupta, Akhil (2000). *Globalization: Some Conceptual Problems for Non-Eurocentric Histories.* Stanford: Stanford University (unpublished paper).

Gupta, Akhil, and James Ferguson (1992). "Beyond 'Culture': Space, Identity, and the Politics of Difference." *Cultural Anthropology* 7(1): 6–23.

———. (1997). "Discipline and Practice: 'The Field' as Site, Method, and Location in Anthropology." In *Anthropological Locations: Boundaries and Grounds of a Field Science,* edited by Akhil Gupta and James Ferguson. Berkeley: University of California Press, 1–46.

Hannerz, Ulf (1967). "Gossip, Networks, and Culture in a Black American Ghetto." *Ethnos* 32: 35–60.

———. (1986). "Theory in Anthropology: Small Is Beautiful? The Problem of Complex Cultures." *Comparative Studies in Sociology and History* 28: 362–367.

———. (1992a). *Cultural Complexity: Studies in the Social Organization of Meaning.* New York: Columbia University Press.

———. (1992b). "The Global Ecumene as a Network of Networks." In *Conceptualizing Society,* edited by Adam Kuper. London: Routledge, 34–56.

———. (1996). *Transnational Connections: Culture, People, Places.* London: Routledge.

———. (1998). "Transnational Research." In *Handbook of Methods in Cultural Anthropology,* edited by H. Russell Bernard. Walnut Creek, London, New Delhi: AltaMira Press, 235–256.

Haquani, Zalmaï (1997). "L'afghanité et l'unité nationale à l'épreuve." *Les Nouvelles d'Afghanistan* 79: 16–17.

Hargreaves Heap, Shaun, Martin Hollis, Bruce Lyons, Robert Sugden and Albert Weale (1992). *The Theory of Choice: A Critical Guide.* Oxford: Blackwell.

Harpviken, Kristian Berg (1996). *Political Mobilization Among the Hazara of Afghanistan: 1978–1992.* Oslo: Department of Sociology.

———. (1997). "Transcending Traditionalism: The Emergence of Non-State Military Formations in Afghanistan." *Journal of Peace Research* 34(3): 271–287.

Harrell-Bond, Barbara, and Efithia Vourtira (1996). "Refugees." In *Encyclopedia of Cultural Anthropology,* edited by David Levinson and Melvin Ember, vol. 3. New York: H. Holt & Co., 1076–1081.

Hart, David M. (1989). "Rejoinder to Henry Munson, Jr.: 'On the Irrevelence of the Segmentary Lineage Model in the Moroccan Rif.'" *American Anthropologist* 91: 765–769.

Hatch Dupree, Nancy (1990). "A Socio-cultural Dimension: Afghan Women Refugees in Pakistan." In *The Cultural Basis of Afghan Nationalism,* edited by Ewan W. Anderson and Nancy Hatch Dupree. London & New York: Pinter Publishers, 121–133.

HCR (1996a). *Convention et Protocole relatifs au statut des réfugiés.* Genève: Haut Commissariat des Nations Unies pour les réfugiés.

———. (1996b). *Statut de l'Office du Haut Commissariat des Nations Unies pour les réfugiés.* Genève: Haut Commissariat des Nations Unies pour les réfugiés.

———. (1997). "Afghanistan: une crise qui s'éternise." *Réfugiés* 108: 1–30.

Hein, Jeremy (1993). "Refugees, Immigrants, and the State." *Annual Review of Sociology* 19: 43–59.

Herzfeld, Michael (1985). *The Poetics of Manhood: Contest and Identity in a Cretan Mountain Village.* Princeton: Princeton University Press.

Heslot, Sylvie (1984–85). *La terminologie de la parenté en Afghanistan: approche di-alectologique.* Paris: Université de Paris III–Sorbonne Nouvelle.

Hobsbawm, Eric (1990). *Nations and Nationalism since 1780: Programme, Myth, Reality.* Cambridge: Cambridge University Press.

Howell, David R. (1982). "Refugee Resettlement and Public Policy: A Role for Anthropology." *Anthropological Quarterly* 55(3): 119–125.

Hudson, Alfred E., and Elizabeth Bacon (1941). "Social Control and the Individual in Eastern Hazara Culture." In *Language, Culture, and Personality: Essays in Honor of Edward Sapir,* edited by L. Spier et al. Menasha: Sapir Memorial Publ. Fund, 239–258.

Huld, Bo, and Erland Jansson, eds (1988). *The Tragedy of Afghanistan: The Social, Cultural and Political Impact of Soviet Invasion.* London, etc.: Croom Helm.

Humlum, Johannes (1959). *La géographie de l'Afghanistan.* Copenhagen: Scandinavian University Books.

Huwyler, Edwin, and François-Xavier Meyer (1979). *The Central Provinces of Afghanistan: A Monography Based on the Available Literature, with an Annotated Bibliography.* Berne: Directorate for Development Cooperation and Humanitarian Aid (unpublished paper).

ICRC (1998). *ICRC Activities in Afghanistan: 1994–5 February 1998.* Geneva: ICRC [Report].

Imperial Gazetteer of India (1991). *Baluchistan.* Lahore: Sang-e Meel. [1st ed.: circa 1903]

Iwamura, Shinobu (1959). *Identification of the Hazara Tribes in Afghanistan.* Tokyo: International Symposium on History of Eastern and Western Cultural Contacts, Unesco.

Iwamura, Shinobu, and Herbert F. Schurmann (1954). "Notes on Mongolian Groups in Afghanistan." In *Silver Jubilee Volume on the Zinbun-Kagaku-Kenkyusyo.* Kyoto: Kyoto University, 480–515.

Jamous, Raymond (1981). *Honneur et baraka: les structures sociales traditionnelles dans le Rif*. Cambridge, London: Cambridge University Press; Paris: Maison des sciences de l'homme.

Janata, Alfred (1990). "Afghanistan: The Ethnic Dimension." In *The Cultural Basis of Afghan Nationalism*, edited by Ewan W. Anderson and Nancy Hatch Dupree. London & New York: Pinter Publishers, 60–70.

Johnson, Chris (2000). *Hazarajat Baseline Study—Interim Report*. Islamabad: UN Co-ordinator's Office.

Kakar, Hasan K. (1973). *The Pacification of the Hazaras of Afghanistan*. New York: Afghanistan Council of the Asia Society.

———. (1979). *Government and Society in Afghanistan: The Reign of Amir 'Abd al Rahman Khan*. Austin; London: University of Texas Press.

Kearney, Michael (1986). "From the Invisible Hand to Visible Feet: Anthropological Studies of Migration and Development." *Annual Review of Anthropology* 15: 331–361.

———. (1995). "The Local and the Global: the Anthropology of Globalization and Transnationalism." *Annual Review of Anthropology* 24: 547–565.

Khosrokhavar, Farhad, and Olivier Roy (1996). *Iran: comment sortir d'une révolution religieuse*. Paris: Seuil.

Kopecky, Lucas-Michael (1982). "The Imami Sayyed of the Hazarajat: the Maintenance of their Elite Position." *Folk* 24: 89–110.

———. (1986). "Die Saiyid und die imamitischen Hazara Afghanistans: Religiöse Vergemeinschaftung und Ethnogenese." In *Die ethnischen Gruppen Afghanistan: Fallstudien zu Gruppenidentität und Intergruppenbeziehungen*, edited by Erwin Orywal.Wiesbaden: L. Reichert, 165–203.

Kunz, Egon F. (1973). "The Refugee in Flight: Kinetic Models and Forms Of Displacement." *International Migration Review* 7(2): 125–146.

———. (1981). "Exile and Resettlement: Refugee Theory." *International Migration Review* 15(1): 42–51.

Labib, Subhi Y. (1969). "Capitalism in Medieval Islam." *Journal of Economic History* 29(1): 79–96.

La'li, 'Alidâd (1993). *Sayri dar Hazârajât*. Qom: Sahâf-i Ihsâni.

Lancaster, William (1997). *The Rwala Bedouin Today*. Prospect Heights: Waveland Press. [1st ed.: 1981]

Lazard, Gilbert (1995). *La formation de la langue persane*. Paris: Peeters.

Lévi-Strauss, Claude (1955). *Tristes tropiques*. Paris: Plon.

Lindholm, Charles (1982). *Generosity and Jealousy: The Swat Pukhtun of Northern Pakistan*. New York: Columbia University Press.

———. (1997). "Logical and Moral Dilemmas of Postmodernism." *Journal of The Royal Anthropological Institute* 3(4): 747–760.

Maitland, P. J. (1891). "The Hazáras of the Country Known as the Hazáraját, and Elsewhere." *Afghan Boundary Commission Report*, vol. 4. Shimla: Government Central Printing Office, 277–450. [Reprint]

Maley, William (1997). "Quel Afghanistan?" *Les Nouvelles d'Afghanistan* 79: 24–26.

Maley, William, ed. (1998). *Fundamentalism Reborn? Afghanistan and the Taliban*. London: Hurst & Co.

Malkki, Liisa H. (1992). "National Geographic: The Rooting of Peoples and the Territorialization of National Identity Among Scholars and Refugees." *Cultural Anthropology* 7(1): 24–44.

———. (1995a). "Refugees and Exile: From 'Refugees Studies' to the National Order of Things." *Annual Review of Anthropology* 24: 495–523.

———. (1995b). *Purity and Exile: Violence, Memory, and National Cosmology Among Hutu Refugees in Tanzania*. Chicago and London: The University of Chicago Press.

———. (1997). "News and Culture: Transitory Phenomena and the Fieldwork Tradition." In *Anthropological Locations: Boundaries and Grounds of a Field Science*, edited by Akhil Gupta and James Ferguson. Berkeley: University of California Press, 86–101.

Ma Mung, Emmanuel (1992). "Dispositif économique et ressources spatiales: éléments d'une économie de diaspora." *Revue européenne des migrations internationales* 8(3): 175–193.

Marcus, George E. (1989). "Imagining the Whole: Ethnography's Contemporary Efforts to Situate Itself." *Critique of Anthropology* 9(3): 7–30.

———. (1992). "Past, Present and Emergent Identities: Requirements for Ethnographies of Late Twentieth-Century Modernity Worldwide." In *Modernity and Identity*, edited by Scott Lash and Jonathan Friedman. Oxford: Blackwell, 309–330.

———. (1995). "Ethnography in/of the World System: the Emergence of Multi-Sited Ethnography." *Annual Review of Anthropology* 24: 94–117.

Marcus, George E., and Dick Cushman (1982). "Ethnographies as Texts." *Annual Review of Anthropology* 11: 25–69.

Marcus, George E., and Michael M. J. Fischer (1986). *Anthropology as Cultural Critique: An Experimental Moment in the Human Sciences*. Chicago, London: University of Chicago Press.

Marsden, Peter (1992). "Afghan in Pakistan: Why Rations Decline." *Journal of Refugee Studies* 5/3–4: 289–299.

Marx, Emmanuel (1990). "The Social World of Refugees: A Conceptual Framework." *Journal of Refugee Studies* 3(3): 189–203.

Massey, Douglas S., Joaquin Arango, Graeme Hugo, Ali Kouaouci, Adela Pellegrino and J. Edward Taylor (1993). "Theories of International Migration: A Review and Appraisal." *Population and Development Review* 19(3): 431–466.

Masson, Charles (1997). *Narrative of Various Journeys in Balochistan, Afghanistan and the Panjab; Including a Residence in those Countries from 1826 to 1838*. New Delhi: Munshiram Manoharlal, 3 vol. [1st ed: 1842]

Mauss, Marcel (1985). "Essai sur le don: forme et raison de l'échange dans les sociétés archaïques." In *Sociologie et anthropologie*. Paris: PUF. [1e éd.: 1923–1924]

Meyer, François-Xavier (1976). "Problèmes de terrain: l'exemple d'un échec en Afghanistan." *Bulletin de la Société suisse d'ethnologie: Problèmes de la recherche sur le terrain vus par des jeunes ethnologues*, numéro spécial: 107–122.

Mintz, Sidney W. (1998). "The Localizing of Anthropological Practice: From Area Studies to Transnationalism." *Critique of Anthropology* 18(2): 117–133.

Mintz, Sidney W., and Eric R. Wolf (1950). "An Analysis of Ritual Co-parenthood (*compadrazgo*)." *Southwestern Journal of Anthropology* 6: 341–368.

Mitchell, J. Clyde (1974). "Social Networks." *Annual Review of Anthropology* 3: 279–299.

Mitchell, J. Clyde, ed. (1969). *Social Networks in Urban Situations: Analyses of Personal Relationships in Central Africa*. Manchester: Manchester University Press.

Monsutti, Alessandro (1996a). "Dehmarda: un village divisé." *Afghanistan Info* 38: 8–9.

———. (1996b). "Le septième anniversaire du Hezb-e wahdat. Bamyan, 2–4 août 1996." *Afghanistan Info* 39: 13–14.

———. (1996c). "Les Hazâras face à la montée des Tâlebân." *Les Nouvelles d'Afghanistan* 74–75: 29–31.

———. (1997a). "La société et les familles afghanes en exil: entre fragmentation et représentation communautaire." *Revue d'histoire des institutions méditerranéennes* 1: 327–331.

———. (1997b). "La quête de reconnaissance des Hazaras." *Les Nouvelles d'Afghanistan* 79: 20–23.

———. (1999). "Guerre et ethnicité en Afghanistan." *Tsantsa* 4: 63–73.

———. (2000a). "The Hazaras of Afghanistan: Coping Through Emigration and Remittances." *ICRC's Forum* 2: 72–73.

———. (2000b). "Nouveaux espaces, nouvelles solidarités: la migration des Hazaras d'Afghanistan." *Les défis migratoires: Actes du colloque CLUSE, Neuchâtel 1998*, edited by Pierre Centlivres and Isabelle Girod. Zurich: Seismo, 333–342.

Moorcroft, William, and George Trebeck (1979). *Travels in the Himalayan Provinces of Hindustan and the Panjab From 1819 To 1825*, 2 vol. Karachi: Oxford University Press. [1st ed.: 1841]

Morton, John (1991). *The Socio-economic Status of Afghan Refugees in Pakistan: A Review and a Research Strategy.* Islamabad: UNHCR.

———. (1994). *Afghan Refugees in Pakistan: Issues of Employment, Repatriation and Assistance*. Islamabad: UNHCR.

Mousavi, Sayed Askar (1998). *The Hazaras of Afghanistan: An Historical, Cultural, Economic and Political Study.* Richmond: Curzon Press.

Munson, Henry, Jr. (1989). "On the Irrevelence of the Segmentary Lineage Model in the Moroccan Rif." *American Anthropologist* 91: 386–400.

———. (1993). "Rethinking Gellner's Segmentary Analysis of Morocco's Ait Atta." *Man* 28(2): 267–280.

———. (1995). "Response to Gellner." *Journal of the Royal Institute of Anthropology* 1(4): 829–832.

Napier, G. C. (1876). *Collection of Journals and Reports from Captain the Hon. G. C. Napier, Bengal Staff Corps, on Special Duty in Persia: 1874*. London: George E. Eyre and William Spottiswoode.

Noelle, Christine (1997). *State and Tribe in Nineteenth-Century Afghanistan: The Reign of Amir Dost Muhammad Khan (1826–1863)*. Richmond: Curzon.

Omidian, Patricia A. (1994). "Life out of Context: Recording Afghan Refugees' Stories." In *Reconstructing Lives, Recapturing Meaning: Refugee Identity,*

Gender, and Culture Change, edited by Linda A. Camino and Ruth M. Krulfeld. Basel: Gordon and Breach Publishers, 151–178.

Omidian, Patricia A., and Juliene G. Lipson (1992). "Elderly Afghan Refugees: Traditions and Transitions in Northern California." In *Selected Papers on Refugee Issues,* edited by Pamela A. Devoe. Washington D.C.: Committee on Refugee Issues (American Anthropological Issues), 27–39.

Orywal, Erwin (1986). "Ethnische Identität—Konzept und Methode." In *Die ethnischen Gruppen Afghanistan: Fallstudien zu Gruppenidentität und Intergruppenbeziehungen,* edited by Erwin Orywal. Wiesbaden: L. Reichert, 73–86.

———. (1988). "Ethnicity—Conceptual and Methodological Considerations." In *Le fait ethnique en Iran et en Afghanistan,* edited by Jean-Pierre Digard. Paris: Ed. du Centre national de la recherche scientifique, 35–40.

Owtadolajam, Mohammad (1976). *A Sociological Study of the Hazara Tribe in Baluchistan (An Analysis of Sociocultural Change).* Karachi: University of Karachi, Department of Sociology.

Pérouse de Montclos, Marc-Antoine (2000). "Réseaux financiers, diasporas et *hawilad:* le rôle clé de la péninsule Arabique entre l'Occident et la Somalie." In *Afrique noire et monde arabe: continuités et ruptures,* edited by Emmanuel Grégoire and Jean Schmitz. Paris: Aube/IRD, 99–116.

Perry, John R. (1975). "Forced Migration in Iran During the Seventeenth and Eighteenth Centuries." *Iranian Studies* 8(4): 199–215.

Peters, Emrys (1990). *The Bedouin of Cyrenaica: Studies in Personal and Corporate Power.* Cambridge: Cambridge University Press.

Petersen, William (1958). "A General Typology of Migration." *American Sociological Review* 23(3): 256–266.

Peyrefitte, Alain (1998). *La société de confiance: essai sur les origines du développement.* Paris: Odile Jacob.

Pirenne, Henri (1963). *Histoire économique et sociale du Moyen Age.* Paris: PUF. [edited by Hans van Werveke]

Pitt-Rivers, Julian (1973). "The Kith and the Kin." In *The Character of Kinship,* edited by Jack Goody. Cambridge: Cambridge University Press, 89–105.

———. (1976). "Ritual Kinship in the Mediterranean: Spain and the Balkans." In *Mediterranean Family Structures,* edited by J. G. Peristiany. Cambridge: Cambridge University Press, 317–334.

———. (1977). *The Fate of Shechem, or, The Politics of Sex. Essays in the Anthropology of the Mediterranean,* Cambridge: Cambridge University Press.

Planhol, Xavier de (1993). *Les Nations du Prophète: Manuel géographique de politique musulmane.* Paris: Fayard.

Poladi, Hassan (1989). *The Hazâras.* Stockton: Mughal Publishing Co.

Polanyi, Karl (1945). *The Great Transformation: The Political and Economic Origins of our Time.* London: Victor Gollancz.

———. (1957). "The Economy As Instituted Process." In *Trade and Market in the Early Empires: Economies in History and Theory,* edited by Karl Polanyi, Conrad M. Arensberg, Harry W. Pearson. New York: The Free Press; London: Collier-Macmillan, 243–270.

Pouillon, Jean (1979). "Remarques sur le verbe 'croire.'" In *La fonction symbolique: Essais d'anthropologie,* edited by Michel Izard and Pierre Smith. Paris: Gallimard, 43–51.

RAASTA (1992). *Afghan Refugees in Karachi: A Preliminary Exploration.* Karachi: Raasta Developpment Consultants.

Rashid, Ahmed (2000). *Taliban: Islam, Oil and the New Great Game in Central Asia.* London and New York: I. B. Tauris.

Ravenstein, Ernest George (1885 & 1889). "The Laws of Migration." *Journal of the Royal Statistical Society* 48(2): 167–235 & 52(2): 241–305. [Reprint: New York: Arno Press, 1976: 165–305]

Reshtia, Sayed Qassem (1997). "Une unité évidente." *Les Nouvelles d'Afghanistan* 79: 27.

REVUE DU MAUSS (1994). *A qui se fier? Confiance, interaction et théorie des jeux.* Paris: La Découverte/MAUSS.

Richmond, Anthony H. (1988). "Sociological Theories of International Migration: The Case of Refugees." *Current Sociology* 36(2): 7–26.

Ridgway, R. T. I. (1983). *Pathans.* Peshawar: Saeed Book Bank. [1st ed.: 1910]

Rist, Gilbert (1998). "Préalables à une théorie générale de l'échange." *Pratiques de la dissidence économique: réseaux rebelles et créativité sociale,* edited by Yvonne Preiswerk and Fabrizio Sabelli. Paris: PUF; Geneva: Nouveaux Cahiers de l'IUED (no. 7), 17–40.

Rizvi, Gowher (1990). "The Afghan Refugees: Hostages in the Struggle for Power." *Journal of Refugee Studies* 3(3): 244–261.

ROBERT R. NATHAN ASSOCIATES, LOUIS BERGER INTERNATIONAL (1989). *Profile of Private Sector Cross-Border Trade Between Afghanistan and Pakistan.* Washington: Robert R. Nathan Associates, Louis Berger International (ms).

Rodman, Margaret C. (1992). "Empowering Place: Multilocality and Multivocality." *American Anthropologist* 94(3): 640–656.

Rosman, Abraham, and Paula G. Rubel (1976). "Nomad-Sedentary Inter-ethnic Relations in Iran and Afghanistan." *International Journal of Middle East Studies* 7: 545–570.

Rouse, Roger (1991). "Mexican Migration and the Social Space of Postmodernism." *Diaspora* 1(1): 8–23.

———. (1992). "Making Sense of Settlement: Class Transformation, Cultural Struggle, and Transnationalism Among Mexican Migrants in the United States." In *Towards a Transnational Perspective on Migration: Race, Class, Ethnicity, and Nationalism Reconsidered,* edited by Glick Schiller, Nina, Linda Basch and Cristina Blanc-Szanton. New York: The New York Academy of Sciences, 25–52.

Roussel, Frédéric, and Marie-Pierre Caley (1994). *Les "Manteqas": le puzzle souterrain de l'Afghanistan.* Peshawar: unpublished paper.

Roy, Olivier (1983). "L'Afghanistan d'est en ouest; compte rendu de voyage 1982." *Les Nouvelles d'Afghanistan* 12–13: 39–41.

———. (1983–84). "La situation au Hazaradjat: la Choura." *Les Nouvelles d'Afghanistan* 16: 10–12.

———. (1985). *L'Afghanistan: Islam et modernité politique.* Paris: Seuil.

———. (1993). "La guerre d'Afghanistan: de la guerre idéologique à la guerre ethnique." *L'Homme et la Société* 17: 85–92.

———. (1997). "Quelle unité pour l'Afghanistan?" *Les Nouvelles d'Afghanistan* 79: 18–19.

RPG (1991). *Afghanistan's Internally Displaced: A Nation Uprooted.* Washington, D.C.: The Refugee Policy Group (ms).

———. (1992). *Afghanistan: Trends and Prospects for Refugee Repatriation.* Washington, D.C.: The Refugee Policy Group (ms).

Safran, William (1991). "Diasporas in Modern Society: Myths of Homeland and Return." *Diaspora* 1(1): 83–99.

Sahlins, Marshall (1965). "On the Sociology of Primitive Exchange." In *The Relevance of Models for Social Anthropology,* edited by Michael Banton. London: Tavistock Publications, 139–236.

———. (1999). "Two or Three Things that I Know about Culture." *Journal of the Royal Anthropological Institute* 5(3): 399–421.

Salzman, Philip C. (1971). "Movement and Resource Extraction Among Pastoral Nomads: the Case of the Shah Nawazi Baluch." *Anthropological Quarterly* 44(3): 185–197.

———. (1978). "Does Complementary Opposition Exist?" *American Anthropologist* 80: 53–70.

———. (1995). "Understanding Tribes in Iran and Beyond." *Journal of the Royal Anthropological Institute* 1: 399–403.

Schnapper, Dominique (2001). "De l'Etat-nation au monde transnational: du sens et de l'utilité du concept de diaspora." *Revue européenne des migrations internationales* 17(2): 9–39.

Schurmann, Herbert F. (1962). *The Mongols of Afghanistan: An Ethnography of the Moghôls and Related Peoples of Afghanistan.* The Hague: Mouton.

Scott, John (1991). *Social Network Analysis: A Handbook.* London: Sage.

Shahrani, M. Nazif (1986). "State Building and Social Fragmentation in Afghanistan: An Historical Perspective." In *The State, Religion, and Ethnic Politics: Afghanistan, Iran, and Pakistan,* edited by Ali Banuazizi and Myron Weiner. Syracuse: Syracuse University Press.

———. (1995). "Afghanistan's Muhajirin (Muslim 'Refugee-Warriors'): Politics of Mistrust and Distrust of Politics." In *Mistrusting Refugees,* edited by E. Valentine Daniel and John Ch. Knudsen. Berkeley, Los Angeles, London: University of California Press, 187–206.

Shalinsky, Audrey C. (1996). "Gender Issues in the Afghanistan Diaspora: Nadia's Story." *A Journal of Women Studies* 17(3): 102–123.

Shami, Seteney (1996). "Transnationalism and Refugee Studies: Rethinking Forced Migration and Identity in the Middle East." *Journal of Refugee Studies* 9(1): 3–26.

Sliwinski, Marek (1989). "Afghanistan: The Decimation of a People." *Orbis: A Journal of World Affairs,* Winter: 39–56.

Spooner, Brian J. (1965). "Kinship and Marriage in Eastern Persia." *Sociologus* 15(1): 22–31.

Stein, Barry N. (1981). "The Refugee Experience: Defining the Parameters of a Field of Study." *International Migration Review* 15(1): 320–330.

———. (1986). "Durable Solutions to Developing Country Refugees." *International Migration Review* 20(2): 264–282.

Street, Brian V. (1984). *Literacy in Theory and Practice.* Cambridge, New York, etc.: Cambridge University Press.
———. (1987). "The Uses of Literacy and Anthropology in Iran." In *The Diversity of the Muslim Community: Anthropological Essays in Memory of Peter Lienhardt,* edited by Ahmed Al-Shahi. London: Ithaca, 28–42.
———. (1990). "Orientalist Discourses in the Anthropology of Iran, Afghanistan and Pakistan." In *Localizing Strategies: Regional Traditions of Ethnographic Writing,* edited by Richard Fardon. Edinburgh: Scottish Academic Press, 240–259.
———. (1992). "Method in our Critique of Anthropology." *Man* 27: 177–179.
TANZIM (1991). *Târix-e melli-e Hazâra.* Quetta: Tanzim-e Nasl-e Naw-ye Hazâra-Moghol, 1980.
Tapper, Nancy (1991). *Bartered Brides: Politics, Gender and Marriage in an Afghan Tribal Society.* Cambridge: Cambridge University Press.
Tapper, Richard (1979). *Pasture and Politics: Economics, Conflict and Ritual among Shahsevan Nomads of Nothwestern Iran.* London: Academic Press.
———. (1983). "Introduction." In *The Conflict of Tribe and State in Iran and Afghanistan,* edited by Richard Tapper. London: Croom Helm, 1–82.
———. (1988). "Ethnicity, Order and Meaning in the Anthropology of Iran and Afghanistan." In *Le fait ethnique en Iran et en Afghanistan,* edited by Pierre Digard. Paris: Ed. du Centre national de la recherche scientifique, 21–34.
———. (1989). "Ethnic Identities and Categories in Iran and Afghanistan." In *History and Ethnicity,* edited by Elizabeth Tonkin, Maryon McDonald and Malcom Chapman. London, New York: Routledge, 232–246.
Tapper, Richard, and Nancy Tapper (1992/1993). "Marriage, Honour and Responsability: Islamic and Local Models in the Mediterranean and the Middle East." *Cambridge Anthropology* 16(2): 3–21.
Tarrius, Alain (1995). "Territoires circulatoires des entrepreneurs commerciaux maghrébins de Marseille: du commerce communautaire aux réseaux de l'économie souterraine mondiale." *Journal des anthropologues* 59: 15–35.
———. (2001). "Au-delà des Etat-nations: des sociétés de migrants." *Revue européenne des migrations internationales* 17(2): 37–61.
Tedlock, Barbara (1996). "Diasporas." In *Encyclopedia of Cultural Anthropology,* edited by David Levinson and Melvin Ember, vol. 1. New York: H. Holt & co., 341–343.
Thesiger, Wilfred (1955). "The Hazaras of Central Afghanistan." *Geographic Journal* 121(3): 312–319.
———. (1956). "Thc Hazarajat of Afghanistan." *Geographical Magazine* 29(2): 87–95.
———. (2000). *Among the Mountains: Travels Through Asia.* London: Flamingo.
Thornton, Thomas H. (1979). *Colonel Sir Sandeman: His Life and Work on our Indian Frontier.* Karachi: Oxford University Press. [1st ed.: 1895]
Timurkhanov, L. (1980). *Târix-e melli-ye Hazâra.* Quetta: Tanzim-e nasl-e naw-e Hazâra-ye Moghol. [translated from Russian, 1972]
Titus, Paul (1996). "Routes to Ethnicity: Roads, Buses, and Differential Ethnic Relations in Pakistani Balochistan." In *Marginality and Modernity: Ethnicity*

and Change in Post-Colonial Balochistan, edited by Paul Titus. Karachi, etc.: Oxford University Press, 273–297.

———. (1997). "Negotiating an Ethnic Landscape: Competition and Cooperation in Balochistan's Transport Industry." *Die Erde* 128: 311–327.

———. (1999). "Global Dismemberments: Siting Afghan Refugees in Networks of Networks." Unpublished paper.

Tölölyan, Khachig (1996). "Rethinking *Diaspora*(s): Stateless Power in the Transnational Moment." *Diaspora* 5(1): 3–36.

Udovitch, Abraham L. (1967). "Credit as a Means of Investment in Medieval Islamic Trade." *Journal of the American Oriental Society* 87: 260–264.

———. (1970). *Partnership and Profit in Medieval Islam.* Princeton: Princeton University Press.

———. (1990). "International Commerce and Society in Mid-Eleventh-Century Egypt and North Africa." In *The Economic Dimension of Middle Eastern History: Essays in Honor of Charles Issawi,* edited by Haleh Esfandiari and Abraham L. Udovitch. Princeton: Princeton University Press, 239–253.

Udovitch, Abraham L., ed. (1981). *The Islamic Middle East, 700–1900: Studies in Economic and Social History.* Princeton: Darwin Press.

UNHCR (1993). *Report on the Repatriation of Afghan Refugees—1992.* Islamabad: UNHCR.

———. (1995). *Country Operation Plan (1995–1996): Pakistan.* Islamabad: UNHCR Branch Office Pakistan.

———. (1998). *Afghan Refugee Statistics,* Islamabad: UNHCR.

UNIDATA (1992). *Afghanistan, Ghazni Province: A Socio-Economic Profile.* Geneva: UNIDATA.

Wallerstein, Immanuel (1974). *The Modern World-System: Capitalist Agriculture and the Origins of the European World-Economy in the Sixteenth Century.* New York: Academic Press, vol. 1.

———. (1980). *The Modern World-System: Mercantilism and the Consolidation of the European World-Economy, 1600–1750.* New York: Academic Press, vol. 2.

———. (1989). *The Modern World-System: The Second Era of Great Expansion of the Capitalist World-Economy, 1730–1840s.* New York: Academic Press, vol. 3.

Webster University (1987). *Afghan Refugees: A Global Concern.* Geneva: Webster University (ms).

Werbner, Pnina (1990). *The Migration Process: Capital, Gifts and Offerings Among the British Pakistanis.* New York, Oxford, Munich: Berg.

White, Jenny B. (1999). "Amplifying Trust: Community and Communication in Turkey." In *New Media in the Muslim World: The Emerging Public Sphere,* edited by Dale F. Eickelman and Jon W. Anderson. Bloomington & Indianapolis: Indiana University Press, 162–179.

Whitten, Norman E., and Alvin W. Wolfe (1973). "Network Analysis." In *Handbook of Social and Cultural Anthropology,* edited by John J. Honigmann. Chicago: Rand Macnally, 717–746.

Wolf, Eric R. (1982). *Europe and the People Without History.* Berkeley, Los Angeles, London: University of California Press.

WORLD BANK (2001). *Afghanistan's International Trade Relations With Neighboring Countries,* http://lnweb18.worldbank.org/SAR/sa.nsf/Attachments/8/dollarsFile/intltrade.pdf.

Yazdâni, Husain 'Ali ("Hâji Kâzem") (1993). *Pozhohishi dar târikh-e Hazârahâ.* Vol. 1. Qom: Châpkhâna-e Mihr. [2nd ed.]

Zetter, Roger (1988a). "Refugees and Refugee Studies–A Label and an Agenda." *Journal of Refugee Studies* 1(1): 1–6.

———. (1988b). "Refugees, Repatriation, and Root Causes." *Journal of Refugee Studies* 1(2): 99–106.

———. (1991). "Labelling Refugees: Forming and Transforming a Bureaucratic Identity." *Journal of Refugee Studies* 4(1): 39–62.

Zolberg, Aristide R. (1981). "International Migrations in Political Perspective." In *Global Trends in Migration: Theory and Research on International Population Movements,* edited by Mary M. Kritz, Charles B. Keely and Silvano M. Tomasi. Staten Island: Center for Migration Studies, 3–27.

Index

R

S

T